MOON

HAN~~~~~~ **W9-BCO-410**

MONTRÉAL
& QUÉBEC CITY

JENNIFER EDWARDS

MONTRÉAL AND QUÉBEC CITY

Lac Mistassini

Mistassmi

167

Chibougamau

Lac Péribonka

109

113

Lac St-Jean

169

Rivière Saguen

Beattyville

113

169

175

Val-D'or

Réserve
Faunique des
Laurentides

Q U É B E C

Réservoir
Gouin

155

175

0   50 mi

0   50 km

Réserve
Faunique la
Vérendrye

Réservoir
Cabonga

Réservoir
Baskating

Réserve
Faunique du
St-Maurice

Réserve
Faunique de
Portneuf

Beaupr

Parc National
de la Mauricie

QUÉBEC CITY

Lévi

Mont-Laurier

Parc du
Mont-
Tremblant

Réserve
Faunique
Mastigouche

131

Shawinigan

117

Ville de
Mont-Tremblant

55

Réserve
Faunique de
Papineau-
Labelle

St-Jovite

St-Agathe-
des-Monts

Trois-Rivières

116

105

309

15

St-Sauveur-
des-Monts

40

112

St-Jérôme

20

Victoriaville

Parc de la
Gatineau

Chelsea

Montebello

148

Lachute

Drummondville

60

Gatineau

17

Mirabel

30

55

OTTAWA

40

Laval

Longueuil

Granby

Sherbrooke

ONTARIO

417

MONTRÉAL

10

31

20

133

Magog

7

Cowansville

Brome

Perth

CANADA

16

USA

11

Lac
Champlain

NEW YORK

87

89

VERMONT

NH

401

Burlington

© AVALON TRAVEL PUBLISHING, INC.

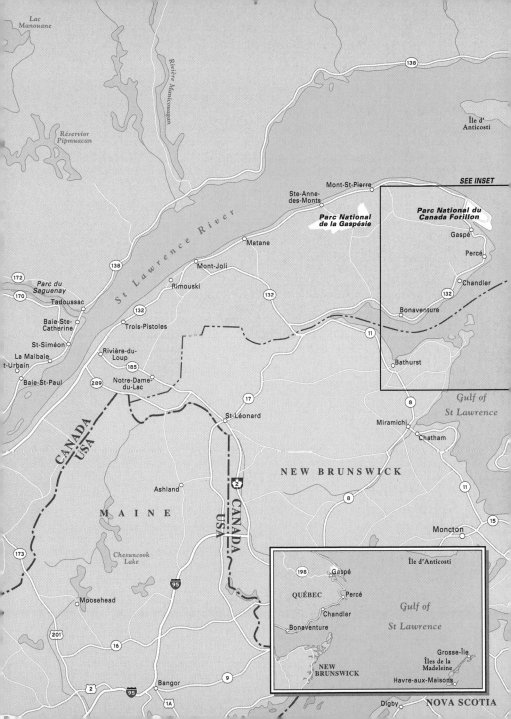

DISCOVER MONTRÉAL & QUÉBEC CITY

There is no other place quite like the province of Québec in North America. A little bit exotic, exceptionally historic, and quite fantastic, this irrepressible pocket of French culture surrounded by a sea of English is a great place to visit for those who like to look back while they move forward.

Whereas the oft-heard complaint about the rest of North America is that it lacks history, in Québec, the history seeps through city streets and country landscapes, it slips off old mansard roofs and church steeples, and it is ultimately responsible for shaping so much of what Québec is today. The province offers a vibrant, living, breathing past, from the provincial capital Québec City, with its strategic cliffside location, fortified walls and preserved buildings, battlegrounds and public squares – where you can almost still hear the sounds of chickens clucking and people

"Our Lady of the Harbor," Chapelle Notre-Dame-de-Bon-Secours

bargaining back and forth – to Montréal with its lively old city, church bells, narrow streets, and looming illuminated cross high atop its landmark Mont Royal.

But there is much more to the province than a chance to look back. Montréal, in particular, is a city known for its fashion savvy, progressiveness, and cosmopolitan nature. Its citizens, it's clear, like to eat, shop, stroll, and take advantage of everything their city has to offer. Montrealers may be more laid-back, but they are also *branché* (plugged in) to what is happening in the rest of the world. Stop for a moment to survey some of the city's cutting-edge design and architecture like the Palais de Congrès, Musée Pointe-à-Callière, and brand new Grande Bibliothèque. Also take note of the boutique hotels, experimental restaurants, and recreational opportunities, and the area's forward-thinking approach becomes

the 1838 Wakefield Mill Inn, Wakefield

abundantly clear. Even Québec City, which will forever be first appreciated for its well-preserved history, has its Old Town but is far from being just a time capsule to be looked at in wonder. It's also a place where locals live, work, raise families, and spend their time.

Beyond its cities, and their particular history and culture, the province and its people are defined by two things: landscape and weather. Québec's main geographical feature is without question its imposing Saint Lawrence River, which in places — such as where the Saguenay Fjord joins it and makes it a rich feeding ground for a spectacular variety of whales — more closely resembles a sea than a river. There are also the many lakes — great for canoeing and summer swims — and the fast-moving rivers, which, for the adventurous, can be explored by kayak and white-water rafts. There are the vast forests, which cover nearly half of the province's territory, the gentle hills, and the high, skiable peaks of places like the Eastern Townships and the Laurentians.

Recognizing its huge potential for recreational tourism and the need for the protection and sustainability of its forests and water-

a roadside attraction on Charlevoix's Route des Saveurs

ways, the province has created a number of stellar parks like Parc National du Mont-Tremblant in the Laurentians and Parc National de la Gaspésie in the Gaspé region. All of Québec's parks offer interpretive centers, equipment rentals, stellar views, campgrounds, and if you want to get a bit cushier, huts and cabins.

Spend any time in Québec, and you'll quickly understand the profound influence the weather has on the people and the place. Virtually a completely different location in summer, spring, fall, and winter, the province yields a completely new experience during each of these times, with new activities, new beauty, and in some ways, new people. Summer is all about taking advantage of the outdoors: camping, road trips, swimming, cycling, and hiking. It's also about hot, steamy nights downtown, having a few beers out on a patio, and attending music festivals. Fall, a fantastic time to visit the province, offers wood smoke and the brilliant colors of the leaves, quiet walks, and reflection. Winter in many ways can seem just as alive as summer, with bustling ski hills, varied cross-country, snowshoeing and skating, and rosy cheeks and roaring

Rocher Percé in the Gaspé: the face that launched a thousand postcards

© SUE MOORE

fires. Spring is a magical time in Québec. The sap starts trickling and the *cabanes à sucre* (sugar shacks) become the most rocking places around. Spring fever hits hard and people enter a sort of "must get out and socialize" trance. The outdoor terraces fill up and even though it's still cold outside, you'll see people spending as much time as they can outdoors.

The round-up conclusion is that you will enjoy Québec any time of year that you go. It's always warm in spirit, hospitable, and despite the distances between places, it's easy to get around. It offers spectacular natural beauty, great food, music, and culture. It has its very French ways, but it is also resolutely North American. It is a special place to the people who live there and will inevitably become one to the people who visit.

the perfect spot for quiet contemplation, Saint Lawrence River

Contents

MAP CONTENTS

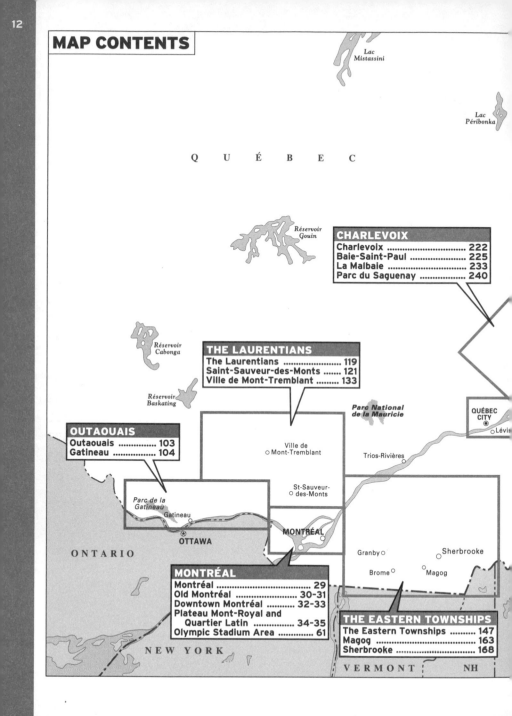

Lac Mistassini

Lac Péribonka

Q U É B E C

Réservoir Gouin

Réservoir Cabonga

Réservoir Baskating

Parc National de la Mauricie

QUÉBEC CITY

Lévis

Ville de Mont-Tremblant

Trios-Rivières

St-Sauveur-des-Monts

Parc de la Gatineau

Gatineau

OTTAWA

MONTRÉAL

ONTARIO

Granby

Sherbrooke

Brome

Magog

NEW YORK

VERMONT   NH

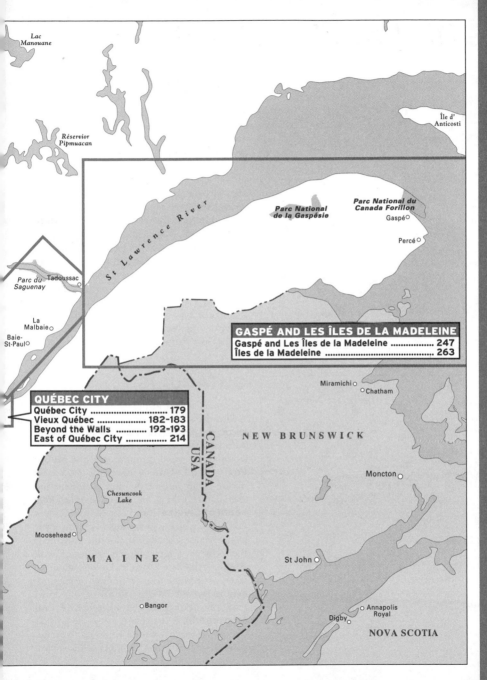

Lac
Manouane

Île d'
Anticosti

Réservior
Pipmuacan

Parc National
de la Gaspésie

Parc National du
Canada Forillon

Gaspé○

Percé○

St Lawrence River

Parc du Saguenay Tadoussac○

La
Malbaie○

Baie-
St-Paul○

Miramichi○
○Chatham

NEW BRUNSWICK

CANADA
USA

Moncton○

Chesuncook
Lake

Moosehead○

M A I N E

St John○

○Bangor

Digby○

○Annapolis
Royal

NOVA SCOTIA

The Lay of the Land

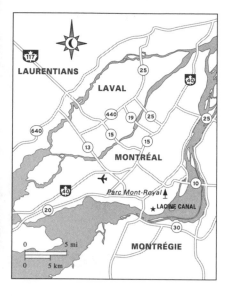

MONTRÉAL

Canada's most cosmopolitan city and North America's most European one is at once an ode to the early days of French colonization and to modern, laid-back sophistication. Bilingual, forward-thinking, and romantic, the inhabitants of this city know how to eat, dance, design, debate, and have a good time. With its many parks, pools, bicycle paths—including its famed **Lachine Canal**—and its beloved **Parc Mont-Royal,** Montréal is a great recreational destination. Then, of course, there's the city's revitalized **old quarter** and its many art galleries and museums, theater groups, and music, dance, and film festivals. It's a city, in short, that always seems abuzz with excitement even during the depths of winter. And if there's one thing that is absolutely certain, it's that Montrealers love their city… and it shows.

OUTAOUAIS

This quiet region in the west of the province is known for two principal attractions. First there's the outstanding **Parc de la Gatineau** with crystal-clear lakes, biking, cross-country skiing, year-round camping, and the **Mackenzie King Estate**—once home to Canada's nature-loving, eccentric Prime Minister. And second, there's the outstanding **Canadian Museum of Civilization.** Located in the city of Gatineau, which is just a stone's throw away from Ottawa, Canada's capital, the museum is the country's biggest cultural institution with riveting exhibits for kids and adults about all facets of Canada. When it comes to accommodations though, no place in this region draws more attention than the revered **Château Montebello,** a massive resort—the world's largest log cabin—with a six-sided fireplace, gorgeous grounds, and a number of year-round recreational activities.

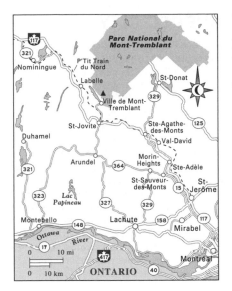

THE LAURENTIANS

Montréal's cottage country and favored skiing destination may be feeling the repercussions of its popularity with major development projects and crowds, but there is always a quiet lakeside spot or mountain view to enjoy. The Swiss-flavored Laurentians are still the place to go for lovers of outdoor adventure. On the menu, you'll find stellar rock climbing in **Val David,** a vast range of cross-country skiing trails near **Morin Heights** and of course, there's the downhill skiing and après-ski fun in places like **Saint-Sauveur** and the famed **Mont-Tremblant.** The Laurentians are also the proud home of the legendary cycling and cross-country skiing trail called the **P'tit Train du Nord,** a 200-km path that cuts through the heart of the region and offers many glimpses into what makes it so special.

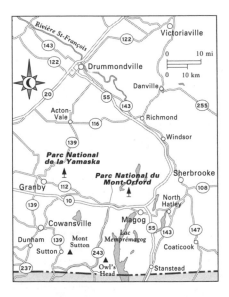

THE EASTERN TOWNSHIPS

Only a short drive from Montréal, Québec's green garden is the place for Sunday drives, cycling tours, and some of the prettiest, gentlest scenery around. With its strong Loyalist heritage, it also has a unique cultural history in the province. Although most of its population is now French-speaking, the majority of its towns like North Hatley, Sutton, and Stanstead have English names, Victorian architecture, and more than a few non-Catholic churches. The Townships are also known for excellent inns, good downhill skiing on such hills as **Mont Orford** and **Owl's Head,** a burgeoning wine scene, and the famous Lac Brome duck, in addition to its round barns, parks and big sparkling lakes. If you do get lost on one of the back roads that make up the Townships' dense network, consider yourself lucky and see where it takes you.

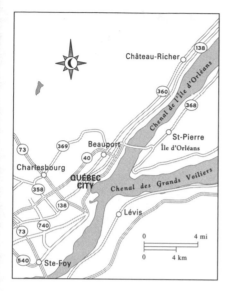

QUÉBEC CITY

Known as the cradle of French civilization in North America, this provincial capital and UNESCO World Heritage site has an impressive list of credentials. But you have to see this architectural and cultural jewel to understand its spectacular worth. In the **Old Town,** the city's earliest beginnings are brought into sharp focus by touring the old fortifications, the historic battleground of the **Plains of Abraham,** and the many museums and monuments. But the history is just as apparent with a casual stroll along the cobblestone streets where almost every turn leads to another reminder of the past. Québec City is not just about history, mind you. Its trendy streets and neighborhoods like **Saint-Roch,** parks, nearby ski hill, sleek shops, and contemporary restaurants, make it a good spot for recreational and fashion-forward pursuits as well.

CHARLEVOIX

Some of Québec's best known painters have fallen under the spell of Charlevoix and its green sloping hills that gently tumble toward the ever-present Saint Lawrence River. Charlevoix is the place to go for hikes, mountain climbs, and river rafting. It offers historic little towns like **Baie-Saint-Paul** and **La Malbaie** and a vast northern section dominated by wilderness and two spectacular provincial parks: **Parc National des Grands-Jardins** and **Parc National des Hautes-Gorges-de-la-Rivière-Malbaie.** You'll also find the best whale-watching opportunities here, thanks to the rich feeding grounds of the Saint Lawrence Estuary. But Charlevoix is becoming most famous for being Québec's gourmet destination. It's got a wealth of locally produced fruit and veggies, cheese, and meats and an impressive array of fine restaurants—all perfect for the foodie travelers.

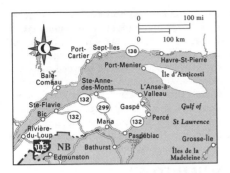

GASPÉ AND LES ÎLES DE LA MADELEINE

With its seaside vistas and craggy coastline, the Gaspé, in the eastern extreme of Québec, is characterized by water and mountains. Some of the province's most beautiful parks reside here, including **Parc National de la Gaspésie,** with its dramatic **Chic Choc Mountains,** and **Parc National du Canada Forillon** with its meadows and beaches. There's also the post-card-famous **Rocher Percé** and the protected northern gannet sanctuary on **Île Bonaventure.** A short flight or ferry ride away rests the gorgeous wind-swept beaches and the iron-red cliffs of the **Îles de la Madeleine,** located in the Gulf of Saint Lawrence. The islands have warm-water swimming, ample camping opportunities, and a population that is laid-back and warm. A haven for musicians and artists, this is the place to kick back and shed your city skin.

Planning Your Trip

Québec, the largest province in a country that is already unfathomably immense, has a fair share of its own distances to cover. Although most of the province's cities, towns, and worthwhile stops are congregated in the south along the border close to the Saint Lawrence River, it can still take plenty of time to take in all that there is to see.

Montréal and Québec City are the province's star attractions, and each one makes a good base from which to explore the surrounding regions. Driving is the best way to get around and explore off-the-beaten-track towns and the provincial and national parks. The highways are generally well maintained (except for the hefty pot hole here and there). Those who aren't wild about driving, especially during winter, and want to get to one location and stay put, can always take the bus or the comfortable train on certain routes.

With just a weekend to spend in the province, limit your visit to either Montréal or Québec City. There is a lot to see in both cities, and you'll be spreading yourself too thin, trying to get to both in the space of just a few days. The ideal time that most visitors allow themselves when visiting both Montréal and Québec City is a week. Give yourself three days in both places and allot two and a half days as travel days. Give yourself 10 days if you want to get a taste of a couple of the other regions in the vicinity, like the Laurentians, Eastern Townships (both just a short drive from Montréal), or Charlevoix (only about one hour away from Québec City). If you want to touch upon all of the province's jewels, a full three weeks will permit a sampling of the cities and all the major tourist regions, and you'll have time for a side trip farther afield to the Gaspé and les Îles de la Madeleine.

In terms of accommodation, there is a wealth of places to stay to suit budgets big and small. The cities offer everything from the typical big chains to independent hotels, plush boutique hotels and B&Bs, while the other regions have a multitude of campgrounds, country inns, and a wide array of B&Bs. Restaurant options are also vast with everything from fast food favorites (*poutine* and burgers) to down-home cooking (meat pie, beans, and ham) and from healthy vegetarian fare to French gourmet meals that showcase all the best local seasonal ingredients. In Montréal, there are quite a few bring-your-own-wine establishments, which add up to huge savings.

WHEN TO GO

Québec is blessed with four distinct seasons, and each one of them has its advantages—although most locals would say that they could certainly handle a little bit less of winter. There's no wrong time to visit the province, but if you do have an aversion to the cold, then you're best off to come during the summer months.

Many people are surprised by just how balmy Québec can be in summer, which typically lasts June–mid-September. The truth is that during July and August, it can be downright muggy, especially in Montréal. Temperatures commonly soar to 30°C and beyond, leading locals to crank air conditioners and seek refuge in public pools. On the whole, though, the summer is a great time to visit. Green, lush, alive, playful, and relaxed, summer is a joyous time in Québec. Naturally, it's also when most Quebecers take their holidays, making public holidays (the first Monday after May 25 for Victoria Day, Saint-Jean-Baptiste on June 24, Canada Day on July 1, and the first Monday in September for Labour Day) busy ones for hotels, parks, and campgrounds. Expect the stores to be closed too.

Winter, that season that is often so dreaded and yet defines Quebecers so thoroughly, starts around mid-November and usually extends well into March. Although the season can be unpredictable and inordinately cold, there are some definite rewards to visiting during this time. There's downhill and cross-country skiing, skating, and dog-sled rides, not to mention the opportunity to hole away in a cozy cabin somewhere with a hot toddy and a warming fire. Road conditions can be somewhat precarious, especially after a bout of freezing rain, but highway workers are quick to sweep and salt the roads. The first snowfall usually happens sometime in December, although frequently it won't stay on the ground until January, the coldest month. The ski season generally lasts from the end of November until April.

For those who want to avoid crowds, the two best times to visit are in spring (April and May) and fall (September and October). By mid-May, the temperatures are warm, the leaves are out, but the hordes of tourists have not yet arrived and school hasn't let out yet. Hotels usually aren't that busy, but you may find that you're too early to appreciate some of the tours and activities, especially outside the cities, that only get started in June. Between mid-March and mid-April is also when the sap starts running, and Quebecers make their annual pilgrimage to the *cabane à sucre* (sugar shack).

Fall is a breathtakingly beautiful time in the province. After Labour Day, things get much quieter, there's a coolness that returns at night and the spectacular fall colors strut their stuff throughout the province. This is a great time to go for hikes and country drives. Thanksgiving in Canada takes place on the second Monday in October.

WHAT TO TAKE

Of course in the winter, you'll need plenty of warm clothes, but dress in layers because people generally compensate for the cold by cranking the heat inside. Bring a warm coat, a scarf,

and a hat that will cover your ears. You'll also want a good pair of mitts and boots that have some lining and treads so that you don't experience any spills on the sometimes-icy streets. Salt, which is very liberally tossed on the roads in winter, can leave stains on boots. If this is a concern, then consider packing along some vinegar, which, mixed with warm water, should get rid of the marks.

If you'll be doing some winter outdoor activities besides just walking around, then also bring some long underwear, thick socks that wick away moisture, and a fleece-lined coat. If you're driving in Québec during the winter months, make sure your car has snow tires or all-season radials, an ice scraper and brush, and even pack along a shovel just in case.

Although there's no real rainy season, it can pour some days, especially in spring, so consider packing a rain jacket. In the summer, bring plenty of shorts, skirts, and T-shirts. Protect yourself against the sun by packing sun block, hats, sunglasses, and some light long-sleeve shirts. If you are heading for a hike in the woods or camping, bring along some bug spray to ward off the mosquitoes. Summer nights at the beginning and end of the season can sometimes be cool, so it's a good idea to pack along a few sweaters or light jackets and warm socks.

The fall can be very cool at night, so bring along a warm jacket (a fleece and anorak are good bets) and plenty of sweaters. Just in case, you may also want to pack some mitts and a hat.

Beyond weather considerations, you need not worry about dress conventions in Québec. It is typically quite casual and open (anything goes), but if you expect to eat at some of the fancier restaurants, then bring some nicer clothes beyond jeans and T-shirts.

Explore Montréal & Québec City

THE BEST OF QUÉBEC IN 10 DAYS

Hitting all the best spots in Québec in only 10 days isn't ideal, but it can be done if you don't get sidetracked. Even if you are planning on just staying in Montréal and Québec City, do try to get out to see some of the outlying regions for a day or two. Each one of them has a unique beauty to offer, as well as scenic drives, parks, inns, and restaurants.

DAY 1

Fly into Montréal-Pierre Elliott Trudeau International Airport and head to a hotel. For the best location, stay in Old Montréal, full of chic boutique properties, or downtown, where many of the chains are.

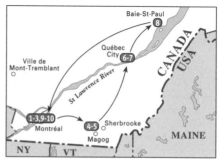

DAY 2

Spend a day in Old Montréal, and tour around the location where the city was born. Visit the **Basilique Notre-Dame,** Montréal's famous church, and spend the rest of the day exploring the small cobblestone streets and ducking into shops, cafés, and art galleries. Have dinner and then head to **Place Jacques-Cartier** to soak in the joyous atmosphere created by the beautifully illuminated buildings, throngs of people, and nighttime buskers.

DAY 3

Head downtown and stroll along **rue Sainte-Catherine,** exploring some of the city's impressive department stores. Stop for lunch and then stroll around the peaceful and aristocratic **Golden Square Mile.** Have a peek through the **McGill University** gates and then keep walking until you reach the **Musée des Beaux-Arts de Montréal.** Spend the afternoon perusing the province's best collection of art. If you have kids along, consider spending the day at the **Olympic Stadium area** instead. You can fill up a whole day here with stops at the fascinating **Insectarium,** a museum dedicated to bugs of all varieties, and the enchanting **Jardin Botanique de Montréal,** the city's legendary gardens. Head to the bohemian **Plateau** for dinner and if your energy hasn't been depleted, hit one of the famed nightclubs along **boulevard Saint-Laurent.**

DAYS 4-5

Pack up your bags and make your way toward the green **Eastern Townships.** Get yourself a nice auberge (inn) in the quaint and bustling towns of **Sutton, Knowlton** or **North Hatley,** and have dinner in the dining room of the inn. The next day, take a leisurely drive along Township roads, making sure you stop at **Saint-Benoît-du-Lac Abbey** for a tour of the grounds and the pretty town of **Frelighsburg.**

DAY 6

Hit the road for the province's capital, **Québec City.** Make yourself comfortable in one of the B&Bs or boutique hotels in the **Old Town.** Head to **rue Petit-Champlain** and explore the many shops that line the historic street. Take the **Funicular** up to the **Château Frontenac,** and go on one of the tours of the landmark building. Have dinner and finish your evening off with some jazz music at the Hôtel Clarendon's **L'Emprise lounge.**

DAY 7

Begin by exploring the **Citadelle** and the **Fortifications** to get the bigger picture of the walled city. This should take the better part of a day. Spend your evening in Québec City's hip new **Saint-Roch** neighborhood. After dinner, stop by the magnificent **Jardin Saint Roch** and take a break by the waterfall, a soothing scene that will calm you before you head to dreamland.

DAY 8

Wake up at a reasonable hour and head east toward the pastoral **Charlevoix,** stopping off at **Basilique Sainte-Anne-de-Beaupré,** Québec's most legendary shrine, on your way. Next stop is the art- and food-centric town of **Baie-Saint-Paul.** Check into your inn and spend the rest of the day exploring the art galleries and shops along rue Saint-Jean-Baptiste. Tonight, have your blow-it-all meal either in town or at one of the restaurants in one of the little inns just outside town.

DAY 9

After breakfast in town, pack up the car and slowly make your way back to Montréal. When you get there, reward yourself with dinner downtown.

DAY 10

Head to Montréal-Pierre Elliott Trudeau International Airport for the flight home.

THE WEEK-LONG OUTDOOR ADVENTURE

The province has some stellar opportunities for outdoor enthusiasts, including major biking trails, mountain climbing, white-water rafting, and hiking. The activities mentioned here combine city and wilderness recreation and are targeted toward summer visitors who are fit and want to combine sightseeing with recreational pursuits.

DAY 1
Arrive at Montréal-Pierre Elliott Trudeau International Airport and head to a hotel in Montréal.

DAY 2
Spend today on Montréal's legendary 14.5-km **Lachine Canal** bike path by starting at the port in Old Montréal. Stop for a light lunch at the **Atwater Market.** You can eat there or bring food along for a picnic by the canal. Continue your ride until you've reached the suburb of Lachine and the **Lachine Lock Visitor Service Centre.** Stop to see the legendary rapids that are the reason why Montréal is located where it is. Make your way back to downtown Montréal.

DAY 3
Hit the highway in the morning and make the short trip to **Saint-Sauveur.** Check into your hotel, get out your bike, and head along the **P'tit Train du Nord,** the mythical 200-km bike trail that winds its way through the Laurentians from Saint-Jérôme to Mont Laurier. On the first day, bike to **Val-David,** stopping off at the public beach at **Lac Raymond** along the way. Stop in Val-David for a light lunch. If biking is not your thing, make the short drive to Val-David and consider an afternoon of rock climbing in this town known as the best place to climb in eastern Canada.

DAYS 4-5
The next morning, drive to **Mont-Tremblant.** Check into your hotel and then take the afternoon to explore the many trails leading to its summit – or take the gondola to the summit and work your way down. Afterwards,

stop for dinner and drinks in the pedestrian village. The next day, head into the **Parc National du Mont-Tremblant,** Québec's biggest park, for a day of canoeing. If you're keen on a more solitary wilderness experience, skip the ski station and head directly to the park. Rent a hut located on a lake so that you can spend the next couple of days hiking, canoeing, and swimming, or head out for a two-day canoe trip.

DAY 6
Make the drive back to Montréal, where you will spend your last night. In the late afternoon, explore **Parc Mont-Royal.** Park your car in one of the lots (or take the city bus that leads up the mountain), and explore the paths, the beautiful cemetery grounds, and Beaver Lake. Finish your visit with a stop at the **Belvédère Kondiaronk** for an incredible view – and a parting glimpse of the city. Reward yourself for all the exercise with an ice cream at the **Chalet du Parc Mont-Royal.**

DAY 7
Head to Montréal-Pierre Elliott Trudeau International Airport for the flight home.

NINE DAYS FOR HISTORY BUFFS

Québec, often described as a little piece of Europe in North America, is a treasure to those who like a healthy dose of history when they travel. This schedule, which focuses on Montréal and Québec City with a little side trip to Île d'Orléans, permits a leisurely pace and hits all the major sights.

DAY 1

Arrive at Montréal-Pierre Elliott Trudeau International Airport and head to a hotel in Old Montréal, which, as the name suggests, is where much of the city's history lies.

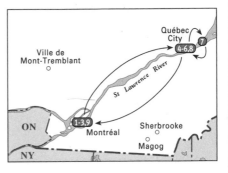

DAYS 2-3

There is a full few days' worth of worthwhile sights in Old Montréal alone, but you should at least make sure your visit includes the charming sailors' church, **Chapelle Notre-Dame-de-Bon-Secours,** which dates back to 1771. The church has a tower that affords a great view of the port and an adjoining museum, the **Musée Marguerite Bourgeoys,** dedicated to the church's founder, also known as the "mother of the colony." You should also hit **Place d'Armes,** the city's historic square, which has at its center a statue of Montréal's founder Paul Chomedey de Maisonneuve and many first-in-the-city buildings all around it. Stop by the **Centre d'Histoire de Montréal** for an exhibit on the city's five main historical eras and the excellent **Musée Pointe-à-Callière** for a subterranean walk through Montréal's first foundations.

DAY 4

Drive to Québec City and head to a hotel or inn in the Old Town. Go to the city's most recognizable building, the **Château Frontenac** for a drink or splurge on dinner. You'll be sitting on the site where Québec City was born. After that, go for a stroll along **Terrace Dufferin** and look out at the view that the city's earliest settlers also gazed out on to make sure that no invaders were drawing near.

DAY 5

Put your walking shoes on and set out to explore Québec City's **Old Town.** First head to **Place Royale,** the old market square that dates back to 1608, and gaze up at the **Fresque des Québécois,** the mural where you'll see portraits of some of the major players in Québec's history. Next, spend a few hours at the **Musée de la Civilisation de Québec** and take in the *People of Québec... Then and Now* exhibit to get the full picture of the city's earliest days. When you leave the museum, head wherever the wind takes you. There are no wrong turns in the Old Town, and you will eventually stumble upon some architectural gem, monument, or museum. Stop for dinner and then head to the narrow **rue Petit-Champlain,** the main drag in what is considered the oldest commercial quarter in North America.

DAY 6

Wake up early and go on a guided tour along the **Fortifications de Québec,** the city's ancient protective walls. Once you're done, spend the rest of the day at the **Parc des Champs-de-Bataille,** exploring the location where the country's most infamous battle between the French and the English took place. Visiting these two places will fill up your day.

DAY 7

Dedicate a full day to touring the beautiful **Île d'Orléans.** Drive around the island taking in the beautiful homes – the best collection of New France residential architecture. Stop by the **Manoir Mauvide-Genest,** a 1734 house that is now a museum chronicling the life of its first residents and **Église Saint-Pierre,** the oldest church on the island built in 1717.

DAY 8

Leave for Montréal in the morning, so that you can spend the afternoon exploring the Golden Square Mile, including the **Musée McCord,** an excellent historical museum, and the **Musée des Beaux-arts de Montréal,** which features works from some of the province's earliest artists.

DAY 9

Head to Montréal-Pierre Elliott Trudeau International Airport for the flight home.

FIVE DAYS FOR FOODIES

Québec is a dream for those who love to wine and dine. From bad-for-you, but oh-so-good junk food to upscale, gourmet French cuisine, Quebecers love to eat and love to eat well. There are two spots in the province especially known for their opportunities to indulge: Montréal and the Charlevoix region. Here is a way to hit some of the highlights.

DAY 1

Arrive at Montréal-Pierre Elliott Trudeau International Airport on Friday night and head to a hotel downtown or in Old Montréal. Book a table at one of the boutique hotel restaurants in Old Montréal like **Verses Restaurant** at the Nelligan or **Cube** at the Hôtel Saint-Paul. If you're in the mood for a little nighttime stroll, hit the charming rue Bernard in Outremont and stop by **Le Bilboquet** for some artisanal ice cream and sorbet in delectable flavors like pear, taffy, and mango-raspberry.

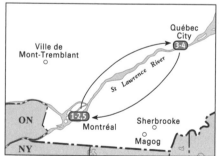

DAY 2

On Saturday morning, head up to the **Jean-Talon Market,** and pick out some fixings for your own picnic. You can find some of the best Québécois specialties here like maple syrup Ice wine, cheeses, *tourtière, pâté,* and local organic fruit and veggies. If you get hungry while you're there, there's a great outdoor crêpe stand. Beer lovers should head to the **McAuslan Brewery** on the Lachine Canal, where you can get a one-hour tour and tasting of the microbrewery's five beers that range from the light and fruity Apricot

Wheat Ale to the dark and robust Oatmeal Stout. Finish your day with a classic French bistro meal at the wonderful **L'Express** on rue Saint-Denis. It's worth it just for the jar of little pickles that they bring to your table.

DAYS 3-4

Wake up early on Sunday morning and head to **Olive+Gourmando** in Old Montréal to pick up a café au lait, some cranberry and lemon poppy seed muffins, and a few sinful chocolate and espresso brownies for the road. Make your way to **Baie-Saint-Paul** in the Charlevoix region, located just 100 km east of Québec City. Settle into your hotel and then explore town. Stop by **Laiterie Charlevoix-Économusée du Fromage** to pick up some exquisite Migneron cheese. Make a reservation at any one of the excellent restaurants, like **Le Mouton Noir** with

its outdoor patio overlooking the river or **Al Dente,** a tiny spot that makes its own excellent fresh pasta. The next day, make some more stops along the **Route des Saveurs,** including **Les Jardins du Centre,** which stocks unusual vegetables like blue potatoes and yellow carrots and other locally grown products. For dinner, try the country-style dining room **Les Saveurs Oubliées,** known for their Charlevoix lamb.

DAY 5

Hit the road for Montréal and if there's time before you leave, head to the Plateau neighborhood and pick up some fresh bagels at **Saint-Viateur Bagel** or **Fairmount Bagel** and some smoked meat at **Schwartz's** or **Lester's Deli.** If you don't have time, both places will also send you a slab via mail. Your friends and family will love you forever.

THE BEST OF WINTER

Contrary to popular belief, Québec is a great place to visit in the winter, especially if you enjoy the outdoors and warming up by the fire at night. Although the weather can be unpredictable, you should be fine if you take precautions while driving and stay put if things look too grim outside. The truth is that the province actually is at its most beautiful under a blanket of fresh snow and that the winter, as much as Quebecers may be loathe to admit, is actually in many ways what defines them.

DAY 1

Arrive at Montréal-Pierre Elliott Trudeau International Airport on a Friday and head to a Montréal hotel. Have dinner in a cozy place like **Restaurant Bonaparte** where you can reserve a seat by the fireplace. Make sure that you are dressed warmly – hat, good coat, mitts – and then catch a ride on a **calèche.** You'll get a tour of the city and be kept toasty under a big fur blanket. Have a warming nightcap before retiring.

DAY 2

After you've had a good hearty breakfast, head downtown to **rue Sainte-Catherine** for some Saturday shopping. Duck down into the **Underground City** where you can roam from store to store without worrying about having your zipper done up. Come up for some air and visit avenue McGill College. The trees that line its meridian are all decked out in white lights and culminate with Place Ville-Marie's beautiful 63-foot-high illuminated tree sculpture. Spend the late afternoon skating at the **Bonsecours Basin Skating Rink.** As the sun goes down and it starts to get dark, you'll get a good view of many of Old Montréal's illuminated buildings. Continue skating until you've worked up your appetite for dinner.

the room in always warm and crowded, or the more upscale **Aux Truffes** for foie gras and fine dining. If you want to extend the evening, there's plenty of late-night fun to be had at one of the thumping nightclubs in and around the village.

DAY 3

Wake up early on Sunday and head up to the Laurentians. Stop in at **Saint-Sauveur** for a quick perusal of the shops along rue Principale before continuing on to **Mont-Tremblant.** Check into a hotel and then strap on your skis for an afternoon heading down the slopes. The evening's activities include an exploration of the Station's pedestrian village, including dinner at a casual après-ski place like **Microbrasserie La Diable,** where

DAY 4

Wake up early and make the trip back to Montréal. If you want to take a good winter souvenir back with you, consider stopping in at **Kanuk** located on rue Rachel in the Plateau before you go. This great shop and factory makes some of the nicest – and warmest – winter gear around, including coats, vests, and sleeping bags. Head to Montréal-Pierre Elliott Trudeau International Airport for the flight home.

MONTRÉAL

The 51-km-long and 14-km-wide island that sits in the middle of the St. Lawrence River, known as Montréal, is a city of many distinctions: the only major French-speaking city in North America, the third-largest francophone city in the world (recently bumped down from second place by Kinshasa), the second-largest city in Canada, and by turn, the most laid-back, the one with the sexiest people, a festival city, bilingual city, and the city that most resembles a European one in North America.

Whatever the characterization, the 3.6 million people who call Montréal home have a lot to be proud of these days. With the years of economic doldrums largely behind it, and the largely French population confident in the strength of its language and culture, Mon-

tréal has opened itself up again in a way not seen since the 1960s and '70s, when the world descended upon it for Expo '67 and the 1976 Summer Olympics. Buildings with daring design, boutique hotels, and cultural institutions are going up, while there is still fervent enthusiasm for the preservation and promotion of the city's heritage.

Not too slick and not too gritty, sophisticated but not snobby, urban but green-loving, Montréal is a city that has come into its own. Ask the locals what they think and you may hear them curse the long, brutal winters, the constantly wrangling politicians, and the potholed streets, but Montrealers have a deep-rooted love for their city that, to anyone visiting, is utterly infectious.

MONTRÉAL

HIGHLIGHTS

(Place Jacques-Cartier: A riot of music, laughter, and buskers, this square in Old Montréal is where the party is all summer long (page 38).

(Basilique Notre-Dame: Light a candle or simply sit quietly and gaze at the bejeweled and elegant grand dame of churches (page 43).

(Musée Pointe-à-Callière: This museum in Old Montréal has exhibits and is itself an exhibit. Tour its foundations to discover all the relics dating to the beginning of the city (page 45).

(Musée des Beaux-Arts de Montréal: With more than 30,000 art objects and a huge Canadian collection, Canada's oldest museum is *the* place in Montréal for art lovers (page 52).

(The Lookouts at Parc Mont-Royal: This landmark oasis in the middle of the city center is the best location to take in views of the city... and for late-night kisses (page 54).

(Oratoire Saint-Joseph: You may not want to climb its almost 300 stairs on your knees, but you will at least want to observe the grandiose, fortresslike oratory that Brother André built (page 55).

(Boulevard Saint-Laurent: Known as "the Main," Montréal's boulevard Saint-Laurent offers up eastern European eats, trendy clothes, and the most active nightlife in the city (page 57).

(Insectarium de Montréal: Bugs aren't icky, they're just misunderstood, claims this temple to creepy-crawlies. See bugs, learn about them, and even taste them (page 62)!

(Lachine Canal: Biking alongside this 14.5-km canal is one of the city's best summertime activities. Get your exercise and learn about the Lachine Rapids, the reason Montrealers now call this island home (page 63).

(Shopping on rue Sainte-Catherine: There may be shopping strips that are more chic, but how many let you shop above ground... and below (page 78)?

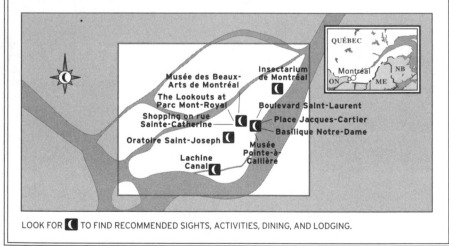

LOOK FOR **(** TO FIND RECOMMENDED SIGHTS, ACTIVITIES, DINING, AND LODGING.

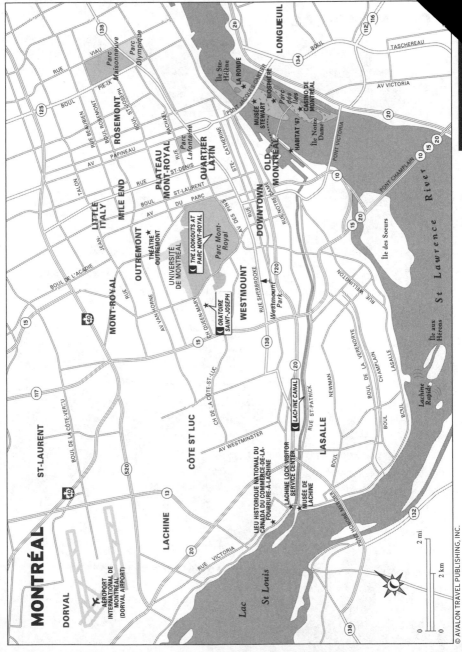

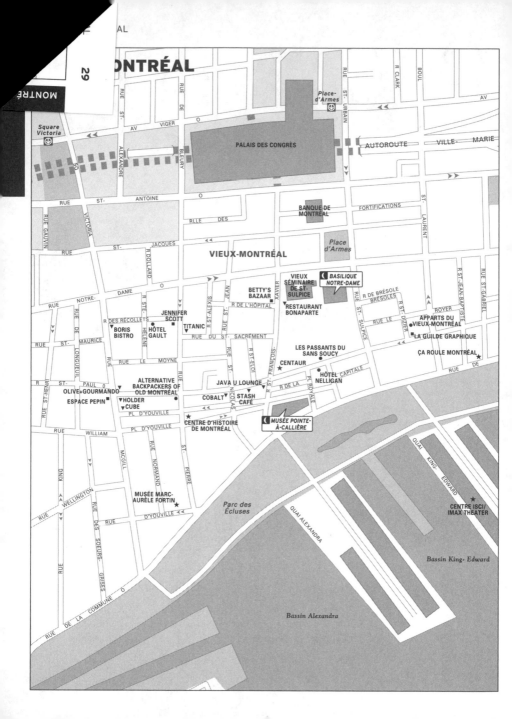

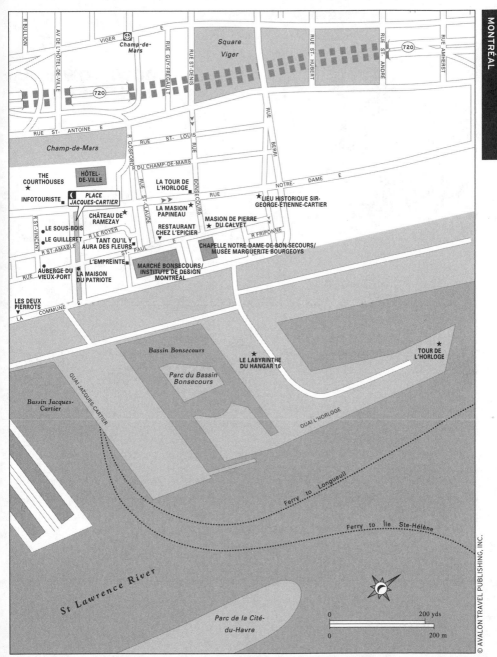

R BULLION
AV DE L'HÔTEL-DE-VILLE
VIGER
Champ-de-Mars
RUE GUY-FRÉGAULT
RUE ST-DENIS
E
Square Viger
RUE ST-HUBERT
RUE ST-ANDRÉ
720
RUE AMHERST

720

RUE ST-ANTOINE E
RUE ST-LOUIS
RUE
BERRI

Champ-de-Mars

R GOSFORD
R DU CHAMP-DE-MARS

THE COURTHOUSES ★
HÔTEL-DE-VILLE
LA TOUR DE L'HORLOGE ★
NOTRE- DAME E

INFOTOURISTE ■
PLACE JACQUES-CARTIER
RUE ST-CLAUDE
BONSECOURS
RUE
LIEU HISTORIQUE SIR-GEORGE-ÉTIENNE-CARTIER ★

CHÂTEAU DE RAMEZAY ★
LA MASION PAPINEAU ★
MASION DE PIERRE DU CALVET ★

● LE SOUS-BOIS
R ST-VINCENT
● LE GUILLERET
R LE ROYER
RESTAURANT CHEZ L'ÉPICIER
R FRIPONNE

R ST-AMABLE
TANT QU'IL Y AURA DES FLEURS ■
ST- PAUL
E
CHAPELLE NOTRE-DAME-DE-BON-SECOURS/ MUSÉE MARGUERITE BOURGEOYS

L'EMPREINTE ■
MARCHÉ BONSECOURS/ INSTITUT DE DESIGN MONTRÉAL

RUE
AUBERGE DU VIEUX-PORT ●
LA MAISON DU PATRIOTE

LES DEUX PIERROTS ▼
LA COMMUNE

Bassin Bonsecours
LE LABYRINTHE DU HANGAR 16 ★
TOUR DE L'HORLOGE ★

QUAI JACQUES-CARTIER
Parc du Bassin Bonsecours

QUAI L'HORLOGE

Bassin Jacques-Cartier

Ferry to Longueuil

Ferry to Île Ste-Hélène

St Lawrence River

Parc de la Cité-du-Havre

0   200 yds
0   200 m

MONTRÉAL

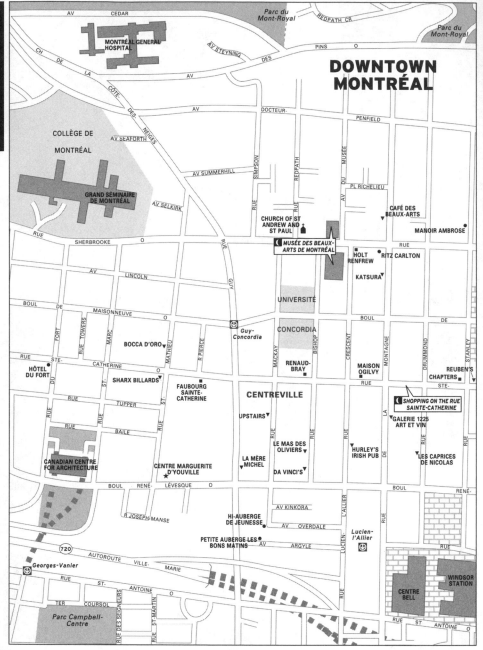

DOWNTOWN MONTRÉAL

Parc du Mont-Royal

Parc du Mont-Royal

MONTRÉAL GENERAL HOSPITAL

COLLÈGE DE MONTRÉAL

GRAND SÉMINAIRE DE MONTRÉAL

AV CEDAR

CH DE LA CÔTE DES NEIGES

AV STEYNING

REDPATH CR

PINS

DES

AV

AV

DOCTEUR-

PENFIELD

PL RICHELIEU

AV SEAFORTH

AV SUMMERHILL

AV SELKIRK

SIMPSON

REDPATH

RUE

DU MUSÉE

CAFÉ DES BEAUX-ARTS

MANOIR AMBROSE

CHURCH OF ST ANDREW AND ST PAUL

MUSÉE DES BEAUX-ARTS DE MONTRÉAL

HOLT RENFREW

RITZ CARLTON

KATSURA

RUE

SHERBROOKE O

RUE GUY

UNIVERSITÉ

RUE

AV LINCOLN

BOUL DE MAISONNEUVE O

Guy-Concordia

CONCORDIA

BOUL DE

DE

RUE FORT

RUE TOWERS

RUE MARC

MATHIEU

R PIERCE

MACKAY

BISHOP

CRESCENT

MONTAGNE

DRUMMOND

STANLEY

BOCCA D'ORO

RENAUD-BRAY

MAISON OGILVY

REUBEN'S CHAPTERS

RUE STE-CATHERINE O

HÔTEL DU FORT

SHARX BILLARDS

FAUBOURG SAINTE-CATHERINE

CENTREVILLE

RUE

STE-

SHOPPING ON THE RUE SAINTE-CATHERINE

RUE TUPPER

UPSTAIRS

GALERIE 1225 ART ET VIN

RUE BAILE

LE MAS DES OLIVIERS

LA MÈRE MICHEL

HURLEY'S IRISH PUB

LES CAPRICES DE NICOLAS

CANADIAN CENTRE FOR ARCHITECTURE

CENTRE MARGUERITE D'YOUVILLE

DA VINCI'S

LA

RUE

DE

BOUL RENÉ-LÉVESQUE O

RENÉ-

R JOSEPH-MANSE

AV KINKORA

L'ALLIER

BOUL

HI-AUBERGE DE JEUNESSE

AV OVERDALE

Lucien-l'Allier

720

Georges-Vanier

AUTOROUTE VILLE-MARIE

PETITE AUBERGE LES BONS MATINS

AV ARGYLE

RUE

RUE

WINDSOR STATION

RUE ST-ANTOINE O

MARIE

ANTOINE O

TER

COURSOL

RUE DES SEIGNEURS

ST-ANTOINE

RUE ST-MARTIN

CENTRE BELL

RUE ST ANTOINE O

Parc Campbell-Centre

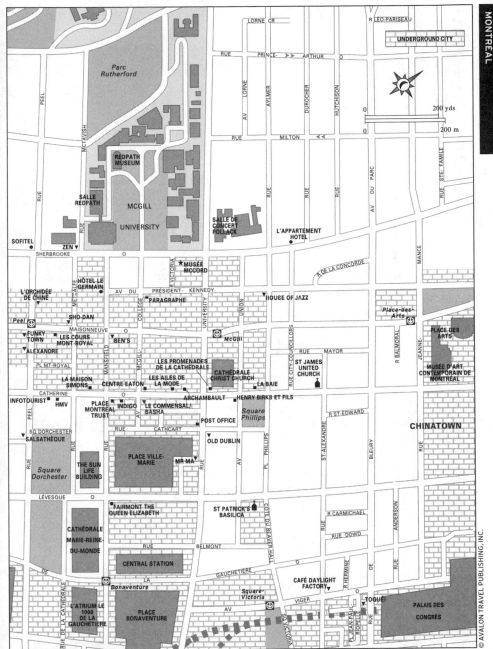

UNDERGROUND CITY
LORNE CR
R LEO-PARISEAU
RUE   PRINCE- >> ARTHUR
Parc
Rutherford
AV LORNE
AYLMER
DUROCHER
HUTCHISON
200 yds
0
0
200 m
RUE   MILTON <<
REDPATH
MUSEUM
RUE
AV DU PARC
RUE STE-FAMILE
SALLE
REDPATH
MCGILL
SALLE DE
CONCERT
POLLACK
L'APPARTEMENT
HOTEL
SOFITEL
UNIVERSITY
ZEN ▼
SHERBROOKE
MANCE
RUE
★MUSÉE
MCCORD
RUE VICTORIA
RT DE LA CONCORDE
HÔTEL LE
GERMAIN
L'ORCHIDÉE
DE CHINE ▼
AV DU   PRÉSIDENT- KENNEDY
PARAGRAPHE
HOUSE OF JAZZ
Place-des-
Arts
Peel ●
SHO-DAN
COLLEGE
UNIVERSITY
UNION
PLACE DES
ARTS
MAISONNEUVE
FUNKY
TOWN ▼
LES COURS
MONT-ROYAL
BEN'S
McGill
MUSÉE D'ART
CONTEMPORAIN DE
MONTRÉAL
ALEXANDRE ▼
MARSFIELD
MCGILL
RUE CITY COUNCILLORS
R BALMORAL
JEANNE-
PL MT-ROYAL
RUE   MAYOR
ST JAMES
UNITED
CHURCH
LES PROMENADES
DE LA CATHÉDRALE
CATHÉDRALE
CHRIST CHURCH
LA MAISON
SIMONS
CENTRE EATON
LES AILES DE
LA MODE
LA BAIE
CATHERINE
ARCHAMBAULT
HENRY BIRKS ET FILS
CHINATOWN
INFOTOURIST ■
HMV
PLACE
MONTRÉAL
TRUST
INDIGO
LE COMMENSAL/
BASHA
Square
Phillips
R ST-EDWARD
ST-ALEXANDRE
PEEL
POST OFFICE
RUE   CATHCART
SQ DORCHESTER
SALSATHÈQUE ▼
OLD DUBLIN ▼
PL PHILLIPS
BLEURY
RUE
THE SUN
LIFE
BUILDING
PLACE VILLE-
MARIE
MR MA
AV
RUE
Square
Dorchester
LÉVESQUE
FAIRMONT THE
QUEEN ELIZABETH
ST PATRICK'S
BASILICA
R CARMICHAEL
ANDERSON
CATHÉDRALE
MARIE-REINE-
DU-MONDE
RUE DOWD
CÔTE DU BEAVER-HALL
RUE
DE
RUE
RUE   BELMONT
CENTRAL STATION
GAUCHETIÈRE
R HERMINE
DE
LA
Bonaventure ●
CAFÉ DAYLIGHT
FACTORY ▼
TOQUÉ ▼
L'ATRIUM LE
1000
DE LA
GAUCHETIÈRE
PLACE
BONAVENTURE
Square
Victoria ●
VIGER
AV
RUE DE LA CATHÉDRALE
VICTORIA
PL JEAN-PAUL
RIOPELLE
RUE
PALAIS DES
CONGRÈS

MONTRÉAL

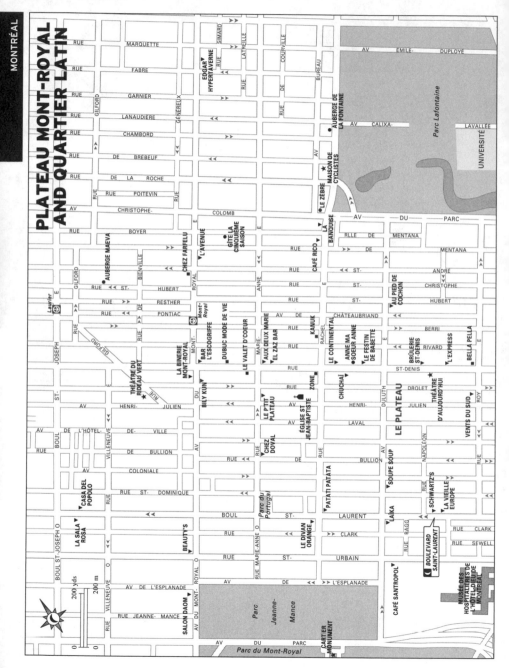

PLATEAU MONT-ROYAL AND QUARTIER LATIN

MONTRÉAL

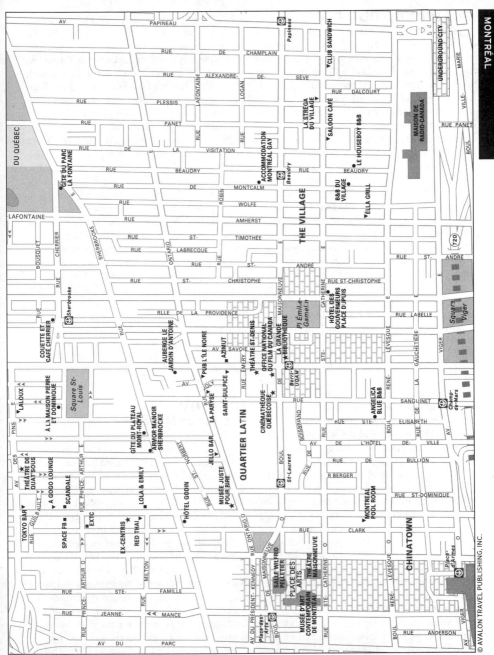

AV

RUE PAPINEAU

RUE DE CHAMPLAIN

RUE ALEXANDRE-DE-SÈVE

LAFONTAINE

LOGAN

RUE PLESSIS

PANET

RUE DE LA VISITATION

RUE

DU QUÉBEC

GÎTE DU PARC LA FONTAINE

RUE BEAUDRY

RUE DE MONTCALM

RUE ROBIN WOLFE

LAFONTAINE

RUE AMHERST

BOUSQUET

CHERRIER

SHERBROOKE

RUE ST- TIMOTHÉE

RUE ONTARIO LABRECQUE

Sherbrooke

COUETTE ET CAFÉ CHERRIER

RUE ST- CHRISTOPHE

RUE

RLLE DE LA PROVIDENCE

RUE DE PINS

Square St-Louis

LALOUX

A LA MAISON PIERRE ET DOMINIQUE

AUBERGE LE JARDIN D'ANTOINE

AZIMUT

PUB L'ÎLE NOIRE

AV SAVOIE

THÉÂTRE ST-DENIS

RUE ÉMERY

OFFICE NATIONAL DU FILM DU CANADA

LA GRANDE BIBLIOTHÈQUE

Pl Émile-Gamelin

HÔTEL DES GOUVERNEURS PLACE D JPUIS

CATHERINE

RUE ST-CHRISTOPHE

ANDRÉ

MAISONNEUVE

RUE LABELLE

Square Viger

GÎTE DU PLATEAU MONT-ROYAL

ARMOR MANOR SHERBROCKE

JELLO BAR

LA PARTYE

SAINT-SULPICE

AV JOLY

CINÉMATHÈQUE QUÉBÉCOISE

Berri-UQAM

RENÉ

ANGELICA BLUE B&B

SANGUINET

Champ-de-Mars

QUARTIER LATIN

LA PARYSE

RUE STE- ELISABETH

THÉÂTRE DE QUAT'SOUS

A GOGO LOUNGE

SCANDALE

AV DES ARTHUR

RUE PRINCE ARTHUR E

LOLA & EMILY

MUSÉE JUSTE POUR RIRE

BOUL St-Laurent

AV DE L'HÔTEL DE- VILLE

RUE DE BULLION

R BERGER

MONTREAL POOL ROOM

RUE ST-DOMINIQUE

TOKYO BAR

RUE GUILBAULT

SPACE FB

EXTIC

EX-CENTRIS

RED THAI

HÔTEL GODIN

RUE NORBERT

RUE ONTARIO O

RUE CLARK

CHINATOWN

ARTHUR O

MILTON

STE- FAMILLE

RUE MAISONNEUVE

DE PRÉSIDENT- KENNEDY

SALLE WILFRID PELLETIER

PLACE DES ARTS

THÉÂTRE MAISONNEUVE

STE CATHERINE

RENÉ-

LEVESQUE

Place-d'Armes

RUE JEANNE- MANCE

Place-des-Arts

MUSÉE D'ART CONTEMPORAIN DE MONTRÉAL

AV DU PARC

BOUL RUE ANDERSON

THE VILLAGE

CLUB SANDWICH

UNDERGROUND CITY

RUE DALCOURT

LA STREGA DU VILLAGE

SALOON CAFÉ

LE HOUSEBOY B&B

ACCOMMODATION MONTRÉAL GAY

Beaudry

BEAUDRY

B&B DU VILLAGE

ELLA GRILL

MAISON DE RADIO-CANADA

RUE PANET

MARIE VILLE-

BOUL

720

ANDRÉ

CHINATOWN

© AVALON TRAVEL PUBLISHING, INC.

PLANNING YOUR TIME

Staying in Montréal for two weeks would not be unreasonable with all the restaurants, attractions, neighborhoods, and bars and clubs to sample, but five days will do in a pinch and six is even better. If you're staying downtown or in Old Montréal, you'll be able to fit in a little more by walking to many of your destinations.

Start off your city visit by heading to the place where it all began, Old Montréal. Check in to one of the B&Bs, or if you can spring for a little more, one of the area's plush boutique hotels. Stay for at least two nights. Start off by visiting **Place-Jacques Cartier** (Champ-de-Mars metro). You'll see the Infotouriste center there; it's a good chance to stock up on brochures, get your questions answered, and get a map to the old town's cobblestone streets. Tour the old sights, Including the Chapelle Notre-Dame-de-Bon-Secours, the Château de Ramezay and its lovely garden and, of course, the magnificent **Basilique Notre-Dame.**

On your next day, stop by the Old Port, and, if you're in the mood for a little 21st-century activity, take in the Centre iSci science center and an IMAX film. Then head over to the western part of Old Montréal, stroll through Place d'Youville, and stop by the tiny Centre d'Histoire de Montréal for a look at its wonderful exhibit *Montréal of a Thousand Faces.* Next, head to the **Musée Pointe-à-Callière** for a tour of its fortifications and a well-executed look at the beginnings of Montréal.

Decamp to a hotel downtown or a B&B in the Plateau neighborhood for the next three days. Spend day three dropping some coin along **rue Sainte-Catherine,** checking out the underground network of tunnels that connect to all the major shopping malls and department stores. Walk through the leafy Golden Square Mile by heading west along rue Sherbrooke and making sure you stop in for a visit to the formidable **Musée des Beaux-Arts de Montréal.**

If you're keen on fitting in some exercise, rent a bike or some inline skates and head to Parc Jean-Drapeau, making sure that you pass by the Lego-block masterpiece, Habitat '67, on your way over. If you're up for something a bit more extensive, then plan for a bike trip along the city's well-used **Lachine Canal.** At the end of the canal, you'll be in the borough of Lachine, home to the famous Lachine Rapids. Getting to Lachine, stopping for lunch, and then heading back downtown will take up the better part of a day.

Head up to the mountain and the **Parc Mont-Royal** in the morning of day five, visit the interpretation center in La Maison Smith, and then visit both lookouts: Belvédère Kondiaronk and Belvédère Camilien-Houde. Head down voie Camilien-Houde toward the Plateau district. Walk down the Main (boulevard Saint-Laurent), have lunch, and if you have time, head over to Saint-Denis for more strolling and shopping and dinner at one of the hundreds of good restaurants in the district.

If you can spend a sixth day, then head over to Parc Olympique and visit the stellar **Insectarium.** There's plenty more to see in this neighborhood called Hochelaga-Maisonneuve, including visiting the Jardin Botanique de Montréal and the Biodôme and taking a cable car up to the top of the "Big O," Montréal's Olympic Stadium.

HISTORY
For Fur or Money

In 1535 Jacques Cartier first set anchor on the shores of Montréal, land that the Algonquin, Huron, and Iroquois had called home for about 8,000 years. Sent by the French king with orders to establish a profitable colonial empire in the New World, as well as a passage to India, Cartier was blocked by the riotous Lachine rapids and forced to set anchor.

With the help of Iroquois guides, Cartier climbed the mountain at the island's center, planted a cross at the top, and christened it Mont Royal. But when he returned to France empty-handed—no gold, no diamonds, no route to the Far East—the king became disenchanted and refused, for the time being, to finance any more trips to the new colony.

After Samuel de Champlain's successful establishment of a fur-trade settlement in Québec City in 1608, France added another notch to its post in 1642 when Paul de Chomedey de Maisonneuve founded Ville-Marie, the settlement that would eventually become Montréal. De Maisonneuve's original mission—to convert the native people to Catholicism—led to the foundation, in quick succession, of hospital Hôtel-Dieu de Montréal, a few churches, and the colony's first school.

As new settlers arrived, the economy built itself on the trade of fur, but French Montréal increasingly found itself in intense competition with the British colonies of New England and later, those up north in the Hudson Bay area. To make matters worse, the Iroquois, who were trading furs with the British, were the French-friendly Hurons' worst enemies. In 1648–1649, the Iroquois went to war with the Huron and wiped them out. Left without its trading partner, Montréal's economy tanked, as did the rest of the colony's. France's deployment of troops to impose peace on the Iroquois resulted in a trading partnership and a revitalization of Montréal's economy. But in 1760, when British troops invaded, the French regime ended. The Treaty of Paris sealed the deal and transferred the territory to the British. So long to La Nouvelle France.

In 1775, Montréal was invaded again—although this time by American Revolutionists seeking independence from England. When a delegation led by Benjamin Franklin came to the city to convince French Canadians to join the fight against the British crown, the French refused to collaborate, helping the English army successfully push the Americans back. Franklin came back to Montréal in 1778 with the same goal in mind and, with the help of a typographer friend named Fleury de Mesplet, launched a newspaper for the American cause called *La Gazette,* which is still published today.

Growth of a Modern "Sin" City

With the construction in the 1820s of the Lachine Canal, which opened the interior to trade, the city's economy again soared. When

Montréal officially incorporated in 1832, it was predominantly English-speaking, thanks to a flurry of immigrants from Ireland, Scotland, and England. The boom also brought in a huge influx of immigrants from Italy, Russia, and Eastern Europe, making Montréal in 1852 the largest city in British North America.

After World War I, Prohibition turned the resolutely wet Montréal into party central for Americans looking for a good time. With its easy access to gambling, prostitution, and a wide array of bars and pubs, freewheeling Montréal became known as "Sin City." But despite the good times, Montréal had a high unemployment rate, worsened still by the stock market crash and Great Depression of 1929. When the city's economy began to recover in the mid 1930s, skyscrapers started going up, causing a major change in the city's skyline.

The Drapeau Era

Not many people would argue that Jean Drapeau, mayor of Montréal from 1954 to 1957 and then again from 1960 to 1986, was the major force behind the transformation of the city into the modern, creative, and innovative one that it is today. Montréal had its international premiere with the successful staging of the World's Fair (Expo '67), which managed to attract 50 million visitors in one summer. The mayor went on to establish a professional baseball team, which he named in honor of the event—the Montréal Expos. He was also responsible for the construction of the city's metro system, Place des Arts, and the successful bid for the 1976 Summer Olympics. While the Olympics did many great things for civic pride and worldwide recognition, it left the city with a massive $1 billion debt, which has just recently been paid off.

Separatism and the City

There's no denying that the rise of the separatist movement took its toll on Montréal. With the violence of the Front de Libération du Québec (FLQ) in the late 1960s and early 1970s, the beginning of the language laws in the mid-'70s, and the resulting great Anglophone exodus, Montréal wasn't a very attractive investment option. The effects of the exodus, the referendums, and two major recessions took their toll on the city. The downtown core became grubby and had plenty of boarded-up storefronts, while residents wondered if the city's snuffed-out spark would ever reignite.

Montréal Today

After a nail-biting close-call election in 1994 and a slowly recovering economy, the city began to focus its attention on reawakening its semidormant talents. It became a major destination for the making of Hollywood films and a leader in animation, managed to avoid the dot-com crash and burn, and saw its real estate market boom.

More recently, Drapeau's dream of uniting the island of Montréal under one municipal government almost became a reality. Despite major local criticism, Montréal followed the lead of Toronto by merging the city's 27 independent municipalities with the City of Montréal under the slogan "One island, one city." Gerald Tremblay became the megacity's first mayor. But English-speaking communities were still unhappy with the arrangement and forced referendums on "demerging." Fifteen of these boroughs regained independence on January 1, 2006.

Sights

OLD MONTRÉAL

Old Montréal's existence has had many phases: birthplace of the city; hub of commercial and political life; neglected, desolate area; and ticky-tacky tourist hub. Today, the one-square-km area stretching from rue Saint-Denis in the east to rue McGill in the west, between the water and the downtown sector, is still a major tourist hub, but it's also a hip and *branché* (in the know) locale with designers aplenty, boutique hotels, contemporary restaurants, and nearly 30 art galleries.

Even with its newfound cool, this is still the spot where history reigns supreme, where wandering the cobblestone streets lets you easily imagine what it would have been like to live during the days of corsets and top hats, candlesticks and calèches. The old town is most alive during the summer when people flock to its churches, museums and historic sites; in contrast, the winter months are serene and almost desolate, providing the increasing number of locals who have moved into the converted warehouse spaces a welcome break from the tourist throngs.

Situated between the water and Montréal's downtown, Old Montréal covers about one square km. Three metro stations offer access to the area. From west to east they are Square-Victoria, Place d'Armes, and Champ-de-Mars. Old Montréal's main streets are rue Notre-Dame, which runs by the Basilique Notre-Dame, and the narrow rue Saint-Paul, but a good way to start your visit is by getting off at Champ-de-Mars metro and heading to the tourist information office just off Place Jacques-Cartier.

◖ Place Jacques-Cartier

The pedestrian focal point of Old Montréal, its heart and tourist hub in the summer, Place Jacques-Cartier is a collision of colors, people, music, and food. During the summer, the cobblestone square that stretches from rue Notre-Dame in the north to rue de la Commune in the south is abuzz with street musicians, jugglers, painters, bar terraces, and truckloads of tourists. Although named for the French explorer, Place Jacques-Cartier is dominated by a monument to Lord Nelson, the British general who triumphed over Napoléon at Trafalgar. Despite numerous attempts by Québec nationalists to get rid of the statue,

BRIGHT LIGHTS, OLD CITY

Wandering through the cobblestone streets of Old Montréal during the day is a chance to imagine what it would have been like to live during the days of New France pleasantries. At night, though, the area takes on even more charm, with the old city's historic buildings beautifully illuminated to showcase their most charming features.

City administrators had what you might call a bright idea when they commissioned, in celebration of the new millennium, urban lighting designer Gilles Arpin to come up with a master plan that would shine light on the area's rich history. Here's a tour of the brilliant results.

Make **Hôtel de Ville** your first stop. Lit up by golden hues on the façade of the main building and bluer, cooler hues on the rooftops, city hall is considered by many the most spectacular building at night. Once you've had your fill, head down Place Jacques-Cartier, taking in the subtly illuminated buildings on either side of the square until you hit **rue Saint-Paul Ouest**. Take a left and head past Marché Bonsecours to the Chapelle Notre-Dame-de-Bon-Secours. Once you are in front,

walk up the tiny rue Bonsecours so you can get the full effect of the lit steeple and the glowing stained glass windows.

Next, head down toward the water, so that you arrive on **rue de la Commune**. Take a look up at the softly lit statues (the Virgin Mary and her angels) that adorn the top of the chapel before heading west on the south side of the street. Here, you'll walk past the wall of luminous limestone buildings that line the south side of Old Montréal.

Once you've hit rue Saint-Sulpice, head north, toward **Place d'Armes**. Arriving at Old Montréal's most historic of historic squares, head straight to the statue at its core. The monument to Maisonneuve, the city's founder, is illuminated at dusk every night. It is quickly followed by the sequenced illumination of all buildings that surround Place d'Armes, in order from the oldest to the newest. From the statue, do a slow 360-degree turn, looking out for the glowing clock atop the Séminaire Saint-Sulpice, the beautiful blue that shines through the windows of Cathédrale Notre-Dame, and the more Gotham-inspired lighting effects of the art-deco Aldred building.

including a failed attempt to blow it up in the 1890s, it remains the oldest in the city. Just a few steps west, you'll find **Infotouriste** (174 rue Notre-Dame Est, 9 A.M.–5 P.M. daily Apr.–June, 9 A.M.–7 P.M. daily June–Sept., 9 A.M.–5 P.M. daily Sept.–Nov., 9 A.M.– 5 P.M. Wed.–Sun. Nov.–Apr.), the primary information office in Old Montréal and the spot to pick up a free map of the area. On the east side of the square is the 1812 **Jardin Nelson** (407 place Jacques-Cartier, 514/861-5731, www.jardinnelson.com, 11:30 A.M.–3 A.M. Mon.–Fri. and 10 A.M.–3 A.M. Sat.–Sun. Apr.–Nov.), which possesses one of the city's best, if often overcrowded, outdoor patios complete with shady trees and jazz music. Leading off the west side of the street is **St. Amable Lane,** a nar-

row street lined with street artists hawking paintings of Montréal street scenes and waiting to do your caricature.

Hôtel-de-Ville

Situated at the top upper right-hand corner of Place Jacques-Cartier, Montréal's Hôtel-de-Ville (275 rue Notre-Dame Est, 514/872-3555, www.old.montreal.qc.ca, 9 A.M.–5 P.M. daily) may look like a peaceful and orderly place, but it belies a tempestuous past. In 1967, French President Charles de Gaulle, who was visiting Montréal during the World's Fair, shouted out from the balcony to the hordes of people gathered below: "Vive le Québec... Vive le Québec Libre!" ("Long live Québec... Long Live Free Québec!"). The shout, repeated all across the province and across the country by the media,

© JENNIFER EDWARDS

Montréal's Hôtel-de-Ville, site of the famous shout out from Charles de Gaulle

fanned the flames of the already burning fires between separatist-leaning Quebecers and Canadian federalists.

Beautiful during the day, but even more so at night when it is lit up, the building was originally designed by Henri-Maurice Perrault. Completed in 1903, but damaged by fire in 1922, it was rebuilt a year later in beaux-arts style, taking the city hall in Tours, France, as a model. Free guided tours are available from Monday to Friday.

The Courthouses

Although Québec City is the provincial capital, the cluster of courthouses around the Hôtel-de-Ville contributes to a feeling of big government, or at least strong conviction, among the city's citizens. At the top of Place Jacques-Cartier, to the left of City Hall, is the **Vieux Palais de Justice** (155 rue Notre-Dame Est), which dates to 1856. Contrary to its neighbor's French architectural flair, this oldest judicial building in Montréal was modeled after London's main post office. Today it houses the city's financial department. The Vieux Palais

was replaced in 1925 with the building across the street, which is now the **Cour d'Appel du Québec** (100 rue Notre-Dame Est). Architect Ernest Cormier, who also designed the Supreme Court of Canada, brought art-deco grandeur and an imposing colonnade to the new justice building. Have a peek inside the lobby to see its ornate ceiling. All judicial affairs moved to their current location in the modern **Palais de Justice** (1 rue Notre-Dame Est). Built in 1971, the dark-glass, 17-story building houses 76 courtrooms, a number of which are filled with Montrealers contesting parking tickets.

Marché Bonsecours

The long, imposing neoclassical limestone building with the 100-foot-high silver dome at the bottom left-hand side of Place Jacques-Cartier is the Marché Bonsecours (350 rue Saint-Paul Est, 514/872-7730, www.marchebonsecours.qc.ca), Montréal's original main market. Considered one of Canada's most impressive buildings when it opened in 1846, the market was designed by architect William Footner and modeled after the Customs House in Dublin. For a time, the building has housed the Canadian Parliament, City Hall, a police station, and a library.

Restored for the city's 350th anniversary in 1992, the sprawling building, which covers 100,000 square feet, now contains an array of expensive shops selling jewelry, clothing, and art. An exhibition hall on the second floor has historic displays and there's also the impressive **Galerie des Métiers d'Art du Québec** (514/878-4637, www.galeriedesmetiersdart.com, 10 A.M.– 6 P.M. daily and 10 A.M.–9 P.M. Thurs.–Fri. spring and summer), a crafts gallery whose mission is to showcase and promote the work of Québec artists, especially those working in glass, textile, and ceramics.

Chapelle Notre-Dame-de-Bon-Secours

Old Montréal's most sentimental and symbolic landmark, the Chapelle Notre-Dame-de-Bon-Secours (400 rue Saint-Paul Est, 514/282-8670, www.marguerite-bourgeoys.com, chapel free, museum $6) was originally built in 1675 under the leadership of Marguerite Bourgeoys. Destroyed by fire in 1754, the chapel was rebuilt in 1771 and given the name the "Sailors' Church" thanks to the harbor-facing rooftop statue of the Virgin Mary. Immortalized in Leonard Cohen's song, *Suzanne,* ("As the sun pours down like honey, on Our Lady of the Harbour..."), the 10-meter-high statue and her surrounding angels are said to safeguard the passage of sailors who pass under her gaze. Many sailors have shown their appreciation by donating miniature ships, some of which still hang in the chapel. Climb the 92 steps up the winding stairs of the chapel's tower and you'll get a beautiful 360-degree panorama of Old Montréal and the harbor.

The adjoining **Musée Marguerite Bourgeoys** (adults $6, students $4, children 6–12 $3) chronicles the life of the saint, also known as the "mother of the colony" and Montréal's foundation. The chapel and museum are open 11 A.M.–5 P.M. Tuesday–Sunday March–Apr., 10 A.M.–5 P.M. Tuesday–Sunday May–October, and 11 A.M.–3:30 P.M. Tuesday–Sunday November–mid-January).

Marché Bonsecours

Historic Homes

Almost directly in front of the Hôtel-de-Ville is the **Château de Ramezay** (280 rue Notre-Dame Est, 514/861-3708, www.chateauramezay.qc.ca, 10 A.M.–6 P.M. daily June–Sept. and 10 A.M.–4:30 P.M. daily Oct.–May, adults $7, students $5, children 5–17 $4), one of the finest examples of a building from the French regime still standing. Built in 1705 for the governor of Montréal, Claude de Ramezay, the house has 15 connecting rooms (ample room was needed for the governor's 16 children) and plenty of artifacts from early colonization days. In the back of the home is the incredibly beautiful **Jardin du Gouverneur** (mid-June–mid-Oct.). Landscaped in an upper-crust New France style, the garden has free entry and is very worthy of a stroll through the fruit trees and the herb and flower gardens and a stop at the outdoor Café du Château.

One of the most photographed buildings in Old Montréal is the beautiful **Maison de Pierre du Calvet** (405 rue Bonsecours, 514/282-1725, www.pierreducalvet.ca). The rough graystone house with red doors and window frames, built in either 1725 or 1770 depending on whom you ask, was originally the home of Pierre du Calvet, a notary who was later jailed for treason for collaborating with the rebels during the American Revolution. The building now houses a small inn and the ornately decorated Les Filles du Roi Restaurant.

On the corner of Bonsecours and Notre-Dame is **La Maison Papineau** (440 rue Bonsecours). Built in 1785 by John Campbell, a British colonel, the house was sold to lawyer Joseph Papineau, father of Louis-Joseph, who went on to lead the Patriots' Rebellion against the British in 1837. The only building in Old Montréal with a wood façade, the house stayed in the Papineau family until 1920. The house was bought in 1964 by Montréal journalist Eric Mclean, who restored it to its former glory and breathed new life into the area by encouraging a spurt of restoration. He sold it to the Canadian government in 1982. The house is likely soon to be turned into a national historic site.

Lieu Historique National du Canada de Sir-George-Étienne-Cartier

Commemorating the life of lawyer and politician Sir Georges Étienne-Cartier, one of the Fathers of Confederation, the Lieu Historique National du Canada de Sir-George-Étienne-Cartier (458 rue Notre-Dame Est, 514/283-2282 or 800/463-6769, www.pc.gc.ca, 10 A.M.–noon and 1 P.M.–5 P.M. Wed.–Sun. Apr.–late May and early Sept.–late Dec., and 10 A.M.–6 P.M. daily late May–early Sept., adults $4, youth 6–16 $2, family $10) is now owned by Parks Canada. Spanning two sides of a duplex, the site pays tribute to Cartier's significant achievements (head of the Conservative Party, main instigator behind the creation of the Grand Trunk Railway, and creator of a new Québec civil code) and provides insight into the pomp and pageantry of Victorian high society.

Old Port

Because of the unnavigable Lachine Rapids farther upstream, this piece of land, now Montréal's Old Port (514/496-7678 or 800/971-7678, www.oldportofmontreal.com), became a natural docking point for ships. Although it is no longer the commercial heart of the city, it remains one of Canada's most important ports.

With the 2.5-km **Parc du Bassin Bonsecours**'s opening in 1981 and with a major rehaul done in 1992, the port has become a desirable place spend an afternoon. It's popular in the winter for its beautiful, big skating rink and in the summer for its many water-focused activities, its **Promenade,** and the **Tour de l'Horloge** (514/497-7678, 10 A.M.–5 P.M. daily early May–early Sept., admission free), a 1922 monument to the sailors lost in World War I with a tower that affords a great view of the port and the Jacques Cartier Bridge. If you want some fun with the kids, try **Le Labyrinthe du Hangar 16** (www.labyrintheduhangar16.com, 11:30–5:30 daily mid-May–late June, 11 A.M.–9 P.M. daily late June 21–late Aug., and 11:30 A.M.–5:30 P.M. weekends late Aug.–late Sept., adults $12, teens

13–17 $11, and children 4–12 $9.50), a maze in a big hangar on the Quai de l'Horloge; participants have to find icons and key words, permitting them to move forward in the search for Omer Saint-Laurent, a kidnapped docker.

Situated in a modern glass building, the **Centre iSci** (514/496-4724 or 877/496-4724, www.centredessciencesdemontreal.com, 9:30 A.M.–5 P.M. Mon.–Fri. and 10 A.M.–5 P.M. Sat.–Sun., adults $10, teens 13–17 $9, children 4–12 $7, families $30) is a dedication to all things scientific, technological, and fun. Interactive exhibits explore space, robots, sound and light, and communication systems. This is also where you will find the **IMAX theater,** a 380-seat theater showcasing 2D and 3D films that explore geographical and natural phenomena.

Two information booths are on the site: one on Jacques Cartier Pier, which is open from early May to late September, and one in the Centre iSci, open from late April to early September.

Maison de Pierre du Calvet

Place d'Armes

If Place Jacques-Cartier is the square that entertains, then Place d'Armes is the one that teaches. Buildings of major historical significance surround this public space, including the Basilique Notre-Dame, the Séminaire de Saint-Sulpice, and the Bank of Montréal. Most spectacular is seeing the square at night, when these buildings are illuminated as a part of the city's master lighting plan.

In the center of the park is a monument to the city's founder, Paul de Chomedey de Maisonneuve, who fought a battle on this very site. At the statue's base are other significant figures in Montréal's history. There are Jeanne Mance, founder of the Hôtel-Dieu Hospital, trader and soldier Charles Lemoyne, army major Lambert Closse with his guard dog, Pilote, and a nameless Iroquois brave.

Vieux Séminaire de Saint-Sulpice

Montréal's oldest building, Vieux Séminaire de Saint-Sulpice (116 rue Notre-Dame Ouest) was built in 1685 to house members of the Sulpi-

cian order, which it still does today. Although the building is closed to the public, it's worth stopping by for a glimpse of its massive clock, said to be the oldest public clock in North America. Dating to 1701, the clock has gears made of wood.

(Basilique Notre-Dame

Forget the minor dent in its distinguished reputation that was Celine Dion's wedding: The Basilique Notre-Dame (110 rue Notre-Dame Ouest, 514/842-2925 or 866/842-2925, www.basiliquenddm.org, 8 A.M.–4 P.M. daily, entry $4) is one of the city's most beautiful and grandiose historical sites. Built between 1824 and 1829 by Irish architect James O'Donnell—a Protestant who later converted to Catholicism so that he could be buried on-site—the church was a replacement for an older one that could no longer accommodate Montréal's booming population.

But not everything was immediately happy after its inauguration. The congregation apparently thought that the interior was too bland, too "Protestant," and so Victor Bourgeau, a church architect, was enlisted to punch things up. The job, which included working on the sanctuary and the pulpit, occupied him until he died. Also, worrying that the church's huge scale—not exactly the most intimate of settings—would deter people from holding weddings and funerals there, the Sulpicians decided to build the small Chapelle du Sacré-Coeur in 1888. It was destroyed 90 years later by fire but was rebuilt shortly after.

Elevated to basilica status in 1982 by Pope John Paul, Notre Dame has really come to be seen as the city's church. Every Christmas Eve, there is a magical mass with a choir—it's always a full house. In 2000, the church was the site of former Canadian Prime Minister Pierre Trudeau's state funeral.

You can get a guided, 20-minute tour of the basilica in English included in the price of admission. There's also the sound-and-light show **And Then There Was Light** (www.therewaslight.ca, adults $10, children 1–17 $5), a presentation on the history of the basilica and the city given from the perspective of James O'Donnell. The show usually takes place twice per night.

Banque de Montréal

Built in 1847 for Canada's oldest bank, the Banque de Montréal (119 rue Saint-Jacques Ouest, 514/877-6810) was designed by François Dollier de Casson, the head of the Sulpicians in Montréal. Taking an impressive stance with its dome and neoclassical façade, the bank is even more striking inside with its dark marble walls, Corinthian columns, a coffered ceiling, and 20-foot statue of Pietas that commemorates the bank's employees who were killed in World War I.

Now serving as head office for the Bank of Montréal, the building welcomes visitors into its lobby for a look around and to its tiny museum, which is dedicated to the early days of banking in the country. Entry is free.

Palais des Congrès

With its multitude of translucent, colored-glass panels, the ultramodern Palais des Con-

the city's famous Basilique Notre-Dame

grès (159 Saint-Antoine Ouest, 514/871-8122, www.congresmtl.com), Montréal's convention center, sits in sharp contrast to the Old Montréal area on whose border it sits. The Palais first began operating in 1983 in response to the city's surge in popularity as a tourist and business destination after the Montréal Olympics in 1976. By the end of the 1990s, though, it was clear that it needed to expand. The government heeded the call and drew up plans to expand the building by double its original size. In December 2002, its unconventionally playful look was unveiled and has received major acclaim worldwide.

Stop by the Palais to have a look at the **Lipstick Forest,** 52 reddish-pink tree trunks that are reproductions of those on avenue du Parc. You should also stop by Place Jean-Paul-Riopelle, right across the street, which features randomly positioned trees—real ones this time—that represent 11 different species. In the middle of the square is a fountain by Riopelle himself called "La Joute," which at night during the summer and fall, puts on a 30-minute spectacle of mist, waterworks, and light effects.

MONTRÉAL

Place d'Youville

The beautiful and peaceful square Place d'Youville, which has been extensively landscaped and refurbished in recent years, is a good place to stop, take a load off, and admire the surroundings. Named after Marguerite d'Youville, the founder of the Grey Nuns, the square now features a crisscrossing of wooden and stone walkways that represent its historical position as a link between the city and the Rivière Saint-Laurent. Just off rue Saint-Pierre, you'll spot the **Centre d'Histoire de Montréal** (335 place d'Youville, 514/872-3207, 10 A.M.–5 P.M. Tues.–Sun. early May–Sept. and Wed.–Sun. late Jan.–early May and Sept.–early Dec., adults $4.50, children 6–17 and students $3, family $13) housed in an out-of-place Flemish-style building once home to the local fire station. The museum features a permanent exhibition of five significant eras in Montréal's history, including first contact and the cultural boom of the 1960s and 1970s. A second permanent exhibit, *Montréal of a Thousand Faces,* is a thoroughly engaging, multimedia exploration of the city's dwellers from various neighborhoods, cultures, and ages.

🄲 Musée Pointe-à-Callière

On the site of the first settlement of Ville-Marie de Montréal, the Musée Pointe-à-Callière (350 place Royale, 514/872-9150, www.pacmusee.qc.ca, 11 A.M.–6 P.M. Tues.–Sun. late June–early Sept. and 11 A.M.–6 P.M. Tues.–Sun. early Sept.–late June, adults $11, students $6.50, children 6–12 $4, families—two adults and two kids—$23), an archaeology and history museum built in 1992, has a sleek, postmodern façade that disguises the stone foundations that lie below and make up its primary exhibits. Many excavations on the site have turned up artifacts from the days when the native people lived there to the settling of Montréal and beyond.

A good multimedia show called *Montréal, Tales of a City...* ushers you into the museum. Then you can explore the rest of the site and the excavations that make up the *Where*

Montréal Was Born exhibit via guided tour or on your own. The top floor of the tower has stunning views of Old Montréal. Check out the gift shop too.

Musée Marc-Aurèle Fortin

Just south of the square, the Musée Marc-Aurèle Fortin (118 rue Saint-Pierre, 514/845-6108, www.museemafortin.org, 11 A.M.–5 P.M. Tues.–Sun., adults $5, students $3, children 12 and under free) is dedicated to one of Québec's most well-known artists, Marc-Aurèle Fortin. Experimenting with new techniques, Fortin was known for painting on canvases that he would prepaint in gray or black to emphasize contrast. Although he received little recognition until after he died, his landscapes of the Gaspé, the Laurentians, and the Charlevoix regions are now highly revered. Every summer, rue Saint-Pierre becomes an outdoor studio, featuring artists painting in Fortin's style.

Cartier Éphémère

Opened in 1994, the Cartier Éphémère (745 rue Ottawa, 514/392 1554, www.quartierephemere.org, noon–8 P.M. Wed. and Fri.–Sun and noon–10 P.M. Thurs., entry $2) is in the old Darling Foundry, just west of the Place d'Youville. The 1880 building is now an immense (about 5,000 square feet) exhibit space and studio dedicated mostly to young artists from Québec. You should check out this cool space in the heart of the multimedia district even if you aren't interested in contemporary art. It's worthwhile just for its ultracool Bar Cluny.

Tours

Touring around Old Montréal and its often-narrow cobblestone streets is best done on foot. Plenty of park benches are scattered about to take the occasional load off. You can also, of course, catch a ride on one of the **calèches,** the horse-drawn carriages that line up in front of the Basilique Notre-Dame. Rides usually last about half an hour and the drivers are typically well-informed and personable.

Two cultural walking tours in Old Montréal are worth mentioning. First is the **Old Montréal Ghost Trail** (514/868-0303 or 877/868-0303, www.phvm.qc.ca, adults $15, students $12, children $7), which offers spooky tours, including one that focuses on the city's most notorious crimes, a historical ghost hunt, and an Old Port ghost walk. The ticket booth is on the Quai Jacques-Cartier. Tours usually depart at 8:30 P.M. and run until 10 P.M. For a more straightforward historical walking tour, try one of the ones offered by **Guidatour** (514/844-4021 or 800/363-402, www.guidatour.qc.ca, adults $15, students $12, children 6–12 $7), which depart twice a day from the Basilique Notre-Dame and last about an hour and a half. Tours are led by historical characters and cover sites around Place d'Armes and Place Jacques-Cartier. The season runs from mid-May to early October.

If you prefer a tour of the nautical type, head down to the Old Port. There's the glass-topped *Bateau Mouche* (514/849-9952 or 800/361-9952, www.bateaumouche.ca, day trip adults $17, students $16, children 2–12 $10, night trip four-course menu lower deck $81, five-course menu upper deck $136), which offers one-hour narrated day trips departing from Quai Jacques-Cartier and jogging around Old Montréal's main piers, past Habitat, and between Île Sainte-Hélène and Île Notre-Dame, and the nighttime dinner and booze cruise, which comes with a meal prepared by Chef Alain Pignard from the Queen Elizabeth Hotel. Departing three times a day from Quai King Edward is **Croisières AML's** (514/842-3871 or 800/563-4643, www.croisieresaml.com, adults $23, students $20, children $10) *Cavalier Maxim,* which offers 1.5-hour narrated tours that run past the Pont Jacques-Cartier and the Boucherville Islands. *Le Petit Navire* (514/602-1000, www.lepetitnavire.ca, adults $13, students $12, children 2–12 $7) is another boat that offers tours of the Old Port, although with only 26 passengers allowed on board, these tours are much more intimate. The tour lasts for 45 minutes and departs every hour from Quai Jacques-Cartier.

DOWNTOWN

When Montréal started to experience tremendous commercial and industrial growth in the 1850s, rue Sainte-Catherine started emerging as the city's main commercial thoroughfare, stealing the thunder from Old Montréal. Today, this 15-km street, which cuts through the city from east to west, also constitutes the heart of the downtown area, which roughly extends from boulevard Saint-Laurent in the east to rue Atwater in the west and from autoroute Ville-Marie in the south to avenue des Pins in the north.

The diversity of the area's buildings—sleek, modern office towers, neo-Gothic churches, Victorian mansions—not to mention its prized Canadian Centre for Architecture, make the district a must for architecture fans. Some of the city's best and biggest museums are also here, including the must-see Musée des Beaux-Arts de Montréal. Then there are the hundreds of restaurants and bars on hand and finally, there's the shopping, a massive network of malls and department stores, most linked together by the antlike tunnels that exist under the surface. This city under the city started with the construction of Place Ville-Marie in 1962. Now, it counts 13 km worth of tunnels, a survival tactic during the city's harsh winters.

Chinatown

At the beginning of the 19th century, Chinese migrants started arriving in Canada to work on the railroads. When the work was done in the 1880s, few could afford the trip home and so settled in the cities. In Montréal, these new residents flocked to the area along rue de la Gauchetière near boulevard Saint-Laurent. For a long time most of the Montréal Chinese community lived here, but nowadays, the community is dispersed throughout the island and this tiny neighborhood has become the commercial heart. Four big red arches, replicas of China's imperial doors, mark the perimeter of the area. On each of these ceremonial gates are inscribed the same words: Facing outward is the word "Chinatown," and

TAKE ME TO THE UNDERGROUND

There's no sense in letting a cold, blustery winter day ruin a good afternoon of shopping and strolling, now is there? Those are precisely the sentiments of many Montrealers – about 500,000 or so of them – who pass through some segment of the Underground City each day, whether it's to go from the metro to an office building, from apartment to grocery store, or simply from mall to mall.

Located between the Peel and Place des Arts metro stations on the green line and between Lucien L'Allier and Place d'Armes metro stations on the orange line, the Underground's passageways cover about 30 km, with 120 exterior access points leading pedestrians down into the maze.

The Underground also consists of 60 residential and commercial complexes, meaning that someone could literally skip the whole winter altogether if the cold wasn't to their liking.

Construction of Montréal's Underground City began in 1962 with the erection of Place Ville-Marie at the foot of avenue McGill College. A tunnel joining Place Ville Marie to Central Station and the Queen Elizabeth Hotel was soon added. Today, 30 percent of all downtown buildings are linked to the underground network, including a multitude of hotels, movie theaters, and banks, as well as corporate headquarters, museums, universities, and the Bell Centre – home of the Montreal Canadiens.

The majority of the underground network is open during the hours of operation of the metro (5:30 A.M.-1 A.M.). Some buildings, however, are open only during business hours. You can obtain a map of the Underground City at any metro station.

---

facing inward are the words "A splendid environment fosters a great people."

Exploring Chinatown is best done on foot because the neighborhood is small and its main street, rue de la Gauchetière, is pedestrian. You'll find numerous restaurants, herbalists, souvenir shops, and a great people-watching square named after China's modern-day founder, Dr. Sun Yat-Sen, along de la Gauchetière. Chinatown's other busy street, boulevard Saint-Laurent, is where you will find most of the food markets.

Place des Arts

The city's main grounds for all kinds of cultural events, Place des Arts (175 rue Sainte-Catherine Ouest, 514/842-2112, www.pda.qc.ca) is a massive cultural complex composed of five concert halls and a huge outdoor plaza that welcomes events such as Les FrancoFolies, the Festival des Films du Monde, and the Festival International de Jazz de Montréal's million-plus fans. It is also home to various cultural organizations such as the Grands Ballets Canadiens, the Opéra de Montréal, and the Orchestre Symphonique de Montréal.

Another initiative of Montréal's most culturally ambitious mayor, Jean Drapeau, the center was inaugurated in 1963 as an initiative to showcase the city's arts and expand the downtown core eastward.

On the rue Jeanne Mance side of the Place des Arts site is the **Musée d'Art Contemporain de Montréal** (185 rue Sainte-Catherine Ouest, 514/847-6226, www.macm.org, 11 A.M.–6 P.M. Tues. and Thurs.–Sun. and 11 A.M.–9 P.M. Wed., admission adults $6, seniors $4, students $3, family $12), the only institution dedicated to contemporary art in Canada. Built in 1992, the museum has a focus on Québec art with two-thirds of its 7,000-piece collection by Québec artists such as Paul-Émile Borduas, Jean-Paul Riopelle, Marcelle Ferron, and Betty Goodwin. The museum also hosts many innovative multimedia installations featuring theatrical, dance, and video. The museum's most famous happening in recent history was its commissioning of performance artist Spencer

Tunick's 2001 photograph of more than 2,000 far-from-camera-shy naked people gathered in front of Place des Arts.

Rue Sainte-Catherine

Through the years, you could always tell how the city was faring financially by walking along the rue University to rue Guy segment of the 15-km rue Sainte-Catherine, Montréal's major shopping thoroughfare. During the recession years of the 1980s and '90s, Sainte-Catherine's scene was bleak: no crowds, empty stores, and constant notices of closures, but today, the street is abustle with activity, restoration, and new development. It's thanks to the municipal government that the city has such an active downtown. While many North American cities were busy setting up shopping malls in the outskirts, Montréal encouraged developers to set up right downtown on street level and below.

Before August 2005, you'd forgive yourself for walking right past **St. James United**

© JENNIFER EDWARDS

Modernity looms over Cathédrale Christ Church on rue Sainte-Catherine.

Church (463 rue Sainte-Catherine Ouest, 514/288-9245, 10 A.M.–4 P.M. Mon.–Fri. mid-May–late Aug., Sunday worship 11 A.M.) and not noticing anything but a rundown section of shops. This 1889 French Gothic–style church, set back from the street, was covered in 1927 by a commercial building running the length of the block in front as a result of a broke parish trying to benefit from the valuable land around it. Almost all that was recognizable of the church on the street front was a bright neon sign bearing its name.

Thanks to major private fund-raising and dollars from the municipal, provincial, and federal governments, the buildings have been torn down to reveal the beauty of the church that once was. The church interior has always benefited from its beautiful Victorian stylings and amphitheater-like layout, especially when it's playing host to concerts by its favorite house band, the world-acclaimed Montréal Jubilation Choir.

Marking the entrance of rue Sainte-Catherine's true shopping district, **Square Phillips,** on rue Sainte-Catherine opposite La Baie d'Hudson, is one of the favorite resting points of shoppers and, given the state of its monument to King Edward VII, of pigeons. Paying tribute to the king who came to Montréal to officiate at ceremonies for the opening of the Pont Victoria in 1860, the statue is also flanked at its base by four figures, including the one in front somewhat ironically called *Armed Peace,* which features a woman holding an olive branch and a half-hidden sword under her skirt. On the west side of the square is Canada's famous and historic jewelry store, Birks.

When the beautiful **Cathédrale Christ Church** (635 rue Sainte-Catherine Ouest, 514/843-6577, 8 A.M.–6 P.M. Sun.–Fri. and 9:30 A.M.–6 P.M. Sat.) was constructed in 1859, its surroundings were far more peaceful and pastoral than the dense Sainte-Catherine setting it occupies today. Now the neo-Gothic Anglican church, situated directly in front of the towering Place de La Cathédrale pink-glass office building, is a constant reminder—and favorite photo op—of Montréal's old-meets-new dichotomy. Sitting directly above Les Promenades de la Cathédrale, an underground mall, the church often hosts summertime music concerts. Have a peek at the lovely tranquil courtyard in back—a favorite spot for office workers on lunch.

Avenue McGill College

Glance up along beautiful avenue McGill College from rue Sainte-Catherine or **Place Ville-Marie** (avenue McGill College at rue Cathcart, 514/861-9393, www.placevillemarie.com), the landmark modern shopping and office complex at its foot, and you'll catch a stunning glimpse of McGill University straight ahead with Mont-Royal in the background. Widened in 1988 so that people could have a clear line of sight, avenue McGill College is actually nicest during the winter, when its middle strip of trees are decked out with white lights. Flanked by modern buildings, the avenue is probably best known for the sculpture *The Illuminated Crowd* on the west side of the street, north of rue Sainte-Catherine. Created by the British-born sculptor Raymond Mason and installed in 1986, the frequently photographed sculpture features a cluster of people, looking and pointing to the other side of the street. Running the gamut of human emotion, the piece seems completely whimsical at first, but get a little bit closer and you'll see that all is not peachy keen.

Boulevard René-Lévesque

Lined with office buildings, this major thoroughfare running east-west through downtown Montréal was, in 1987, caught in the middle of a major struggle between some English- and French-speaking Montrealers. The street was originally called Dorchester to honor the first Québec governor after the British Conquest. But after the province's legendary premier and father of the sovereignty movement, René Lévesque, died in 1987, the city motioned to rename the street after Lévesque. You guessed it: A major uproar ensued and today some stubbornly resolute Anglophones still refer to the street as Dorchester. Tellingly, the section of the boulevard that runs through Westmount has kept the name Dorchester.

Back toward the eastern side of downtown is Montréal's first anglophone Catholic church, **St. Patrick's Basilica** (460 boulevard René-Lévesque Ouest, 514/866-7379, www.stpatricksmtl.ca, 9 A.M.–6 P.M. daily). Better known as "the Irish Church," it was constructed to serve the need of the numerous Irish immigrants who arrived in the city en masse during the potato famine. Built in Gothic Revival splendor, the church first opened on St. Patrick's Day, March 17,1847, and is considered one of the country's finest examples of this architectural style. The church is known for its peaceful grounds, woodwork, including pine columns and red oak pews, and its oil painting collection and 10-bell chimes.

The Sun Life Building (1155 rue Metcalfe, www.sunlifebuilding-montreal.com), erected between 1913 and 1933 for the powerful insurance company Sun Life, was for many years the tallest building of the British Empire. Its impressive size—it measures 122 meters in height and counts 24 floors—stoic colonnades and beaux-arts style made it one of the most prestigious office buildings in the city and often a bitter reminder to French Montrealers of the positions of power held by Anglophones. Even more impressive is the fact that during World War II, the building's basement vaults protected the crown jewels of England as well as the gold bullion of the Bank of England. But the Sun Life Company doesn't live here anymore. After the election of the Parti Québécois in 1976, company executives announced it would move to Toronto for fear of separatism. René Lévesque reportedly responded with his typical aplomb, calling them "sons of bitches."

Just east of the Sun Life Building and south of the tourist information center lies **Square Dorchester.** The square was originally named Dominion, but those feeling sorry for the old lord after his name came off the street signs of the rechristened boulevard René-Lévesque rallied to at least give him a square. The shady green spot with picnic tables and benches receives a massive pilgrimage of lunch munchers every weekday during the summer. Three monuments can be found within the square's confines: one dedicated to the memory of the soldiers killed during the Boer War, another of Scottish poet Robert Burns, and a third of the late great Canadian prime minister, Sir Wilfrid Laurier.

Many longtime Montrealers still stop for a look at the 13 patron saint statues that grace the rooftop of **Cathédrale Marie-Reine-du-Monde** (1085 rue de la Cathédrale, 514/866-1661, www.cathedralecatholiquedemontreal.org, 7 A.M.–7:30 P.M. Mon.–Fri.). When Bishop Ignace Bourget decided it was time for the Catholic Church to gain some ground in this British-dominated neighborhood and boldly (some would say arrogantly) went ahead with plans to build a smaller replica of St. Peter's Basilica in Rome, the plans sparked a major controversy, but he went ahead anyway. Although architect Victor Bourgeau, who also created the interior of the Basilique Notre-Dame, did not think it possible to re-create St. Peter's on such a smaller scale at first, he finally acquiesced. Building construction began in 1870 and took 24 years to complete because of a constant shortage of funds. Beyond the roof statues, the cathedral's main features are its high dome and imposing baldachin over the altar, a scale model of Bernini's in St. Peter's.

Heading west on René-Lévesque, you'll notice a big graystone complex on the right. It's the **Centre Marguerite d'Youville** (1185 rue Saint-Mathieu, 514/937-9501, 1:30–4:30 P.M. daily), the motherhouse of les Soeurs Grises (the Gray Nuns) order founded by Marguerite d'Youville, the first Canadian-born saint, to help care for the sick, the elderly, and the poor. The convent also served as a school and a hospital until the 1960s, when the government forced it to separate its religious teachings from its charitable work. The center houses a museum dedicated to the life and work of d'Youville.

The acclaimed **Canadian Centre for Architecture** (1920 rue Baile, 514/939-7026, www.cca.qc.ca, 10 A.M.–5 P.M. Wed. and Fri.–

Sun. and 10 A.M.–9 P.M. Thurs., adult $10, students $5, children 6–12 $3, admission free Thurs. after 5:30 P.M.), founded in 1979 by architect and Seagram liquor heir Phyllis Lambert, is both a museum and an architectural study center. The building incorporates a new U-shaped, gray limestone building and the 1874 mansion of railroad magnate Baron Thomas Shaughnessy, one of the few mansions that wasn't destroyed by the widening of boulevard René-Lévesque in the 1950s. The CCA's exhibits sometimes focus on accessible topics such as Montréal's architecture boom during the 1960s, but it can also feature some pretty heady matters such as the exploration of "a new sensorial approach to urbanism." But, even if you consider yourself an architectural neophyte, just visiting the site makes for a pleasant diversion. Make sure you take in the Sculpture Garden in front of the autoroute Ville-Marie.

Rue de la Gauchetière

A fine example of Romanesque Revival architecture designed by the renowned hotel architect Bruce Price (he of Québec City's Château Frontenac), **Windsor Station** (1160 rue de la Gauchetière Ouest, 6:30 A.M.–10:45 P.M. Mon.–Fri., 9:30 A.M.–11 P.M. Sat. and 1 P.M.–9 P.M. Sun.) has an illustrious past, although you wouldn't necessarily know it by the quiet stance it holds today. Opened in 1890 with the slogan "Beats all creation, the new CPR Station," the building served as the eastern hub of the Canadian Pacific Railway but is now strictly used for local commuter trains.

Windsor station is adjacent to the **Centre Bell** (1260 rue de la Gauchetière Ouest, 514/932-2583), the new, but somewhat soulless, 21,500-seat center that hosts the city's hockey team, the Canadiens. During a closing ceremony at the beloved Forum on rue Sainte-Catherine and rue Atwater, previous Canadiens legends were invited on stage. The procession, which featured a 10-minute standing ovation when Rocket Richard took the floor, was one of the most moving nights in Montréal hockey history. Opened in 1996, the Centre Bell also hosts most of the city's big-ticket music concerts.

A little bit farther south on rue Saint-Jacques is the **Planétarium de Montréal** (1000 rue Saint-Jacques Ouest, 514/872-4530, www.planetarium.montreal.qc.ca, English *Night Sky* show 7:15 Fri.–Sun., adults $8, students $6, youth 5–17 $4), formerly known as Dow Planetarium. Set up by Montréal mayor Jean Drapeau in the 1960s (one of many cultural institutions), the Planétarium's Théâtre des Étoiles (Star Theater) seats 385 people in a circle around the Zeiss projector, which is capable of reproducing the night sky from anywhere on Earth. *Night Sky* is the 45-minute celestial show that plays every evening, while temporary shows play in the afternoon.

GOLDEN SQUARE MILE

At the turn of the 19th century, 70 percent of Canada's wealth was resting in the hands of a predominantly Scottish-populated area centered between rue Sherbrooke to the south, foreign embassy–lined avenue du Docteur Penfield to the north, rue Aylmer in the east, and chemin de la Côte-des-Neiges to the west. The area's grandiose mansions, Protestant churches, and wealthy anglophone residents led people to start referring to the area as the Golden Square Mile. Many architectural gems still dot aristocratic rue Sherbrooke, and with the street's upscale fashion boutiques, art galleries, and antiques dealers, it makes for a very refined and cultured walk.

Musée McCord d'Histoire Canadienne

A passionate historian and collector, lawyer David Ross McCord realized his life dream when he opened the Musée McCord (690 rue Sherbrooke Ouest, 514/398-7100, www.mccord-museum.qc.ca, 10 A.M.–6 P.M. Tues.–Fri., 10 A.M.–5 P.M. Sat.–Mon., adults $10, students $5.50, children 6–12 $3) in 1921. Opened in a building provided by McGill University, the history museum is considered one of North America's most significant. The museum is noted for its First

Musée McCord

Nations collection, its mind-boggling, huge archive of photographs of Canadian people, landscapes, and events taken by William Notman's studio during the years 1850–1930, and its impressive costume and textile collection from 1726 to the present day.

McGill University

At the end of the avenue McGill College, past the Roddick Memorial Gates, sits the beautiful, leafy campus of McGill University (845 rue Sherbrooke Ouest, 514/398-6555, www.mcgill.ca), contained in 80 buildings on 80 acres of land. Inaugurated in 1829, the school was named after fur-trade merchant James McGill, who bequeathed his 46-acre estate and fortune to the creation of the university. Today, McGill University is considered one of the country's most prestigious institutions and has one of the most international student bodies in North America. Its students are a proud lot, often sporting McGill sweaters or bags, something you'll rarely see among students of other Québec universities.

At the top of the walkway, leading up from the gates on rue Sherbrooke, is the **Arts Building,** the oldest structure on campus, dating to 1839. The campus's green setting and architectural gems have made it a favored spot for a slew of movies, including Robert De Niro's *The Score,* Ben Affleck's *The Sum of All Fears,* and John Travolta's abysmal Scientology movie, *Battlefield Earth.*

To the left of the Arts Building is the university's Greek Revival **Redpath Museum** (859 rue Sherbrooke Ouest, 514/398-4086, 9 A.M.–5 P.M. Mon.–Thurs. and 1 P.M.– 5 P.M. Sun., www.mcgill.ca/redpath), a temple to the natural world. Opened in 1892 thanks to financial backing by sugar tycoon Peter Redpath, the building was commissioned to celebrate 25 years of service from McGill's principal Sir William Dawson. The museum's collection was actually built around an assortment of rocks, birds, and butterflies that Dawson brought with him when he started at the school. The third floor is the museum's most fascinating; it includes an ethnology exhibit

with mummies from ancient Egypt and art and musical instruments from Africa, along with a great view of the museum's grand hall below.

(Musée des Beaux-Arts de Montréal

What started out as the Art Association of Montréal in 1860 officially turned into the Musée des Beaux-Arts de Montréal (1379-80 rue Sherbrooke Ouest, 514/285-2000 or 800/899-6873, www.mbam.qc.ca, 11 A.M. to 5 P.M. Tues.–Sun., permanent collection free, temporary exhibits adults $12, students $6, children under 12 free) in 1947, making it the oldest museum in the country. With an art collection of more than 30,000 objects from all around the world and a Canadian collection said to be the finest in the country, the museum received some major relief when in 1991 it got a much younger partner, the Jean-Noël Desmarais Pavilion.

Habitat 67 architect Moshe Safdie designed the postmodern Jean-Noël Desmarais Pavilion, which moved in just across the street. The sleek glass-fronted building doubled the exhibition space of the original and gave the museum a more contemporary face.

The buildings are linked by an underground tunnel, which itself is lined with artwork. There is an impressive book and gift shop in the Jean-Noël Desmarais Pavilion—a good opportunity to pick up a souvenir gift if you need one—as well as the Café des Beaux-Arts, which serves contemporary French food.

Church of St. Andrew and St. Paul

The neo-Gothic Church of St. Andrew and St. Paul (3415 rue Redpath, 514/842-3431, www.standrewstpaul.com, service 11 A.M. Sun.) is a result of the uniting of two congregations that date to the mid-1800s. The present church was constructed in 1932 and is one of the most important vestiges of Scottish heritage in the Golden Square Mile. The many beautiful stained-glass windows depict the history of the church and all the traditional scenes of the life of Jesus with one difference: The three

MONTRÉAL

© JENNIFER EDWARDS

the postmodern Jean-Noël Desmarais Pavilion at the Musée des Beaux-Arts de Montréal

wise men are depicted as an Inuit, an Indian, and a fur trader. Another interesting detail is outside on the church tower. Look up and you may be able to make out some frogs. Apparently, in medieval times, the not-easy-being-green amphibians were regarded as symbols of protection against evil spirits. To the right of the church is a little garden established for quiet meditation.

Grand Séminaire de Montréal

One of the nicest city walks you can take is along rue Sherbrooke starting from avenue McGill College and then heading west to the Grand Séminaire de Montréal (2065 rue Sherbrooke Ouest, 514/935-1169, www.gsdm.qc.ca). Turn in at the gates and you'll be in one of the oldest gardens in North America. The grounds and the lovely old graystone school, built by the Sulpician order as a training ground for future priests, is also home to the Collège de Montréal. The incredibly lovely 520-foot-long basin, thought to be built between 1731 and 1747, has rows of trees

built along either side. You can take a guided historical and natural tour of the property during the summer at 1 P.M. and 3 P.M. or just stop in for a quiet picnic.

PARC MONT-ROYAL

If there is one spot that every Montrealer would agree is worth taking in, it's the 343-acre Parc Mont-Royal, or "the Mountain" as people plainly call it. Rising 223 meters from the city center (no buildings in downtown Montréal are allowed to exceed this), the Mountain, with its illuminated cross, lookouts, and parklands is the city's main landmark and its heart. All year long, Montrealers visit the mountain to walk, run, bike, cross-country ski, have lunch, visit the graves of loved ones long passed away, or simply to look out over their city and remind themselves of why they live where they do.

Named by Jacques Cartier when he first climbed it in 1535, the mountain actually owes its designation as a park to the public outcry that resulted when a landowner on the premises cut down all his trees for firewood. The city swiftly put the land aside and many years later hired Frederick Law Olmsted, the landscape architect behind Central Park in New York City, to design the park, which officially opened in 1876. The chemin Olstead, a winding set of trails, is a testament to his legacy.

The scene on the mountain today is a little different. On the first hot Sundays of the summer, mobs of young folk gather around the George Étienne Cartier monument just off avenue du Parc to groove to the sound of the tam-tams, an assembly of impromptu bongo players. This hippy-happy ritual may not be to everyone's liking, but it's testament to the relaxed, community spirit that is so much a part of Montréal.

The most popular entry points for visitors on foot are the chemin Olstead, which begins right by the Cartier Monument on avenue du Parc, and the Peel Steps, which run from avenue des Pins and lead directly to the Kondiaronk Lookout. By car, there's voie Camillien-Houde, which also begins at avenue du Parc, or rue Remembrance, which leads into the park from the north side of Westmount. There are five parking lots in the park that charge $1.25 per hour or $3.75 per day and you'll find street parking on some of the north-end streets.

For those visiting via public transportation, your best bet is to go to Mont-Royal metro and grab Bus 11. It stops at the base of the Mountain on avenue du Parc and runs along voie Camillien-Houde to the lookout and to Beaver Lake.

For visitor information and interpretation, check out **Centre de la Montagne** (1260 chemin Remembrance, 514/843-8240, www.lemontroyal.qc.ca, 9 A.M.–6 P.M. Mon.–Fri. and 9 A.M. to 8 P.M. Sat.–Sun.), half way between Beaver Lake and the Chalet du Parc Mont-Royal. The visitors center is housed in La Maison Smith, an 1858 house once owned by one of the landowners who called the Mountain home. There's a permanent exhibition there called *Monte Real, Monreale, Mont Royal, Montréal*, which chronicles the history of the Mountain. There's also a

boutique and a café with healthy soups and sandwiches. Tours of the mountain summit are offered during the summer.

Georges-Étienne Cartier Monument

The Georges-Étienne Cartier Monument on avenue du Parc honors Georges-Étienne Cartier, one of the fathers of Confederation and right-hand man to John A. Macdonald, the first prime minister of Canada. The lovely monument, which is capped by an angel, is perhaps most famous for being the rendezvous point of the Sunday afternoon tam-tams, a gathering of bongo players, dancers, and Frisbee throwers, among others. It's also the starting point of the chemin Olmsted.

The Cross

On the summit of the Mountain stands Montréal's famous 98-foot cross, erected in 1924 to commemorate one farther down the hill that was put up by Paul de Chomedey de Maisonneuve when Montréal was spared from flooding on Christmas Day, 1642. In 1992, in time for Montréal's 350th anniversary, the city replaced the original incandescent white bulbs with fiber optics, capable of changing the cross's color from blue to red to purple. It's only for significant events that the cross will shine anything but white, such as the purple that it shone when Pope John Paul died. It is possible to walk and bike up to the cross, but the best way to admire it is from the city center below when it lights up at night.

【 Lookouts

The Mountain's main lookout is the **Belvédère Kondiaronk**, constructed in 1908 but officially named in 1998 in commemoration of the Huron chief who brokered a 1701 peace deal between the French, Hurons, and Iroquois. The concrete-pad lookout, which extends from the Chalet du Parc, offers the best view of downtown, the river, the south shore, and, on a clear day, Vermont's mountains. Look for the metal arrows on the belvedere stone to identify some of the city's main spots and three of the city's bridges: Jacques-Cartier in the east and Victoria and Champlain in the west.

A second lookout is the **Belvédère Camilien-Houde**. It's accessible by car via the voie Camilien-Houde, a road named after a former mayor of Montréal who, ironically, was vehemently opposed to any kind of road that would run through the park. With parking, this lookout is the favored spot for nighttime make-out sessions. You'll see the Olympic Stadium, the Plateau Mont-Royal, and the east side of the city from here.

Chalet du Parc Mont-Royal

The Chalet du Parc Mont-Royal (514/872-3911) was built by Aristide Beaugrand-Champagne in 1932 to replace an older one that risked crumbling to the ground. Inside the hall, you can take a peek at the paintings that adorn the walls, chronicling several moments of Montréal history, or cool down with an ice cream in summer or warm up in winter. The hall frequently hosts classical music concerts.

Cemeteries

The two cemeteries in Parc Mont-Royal make for a pleasant afternoon stroll, and, if you're not squeamish about the company, a quiet picnic. There's the 343-acre **Cimetière Notre-Dame-des-Neiges** (4601 chemin Côte-des-Neiges, 514/735-1361, www.cimetierenddn.org), the largest cemetery in Canada. More than 900,000 people have been buried here since its inception in 1854, including some of the city's most famous figures: hockey great Maurice Richard, Mayor Jean Drapeau, and poet Emile Nelligan. Known for its landscaping and variety of deciduous trees (red oak, silver and Norwegian maple), the cemetery also has 55 km of roads crisscrossing the grounds.

The Mountain's other cemetery is the smaller, non-Catholic **Cimetière Mount-Royal** (1297 chemin de la Forêt, 514/279-7358, www.mountroyalcem.com), which covers 165 acres of ground. Not as orderly as its companion, this cemetery has more of a natural, gardenlike feel with 43 km of pathways. There are

woodlands on the premises, as well as many fruit trees. Legendary writer Mordecai Richler and brewer John Molson are buried here.

Beaver Lake

The small, circular Beaver Lake was built in 1937 as part of a job-creation project for unemployed workers of the Depression. It is only partially man-made, as there was actually a small lake already there, filled with old beaver lodges—hence the name. Today the shallow pool is a favored summertime spot for family picnics. During the summer, people catnap on the gentle slope that leans toward it, rent pedal boats, or line up for ice cream at the kitschy '50s-looking pavilion, which, along with the lake, are due to undergo major renovations. During the winter, the lake becomes a skating rink and the pavilion becomes the place to rent skates or skis or to warm up with hot chocolate.

AROUND THE MOUNTAIN
◖ Oratoire Saint-Joseph

Sitting on the slopes of Mont-Royal, the massive Oratoire Saint-Joseph (3800 chemin Queen Mary, 514/733-8211, www.saint-joseph.org) cuts an impressive figure. Looming like a fortress with its 195-foot domed church, this is actually the largest shrine in the world dedicated to Joseph, Jesus's father, and the second-tallest after Saint Peter's in Rome. But the reason for its existence and the reason so many of the two million annual visitors come is because of one man, Brother André.

Born in 1845, André Bessette, the son of poor farmers, worked as a porter before joining the Congregation of the Holy Cross in 1870. The monk quickly became known for his curative powers and was able to build a small chapel in 1904 on the site where the oratory now sits. As word got out about his ability to heal and massive pilgrimages to his chapel began, the slight priest petitioned for funds to build an oratory. Work began on the oratory in 1924 but was only completed about 30 years after Brother André's death in January 1937; reportedly one million people

O BROTHER, WHERE ART THOU?

Montréal's beloved Brother André may have been a man of tiny stature, but his dreams and his heart were huge. His legendary piety and reputation as a miracle worker for the sick and suffering made him a saint among Montrealers long before he was beatified by Pope John Paul II in 1982. When he died in 1937 at the age of 92, a whopping one million people visited his casket.

Its no wonder that the city was in utter shock when they woke up one morning in 1973 to the news that Brother's André's heart, which had been preserved and on display in the Oratory, was reported stolen. The thieves eventually called in a ransom: They wanted $50,000 to ensure the safe return of the Oratory's most precious and famous relic. Indignant, the church immediately refused.

For more than a year, no clues as to the heart's whereabouts turned up. Then one day just before Christmas in 1974, a lawyer received an anonymous call saying that the heart was located in a locker in the basement of an apartment building. Police went to the locker and positively identified the glass-boxed heart as that of Brother André. The identity of the thieves, however, was never found out.

Today, Brother André's heart is back on display in the Oratory, where it's watched over a tad more closely.

mourned the miracle worker's death. He was beatified by the pope in 1982.

Today, the neoclassical building is composed of a primitive chapel, the pretty crypt, a votive chapel with an array of crutches and canes left behind by the cured, a museum with an impressive religious art collection, and, of course, the huge basilica, which is actually a bit underwhelming inside with its '50s-style modernity. What is most impressive is that pilgrims can still be seen ascending the 283 stairs on their knees. Hope they have knee pads...

Westmount

With its predominantly anglophone population and wealth, Westmount (westmount.ville.montreal.qc.ca), actually situated due south of the mountain, is the wealthiest borough in Montréal and at one time the weathiest in the country, and it is often snubbed by Montrealers of more meagre means. True, the mansions of Upper Westmount, those on the slopes of Mont-Royal, are breathtaking in their stately opulence and count some of the country's most prominent citizens as residents, including former Prime Minister Brian Mulroney and Québec Premier Jean Charest, but the borough with its active rue Sherbrooke is slowly becoming more inclusive.

If you have a car and enjoy gazing at the way the other half live, go for a cruise along the streets that make up the area north of Summit Circle. Otherwise, you can have a stroll down **avenue Greene,** with its superposh boutiques, toward **Westmount Square** (1 carré Westmount, 514/932-0211), the Ludwig Mies van der Rohe–designed, tinted-glass, three-tower building constructed in 1967.

Westmount is also known for its section of rue Sherbrooke, a leafy, high-end boutique- and restaurant-lined section of the street. The borough's green lung and its heart is **Westmount Park.** This pretty 26-acre park has a big playground, wading pool, and baseball diamonds, but its most attractive feature is the waterway that winds through the park, past grassy hills, benches, and shady trees. On the western edge of the park sits the lovely **Westmount Library** (4574 rue Sherbrooke Ouest, 514/989-5300, www.westlib.org, 10 A.M.–9 P.M. Mon.–Fri. and 10 A.M.–5 P.M. Sat.–Sun.). In existence since 1899, the library went through major renovations and additions in 1995, but the original Findlay Room remains intact with its columns, lead-glass windows, and green table lamps. Right nearby, you'll find the pretty little greenhouse.

Outremont

Directly on the other side of the mountain from Westmount, Outremont (outremont.ville.montreal.qc.ca) is actually sometimes referred to as the "French Westmount." Featuring stately homes, especially in those areas closest to the Mountain, Outremont is home to some of Montréal's wealthiest Francophones. It is also home to a large share (more than 6,000) of the city's Hasidic community. Outremont is probably best known for its parks and two main shopping streets: avenue Laurier, the destination for the French upper crust with its patisseries, cheese shops, and French-designer boutiques, and avenue Bernard, the more culturally diverse strip with Jewish bakeries and sushi shops.

If you're around this neck of the woods on a Sunday evening, check out **Parc Saint-Viateur.** This lovely park situated on avenue Bloomfield, just south of avenue Bernard, has a winding waterway and footbridge but is best known for its weekly tango lessons during the summer. The mix of young and old, beginners and accomplished congregating in the gazebo to dance to tango music is magical.

PLATEAU MONT-ROYAL

Montréal's Plateau Mont-Royal neighborhood, named for its plateaulike position at the bottom of Mont-Royal, is the one that best reflects the city itself. Casual, artistic, colorful, playful, and urban, the Plateau is the stomping ground of the city's artists, intellectuals, students, and immigrants. Immortalized in the novels of Mordecai Richler and the plays of Michel Tremblay, the Plateau was originally a mainly working-class neighborhood known for its Jewish delis and Portuguese rotisseries along boulevard Saint-Laurent. All that started to change when artists started moving in, taking advantage of its leafy streets, roomy triplexes, wrought-iron staircases, and neighborhood cafés, not to mention its cheap rents. Suddenly, in the late 1980s the Plateau exploded on the scene and was being praised by the people who matter as one of the hippest and best neighborhoods in the world to live.

Although attention brought high rents and some gentrification, the Plateau is still a place where the pace is a little slower, where people linger over coffee and beer on an outdoor terrace, where parents push kids in strollers for early evening walks, and where the nightlife is the most swinging on the island. The Plateau's three major thoroughfares are boulevard Saint-Laurent, also known as the Main, avenue du Mont-Royal, and rue Saint-Denis. Each street has a completely different feel, and each offers a huge array of shops, bars, cafés, and restaurants. Many other streets on the Plateau deserve to be explored: Duluth and Prince-Arthur for their pedestrian-friendliness and busy nighttime scenes, the bourgeois streets around Square Saint-Louis for their beautiful Victorian homes, and the narrow residential streets such as rue Drolet and Henri-Julien for their colorful packed-in duplexes, all monuments to the rich and vibrant history of this fascinating area.

The four metro stations, which are situated in the general Plateau area, are Mont-Royal station to the north, Saint-Laurent and Berri-UQAM in the south, and Sherbrooke in the east. Get off at Mont-Royal metro station to explore the shops and restaurants along avenue Mont-Royal, Saint-Laurent metro to explore boulevard Saint-Laurent, Berri-UQAM metro to explore the Quartier Latin, and Sherbrooke metro for Parc Lafontaine in the middle section of rue Saint-Denis.

As for buses, you can catch the 55, which travels north up Saint-Laurent and south along rue Saint-Urbain. The 24 runs along rue Sherbrooke, hitting the south side of Parc Lafontaine, the 144 runs along des Pins until Sherbooke metro station, while the 30 travels a good part of Saint-Denis. For all bus and metro maps and information, see www.stcum.qc.ca or call 514/STM-INFO (514/786-4636).

(**Boulevard Saint-Laurent**

Although other streets may have an older history and may be prettier, most Montrealers would agree that boulevard Saint-Laurent is the heart and soul of city. Also known as "the

Main," this old divide between English-speaking Montréal (to the west) and French-speaking Montréal (to the east) also splits the city in half so that addresses start from it and ascend in opposite directions.

Magical, cool, and at once frenzied and laid-back, Saint-Laurent, the city's first boulevard, has traditionally been the landing point for several waves of immigrants, including Eastern European Jews, Greeks, Italians, Portuguese, and Chinese, and later on West Indians, Africans, Latin Americans, and East Indians. Today, the Main is still the best place to get a smoked meat and a cola, a falafel, some dim sum, a steak, or sushi. You can go to trendy nightclubs or sweaty salsa dance boxes and shop at dollar stores or high-end boutiques. Give yourself an afternoon, an evening, and an appetite, to explore it.

With its numerous bring-your-own-wine restaurants, terraces, street performers, and outdoor cabarets, **rue Prince Arthur** running east off Saint-Laurent is fully animated during the summertime. A walk down this pedestrian street with its antique lampposts and fountain is a must. Grab a seat and sip sangria on one of the street's many terraces, which are great for people-watching and soaking in the scene. You may want to opt for Saint-Laurent or Saint-Denis for dinner, however, as for the most part the food in the restaurants along Prince Arthur (typically Greek, Portuguese, and Italian) have a touristy blandness.

Rue Saint-Denis

The busy, more upscale, and French-flavored rue Saint-Denis, between boulevard Saint-Laurent and rue Saint-Hubert, developed in the mid-19th century when Quebecers left the countryside to work in Montréal factories. This new community clustered around rue Saint-Denis, forming the beginnings of the Plateau. Today the street is home to a multitude of cafés, restaurants, and bars, many of which were transformed from old Victorian homes and feature beautiful back terraces. It has an active nightlife and is also a favored location for Québec designers, specialty food shops, cool furniture and home accessory shops, and many French-language book stores.

© JENNIFER EDWARDS

Beautiful residences surround Square Saint-Louis.

Just north of rue Sherbrooke on the west side of rue Saint-Denis, **Square Saint-Louis** is a pretty if slightly gritty public park, where folk gather quietly by the fountain during the day and somewhat more raucously at night. What makes this spot so worthy of a visit is less the park itself and more the architectural treasures that surround it. In 1880, when the park was constructed on the site of a former reservoir, it attracted the French bourgeoisie, who built magnificent Victorian homes in the vicinity. Magnificent houses with colorful roofs and turrets and majestic walk-ups also attracted many of the city's artists, including Michel Tremblay, Émile Nelligan, and filmmakers Claude Jutra and Gilles Carle.

Just west of rue Saint-Denis is the majestic **Église Saint Jean-Baptiste** (4237 rue Henri-Julien). The original church was built in 1874 but destroyed by fire in 1898. It was reconstructed and burned down again in 1911. The third time proved to be the charm and the church has remained intact since 1914. Named after Saint Jean-Baptiste, the patron saint of French Canadians, the huge church's ornate, neobaroque interior is well worth a peek. Its massive organ was built by the Casavant Brothers.

Avenue du Mont-Royal

If boulevard Saint-Laurent is the heart of Montréal, then avenue du Mont-Royal is the heart of the Plateau. Calmer and more residential feeling than the Plateau's other two main streets, the avenue is still a major commercial thoroughfare for nearby residents. But the street hasn't always been a commercial success. In 1959, when repairs to natural-gas lines caused the street to close down for an extended period, merchants fed up with the lost business decided to relocate, leaving the street barren. This drought lasted until the 1980s, when the larger Plateau neighborhood became regarded as a hip place to live. Under a revitalization incentive called Opération Commerce, the street blossomed into the gem it is today. With its music, book-, and many second-hand stores (*friperies*) and many bars and restaurants, av-

enue Mont-Royal is a good destination to while away a few hours.

Surrounded by Victorian houses, the leafy **Parc Lafontaine** (rue Sherbrooke Est, Papineau, Rachel, and avenue du Parc La Fontaine), just south of avenue Mont-Royal, is the playground for residents of the Plateau. With two big linked ponds, a fountain, huge trees, walking paths, tennis courts, and picnic tables, this oasis in the middle of the city is a well-used and appreciated spot, especially on summer weekends. Montrealers visit the park to picnic, walk, jog, and play tennis, soccer, and *pétanque,* the French version of bocce. During the winter the park's pond is transformed into a huge skating rink.

QUARTIER LATIN

South of Plateau Mont-Royal, surrounding l'Université du Québec à Montréal (UQAM) and lower rue Saint-Denis, lies the Quartier Latin. This area, which contains most of the district's cultural attractions and which is a major student hub, owes its name to Paris's Quartier Latin. The Parisian neighborhood housed the Université de Sorbonne, which conducted its courses in Latin, hence the name.

At the beginning of the 19th century, Montréal's Quartier Latin was a modest agricultural community with an orchard plantation as its center. After the construction of Église Saint-Jacques in 1823 and a property boom in the 1860s, the community began to thrive.

The Université Laval (later the Université de Montréal) erected a campus here in 1893 and remained here until it built its massive property on the western slope of Mont-Royal in the early 1940s. It was at the end of the 1960s, when l'UQAM decided to occupy the empty space, that the area was coined Quartier Latin. Home to an active student scene, a number of boutiques, restaurants, and bars, the Quartier Latin also features 20 cultural institutions, including eight theaters and four cinemas.

Musée Juste pour Rire

The Musée Juste pour Rire (2111 boulevard Saint-Laurent, 514/845-4000, www.hahaha.com, adults $9, children 4–12 $5) is the brainchild of entrepreneur Gilbert Rozon and the result of his desire to expand the success of the Festival Juste pour Rire into something more permanent. At the outset, the museum, built in a converted brewery, was dedicated exclusively to funny business but has since expanded to include different exhibitions related to entertainment. Still, comedy is what this place does best and the Comedy Hall of Fame, with 100 clips of the best routines from 100 renowned comics, is a great way to spend a rainy afternoon. The museum is open only during temporary exhibitions, though, so your best bet is to check out its website for a listing of events.

La Grande Bibliothèque

It's an uncommon sight to witness people standing in line at a library, but this is exactly what happened when La Grande Bibliothèque (475 boulevard de Maisonneuve Est, 514/873-1100, www.bnquebec.ca, 10 A.M.–10 P.M. Tues.–Fri., 10 A.M.–5 P.M. Sat.–Sun.) opened its doors in the spring of 2005. With an exterior made from glass and copper, the library cuts an impressive figure, but inside is where the library really shines, with its more than one million books, not to mention its digital collection and large selection of microform and audio resources. There is a special emphasis placed on Québec's publishing heritage as well as anything written about Québec throughout the globe. The news section is open 10 A.M.–midnight every day.

NORTHWEST OF THE PLATEAU
Mile End

You may already be familiar with Mile End if you've read any of Mordecai Richler's books, many of which take place in this area near rue Saint-Urbain. Between the Plateau and Outremont boroughs, Mile End has become Montréal's newest, coolest neighborhood. Given its name because getting to the racetrack that used to be here in the late 1800s required zigzagging along a mile-long path, Mile End is a multicultural neighborhood, probably most fa-

THE MONTRÉAL TRIPLEX

If there's one building that epitomizes Montréal's residential architecture, it's the triplex. As Montréal as the brownstone is New York, the stately stone or brick triplexes, with their balconies and prominent, often ornamental, wrought-iron staircases, are some of the most photographed buildings in the city.

Montréal's triplex boom began in the late 1800s when immigrants from Europe started arriving in droves, settling into neighborhoods like Mile End, the Plateau, and Little Italy. Today, it's not uncommon to see first generation immigrants from that time still living on the first floor of the triplex, renting out the second and third floors to successive generations. But even more common these days is to see young professionals with money to spare, snatching up the buildings, renovating them, and then dividing them into condos.

Urban architects praise the Montréal triplex. They claim that while still allowing high-density living, the triplex builds a stronger sense of community by giving each resident a front door on the exterior of the building and hence, more interaction with the street. See, good things can happen in threes.

mous for its two world-renowned bagel shops, **Saint-Viateur Bagel** (263 rue Saint-Viateur Ouest, 514/276-8044, open 24 hours daily) and **Fairmount Bagel** (74 rue Fairmount, 514/272-0667, open 24 hours daily). Be prepared for a heated discussion with locals about who makes the better bagel—it's serious business in this city.

Little Italy

As Montréal's third-largest ethnic community, Italians have claimed the area bordered by the quadrangle of rue Saint-Zotique, boulevard Jean-Talon, rue Drolet and rue Marconi as their own. Although Little Italy is well known for its shops and parks, the main reason people visit the area is, natch, for the Italian food. (See the *Food* section of this chapter.)

When you've finished your meal, stretch your legs by taking a stroll through the neighborhood, stopping off at Parc Dante (rue Dante, near Alma). Named after famed medieval poet Dante Alighieri, this is a favorite meeting place for the Italian community. The park plays host to a variety of festivals throughout the year. Adjacent to the park is the beautiful **Église La Difesa** (6800 rue Henri-Julien, 514/277-6522), built in 1919. Although it's not open to the public, it's worth a look from the outside. And of course, don't forget to visit the city's famed **Jean-Talon Market** (7075 rue Casgrain, 514/277-1588, www.marchespublics-mtl .com, 7 A.M.–6 P.M. Mon.–Wed., 7 A.M.–8 P.M. Thurs.–Fri., and 7 A.M.–5 P.M. Sat.–Sun.) in the middle of Little Italy. Fresh fruit, veggies, and flowers are the market's specialties with a ring of cheese, meat, fish, and specialty stores that surround it.

OLYMPIC STADIUM AREA

In the east end of Montréal in the Hochelaga-Maisonneuve district, this grouping of sights is a great spot for families. Dominated by the leaning tower and oval bubble of the Stade Olympique, the area is also well-known for its botanical gardens, Insectarium, and the Château Dufresne.

To get there, take the metro's green line out to the Viau station, which is right beside the Stade Olympique. You can also get off at the Pie-IX station, named after Pope Pius IX (pronounced Pee-neuf), to visit the Château Dufresne and the Jardin Botanique.

During the summer, there's a free minitrain that runs through the site, stopping at four locations (the Viau metro station, the Biodôme, Parc Olympique, and the Jardin Botanique). It takes 30 minutes to make the full circle.

Stade Olympique

Referred to by locals as the "Big O," the Stade Olympique (4141 avenue Pierre-de-Coubertin,

514/252-4141, www.rio.gouv.qc.ca) was designed and built for the 1976 Olympic Summer Games by architect Roger Tallibert. Also home to the Montréal Expos before the baseball team was transferred to Washington after the 2004 season, the $1 billion building has been plagued with problems since its construction and has been termed the "Big Owe" as it took till 2006 to pay it off. In 1999, the stadium's original retractable roof was replaced by a permanent cover after some of the support beams snapped and a huge concrete slab fell to the ground almost 10 years before. The stadium is now used for a variety of events, including exhibitions, Motocross, marathons, Alouettes football games, and even monster truck shows. The stadium also houses a sports center, which includes a publicly accessible Olympic pool (1:30 P.M.–8 P.M. Mon.–Fri. and 1 P.M.–4 P.M. Sat.–Sun., adults $3.50, children 17 and under $2.50, students and seniors $2.65).

You can also take the cable car up the building's inclined tower (the world's tallest tilting structure) to the Montréal Tower Observatory, where, on a clear day, you can get an exceptional view of the city (and sometimes even the Laurentian mountains).

Biodôme de Montréal

The former bike-racing stadium is now the Biodôme de Montréal (4777 avenue Pierre-de-Coubertin, 514/868-3000, 9 A.M.–5 P.M. Tues.–Sun. early Sept.–Feb., 9 A.M.–5 P.M. daily mid-Mar.–late June, 9 A.M.–6 P.M. daily late June–early Sept., adults $12, students 18 and older $9, children 5–17 $6), a half-zoo, half-museum that examines the flora and fauna of four different ecosystems. Stroll though a tropical forest with its birds, bats, iguanas, vines, and dense bush, and then it's off to a Laurentian forest with its maple trees, rocky outcrops, porcupines and otters, beavers and lynx. In the St. Lawrence marine ecosystem you'll find pools and aquariums of sturgeon, starfish, crab, and sea birds, while the polar worlds of the Arctic and Antarctic contain penguin, puffin, and other arctic birds. Kids particularly love watching the penguins race around in the water and lining up to be fed their dinner of fresh fish.

Jardin Botanique de Montréal

Founded in 1931 by Mayor Camilien-Houde, the immense Jardin Botanique de Montréal (4101 rue Sherbrooke Est, 514/872-1400, 9 A.M.–5 P.M. Tues.–Sun. Nov.–mid-May, 9 A.M.–6 P.M. daily mid-May–mid-Sept., 9 A.M.–9 P.M. daily mid-Sept.–mid-Oct., adults $12, students 18 and older $9, children 5–17 $6) is one of the world's largest with more than

22,000 plant species, 10 greenhouses, and 30 theme gardens, including the famous **Chinese Garden,** which was created as a joint effort between the City of Shanghai and the Jardin Botanique de Montréal and required a crew of 50 Chinese craftsmen to assemble.

The **Arboretum,** home to more than 7,000 species of trees and shrubs in 45 main collections, is another of the Jardin Botanique's must-see attractions. It covers more than half of the grounds (40 hectares) and is particularly lovely in the fall when the exceptional orange, red, and yellow colors pop out. Winter in the arboretum is also enchanting, especially for avid bird-watchers and cross-country ski enthusiasts.

◖ Insectarium de Montréal

Within the Jardin Botanique grounds, the fascinating Insectarium de Montréal (4581 rue Sherbrooke Est, same hours and rates as the Jardin Botanique) is an ode to squiggly, creepy-crawly creatures from around the world. Live collections display more than 100 species, including beetles, butterflies, cockroaches, caterpillars, butterflies, grasshoppers, and spiders—all in an array of shapes, sizes, and colors. If you're visiting in late August or early September, don't miss the tagging and release of monarch butterflies. For the daring, there are also the insect tastings, which include chocolate-covered ant tastings and crunchy roasted crickets. Yum! If you go during the school season, you may want to consider visiting on the weekend or a weeknight, as weekdays are usually busy with schoolkids.

Château Dufresne

Although it's overshadowed by the Parc Olympique sights, the Château Dufresne (2929 avenue Jeanne d'Arc, 514/259-9201, www.chateaudufresne.qc.ca, 10 A.M.–5 P.M. Thurs.–Sun. adults $6, students $5, children $2.50) provides an interesting glimpse into the lives of the French bourgeoisie. Constructed in 1915 by the two sons of successful shoe manufacturer Victoire du Sault Dufresne, the beaux-arts mansion, which cost a cool million to build—a fortune at the time—is actually two adjoining homes. The brothers, Oscar and Marius Dufresne, lived here with their families among the lavish wood staircases, murals by famous church artist Guido Nincheri, plush salons, and a Turkish smoking room.

(LACHINE CANAL

Montréal's early settlers immediately began looking for ways to avoid the Lachine Rapids. In 1670, François de Salignac, a Sulpician Seminary superior, first envisioned building a canal from Montréal to Lachine. But his successor, François Dollier de Casson, brought the plan to fruition. By emphasizing that a canal could power the city's mills as well as facilitate shipping, he eventually persuaded the powers that be to proceed with the project. Although construction began in 1689, it was interrupted twice—at first because of an Iroquois attack on Lachine, and then because of a lack of funds—and was completed only in 1825, thanks to the deep pockets of prominent merchant and Bank of Montréal founder John Richardson.

At the time, Montréal was itching to become North America's trade hub and the 14.5-km canal stretching from the Old Port to Lac Saint-Louis in Lachine made that dream possible. The southwestern part of the city was transformed into a cradle of industrialization as a result. The waterway was widened in the late 1930s to allow for wider boats, but heavy traffic and increasingly wider ships led to the creation of the more accommodating St. Lawrence Seaway in 1970 and, subsequently, the canal's closing.

During the 1980s the canal was an unsightly spot with a mass of junk piling high. Rumor has it that more than 80 scrap cars were pulled from its shallow depths. In 1997 Parks Canada launched a major revitalization project and reintroduced pleasure boating in 2002. Today the canal is best known for its historical landmarks, attractive urban housing projects, and many recreational and leisure opportunities, including, according to many locals, the sweetest spot in the city for a picnic.

To get to the Lachine Canal via metro, get off at the Square-Victoria stop for the Old Port Locks Sector, Lionel-Groulx for the Atwater Market sector, and Charlevoix for the Saint-Gabriel Lock. Bicycles are permitted on the metro daily 10 A.M.–3 P.M. and after 7 P.M. on the first cars of the train. You can get to the Lachine sector of the canal via the 195 bus that departs from Angrignon metro. If you want to drive to the canal, there are plenty of parking lots, some of which are free of charge. You'll find a lot for the Old Port sector on rue de la Commune near rue du Port, one for the Atwater Market sector near the rue Notre-Dame and rue Atwater intersection, and one for the Lachine Lock sector at rue Du Canal.

Old Port to Atwater

The upstream entrance to the Lachine Canal begins in the Old Port at locks 1 and 2 where rue de la Commune and rue McGill converge. While there, you can stop by the new **Café des Éclusiers** (514/496-0109, 11:30 A.M.–11 P.M. Mon.–Wed. and Fri.–Sun. and 11:30 A.M.–1 A.M. Thurs. May–Sept.), a restaurant-bar, to watch the boats going through the locks.

The next lock stop leads into the Saint-Gabriel sector, the industrial heart of the canal. The area is dominated by the massive red-brick **Redpath sugar refinery,** once the largest industrial complex in Montréal. Back in the 1840s, the company's founder, John Redpath, had worked on the construction of the canal. The building was abandoned in 1980 when the company moved to Toronto, and there was an initial push to convert it into a museum devoted to the canal's industrial past. The plan fell through and the building has since been converted into condos.

The next major stop along the canal is the **Atwater Market** (138 avenue Atwater, 514/937-7754, www.marchespublics-mtl.com, 8 A.M.–6 P.M. Mon.–Wed., 8 A.M.–8 P.M. Thurs., 8 A.M.–9 P.M. Fri., 8 A.M.–5 P.M. Sat.–Sun.), one of Montréal's two major food markets. Housed in an art deco building, Atwater Market has been open since 1933. Having gone through major gentrification in recent years, Atwater carries all the regular fruit and veggies, seafood, meats, and cheeses, but also several gourmet products such as fine chocolates and fresh pasta.

Once you've had a nosh, it may be time to stop for a beer at **La Brasserie McAuslan** (rue Saint-Ambroise, 514/939-3060, www.mcauslan.com, 4 P.M.–9 P.M. Wed.–Fri. and noon–6 P.M. Sat.–Sun.). Dating to 1989, the brewery has become Québec's biggest. There's a great outdoor patio overlooking the canal where you can sample one of the five brews it has on tap (go for the excellent Apricot Wheat Ale if you like a fruity tinge to your suds). You can also do a one-hour brewery tour if you're so inclined.

Lachine

At the end of the canal (or the beginning depending on which way you've come) is the quiet and prosperous borough of Lachine—named as such because one of the first seigneurs in the area, Robert Cavalier de la Salle, was convinced that he could find a passage to the Far East. His many attempts led his contemporaries to refer to the area in mockery as "La Chine." The **Lachine Lock Visitor Service Centre** (500 chemin des Iroquois, 514/364-4490, 9:30 A.M.–5 P.M. daily mid-May to early Sept.) has guides to tell you about every Lachine Canal detail imaginable and a photographic exhibit chronicling the canal's history. Right next door is the **Lieu Historique National du Canada du Commerce-de-la-Fourrure-à-Lachine** (1255 boulevard Saint-Joseph, 514/637-7433, 9:30 A.M.–12:30 P.M. and 1 P.M.–5 P.M. daily early Apr.–early Oct. and Wed.–Sun. mid-Oct.–late Nov., adults $4, youth $2). In a beautiful old 1803 stone warehouse where fur pelts brought back from expeditions upriver were stored, this historic site commemorates Montréal's flourishing fur industry during the 18th and 19th centuries. Just across the bridge is the **Musée de Lachine** (1 chemin de Musée, 514/634-3471, 11:30 A.M. -4:30 P.M. Wed.–Sun. Apr.–Dec.), which lays claim to the oldest building in Montréal, the Mayson LeBer-LeMoyne, built be-

tween 1669 and 1685. The museum itself and the other buildings on the property serve as archaeological site, exhibit area for historical artifacts, contemporary art gallery, and abstract sculpture garden.

Although the **Lachine Rapids** are not as treacherous today as they would have been at the time of colonization, when they stopped explorers in their tracks and forced them to settle, they still pose a hearty challenge to whitewater rafters and kayakers. In contrast to the furious waters, the shore by the rapids is so serene—with its huge, sweeping willow trees and bird refuge—that it's become a favored spot for wedding photographs. The area, actually a park called **Parc des Rapides** (corner boulevard LaSalle and 6e Avenue, 514/367-6351) has a lookout and interpretive panels, chronicling the history and natural characteristics of the mighty rapids.

Tours

If you want to meander along the Lachine Canal and don't have your own pleasure craft, you can try out **Croisières Canal de Lachine** (footbridge near Atwater Market, 514/846-0428 or 866/846-0448, www.croisierecanaldelachine.ca, historical cruise adults $17, students $14, children 4–14 $10). The nonprofit tour operator offers two-hour historical cruises with a Parks Canada interpreter aboard *L'Éclusier*, a glassed-in, 63-foot, biodiesel-fuel boat that meanders along the canal, departing twice a day during the summer. The outfit also offers a breakfast tour followed by a visit to a farm or vineyard and a two-hour tasting cruise with a tour and beer sampling at the McAuslan Brewery and lunch in the Ambroisie restaurant.

Every Sunday during July and August, **Parks Canada** (514/496-5379, www.pc.gc.ca) organizes various outings along the Lachine Canal with a historical focus. Activities include a dragon-boat expedition ($12), which starts with a lesson on how to navigate the vessel and then continues with a historical tour of the canal, a free guided historical bike tour, and free interpretive explorations of the

Côte-Saint-Paul Lockstation and the workshops, mills, and basins along the Peel side of the canal. Most activities have a morning and afternoon session.

PARC JEAN-DRAPEAU

Covering 268 hectares on two islands in the middle of the St. Lawrence, Parc Jean-Drapeau is Montréal's largest and most recreationally diverse park. The park was named after Jean Drapeau, Montréal's energetic and ambitious mayor, who brought Expo '67 to the city and used the islands as a stunning stage from which to showcase the Games and accommodate its 45 million visitors. Île Ste-Hélène, originally named in 1611 by French explorer Samuel de Champlain to honor his 12-year-old wife (!), Hélène Boulle, and Île Notre-Dame, the artificial island built out of excavated rubble from the underground metro system, became, for one short moment, the most exciting place on earth.

Although the spotlight has shifted, the two islands have been quietly celebrated by Montrealers ever since. They go there to walk, cycle, inline skate, and, of course, play the slots, put on their best poker faces, and watch cars race. But the legend and impact of Expo '67 lingers still. To reach the islands, you can either take the Pont Jacques-Cartier, which offers access to Île Sainte-Hélène or Pont de la Concorde, which will take you to Île Notre-Dame. There are five parking lots on the islands, which all cost $10 (except for the lot at La Ronde, which costs $12) for a full day during high season.

If you want to go by metro, use the yellow line from Berri-UQAM station to Jean-Drapeau, which will let you out on Île Sainte-Hélène. From there, you can catch the 167 bus, which tours the entire park before ending at the casino. Buses run about every 15 minutes between 9 A.M. and 1 A.M.

To cycle over to the park, you can use the reserved lanes along both bridges from Montréal or a bike link from the south shore along the Pont Victoria April 15–November 15.

Finally, you can take a ferry across to the park by taking one of the shuttles operated by **Navettes Maritime du Saint-Laurent** (514/281-8000, www.navettesmaritimes.com, adults and children 6 and up $4.50). The shuttles depart Quai Jacques-Cartier in Old Montréal and leave every hour daily late June to early September and on weekends late May to late June and early September to early October.

For information on Parc Jean-Drapeau, you can visit the **information center** (514/872-6120, www.parcjeandrapeau.com, 10 A.M.–6:30 P.M. daily mid-June–late Aug.) near the Passerelle du Cosmos bridge on Île Notre-Dame. At the center, pick up a tourist map of the park (most of all so that you know where all the bathrooms are) and find out about all the activities. There are ATMs on the islands at the Casino de Montréal, La Ronde, and the chalet at the beach.

Habitat '67

Although technically part of the mainland, the pyramid of Lego blocks called Habitat '67 that you may see from one of the Old Port piers is on a spit of land called Cité du Havre,

Moshe Safdie's unique Habitat '67 was built for the World Fair.

MONTRÉAL

The iconic geodesic dome from Expo '67 is now home to Biosphère.

© JENNIFER EDWARDS

just before Pont de la Concorde makes the crossing over to Île Ste-Hélène.

Moshe Safdie was only 26 and fresh out of McGill's architecture school when his thesis was selected as the spotlight project of the Montréal World Fair, Expo '67. Called Habitat, the 158-apartment complex, created out of over 300 prefabricated concrete blocks, was designed as a solution to high-density living, demonstrating that a great number of people can live in close proximity and yet still reap the pleasures of privacy and space. When the cube-stacked building was unveiled just before Expo, it created a huge stir, with as many people loving the place as hating it. Most architects praised the design, however, and Safdie became an internationally recognized name. Safdie also designed the new Musée des Beaux Arts and the National Gallery of Canada. You can catch a peek of the complex as you cross Pont de la Concorde heading over to Île Sainte-Hélène, but the best vantage point is from the road and bike path that runs just in front.

Biosphère

Along with Habitat, the towering geodesic dome on Île Sainte-Hélène called Biosphère (160 chemin Tour-de-l'Isle, 514/283-5000, www.biosphere.ec.gc.ca, noon–5 P.M. Mon. and Wed.–Fri. mid-Sept.–mid-June and 10 A.M.–6 P.M. mid-June–mid-Sept., adults $10, students $7.50, youth 7–17 $5, children under 6 free) has come to be viewed as a symbol of Montréal and its innovation and prosperity. Designed by architect Buckminster Fuller for use as the American Pavilion during Expo, the steel-frame structure, which weighs 600 tons, was originally covered with transparent acrylic panels. About 10 years after the fair, when some repairs were being done, a fire destroyed the outer layer and it was never replaced. Instead, a museum was installed within the dome in 1995. Run by Environment Canada, the museum highlights, through the use of interactive exhibits, the importance of water and the balancing of the ecosystem.

Trilogie

Starting near Biosphère is a new trail with interpretive panels called Trilogie, which was conceived to allow visitors to take in three wetland areas in the park, including the water-purification system at Biosphère, the pond filters on Île Notre-Dame, and the peat bog at the Jardins Floralies.

Complexe Aquatique

Officially opening to the public in the summer of 2006, the enormous Complexe Aquatique (514/872-6120, www.parcjeandrapeau.com) is one place where you won't be fighting for lap space. Built in the 1950s, the complex was renovated and swimming pools—a competition pool, a warm-up pool, and a diving pool—were added in time for the city's hosting of the 2005 FINA World Aquatic Championships. Now, the complex offers the ideal setting for training camps, competitions, or a leisurely afternoon doggie paddle.

Restaurant Hélène de Champlain

Just up from Biosphere is the islands' sole official restaurant, Hélène de Champlain (200 Tour de l'Isle, Île Ste-Hélène, 514/395-2424, www.helenedechamplain.com, mains $16–39), a fancy-pants French restaurant in a large former sports chalet built for the island in 1938. The Norman-style building was converted into a restaurant in 1955 and hosted many heads of state during Expo '67. Behind the restaurant is a rose garden with hundreds of varieties.

Tour de Lévis

Built in the 1930s, the 92-foot Tour de Lévis was named after the last French commander left standing during the 1760 British Conquest; he burned his flags rather than hand them over to the British. Originally a water reservoir, the renovated building now houses a staircase with 157 steps, which lead to an observation deck with an incredible 360-degree view of Parc Jean-Drapeau, the island of Montréal, and the river.

Musée Stewart

On the western (or Montréal) side of the island, you'll find the Musée Stewart (20 rue Tour-de-l'Isle, 514/861-6701, www.stewart-museum.org, 10 A.M.–5 P.M. Mon. and Wed.–Sun. Oct.–mid-May and 10 A.M.–5 P.M. daily mid-May–early Oct., adults $10, students $7, children under 7 free) on the old grounds of Fort de l'Île Ste-Hélène, a fort built by the British to safeguard Montréal from hungry Americans. The museum, in the old arsenal, was conceived in 1970 thanks to a donation from the personal collection of philanthropist, historian, and president of Macdonald Tobacco, David Macdonald Stewart. Today, the museum focuses on the history of New France and the influence of European civilizations through a broader collection of documents, maps, antique weapons, and household items dating as far back as 16th century.

La Ronde

It used to be that La Ronde (22 chemin Mac-Donald, 514/397-2000, www.laronde.com, 10 A.M.–8 P.M. daily late May–mid-June, 10 A.M.–10:30 P.M. daily mid-June–early Sept., 10 A.M.–7 P.M. Sat.–Sun. early Sept.–late Sept., and 5 P.M.–9 P.M. Fri., noon–9 P.M. Sat., and noon–8 P.M. Sun early–late Oct., adults and children 12 and older $30, children 3–11 $20) had an endearing but seedy side with creaky rides and guys with tight jeans and cigarettes operating the rides. Nowadays with the amusement-park conglomerate Six Flags having taken over, the province's largest amusement park is all straightforward, ultraslick adrenaline-inducing entertainment.

The park got its start during Expo '67 and at least one ride, the Minirail, an exploratory train that circles the park, dates from that time. But it pales in comparison to some of the park's other offerings, most notably the thrill rides such as the classic Monster roller coaster, which at 40 meters is the highest wooden roller coaster in the world, the Cobra, a stand-up roller coaster, and the Vampire, an inverted roller coaster, which reaches speeds of

80.5 km an hour. Of course, the park has a Ferris wheel, but this one, at a height of 45 meters, is a veritable thrill-ride itself.

Circuit Gilles-Villeneuve

In early June, Parc Jean-Drapeau's peace and quiet is interrupted by the roaring sounds of the **Grand Prix du Canada** (514/350-0000, C.P. 248, Station Place d'Armes, 514/350-0000, www.grandprix.ca, general admission Fri. $25, Sat. $40, Sun. $60, 3 days $90), the Formula One event that hosts the world's best race-car drivers and thousands of racing fans. The 4.4-km circuit on Île Notre-Dame was built in 1978 and named after Gilles Villeneuve, the famous race-car driver from Québec (and father of Jacques Villeneuve), who won his first F1 race on the track in 1978 but who died during a qualifying lap at the Belgian Grand Prix in 1982. The circuit is home to a second event, the **Molson Indy** (514/397-4639, www.molsonindy.com), which takes place over three days in late August. Although it doesn't get nearly the limelight of the Grand Prix, the Indy attracts a very respectable crowd (more than 100,000).

Circuit Gilles-Villeneuve is far from abandoned once the racing is over, though. It's open year-round to cyclists, inline skaters, and walkers who want to revel in one of the quietest spots in the city. The circuit passes the **Bassin Olympique,** the basin built for the 76 Olympics' water sports, which today hosts several events including rowing, canoeing, and dragon-boat races.

Jardins Floralies

The beautiful Jardins des Floralies are 25 hectares of mature gardens that were designed by international landscape artists for the International Floralies horticultural fair in 1980 and that have been lovingly maintained ever since. Enjoy a picnic or take a paddleboat ride in the canals that meander through the gardens, which are divided into 12 sections dedicated to various countries (United States, Italy, France, Mexico, Israel, etc.) and provinces (Québec, Ontario, Alberta).

Casino de Montréal

Between the Jardins des Floralies and the Lac des Régates sits the gleaming Casino de Montréal (1 avenue du Casino, 514/392-2746, www.casino-de-montreal.com, 24 hours daily). Housed inside the former French and Québec Expo '67 pavilions, the casino was opened in 1993 and drew huge crowds—actually twice as many people as were originally anticipated—forcing it to quickly expand. There are five floors of games, including a mind-numbing 3,000 slot machines and 120 gaming tables for blackjack, roulette, Sic Bo, Caribbean stud poker, and Pai Gow poker.

The casino also houses a performance hall, which hosts nightly musical revues, concerts, and comic performances. There are also four restaurants and four bars to choose from. Restaurants include the ultraupscale, five-diamond Nuances, La Bonne Carte for a buffet lunch or dinner, Via Fortuna, an Italian bistro, and L'Entre-Mise, which serves casual fare, including Montréal smoked meat.

Beach

On the western tip of Île Notre-Dame, not far from the Pont Victoria heading to the south shore, is a fine-sand beach (10 A.M.–7 P.M. mid-June–late Aug., adults $7.50, after 4 P.M. $4.50, children 6–13 $3.75, after 4 P.M. $2.50, children under 5 free, family pass $19) where Montrealers find a little summer respite from the concrete and traffic of the city. Patrolled during the summer, the beach's man-made lake, Lac des Régates, is crystal-clear thanks to its elaborate filtration system. There's a water-sports pavilion where you can rent beach chairs, canoes, kayaks, sailboards, and pedal boats.

Piknic Électronik

For something a little less testosterone-revving than car-racing events, Île Sainte-Hélène also hosts the Sunday-afternoon Piknic Électronik (www.piknicelectronik.com, 1 – 8 P.M. Sun. late May–late–Sept., admission $5, children under 14 free), a chance to listen to electronic music in the great wide open instead of a musty, dark club. The event takes place around Calder's sculpture just up from the metro station and features some of the city's best DJs. There's a constructed dance floor and a sea of blankets and people playing Frisbee and hackisack.

Sports and Recreation

BIKING
Lachine Canal
The Lachine Canal can take most of the credit for Montréal's appointment to North America's most bike-friendly city by *Bicycling* magazine in 1999. Opened in 1977, the 14.5-km canal path is one of Montréal's oldest and most popular. Almost entirely flat, the divided path is an easy ride, and an experienced cyclist should be able to get from one end to the other in about an hour. The canal is also part of the larger **Pôle des Rapides** (514/364-4490, www.poledesrapides.com, late June–mid-Oct.)—100 km of cycling paths covering Lachine, LaSalle, the Sud-Ouest, and Verdun boroughs. The information center for the circuit is at Quai 5 on the Lachine Canal.

Parc Jean-Drapeau
The Circuit Gilles-Villeneuve on Île Notre-Dame also makes for an extremely pleasant afternoon cycle or inline skate trip. To get to the circuit you need to first make it to Île Sainte-Hélène via Pont Jacques-Cartier in the Old Port, Cité du Havre's Pont de la Concorde (both bridges have biking paths), or the Jean-Drapeau metro station. The island actually has 15 km worth of trails, including the Gilles-Villeneuve circuit and ones that take in the Jardins Floralies and the route around the Olympic Basin.

Bike Shops
If you are looking to rent a bike or inline skates, you can visit **Ça Roule Montréal** (27 de la Commune Est, 514/866-0633, www.caroulemontreal.com, bike weekdays hour/day $7/$22, weekends hour/day $7.50/$25) in Old Montréal at the bottom of

boulevard Saint-Laurent. You can go it alone or opt for one of the store's guided tours, which require a minimum of six participants.

At the intersection of two bikeways, the **Maison des Cyclistes** (1251 rue Rachel Est, 514/521-8356, ext. 344, 8:30 A.M.–8 P.M. Mon.–Fri. and 9 A.M.–7 P.M. Sat.–Sun.) is adjacent to the park. This mecca of all things relating to Montréal and cycling houses the provincial biking association Vélo Québec as well as Café Bicicletta, an Italian-style café with light snacks including bagels, panini, and empanadas. Drop by if you have any questions about biking routes in Montréal or just to hang with the cycling crowd.

BOATING AND KAYAKING
Lachine Canal
By the Atwater footbridge is **H2O Adventures** (514/842-1306 or 877/935-2925, www.aventuresh2o.com, solo kayak $15/hr., tandem kayak $25/hr., pedal boat $10/hour and electric boat $35/hour), a large rental and touring outfit that rents out kayaks, pedal boats, and small electric boats and offers courses in sea kayaking.

Lachine Rapids
Think you have the mettle to face the rapids that stumped the early colonists? Well, a number of white-water rafting operators can take you out to test your skill. There's **Les Descentes sur le Saint-Laurent** (8912 boulevard LaSalle, 514/767-2230 or 800/324-7238, www.raftingmontreal.com, rafting adults $40, teens 13–18 $34, children 6–12 $23, jet-boating adults $48, teens 13–18 $38, children 8–12 $28), a jet-boating and rafting company near the Pont Mercier

that offers high-adventure and more family-oriented expeditions on the rapids. Departing from the Old Port is **Saute-Moutons** (47 rue de la Commune Ouest, 514/284-9607, www.jetboatingmontreal.com, rafting adults $55, teens 14–18 $45, jet-boating adults $55, teens 13–18 $45, and speedboating adults $22, teens 13–18 $18), which offers rafting, jet-boating, and speedboating trips along the St. Lawrence toward Lachine, culminating in a "rodeo-style" rapids experience.

Parc Jean-Drapeau

To take to the water in and around Parc Jean-Drapeau, pay **Option Plein Air** (514/872-0199, www.optionpleinair.com, sailboards and kayaks $14/hour, canoes and pedal boats $16/hour) a visit. Situated by the Bassin Olympique on Île Notre-Dame, the nonprofit center offers sailing lessons and dragon-boat racing. The center is also responsible for the management of the canoe, kayak, pedal boat, and sailboard rentals at the Pavillon Nautique at the beach.

ICE-SKATING
Old Port

Few would argue that there is a finer winter activity in the city than skating at the half-kilometer **Bonsecours Basin Skating Rink** (Basin Bonsecours, 11 A.M.–9 P.M. Mon.–Wed., 11 A.M.–10 P.M. Thurs.–Sun., adults $4, children 6–12 $3, family $12). At night, the lights from the Marché Bonsecours shine bright, while music such as jazz and classical are piped through the loudspeakers. A shop on-site called Patin Patin offers skate rentals and sharpening.

Beaver Lake Rink

From sea level to mountaintop, Parc Mont-Royal's Beaver Lake Rink has a more subdued, woodsy surrounding. It's a popular spot, and the number of skaters outgrew the small man-made lake, so the city set to work on increasing the rink's size in 2005. It also improved the retro-looking and retro-serviced pavilion next to the lake, so that warming up and stopping for a bite to eat at the snack bar is a now a much more pleasant experience.

L'Atrium le 1000 de la Gauchetière

In the 51-story skyscraper on rue de la Gauchetière is Montréal's year-round skating rink, L'Atrium le 1000 de la Gauchetière (1000 rue de La Gauchetière Ouest, 514/395-0555, 11:30 A.M.–6 P.M. Tues.–Fri. and Sun. and 11:30 A.M.–7 P.M. Sat. with a dance and skate 7 P.M.–10 P.M.). With natural light pouring in from the glass-dome ceiling and the glow from the food shops that surround it, the rink has a bright setting despite being indoors. On Saturday nights, the place turns on its roller-skating style and brings in a DJ.

Entertainment and Events

BARS AND CLUBS
Old Montréal

Old Montréal isn't where you want to be if you're interested in clubbing. The area is better suited for those wanting a quiet drink in a sleek boutique hotel setting or those who want some traditional sing-along fun. Some of the boîte à chansons places can get a little rowdy at night, but if you're up for some sing-along songs and beer by the pitcher, they can be a lot of fun. Probably Old Mon-tréal's most famous rowdy spot is **Les Deux Pierrots** (104 rue Saint-Paul Est, 514/861-1270, 8 P.M.–3 A.M. Fri.–Sat.). In existence for more than 30 years, the bar features singer-songwriters in the Québécois vein. From 4 to 8 P.M., Le Pierrot has a live group called Cubason that plays Caribbean beats. Local hangout **Cobalt** (312 rue Saint-Paul Ouest, 514/842-2960, www.cobalt-montreal.com, 11:30 A.M.–3 P.M. Mon. and Wed.–Sun.) is a café, bistro, and lounge all rolled into one with an easygoing ambience, Monday nights are reserved for DJs while the weekends feature musical jazz brunches with live jazz and your choice of pancakes, French toast, or frittata. A handful of sandwich and salad dishes are on the menu (panini, smoked salmon on a bagel, and mixed greens salad with emmental and grilled cashews).

Downtown

For people who like to see and be seen, **rue Crescent,** with its mix-and-mingle pubs and fashion-savvy clientele, is the party destination of downtown. It's the official location for all the major partying done during the Grand Prix weekend, and year-round it's a place where tourists and mostly anglophone Montrealers head out to cruise.

Some locals will try to dissuade you from heading to Crescent because it rides low on flair and creativity. That being said, it's still worth a stroll at night and perhaps a stop on a sunny afternoon at one of its many streetfront patios. An exception on the Cresent strip is **Hurley's Irish Pub** (1225 rue Crescent, 514/861-4111, www.hurleyirishpub.com, 11 A.M.–3 A.M.). One of the city's favorite Irish pubs, Hurley's has live music every night starting at 9:30 P.M. and cozy lounge sections, a terrace, and a courtyard. Get yourself a pint of Guinness and the world is a better place. Another anomaly is the brew pub **Brutopia** (1219 rue Crescent, 514/393-9277, 3:30 P.M.–3 A.M. daily), which offers six beers brewed on the premises, a relaxed environment, and great bands. There are two terraces, one out front and a shaded one in back.

The legendary **Old Dublin** (1219A rue University, 514/861-4448, 11:30 A.M.–3 A.M. daily) rises proudly from its parking lot setting. There's nothing shiny and cute about this Irish pub—it's got a low ceiling and not much in the way of décor. But it is where all the traditionalists go, where there are more than 20 beers on tap and more than 15 hamburger varieties, and where the music is almost always good. For Latin dance lovers, the '70s style **Salsathèque** (1220 rue Peel, 514/875-0016,

10 P.M.–3 A.M. Wed.–Sun., $5 cover charge on Fri. and Sat.) is the place to shake your hips and get down. There are plenty of disco balls and an illuminated *Saturday Night Fever* dance floor and there are also salsa demonstrations. It's loud and a bit of a meat market, but on the right night, it can be loads of fun. Another disco haven is **Funky Town** (1454A rue Peel, 514/282-8387, 11 P.M.–3 A.M. Thurs.–Sat.) just up the street. This place also has a dance floor that lights up, but it is more consistent with its '70s hits lineup. If you like playing pool, **Sharx Billards** (1606 rue Sainte-Catherine Ouest, 514/934-3105, www.sharx.ca, 11 A.M.–3 A.M., $10/hour, $20 deposit requested) on the corner of rue Guy is one of the city's most well-reputed and popular billiards bars. The two-floor **Galerie 1225 Art et Vin** (1225 rue de la Montagne, 514/395-1225, 10 A.M.–10 P.M. Tues.–Fri., 11 A.M.–10 P.M. Sat.) is an art gallery and wine bar under one roof. With exposed brick and a marble fireplace, the atmosphere is warm and casual. Art exhibits change every month.

Plateau Mont-Royal

Clubbing is a necessary part of any Montrealer's upbringing. And the place that he or she (both English and French) will turn to first is inevitably boulevard Saint-Laurent. Groups of people from the young to the middle-aged (although they are more scarce) stroll the strip in search of whatever party seems to be in full swing. Some spots have notorious lineups with bouncers who act as if they're on the selection committee for admission to heaven.

A Gogo Lounge (3682 boulevard Saint-Laurent, 514/286 0882, 5 P.M.–3 A.M.) would be the preferred stop of Austin Powers if the Groovy One were to hit Montréal. With plenty of cocktails and menus printed on old vinyl records, psychedelic colors, and 1960s furniture, this laid-back spot is a tongue-and-cheek throwback to '60s kitsch. Austin wouldn't appreciate the '70s and '80s music selection, though. Get decked out for a night at the **Tokyo Bar** (3709 boulevard Saint-Laurent, 514/842-6838, 10 P.M.–3 A.M. daily), which sports white-leather sofas, a red dance floor, kitschy Asian décor, and a terrace overlooking the Main. Frequented by the young and the jet set, this club plays booming house, hip-hop, or disco music depending on the evening. With its hanging lanterns, retro-chic décor, and huge selection of martinis, **Jello Bar** (151 rue Ontario Est, 514/285-2621, 9 P.M.–3 A.M. Thurs. and Sat., 5 P.M.–3 A.M. Wed.–Fri.) is an institution in Montréal and of one the few places where you may be unapologetically refused at the door if you are younger than 21 years old (or too badly dressed). But with its DJs and the occasional live band rocking the house with funk, R&B, salsa, and house, once you get in, you'll find the club boisterous, friendly, and relaxed.

Behind a nondescript door is the free-spirited, eclectic, and sometimes wild dancing club **Salon Daomé** (141 avenue Mont-Royal Est, 2nd floor, Thurs.–Sun., cover $6). With its tribal décor, salsa, Haitian, soul, and funk music, this is the place to let loose and blow some steam. Go to discothèque **El Zaz Bar** (4297 rue Saint-Denis, 514/288-9798, 2nd floor, 3 P.M.–3 A.M. daily, $2 cover charge Sun.–Wed., $4 Thurs.–Sat.), or simply "Zaz" to regulars, if you are younger than 25 and looking for action. With its tiny, packed dance floor and pool table at one end of the room, there are plenty of opportunities to rub shoulders.

The Plateau is packed with quiet and not-so-quiet neighborhood bars farther north on Saint-Laurent, on rue Mont-Royal, rue Saint-Denis, and spots in between. One of the best for laid-back, cool ambience has to be **Bily Kun** (354 rue Mont-Royal Est, 514/845-5392, 3 P.M.–3 A.M. daily), where you're just as likely to hear a philosophical discussion as you are a debate about which local bands rock the hardest. Open since 1998, Bily Kun ("white horse" in Czech) has subdued lighting, high ceilings, and a tiled floor, but it is recognized foremost for its mounted ostrich heads that decorate the walls. The opening of **Edgar Hypertaverne** (1562 avenue du Mont-Royal Est, 514/521-4661, 3 P.M.–3 A.M. daily) was seen as a little revolution in Montréal's night-

life history. Untraditionally located a bit east of the Plateau, this hip bar with sleek, modern décor and house music attracts a fashionable crowd that would otherwise never see fit to move beyond Saint-Laurent. In the Quartier Latin, the **Pub L'Île Noire** (342 rue Ontario Est, 514/982-0866, 3 P.M.–3 A.M. daily) is renowned for its huge variety of scotch. But you don't have to be a connoisseur or even like scotch to go. The pub is also a great place to quietly enjoy one of the 14 beers it has on tap. So loyal are the young, artsy fans of **Laïka** (4040 boulevard Saint-Laurent, 514/842-8088, 8:30 A.M.–3 A.M. Mon.–Fri. and 9 A.M.–3 A.M. Sat.–Sun.) that they would consider it sacrilegious to drink anywhere else. This cool but relaxed spot on Saint-Laurent and Duluth opens its windows during the summertime so that you can catch the atmosphere of the street from the inside. Good, affordable food and drinks and in-house DJs make this lounge one of the best spots on the Main. Even if rue Saint-Denis's legendary **Saint-Sulpice** (1680 rue Saint-Denis, 514/844-9458, 11:30 A.M.–3 A.M. daily) is trampled on by every succession of just-legal generation of Montrealers, there is still a very good reason to stop by: the terrace. Behind the building and hidden from the street, the Saint-Sulpice boasts the biggest, busiest, and sunniest terrace of the city with fountains and countless tables.

Mile End

For a fun night out, try **Mile End Bar** (5322 boulevard Saint-Laurent, 514/279-0200, www.mileendbar.com, 5 P.M.–3 A.M. Tues.–Fri., 8 P.M.–3 A.M. Sat.), a cool three-floor bar and restaurant that specializes in tapas and oysters. The first floor is especially popular for its *5 à 7* (happy hour), but eventually, the crowd makes its way up to the second floor for dancing. Large audiovisual screens (the kind your teacher used in science class) are situated throughout the bar showing funky, retro videos. The third floor is like a balcony, where voyeurs can observe the party below. It also has a lounge with comfy oversized chairs. If you're a fan of whisky, cigars, and a Casablanca-like setting, you'll love the relaxed sophistication of the **Whisky Café** (5800 boulevard Saint-Laurent, 514/278-2646, 5 P.M.–3 A.M. Mon.–Fri., 6 P.M.–3 A.M. Sat., 7 P.M.–3 A.M. Sun.). This sumptuous lounge known for its leather booths, wooden blinds, and stainless steel waterfall urinals in the men's (you'll catch many women sneaking in for a peek), has more than 100 single malts on the menu and a fine selection of port and wine.

LIVE MUSIC
Downtown
Previously known as Biddle's, the **House of Jazz** (2060 rue Aylmer, 514/842-8656, 11:30 A.M.–12:30 A.M. Mon.–Wed., 11:30 A.M.–1:30 A.M. Thurs., 11:30 A.M.–2:30 A.M. Fri., 6 P.M.–2:30 A.M. Sat., and noon–12:30 A.M. Sun.) is considered to be Montréal's most important jazz club. Touring jazz musicians will often make the stop at this club, also famed for its lip-smacking ribs. Another favored jazz stop is **Upstairs** (1254 rue MacKay, 514/931-6808, noon–1 A.M. Mon.–Thurs., noon–3 A.M. Fri., 5 P.M.–3 A.M. Sat., and 5 P.M.–1 A.M. Sun.). A little bit more casual and cozy than House of Jazz, Upstairs is a favored hangout of Concordia students and hard-core jazz lovers. There's live music every night starting at 9 P.M. and an array of grilled meats on the menu.

Plateau Mont-Royal
If you're itching to hear some local bands, two spots on the Main are worth mentioning. One is **Le Divan Orange** (4234 boulevard Saint-Laurent, 514/840-9090, 11 A.M.–3 A.M. Tues.–Sun.), just north of Rachel. This spacious but cozy venue has wood floors, couches, a vegetarian menu, and a stage that has seen the likes of some of Montréal's most promising folk, roots, rock, and alt-country bands. Just up the street, **Casa del Popolo** (4873 boulevard Saint-Laurent, 514/284-3804, cover charge) has a similar vibe, although it's much smaller. Its endearing grunge-meets-art décor, good food, cheap beer, and excel-

lent mix of live music, spoken word, and DJs makes La Casa one of the most original and creative venues in town. Over on Saint-Denis, **Bar L'Escogriffe** (4467A rue Saint-Denis, 514/842-7244) is the city's only other venue downtown to hear regular jazz music. Although jazz is but one of the musical genres played here, it's a welcome addition to the city's unreasonably tiny live jazz music scene.

THEATERS AND CONCERT HALLS
Old Montréal
Inside the Old Stock Exchange building, Montréal's leading English-language theater, the **Centaur** (453 rue Saint-François-Xavier, 514/288-3161, www. centaurtheatre.com), has been mounting classic and contemporary plays since its foundation in 1969, including the renowned annual Children's Series. The theater received some major recognition when in 1979 it mounted David Fennario's play *Balconville,* a chronicle of two poor residents, one Anglophone, the other Francophone, of the gritty Pointe-Saint-Charles neighborhood. The show became a hot ticket in Montréal and even went on to tour Europe. In the fall of 2005 a follow-up production, called *Condoville,* was presented at the Centaur revisiting the characters and the Pointe.

Downtown
The megacomplex of **Place des Arts** (175 rue Sainte-Catherine Ouest, 514/842-2112, www.pda.qc.ca) holds five theaters, including Salle Wilfred-Pelletier, Théâtre Maisonneuve, Théâtre Jean-Duceppe, Studio-Théâtre, and the Cinquième Salle. The variety of facilities and seating capacities permit them to hold events year-round, which vary from performances by the resident Les Grands Ballets Canadiens, the Montréal Symphony Orchestra, and the Opéra de Montréal.

Outremont
Now owned by Equipe Spectra (the same people behind the jazz festival and Les Francofolies), **Théâtre Outremont** (1240

avenue Bernard Ouest, 514/495-9944, www.theatreoutremont.ca) is a 1929 theater that has hosted some of Québec's most beloved acts and now shows a varied lineup of music, theater, film, and dance, although most of it is in French. It is also home to Micro-Café, a gourmet café with a great outdoor terrace for people-watching.

Plateau Mont-Royal

It's not surprising that there are a slew of theater companies in the Plateau. After all, this is the neighborhood where one of Montréal's most-famous playwrights and novelists, Michel Tremblay, grew up and wrote his six-volume tome *Les chroniques du Plateau Mont-Royal.*

More than 50 years old, the small **Théâtre de Quat'sous** (100 avenue des Pins Est, 514/845-7277, www.quatsous.com) is one of Montréal's most best-loved theater venues. Situated in a beautiful Victorian building that was once a synagogue, it hosts experimental and intellectual French-language plays. The **Théâtre Saint-Denis** (1594 rue Saint-Denis, 514/849-4211, www.theatrestdenis.com) is one of the city's foremost concert halls. Built in 1915, the theater has been used alternately as a French-language cinema and a music venue for operas, orchestras, and jazz and popular music. Major renovations were done in 1990, turning the theater into two halls: the 2,353-seat Saint-Denis 1 and the 980-seat Saint-Denis 2. The **Théâtre du Rideau Vert** (4464 rue Saint-Denis, 514/844-1793, www.rideauvert.qc.ca) was founded in 1949 by Yvette Brind'Amour and Mercedes Palomino during a time when theaters opened and closed with the change of the seasons. Since then, the theater has presented more than 300 productions, focusing mostly on classic plays and the works of emerging local artists. Félix Leclerc's *Sonnez les matines* and Michel Tremblay's *Les belles-sœurs* were all shown here for the first time. Created in 1968, the **Théâtre d'Aujourd'hui** (3900 rue Saint-Denis, 514/282-3900, www.theatredaujourdhui.qc.ca) is the only venue dedicated exclusively to Québec works. Since its foundation, the theater has

mounted plays by more than 140 Québec playwrights, including Michel Marc Bouchard's *Les muses orphelines.*

Casino

Extending across three buildings, the **Casino de Montréal** (1 avenue du Casino, 514/392-2746, www.casino-de-montreal.com, 24 hours daily) in Parc Jean-Drapeau is one of the world's biggest and flashiest casinos. In addition to its 3,000 slot machines and 120 gaming tables, the casino has a 500-seat cabaret-style concert hall and four restaurants.

CINEMAS
Downtown

Montréal's downtown has always had a good selection of movie theaters, although some of its classic ones have shut down in recent years and have been replaced by big multiplexes. The one inside the **Centre Eaton 6** (705 rue Sainte-Catherine Ouest, 514/866-0111), the **Paramount Montréal** (977 rue Sainte-Catherine Ouest, 514/842-5828), and the huge **AMC Forum 22** (2313 rue Sainte-Catherine Ouest, 514/904-1250) near Atwater all show first-run movies in both English and French. Back toward the heart of downtown is **Le Parisien** (480 rue Sainte-Catherine Ouest, 514/866-0111), an older theater originally built in 1917, which has undergone several renovations. This theater shows mainly French-language films. To get the latest movie listings, you can pick up one of the free weeklies, *Mirror* or *Hour,* or if you have access to the Web, check out www.cinemamontreal.com.

Quartier Latin

Created to promote and preserve film and television from all over the world (but with a special focus on Québec and Canadian films), the sleek **Cinémathèque Québécoise** (335 boulevard de Maisonnneuve Est, 514/842-9768, www.cinematheque.qc.ca, adults $6, students $5, children 6–15 $3) has a bank of 35,000 films, 25,000 TV programs, and just about every book ever published on the subject of film, TV, and video. Every Friday night, the cinematheque screens silent movies accompanied by live piano, and every Thursday night is reserved for an animation screening. Special film and TV showings are typically focused on a genre of film or TV or the culmination of a director or an actor's work. The cute Café-Bar in the building is a good spot for an after-screening cocktail.

On the corner of boulevard de Maisonneuve and rue Saint-Denis is the Montréal branch of the **Office National du Film du Canada (ONF)** (1564 rue Saint-Denis, 514/496-6887, www.nfb.ca, noon–9 P.M. Sat.–Sun., films $2 per hour, adults $3 for one hour or $5.50 for two hours, children and students $2 for one hour or $3.50 for two hours). Part of the complex includes the **Cinérobothèque,** the ONF's screening center, where all of its 8,200 films can be viewed in one of the private units, which come in various sizes, suitable for one person, two people, or larger groups. The center takes its name from Ernest, the robot-projectionist responsible for finding and playing the requested movies. Ernest, in turn, was named after Ernest Ouimet, who founded the Ouimetoscope, North America's first movie house.

Plateau Mont-Royal

Opened in 1999, **Ex-Centris** (3536 boulevard Saint-Laurent, 514/847-2206, www.ex-centris.com, noon–midnight daily, adults $10 or $7.50 before 6 P.M. and on Mondays, students under 12 $6) is a production and screening facility for independent, experimental, and new media works. The creation of Daniel Langlois, founder of Softimage, a successful multimedia company responsible for special effects in movies such as *Jurassic Park, Titanic,* and *Men in Black,* Ex-Centris hosts various events, but the easiest way to discover the futuristic building is to drop by to see a movie.

FESTIVALS AND EVENTS

There is a span of weeks between late June and early August when Montréal seems to be bursting at the seams with people, parties, and music. This is festival season, when different events—jazz music, race-car driving, comedy—run one right after another in a dizzying progression.

Summer

For five days at the beginning of June, North America's largest beer event, the **Festival Mondial de la Bière** (2236 rue Beaubien Est, 514/722-9640, www.festivalmondialbiere.qc.ca, admission free, tasting coupons $1 each) suds up downtown Montréal. A contest and massive beer sampling, the festival takes place at Windsor Station and includes beer tents with microbrews from around the world—a majority of which come from Canada. There are also gourmet food vendors, DJs, and live music playing in the courtyard, along with seminars on beer-and-cheese pairings.

One of the world's largest cycling tours (30,000 participants in 2005) is the **Tour de l'Île** (1251 rue Rachel Est, 514/521-8356 or 800/567-8356, www.velo.qc.ca), an annual, beginning-of-June relaxed bike ride that has participants covering a distance of 45 km through various Montréal neighborhoods and boroughs. Organized by Vélo Québec, a powerful nonprofit organization dedicated to all things bicycle, the tour's route around the island of Montréal changes every year.

Montréal almost lost its glam Formula One event, the **Grand Prix du Canada** (C.P. 248, Station Place d'Armes, 514/350-0000, www.grandprix.ca, general admission Fri. $25, Sat. $40, Sun. $60, three days $90), in 2004 when the federal government refused to allow tobacco advertising during the event in accordance with its antismoking legislation. Teams agreed to take cigarette ads off their cars, but the government had to kick in about $12 million in compensation. Started in 1967, the event found its permanent home on Île Notre-Dame in Montréal in 1978, the year that Québec native Gilles Villeneuve won the race. When Villeneuve died in the Belgian Grand Prix in 1982, the track was renamed the Circuit Gilles-Villeneuve. Today, the race, held in June, is a favorite of Hollywood stars and car-racing enthusiasts who prefer Montréal's more European leanings over Indianapolis.

Held on Wednesdays and Saturdays from mid-June to the end of July, **L'International des Feux Loto-Québec** (22 chemin Macdonald, Île Sainte-Hélène, 514/397-2000, www.internationaldesfeuxloto-quebec.com, show starts at 10 P.M., tickets $21–42) features an international pyromusical competition with a launch site at La Ronde. Each participating country has 30 minutes to wow the panel, which judges on synchronization, musical score, color, and special effects. Before and after the show, the festival also features an array of live concerts with a lineup of Québécois artists and tribute bands. Although tickets include access to La Ronde amusement park rides, many people opt for the free viewing points from Pont Jacques-Cartier and the Old Port.

Québec's national holiday, the **Fête Nationale du Québec** (82 rue Sherbrooke Ouest, 514/849-2560, www.cfn.org) takes place every year on June 24. Official Montréal celebrations include an annual parade along rue Notre-Dame, which becomes a rolling sea of blue and white, the colors of the Québec flag, historical and musical events in Old Montréal, and a big evening concert at Parc Maisonneuve. One of the best ways to take in the festivities, however, are at the smaller neighborhood celebrations where small stages are set up, often in the middle of the street.

The world's largest, and many would say its best, jazz festival, the **Festival International de Jazz de Montréal** (822 rue Sherbrooke Est, 514/871-1881 or 888/515-0515, www.montrealjazzfest.com) takes place for 12 days, beginning on the evening of the last Thursday in June. Featuring an army of local, national, and international musicians (Chick Corea, Ella Fitzgerald, Tony Bennett, Etta James, Prince, Lauryn Hill, and Diana Krall), paid indoor concerts and free outdoor concerts are presented in and around Place des Arts. Some people have argued that the festival has stretched the borders of jazz too wide,

while others say that by doing so, it has been able to attract younger audiences.

With humble beginnings, the festival **Juste pour Rire** (2101 boulevard Saint-Laurent, 514/845-2322 or 888/244-3155, www.hahaha.com) has grown from a four-day event featuring 16 francophone artists to almost a monthlong festival with more than 700 artists from around the world, not to mention its museum, stage, and television shows. Starting in early July, big-name comedians (Bob Newhart, Adam Sandler, Dame Edna), lesser-known artists, and street performers strut their stuff for more than two million spectators in more than 20 indoor venues and along rue Saint-Denis. Two of the favorite parts of the festival are the annual Twins Weekend, which features twins, triplets, quadruplets, and so on, marching in a parade and taking part in physical and mental challenges, and La Grande Bouffe, which takes place on the final weekend of the festival. It's a free meal (in the past the main course has featured a giant omelette and ham and potatoes) at which a chef and servers feed approximately 1,000 people per seating.

Montréal's tribute to French culture from around the world is **Les FrancoFolies** (822 rue Sherbrooke Est, 514/876-8989 or 888/444-9114, www.francofolies.com), a 10-day musical celebration starting the last Thursday in July. Started in 1989 by Alain Simard, the same person behind the jazz festival, Les Francofolies has grown into one of Montréal's best showcases of Québécois talent, both new and old. The festival also takes place in and around Place des Arts with various free outdoor stages and indoor concerts.

Montréal's Gay Pride celebrations, **Divers/Cité** (4067 boul. Saint-Laurent, Bureau 300, 514/285-4011, www.diverscite.org), take place over a week, starting on the last Saturday in July. The festival features a slew of outdoor music concerts and dance parties, the Pride Parade, which meanders along boulevard René Lévesque, and Le Grand Rendez-Vous, where various Gay and Lesbian organizations set up booths to inform the public of their services.

Fall

The newest event organized by the all-powerful Spectra group (jazz festival, FrancoFolies) is the **Festival International de Films de Montréal** (822 rue Sherbrooke Est, 514/288-6730 or 866/901-3436, www.montrealfilmfest.com), a film festival launched in 2005. With ex-Berlin and Venice film festival chief Moritz de Hadeln at the helm, the week-long festival, held from mid- to late September (although this will likely change in future years), promises to have the clout needed to attract big-name directors. Films are screened on rue Saint-Denis in the heart of the Quartier Latin.

Extending for a week in early October, the **Black and Blue Festival** (1-1307 rue Sainte-Catherine Est, 514/875-7026, www.bbcm.org) is one of the world's largest gay events. Started in 1991, the festival features a series of huge dance parties such as the Jock Ball, the Leather Ball, and the Military Ball, as well as a health summit and a multitude of seminars, exhibitions, and sporting events. A significant share of the festival's proceeds go to groups helping people live with HIV/AIDS and to gay and lesbian support groups.

Although competition for Montréal festival-goers is rife, the **The Festival du Nouveau Cinéma** (3530 boulevard Saint-Laurent, 514/282-0004, www.nouveaucinema.ca) has been operating peacefully and successfully for more than 30 years, making it Canada's longest-running international film festival. Starting in mid-October and running for 11 days, the festival screens alternative and independent films in theaters in the Plateau district and downtown.

Winter

It may be only the brave—or crazy—who visit Montréal during February, but at least there is one event that melts away everyone's winter chills. It's the **Festival Montréal en Lumière** (822 rue Sherbrooke Est, 514/288-9955 or 888/477-9955, www.montrealenlumiere.com), celebrated for 11 days in the latter half of February. Billing itself as three festivals wrapped into one, Montréal en Lumière features gastronomic, musical, and artistic activities. The "light" part refers to the outdoor concerts' light shows and pyrotechnics.

Shopping

OLD MONTRÉAL

Once the domain of not much more than tacky souvenir shops, Old Montréal has become much more sophisticated in its old age. While you'll still find plenty of Indian dolls and "Kiss Me, I'm French" T-shirts, many more original offerings are on hand.

Art

It's fine to stroll down **St. Amable Lane** to people-watch and enjoy the scene, but beware of mediocre artists attempting to hawk their ink and watercolor street scenes for a price that is absurdly high. In fact, there are quite a few mediocre art stores in the old town, but there are a few that are much surer bets. In the Marché Bonsecours, the **Institut de Design**

Montréal (390 rue Saint-Paul Est, 514/866-2436) showcases unique items from students of Montréal's design school and from international designers. **La Guilde Graphique** (9 rue Saint-Paul Ouest, 514/844-3438, www.guildegraphique.com) is a gallery and shop featuring 3,000 original works by contemporary artists, predominantly in print form. Founded in 1963, the shop including drawings, etchings, and lithographs. The store has an old hand-operated press with photos explaining the process. Some beautiful etchings featuring Montréal scenes make for a good souvenir or gift. The full-scale nude paintings in **Espace Pepin** (350 rue Saint-Paul Ouest, 514/844-0114, www.pepinart.com) may not be to everyone's liking, but artist Lysanne

Pepin's apartment-like concept store, where each room is decked out with the artist's paintings and home furnishings—linens, candles, tables—of other Canadian designers, makes for an interesting shopping experience and a feast for the eyes.

Clothing

Betty from **Betty's Bazaar** (444 rue Saint-François-Xavier, 514/369-2212, www.bettysbazaar.com, 11 A.M.–5 P.M. Mon.–Wed., 11 A.M.–7 P.M. Thurs.–Fri., 10 A.M.–5 P.M. Sat., and noon–5 P.M. Sun.) travels the globe in search of the cutest cocktail dresses, jackets, shirts, and accessories. The store—predominantly pink with mauve velour drapery—is an ode to all things girly. Services such as makeovers, shopping nights, and personalized shoppers are also offered. A collaboration between married designers Jennifer Kakon and Scott Richler, **Jennifer Scott** (438 rue Saint-Pierre, 514/844-2255, 10 A.M.–6 P.M. Mon.–Sat.) is another glam shop featuring a luxurious line of clothing, jewelry, handbags, and furniture. All the items are artfully arranged in a minimalist, airy shop and if you stop by you might catch a celebrity surveying the wares.

Gifts

There are a lot of tacky souvenir shops in Montréal trying to sell innocent tourists cheap moccasins and T-shirts with wolves on them, but **Tant qu'il y Aura des Fleurs** (347 rue Saint-Paul Est, 10 A.M.–6 P.M. Mon.–Wed. and 10 A.M.–9 P.M. Thurs.–Sun.) is definitely not one of them. This store features tasteful gifts such as jewelry, glasses, and tablecloths. Right nearby is **L'Empreinte** (272 rue Saint-Paul Est, 514/861-4427), a Québec artists' collective that features ceramics, crafts, glassware, and some clothing. A great spot to pick up a historic souvenir is the **Musée Pointe-à-Callière gift shop** (350 place Royale, 514/872-9150, www.pacmusee.qc.ca, 11 A.M.–6 P.M. Tues.–Sun. late June–early Sept. and 11 A.M.–6 P.M. Tues.–Sun. early Sept.–late June). The boutique has reproduction artifacts, Victorian jewelry, model boats,

maps, and a wide variety of books. Then there's the clock oasis, **La Tour de L'Horloge** (340 rue Notre-Dame, 514/529-5456, www.latourdelhorloge.com, 11 A.M.–7 P.M. Tues.–Wed., 11 A.M.–9 P.M. Thurs.–Fri, 10 A.M.–6 P.M. Sat., and noon–6 P.M. Sun.), which stocks an amazing array of unique clocks, from designer to museum pieces. There's a selection of Montréal-made clocks as well.

◖ RUE SAINTE-CATHERINE

Montréal's commercial heart is downtown's rue Sainte-Catherine. On Saturdays and Sundays, especially during warm weather, the street is packed with people strolling around, ducking into shops on either side. During the winter, the street is still busy, but more people are apt to make their way to the various shopping malls via the massive network of underground tunnels. Most of the stores and malls in the downtown area are open from 10 A.M. to 6 P.M. on Monday and Tuesday and extend their hours until 9 P.M. from Wednesday to Friday. Saturday hours are typically 9 A.M. to 5 P.M., while Sunday's are 10 A.M. to 5 P.M.

Malls

Starting from the eastern edge of the downtown district, the first mall that you come to is the completely undergound **Les Promenades de la Cathédrale** (625 rue Sainte-Catherine Ouest, 514/849-9925), which is directly below the Cathédrale Christ Church. This mall is one of the smaller ones with just over 50 stores, including the country's largest Linen Chest store. Next comes the **Les Ailes de la Mode** (677 rue Sainte-Catherine Ouest, 514/282-4537, www.lesailes.com) and its swanky selection of items from clothing to lingerie, cosmetics, and housewares. The biggest mall on the strip is the **Centre Eaton** (705 rue Sainte-Catherine Ouest, 514/288-3710, www.centreeatondemontreal.com). It has all the major American and Canadian clothing stores, such as the Gap, Jacob, Old Navy, and Benetton, plus six cinemas. It links to the west with **Place Montréal Trust** (1500 avenue McGill College, 514/843-

8000, www.placemontrealtrust.com). This mall has a massive fountain and atrium and stores such as designer-discount store Winners, the books and music store Indigo, and Spanish fashion giant Zara. Due south from there, at the bottom of McGill College, is the city's paean to modern architecture, better known as **Place Ville-Marie** (avenue McGill College at rue Cathcart, 514/861-9393, www.placevillemarie.com). Constructed in 1964, the building known for its rotating beacon that sweeps through the city at night and for having one of the first underground shopping courses in the world, has a good array of shops and a high-end food market called Mövenpick. Head back up to rue Sainte-Catherine and then a bit north of the street, and the next mall you'll come to is **Les Cours Mont-Royal** (1550 rue Metcalfe, 514/842-7777). This beautiful courtyardlike mall contains high-end European clothing boutiques and design shops. The lone mall not connected via underground tunnel is the **Faubourg Sainte-Catherine** (1616 rue Sainte-Catherine Ouest, www.lefaubourg.com). This department store made quite a splash when it first opened in 1986 with its mix of cafés, restaurants, small specialty stores, and fruit and veggie stands. It's close to Guy metro station.

Department Stores

With one exception, Montréal's department stores are perennial institutions. Starting from the west is **La Baie** (585 rue Sainte-Catherine Ouest, 514/281-4422, www.labaie.com, 9:30 A.M.–7 P.M. Mon.–Wed., 9:30 A.M.–9 P.M. Thurs.–Fri., 8 A.M.–5 P.M. Sat, 10 A.M.–5 P.M. Sun.), the storefront of the Hudson's Bay Company, Canada's oldest corporation, which started out in the fur trade in 1670. On the department store's seven floors, you'll find clothes (everything from white tube socks to high-end designer labels), accessories, shoes, makeup, and housewares at reasonable... and less reasonable... prices.

The newest, and most successful, kid on the block is **La Maison Simons** (977 rue Sainte-Catherine Ouest, 514/282-1840,

www.simons.com, 10 A.M.–7 P.M. Mon.–Wed., 10 A.M.–9 P.M. Thurs.–Fri., 9:30 A.M.–5 P.M. Sat., noon–5 P.M. Sun.). Offering its own line of affordable clothes under the label Twik and many designer lines, the old Québec City–based business waited an incredibly long time to venture into the province's biggest city. When it did, Montrealers flocked to the store, buying up its casual clothing, wide selection of accessories (the hats usually offer a few wild choices), sportswear, lingerie, and bath and bed linen.

Up north on Sherbrooke, **Holt Renfrew** (1300 rue Sherbrooke Ouest, 415/842-5111, www.holtrenfrew.com, noon–5 P.M. Sun., 10 A.M.–6 P.M. Mon.–Wed., 10 A.M.–9 P.M. Thurs.–Fri., 9:30 A.M.–5 P.M. Sat.) is Montréal's mecca of ultrachic, ultraexpensive clothing. The store, with its classic art deco style, was first opened in 1937. In the basement, you'll find a little café where elegant older ladies come to sip tea or mineral water. The store has all the designer lines, makeup counters, and accessories. Built in 1912 in pure Victorian grandeur, the newly renovated **Maison Ogilvy** (1307 rue Sainte-Catherine Ouest, 514/842-7711, www.ogilvycanda.ca) houses numerous luxury fashion shops and an excellent books section. Ogilvy's—as you'll still hear most people refer to it—is probably most famous for its Christmas window, which features a bevy of mechanical stuffed animals frolicking in the snow.

Books and Music

English-language book stores in downtown Montréal include **Chapters** (1171 rue Sainte-Catherine, 514/849-8825, www.chapters.ca, 9 A.M.–10 P.M. Mon.–Thurs., 9 A.M.–11 P.M. Fri.–Sat., and 10 A.M.–9 A.M. Sun.) and **Indigo** (1500 avenue McGill College, 514/281-5549, www.indigo.ca, 9 A.M.–11 P.M. daily), actually owned by the same person. Both bookstores stock a good selection of local, Canadian, and international books of fiction and nonfiction. There is also the bilingual **Paragraphe** (2220 avenue McGill College, 514/845-5811, www.paragraphbooks.com, 7 A.M.–11 P.M. Mon.–Fri. and 9 A.M.–11 P.M. Sat.–Sun.), a much

A TALE OF TWO MARKETS

Montréal is the proud home to two fabulous outdoor food markets: the Jean-Talon Market, right in the middle of Little Italy, and the Atwater Market, located on the border of posh Westmount and far-less-posh, but colorful, Saint-Henri. The markets are where Montrealers loyally come to get their strawberries in the summer, their pumpkins in October and their Christmas trees in December.

Both feature a swirl of sights, sounds, and smells, especially on weekend mornings when the fruit and veggie stands, cheese shops, seafood stands, bakeries, and delis are alive with conversation, cha-chinging cash registers, and beckoning hollers to passersby.

The Jean-Talon Market was initiated by the city in 1933 to appease the growing economic concerns during the Depression. It was originally known as Shamrock Market, built on an old bus terminus to Laval. The Atwater Market was also built in 1933, and it too provided much needed employment to hundreds of people.

But despite their similar history, pointing out the differences between the two is a favorite topic of conversation in Montréal. Inevitably a mention of one, as in "Oh, I went to Atwater this weekend to pick up some prosciutto" will bring up the other, as in "Well, I found the best prosciutto I've ever tasted at Jean-Talon."

The most common characterization is that Atwater is trendy and snobby, while Jean-Talon is a bit run down but far more authentic. But the truth is that the food tastes great at both... so make two trips.

---

smaller, more selective, bookstore, popular with McGill University students.

French-language bookstores include **Archambault** (500 rue Sainte-Catherine Est, 514/849-6201, www.archambault.ca, 9:30 A.M.–9 P.M. Mon.–Fri., 9 A.M.–5 P.M. Sat., and 10 A.M.–5 P.M. Sun.), which has two other stores on Sainte-Catherine—one in Place des Arts and another in Les Aisles department store—and **Renaud-Bray** (1432 rue Sainte-Catherine Ouest, 514/876-9119, 10 A.M.–6 P.M. Mon.–Wed., 10 A.M.–9 P.M. Thurs.–Fri., 10 A.M.–6 P.M. Sat., and noon 5 P.M. Sun.). Most of these stores also carry music CDs, but for the best selection, head over to the temple of disks, **HMV** (1020 rue Sainte-Catherine Ouest, 514/875-0765, 9:30 A.M.–9 P.M. Mon.–Fri., 9 A.M.–5 P.M. Sat., 10 A.M.–5 P.M. Sun). You can often listen to local artists' CDs on the listening stations.

Jewelry

If you are a fan of the movie *Breakfast at Tiffany's*, **Henry Birks et Fils** (1240 rue Philips Square, 514/397-2511) is for you. Almost worth buying something solely to get one of the famous blue boxes with the rampant lion, the existence of this store dates to 1894. The luxurious interior of the building showcases a wealth of mostly gold jewelry and is one of the first stops for couples picking out their wedding rock.

WESTMOUNT AND OUTREMONT

As Sherbrooke in Westmount starts venturing into its more store-heavy section, have a look for **Ben and Tournesol** (4915 rue Sherbrooke Ouest, 514/481-5050), a fun little shop with stationery, jewelry, and Montréal's famous Matt and Nat handbags. Nearby is **Hollinger Collins Gallery** (4928 rue Sherbrooke Ouest, 514/484-5444, www.heidihollinger.com). Heidi Hollinger is the Montréal photographer who moved to Russia and was able to talk her way into getting very close and personal photos of some of Russia's most intimidating politicians, including an underwear-clad Vladimir Zhirinovski. The gallery sells comtemporary artwork, including paintings, prints, and photographs.

Over on avenue Laurier in Outremont, check out **Les Touilleurs** (152 avenue Laurier, 514/278-0008, www.lestouilleurs.com) if you're passionate about your kitchenware. This store is known for its high-design items, chef demonstrations, and tastings.

PLATEAU MONT-ROYAL

Away from the big chains, rue Saint-Denis and boulevard Saint-Laurent are known for their designer boutiques and cool design shops. This is the place to find items from local designers or smaller, exclusive boutiques. A good shopping itinerary on rue Saint-Denis starts at the intersection of avenue Mont-Royal (Mont-Royal metro) and continues until avenue des Pins. On boulevard Saint-Laurent, it's best to begin on rue Sherbrooke (a couple of blocks north of Saint-Laurent metro) and walk toward rue Rachel (this is the section where the majority of shops are). If you don't mind digging a little for the perfect outfit, a plethora of second-hand stores can be found all along avenue du Mont-Royal.

Clothing

Founded in 1979, **Scandale** (3639 boulevard Saint-Laurent, 514/842-4707, 11 A.M.–6 P.M. Mon.–Wed., 11 A.M.– 9 P.M. Thurs.–Fri., 11 A.M.–5 P.M. Sat., noon– 5 P.M. Sun.) showcases the wildly beautiful creations of Québec designer George Lévesque, known to stop many people in their tracks when they see his latest designs in the window. The shop also sells lingerie and second-hand clothing from Paris for men and women. **Dubuc Mode de Vie** (4451 rue Saint-Denis, 514/282-1462, www.dubucstyle.com, 10:30 A.M.–6 P.M. Mon.–Wed., 10:30 A.M.–9 P.M. Thurs.–Fri., 10:30 A.M.–5 P.M. Sat.) is owned by Québec designer Philippe Dubuc, who made his reputation creating elegant and romantic suits for the modern man. Since opening his store in the heart of the Plateau in 1995, this successful designer has also opened boutiques in New York and Toronto. For the young fashionistas, clothing store **EXTC** (19 rue Prince-Arthur Ouest, 514/282-1083, 10 A.M.–7 P.M. Mon.–Wed., 10 A.M.–9 P.M. Thurs.–Fri., 10 A.M.–7 P.M. Sat., and noon–7 P.M. Sun.) is one of Montréal's coolest fashion secrets. This little boutique offers a large variety of jeans and other trendy

threads at reasonable prices. **Space FB** (3632 boulevard Saint-Laurent, 514/282-1991, www.spacefb.com, 11 A.M.–9 P.M. Mon.–Fri., 11 A.M.–midnight Sat., noon–7 P.M. Sun.) is home to the creations of François Beauregard, a designer who gained public attention with his comfortable and casual outfits in various colors and cuts. With reasonable prices for designer wear, the store is a good bet if you're seeking youthful clothing, particularly sweatshirts, T-shirts, jackets, and skirts. Going to **Lola and Emily** (3475 boulevard Saint-Laurent, 514/288-7598, www.lolaandemily.com, noon– 7 P.M. Mon.–Wed., noon–9 P.M. Thurs.–Fri., noon–6 P.M. Sat.–Sun.) is like visiting an old girlfriend. The store promotes young upcoming designers and is strewn around what seems like a cozy, girly apartment. Everything in this spacious loft, from the furniture to the fashion, is for sale.

Kanuk (485 rue Rachel Est, 514/284-4494, www.kanuk.com, 9 A.M.–6 P.M. Mon.–Wed., 9 A.M.–9 P.M. Thurs.–Fri., 10 A.M.–5 P.M. Sat., noon–5 P.M. Sun.) is a Québec-born company specializing in high-quality winter coats. From parkas to anoraks, vests and raincoats, this store has acquired a great reputation among outdoorsy locals—its coats are considered expensive but a solid investment. **Azimut** (1781 rue Saint-Denis, 514/844-1717, www.azimut.ca, 9 A.M.–6 P.M. Mon.–Wed., 9 A.M.–9 P.M. Thurs.–Fri., 9 A.M.–5 P.M. Sat., noon–5 P.M. Sun) is also loved by Montrealers for its high-quality collection of outdoor clothing. Selling popular brands such as North Face, Columbia, Timberland, and Merrell, this shop not only sells warm winter coats, but also shoes, purses and bags, and watches.

Other

Zone (4246 rue Saint-Denis, 514/845-3530, 10 A.M.–6 P.M. Mon.–Wed., 10 A.M.–9 P.M. Thurs.–Fri., 10 A.M.–5:30 P.M. Sat., and 10 A.M.–5 P.M. Sun.) is a colorful and modern housewares shop featuring items largely made by Québec designers. From wee kitchen gadgets to vases, clocks, lamps, cutlery, and bigger furniture items, this is Québec's answer to

Ikea—albeit on a hipper and much smaller scale. **Le Valet d'Coeur** (4408 rue Saint-Denis, 514/499-9970, 11:30 A.M.–6 P.M. Mon.–Wed., 11:30 A.M.–9 P.M. Thurs.–Fri., 10 A.M.–5 P.M. Sat., and noon–5 P.M. Sun.) is a treasure trove of toys and games from all corners of the globe. The store is packed with all kinds of games in French and in English: role-playing games, society games, puzzles, cards, and on and on. **Bella Pella** (3933 rue Saint-Denis, 514/845-7328, and 1201A avenue Mont-Royal Est, 514/904-1074, www.bellapella.com, 11 A.M.–6 P.M. Mon.–Wed., 11 A.M.–9 P.M. Thurs.–Fri., 11 A.M.–5 P.M. Sat.,

and noon–5 P.M. Sun.) means "nice skin" in Italian and that's exactly what this store is dedicated to: skin products made the Italian way. With the feeling of an apothecary, the store's largely homemade soaps, lotions, gels, and bath salts use ingredients such as lavender, green tea, olive oil, vanilla, and goat's milk. For cards, kitchen objects, beauty products, and gadgets with style and a dash of cheekiness, visit **Chez Farfelu** (843 avenue du Mont-Royal Est, 514/528-6251), a gift and party shop with unique knickknacks that run from tasteful to coy to raunchy. You can spend the better part of an hour in here just browsing all the wares.

Accommodations

OLD MONTRÉAL

Set up in beautiful, old 18th- and 19th-century converted warehouses, factories, and homes, the accommodation offerings in Old Montréal are plentiful, especially for those who have the cash to spare. Slim on the midrange options, the area has a handful of inexpensive hostels and B&Bs on one end and a high preponderance of well-appointed boutique hotels on the other. Depending where you stay, it can be noisy and stay noisy until well beyond 3 A.M., when the partiers pour out of the clubs.

$50-100

Situated in an old 1875 warehouse in Place d'Youville, the **Alternative Backpackers of Old Montréal** (358 rue Saint-Pierre, 514/282-8069, www.auberge-alternative.qc.ca, dorm $20 per person, private room $55 d) is a cozy, well-run youth hostel. With handmade beds and restored doors and furniture that were salvaged from curbside trash, the place has a funky, eclectic feel tempered by the tastefully arched windows, stone walls, and wood floors. A communal/ecological philosophy permeates the place—recycling is actively practiced and donations are collected for local and international charities. There's free high-speed Internet. In another gorgeous build-

ing—this time an old tobacco factory—◖ **La Maison du Patriote** (169 rue Saint-Paul Est, 514/866-0855, www.lamaisondupatriote.com, $85–125 d), an inn/B&B with seven rooms, is great value for Old Montréal. Many of the rooms feature exposed stone walls and French windows—although some of the ones facing out onto rue Saint-Paul can get noisy when the clubgoers pour out at 3 A.M. If this is a concern, grab one of the rooms that face the courtyard instead. Bathrooms are shared. Situated in back of Le Guilleret, **Le Sous-bois** (431 rue Saint-Vincent (courtyard), 514/879-1394, www.lesousbois.com, dorm $34 per person, private room $86 d) is a rustic youth hostel that has the capacity to house up to 50 people. Although it probably doesn't sound terribly appealing to read that the bunk beds have been built with scrap wood, somehow the makeshift quality adds to the charm of the place. There are huge floor-to-ceiling windows and a sunny kitchen. Linens, coffee, breakfast, and Internet are all free of charge.

$100-150

Run by the same people as La Maison du Patriote, **Le Guilleret** (431 rue Saint-Vincent, 514/879-1394, www.leguilleret.com, $185–245 d) is in an old white house, dating to 1760, with red door and window frames. Originally the residence of a sheriff, the house has six fireplaces, three salons, wood posts, encasement windows, and incredibly thick walls. Although the décor is somewhat spartan, the rooms are still charming.

$150-200

Once a small warehouse dating to 1723, the building that houses **Les Passants du Sans Soucy** (171 rue Saint-Paul Ouest, 514/842-2634, www.lesanssoucy.com, $140–175 d) is now a small three-story inn filled with antiques, romantic furnishings, and a lobby that doubles as an art gallery. There are only eight rooms and one suite in the building, making for a more intimate, get-to-know-your-neighbors stay. Breakfasts feature the owner's freshly baked croissants, omelettes, French toast, yogurt, and good, strong coffee.

Over $200

The gorgeous apartments at **Apparts du Vieux-Montréal** (405 rue Saint-Dizier, 514/908-0946, www.a-v-m.org, $195–275) all have exposed beams, stone walls, wood floors, and big windows. The big advantage is that they also have kitchenettes, allowing guests to have the stylish digs and Old Montréal address and to save some bucks by opting to eat in from time to time. Some rooms have fireplaces. Émile Nelligan, Québec's sad, wistful, brilliant poet, is the spirit behind the cool and understated **C Hôtel Nelligan** (106 rue Saint-Paul Ouest, 514/788-2040, www.hotelnelligan.com, $190–295 d), consisting of two adjoining buildings and a gorgeous courtyard in the middle. The boutique hotel's 64 plush rooms are done up in chocolates and creams with hints of red and each has a wall containing passages from Nelligan's poems. You can dine on-site at the hip Verses Restaurant, which serves contemporary French cuisine. With its riverfront view, **Auberge du Vieux-Port** (97 rue de la Commune Est, 514/876-0081 or 888/660-7678, www.aubergeduvieuxport.com, $200–270 d) has more of an airy feel than other Old Montréal accommodations. It's got all the signature features of old buildings in the area: stone walls, exposed beams, wood floors, and beautiful, big windows, yet the rooms here are more spacious. There's a rooftop terrace that overlooks the Old Port.

The **C Hôtel Gault** (449 rue Sainte-Hélène, 514/904-1616 or 866/904-1616, www.hotelgault.com, $230–550 d) may have a gorgeous stone Second Empire exterior, but behind the façade of this former carpet factory is a temple to sleek design and modernism. With minimal and spacious rooms featuring wood and concrete surfaces, designer chairs, bright woolen rugs, and bathroom with a huge tub and marble shower, the Gault is for the ultrahip who make no bones about wanting to be pampered. Not far away on rue McGill is another famed Old Montréal designer boutique hotel: the **Hôtel Saint-Paul** (355 rue McGill, 514/380-2222 or 866/380-2202, www.hotelstpaul.com). The lobby is serene, but übercool with its cream hues, illuminated alabaster fireplace, trip-hop tunes, and beautiful people. The rooms are spare but funky with faux-fur throws, leather headboards, and the occasional cow-print chair. The restaurant on the premises, **Cube,** is famed for its innovative cuisine.

DOWNTOWN

Some lower-fare options are in the downtown area, but unsurprisingly, most of the hotels, which are often part of a chain, tend to run toward the pricey. If you book enough in advance or in the off-season, some bargains are to be had.

$50-100

In the tradition of the hostelling international establishments, the large white and red **HI-Auberge de Jeunesse** (10 rue Mackay, 514/843-3317 or 866/843-3317, www.hostellingmontreal.com, dorm $25–29, rooms $37–75 d) is an easy way to save money in a friendly environment. Situated somewhat ironically in the middle of Montréal's business sector, the hostel has a very youthful, party atmosphere. Organized activities include guided bike tours and pub crawls and trips to the tam-tams in Parc Mont-Royal. The rooms are clean but quite cramped. **(McGill University Residences** (514/398-5200, www.mcgill.ca/residences/ summer, $65–75 d) are one of the best places to stay for those on a budget. The university offers accommodation from mid-May to mid-August in three locations: just north of campus, on University near Sherbrooke, and close to Atwater Market. Cafeterias and laundry rooms are available and for an extra fee, you can have access to McGill's gym. Situated in an 1875 Victorian house, **Le Simone** (1571 rue Saint-André, 514/524-2002 or 888/849-8866, www.lesimone.com, $70–80 d) is a bed-and-breakfast that has 10 simple rooms at reasonable prices for the downtown area. Its Internet access is free and it includes a decent continental breakfast with the price of the room. Call in advance, as $20 can be added on event-filled weekends. Also in a Victorian house, the 22-room graystone guesthouse **Manoir Ambrose** (3422 rue Stanley, 514/288-6922, www.manoirambrose.com, $70–130 d) is near McGill University on a nice and relatively quiet part of rue Stanley. Rooms have somewhat dated red floral curtains and bedspreads and some have nice bay windows.

$100-150

On the eastern edge of the downtown area, the beautiful **(Petite Auberge les Bons Matins** (1401 rue Argyle, 514/931-9167 or 800/588-5280, www.bonsmatins.com, $119–229 d) is an artist's dream overnight stay. Full of color, imagination, and tastefulness, the rooms each have an individual character, as well as brick walls and rough hardwood floors. Some rooms have a fireplace and a private terrace. The location of the **Hôtel du Fort** (1390 rue du Fort, 514/938-8333 or 800/565-8333, www.hoteldufort.com, $125–135), close to autoroute Ville-Marie, isn't the nicest, but it is extremely accessible. For a four-star modern hotel right downtown, it also offers extremely good value.

$150-200

You might think that **L'Appartement Hotel** (455 rue Sherbrooke Ouest, 514/284-3634 or 800/363-3010, www.appartementhotel.com, $153–173 d) was a regular apartment building if you didn't know otherwise, but this red-brick high-rise actually has 126 suites and studios. The rooms really aren't anything special, but there is a good indoor rooftop swimming pool and of course, the location is great.

Over $200

Some very swank and very expensive hotels are in downtown Montréal and the **Sofitel** (1155 rue Sherbrooke Ouest, 514/285-9000 or 877/285-9001, www.sofitel.com, $239–259 d) is one of them. The luxurious French (from France) chain built this modern glass building with 258 rooms right in the middle of the Golden Square Mile. Also in the neighborhood is that ode to classic luxury, the **Ritz Carlton** (1228 rue Sherbrooke Ouest, 514/842-4212 or 800/363-0366, www.ritzcarlton.com, $245–370). Opened in 1912, this Ritz is one of Canada's oldest hotels and the first of its kind in North America. The 229-room, ornately decorated hotel has had its share of superstar guests through the years, including Mary Pickford, the shah of Iran, and the Rolling Stones. It was also the location of Elizabeth Taylor and Richard Burton's first wedding in 1964. Rooms generally overlook the garden out back or rue Sherbrooke. Traditional high tea and finger sandwiches are served every afternoon in the Café de Paris. The **Fairmont the Queen Elizabeth** (900 boulevard René-Lévesque Ouest, 514/861-3511 or 800/257-7544, www.fairmont.com, $219–299) or "Queen E" as it is commonly referred to, is Montréal's other superstar hotel. Naturally, it has played host to Queen Elizabeth, but also to Indira Gandhi, Jacques Chirac, and the Dalai Lama. The hotel remains best known for many as the place where John Lennon and Yoko Ono staged their famous 1969 bed-in and recorded "Give Peace A Chance." The room, suite 1742, where the couple stayed and invited a swarm of media can still be rented for the evening. With its 1,039 rooms, connection to the underground network, and proximity to the train station and financial center, the hotel has become a natural choice for business travelers. There's a health club on-site and three restaurants, including the classic, old-school Beaver Club. Once an office building, the 100-room ◖ **Hôtel Le Germain** (2050 rue Mansfield, 514/849-2050 or 877/333-2050, www.hotelboutique.com, $275–295) is now a gorgeous boutique hotel through and through. The décor is serene with earth-tone colors, dark woods, and wicker offsetting the creamy walls and the service is friendly and attentive. There's also a great panoramic view of downtown.

PLATEAU MONT-ROYAL

Accommodation in the Plateau Mont-Royal area consists primarily of B&Bs and small independent hotels. Staying in the area in a small B&B will give you a real flavor of Montréal beyond the tourist hub of Old Montréal and the downtown area.

$50-100

Owned by the same people, **Gîte du Parc La Fontaine** (1250 rue Sherbrooke Est, 514/522-3910 or 877/350-4483, dormitory $25, room $55–80) and **Gîte du Plateau Mont-Royal** (185 rue Sherbrooke Est) are good choices for youth and budget travelers. Both places offer clean, four- and six-bed dormitories, laundry service, kitchens, outdoor terraces, and Internet access. A continental breakfast is included in the price of your stay. **Auberge Maeva** (4755 rue Saint-Hubert, 514/523-0840, www.aubergemaeva.com, dormitory $22, private room $40–50) is a friendly youth hostel on one of the nicest streets of the Plateau Mont-Royal. Dormitories suit three to six people and are clean, if a little bit cramped. There's a bright communal kitchen, a terrace out back, and a TV room in the basement. Bike rentals are also available at a charge of $5 per day. **Couette et Café Cherrier** (522 rue Cherrier, 514/982-6848, www3.sympatico.ca/couette, $80–105) is a tasteful option near Parc La Fontaine. Dec-

orated in brown and beige tones with plenty of wood and brick, the B&B has a lounge with a fireplace on the first floor and a terrace for sunbathing on the third floor. The owners speak French, English, and Spanish. ◖ **À la Maison Pierre et Dominique** (271 Square Saint-Louis, 514/286-0307, www.pierdom.qc.ca, $75–100) has one of the best locations in the city, facing Square Saint-Louis. There are only five rooms here (some single, some double), but each one is done up in beautiful French country décor, including antique furniture and folk art.

$100-150

One of the nicest and newest spots, perfect for business travelers and those on a budget who don't want to sacrifice style, is ◖ **Anne ma soeur Anne** (4119 rue Saint-Denis, 514/281-3187 or 877/281-3187, www.annemasoeuranne.com, $80–130), part boutique hotel, part studio. The 17 minimalist but warm rooms include workstations that fold up into the walls, tiny kitchenettes, and private bathrooms. Croissants are brought up to your door every morning. Jean-Yves is the friendly owner of the pleasant **Gîte La Cinquième Saison** (4396 rue Boyer, 514/522-6439, www.cinquiemesaison.net, $90), on a quiet and leafy street just off avenue Mont-Royal. There are four rooms on offer, each named after a season with the appropriate colors and décor to match. The breakfasts, featuring fresh baked bread and muffins, are very good. In the heart of the Quartier Latin, ◖ **Angelica Blue Bed and Breakfast** (1213 rue Sainte-Élizabeth, 514/844-5048, www.angelicablue.com, $85–155) has five beautiful sunny rooms (Mexican, Victorian, Royal, Vienna, and Arctic) with high ceilings, exposed brick walls, and pine floors. There is a cute bistro where breakfast is served and a parlor with a mishmash of furniture prints and styles that somehow all seems to work. Also in the Quartier Latin on rue Saint-Denis is **Auberge Le Jardin d'Antoine** (2024 rue Saint-Denis, 514/843-4506, www.hotel-jardin-antoine.qc.ca, $94–180), a Victorian inn with 25 flowery rooms, with only two overlooking the street. Close to plenty of bars and restaurants, the inn is surprisingly peaceful and has a quiet patio out back. Some bathrooms are equipped with a whirlpool bath. Although it looks as if the old graystone **Armor Manoir Sherbrooke** (157 rue Sherbrooke Est, 514/845-0915, www.armormanoir.com, $100–110) and its dominating turret could use a bit of a scrub, the inside is bright and clean. With lovely old mirrors, chandeliers, moldings, and fireplaces, the place shows off its previous existence as an old manor. The location on rue Sherbrooke, just east of boulevard Saint-Laurent, is very handy.

$150-200

The extremely tasteful 【 **Le Zèbre** (1125 rue Rachel Est, 514/528-6801, www.bblezebre.com, $80–190) is in a Victorian house situated right in front of Parc La Fontaine. The four rooms are luxurious with marble bathrooms and balconies or bay windows. Each one has its own special feature, but all are delightful. Only two of the rooms have private bathrooms. Also situated in a Victorian house just down the street is **Auberge de La Fontaine** (1301 rue Rachel Est, 514/597-0166 or 800/597-0597, www.aubergedelafontaine.com, $120–224). This inn has 21 colorful, comfortable rooms, some of them with views overlooking the park. Guests have access to the inn's kitchen and its appliances, and they can also snack on the cheeses, crackers, and cookies left out. For more of a straightforward hotel setting, try the **Hôtel des Gouverneurs Place Dupuis** (1415 rue Saint-Hubert, 514/842-4881 or 888/910-1111, www.gouverneur.com, $149–184), a large hotel with 322 spacious rooms, indoor pool, sauna, fitness club, a bar, and a restaurant. The hotel is at the corner of rue Sainte-Catherine and rue Saint-Hubert and is also directly connected to the metro line, which, of course, is handy during the winter.

Over $200

The 【 **Hôtel Godin** (10 rue Sherbrooke Ouest, 514/843-6000 or 866/744 6346, www.hotelgodin.com, $200–500) is one of the newest boutique hotels of the bunch. It's got a terrific location, right at the bottom of the club- and restaurant-heavy section of boulevard Saint-Laurent on rue Sherbrooke. The 136-room hotel is known for its very contemporary décor, designer furniture, and daring color scheme, featuring grays and beiges with sudden hits of reds and purples. Part of the hotel is in a historic art nouveau 1915 building, the first one in Montréal to be fashioned out of reinforced concrete, while the rest of the hotel is thoroughly sleek and postmodern. A bridge above the on-site gourmet restaurant links the two. There's a chic bar too.

THE VILLAGE

The city's Gay Village is known for its multitude of B&Bs, most of them clean, stylish, and friendly. If you're booking a date during the Divers/Cité festival make sure that you book way in advance.

$50-100

Accommodation Montréal Gay (1607 rue Montcalm, 514/524-8789, www.accommodationmontrealgay.com, $60–100 d) is a charming bed-and-breakfast in the cozy home of Mario and Jacques. In addition to the inn's five standard rooms, there are three apartments available for rent (prices vary depending on length of stay). 【 **Bed & Breakfast du Village** (1279 rue Montcalm, 514/522-4771 or 888/228-8455, www.bbv.qc.ca, $65–85 d) is in the heart of the Gay Village and features five rooms, as well as a suite with two bedrooms. The inn has a quaint living room and a cute terrace, complete with a variety of potted plants, as well as an outdoor hot tub. Gym facilities are also available on-site. **Le Houseboy Bed and Breakfast** (1281 Beaudry, 514/525-1459, www.lehouseboy.com, $65–120 d) features five smokefree rooms and a scrumptious array of gourmet breakfasts, including homemade waffles and blueberry crêpes, frittata with veggies, and ciabatta bread. Guests can eat indoors in the delightful little dining room or have breakfast on the terrace by the garden. The inn also has an indoor hot tub.

$100-150

L'Auberge Universel (5000 rue Sherbrooke Est, 514/253-3365 or 800/567-0223, www.auberge-universel.com, $90–155 d) offers 229 rooms and suites in a classy, yet intimate, setting. The hotel's restaurant, Le Stadium Club, named after the establishment's proximity to the Olympic Stadium, specializes in Italian cuisine. Diners can relax in the bar lounge after dinner or visit the sauna or heated pools (indoors and outdoors).

$150-200

☐ Hotel Champ-de-Mars (756 rue Berri, 514/844-0767, www.hotelchampdemars.com, $155–195 d) is close to the eastern main entrance of the Old Port. This classy hotel consists of 25 rooms and one suite. Guests can choose from among nine different styles of rooms—whatever suits their taste. For those wanting more than the usual continental-style breakfast, the hotel has a restaurant, open daily 8–11 A.M., serving complete breakfasts at a reasonable price.

Food

OLD MONTRÉAL

As you can well imagine, a wealth of restaurants are in this city's tourist heart. Plenty are average, featuring bland, nondescript menus that could be experienced anywhere in North America. A few, though, are stellar, especially the small bakery/coffee shops, French restaurants, and the few that push the limits with inventive, contemporary cuisine.

Cafés

Right across the street from the Marché Bonsecours, **☐ Olive+Gourmando** (351 rue Saint-Paul Ouest, 514/350-1083, www.oliveetgourmando.com, 8 A.M.–6 P.M. Tues.–Wed and Fri.–Sat. and 8 A.M.–11 P.M. Thurs., lunch $8–10) is one of the city's best loved cafés—not only for its warm, convivial atmosphere, gourmet fresh-baked bread (the olive and cheese bread and apricot bread are incredible!), and lunchtime paninis, but also because it had the foresight and mettle to set up shop in the mid-1980s, helping bring new life to a neighborhood that at the time was run-down and depressed. The café has recently started opening for dinner on Thursday nights—it's one of those rare places in Old Montréal where parents and kids can find a little gourmet that they all like. It's open only during regular working hours, which means that **Titanic** (445 rue Saint-Pierre, 514/849-

0854, 7:30 A.M.–4:30 P.M. Mon.–Fri, mains $12) is a popular spot for people who work and live in the neighborhood. This below-street-level, but still sunny, place is also a great place to munch on a gourmet t. Old Montréal's newest café is **java u lounge** (191 rue Saint-Paul Est, 514/849-8881, www.java-u.com, 11 A.M.–3 P.M. Mon. and 11 A.M.–3 A.M. Tues.–Sun.), a modern locale with Parisian-type coffees and gourmet Italian panini. Java u actually started at Concordia University in 2002 and now has several franchises in the United States and the rest of Canada. This location has live music on Sundays and DJs Wednesday through Saturday.

French

Over on McGill, you'll find **Boris Bistro** (465 rue McGill, 514/848-9575, www.borisbistro.com, mains $13–19), a bar/bistro with original spins (triple-decker duck sandwich) and typical, but tasty, French fare (braised rabbit, duck confit). If you're there in summer, make sure you sit in the lovely and lush courtyard out back. On the same street, you'll find **☐ Holder** (407 rue McGill, 514/849-0333, noon–11 P.M. Mon.–Thurs. and noon–midnight Fri.–Sun., mains $14–40), a busy, immense brasserie situated in the corner of a stately office building, previously occupied by the Bank of Montréal. The restaurant's handsome décor features dark wood and a copper-plated bar, while the menu is indisputably French: veal liver with onions, steak *frites* and homemade foie gras. Excellent service, a romantic setting, and classic yet simple French cuisine have made **Restaurant Bonaparte** (447 rue Saint-François-Xavier, 514/844-1448, www.bonaparte.com, noon–2:30 P.M. and 5:30–10 P.M. Mon.–Fri., and 5:30–10 P.M. Sat.–Sun., mains $19–30) one of Montréal's best French restaurants, well worth the higher prices. Expanding across three halls decorated in the Empire style of Napoléon's time, the restaurant offers such dishes as lobster bisque, duck paté, veal medallions, and beef tartar. If you're heading out on a date, go here and you'll be well rewarded.

Contemporary

And then there's **Cluny's Art Bar** (257 rue Prince, 514/866-1213, 7:30 A.M.–5 P.M. Mon.–Wed. and 7:30 A.M.–9 P.M. Thurs.–Fri., mains $5–12). Named after a dog who once roamed the streets of Old Montréal, this cafeteria-style bistro is for people who enjoy chatting about art in a hip postindustrial atmosphere. Menu items feature sandwiches, chicken, salads, and antipasti.

Famous local chef Laurent Godbout's **Restaurant Chez L'Epicier** (311 rue Saint-Paul Est, 514/878-2232, www.chezlepicier.com, 11:30 A.M.–2 P.M. and 5:30–10 P.M. Mon.–Fri. and 5:30–10 P.M. Sat.–Sun., mains $21–35) has garnered a lot of acclaim through the years for its inventive take on French classics—often infusing them with Asian flourishes. There's an impressive wine cellar with more than 2,000 bottles and an adjoining gourmet food boutique where you can buy all kinds of exclusive Québec products, including meats, cheeses, sauces, and oils. Legendary for its innovative cuisine, oh-so-stylish patrons, and sleek surroundings, **Cube** (355 rue McGill, 514/876-2823, www.restaurantcube.com, noon–2 P.M. and 6–11 P.M. daily, mains $30–40) has been a

GARÇON, LE CORKSCREW?

The envy of many other cities in Canada, Montréal has plenty of bring-your-own-wine restaurants where it's cool to brown bag your booze. You'll notice them by the sign they usually have in the window, stating that they are BYOW. Many of these restaurants are located in the Plateau area, especially on rue Prince-Arthur and avenue Duluth.

Before heading to the restaurant, duck into a *dépanneur* (convenience store) or a grocery store and pick out the best looking red or white. These places are allowed to sell alcohol until 11 P.M. If you have a more refined palette or are looking for a greater selection of wines, stop by the Société des Alcools du Québec (SAQ). These government-run stores with the square burgundy logo are usually open seven days a week, but hours vary.

Bars and restaurants serve alcohol 11 A.M.–3 A.M., with the exception of beer halls (brasseries), which serve liquor 8 A.M.–1 A.M. The legal drinking age in Québec is 18 years old.

hot spot since it opened in the summer of 2001. Eating here will hit your wallet hard, but if you're wanting bold, contemporary cuisine and an ambience so hip it consistently draws celebrities such as Robert De Niro and Catherine Deneuve, then this is your place.

Other

Stash Café (200 rue Saint-Paul Ouest, 514/845-6611, www.stashcafe.com, 11:30 A.M.–10 P.M. daily, mains $10–16) is a Montréal institution, known for making some of the best borscht, pierogies, and cabbage rolls in the city. While the food is all Old World Poland, the setting is all Old Montréal: stone walls, exposed wooden beams, and worn wooden benches. If it's in season, be sure to try the marinated wild boar, a recipe that originated with the owner's grandmother. Just down the street is **Restaurant Gandhi** (230 rue Saint-Paul Ouest, 514/845-5866, www.restaurantgandhi.com, noon–2:30 P.M. and 5–10 P.M. Mon.–Fri and 5–10 P.M. Sat.–Sun., mains $10–21), a pretty Indian restaurant with yellow walls and big street-front windows that has an accessible menu, allowing diners to match the curry with the meat. Other menu items include samosas, tandoori duck, lamb *korahi,* and *phirni* (rice pudding).

DOWNTOWN

An enormous number of places to eat are in the downtown district thanks to the shoppers and the people who work there. From food courts in the shopping malls to independent fast-food chains to cafés that soothe tired shoppers' tootsies to fine French fare, there is everything your little heart could desire. It does get quite busy downtown on weekends, so reserving is a wise idea.

Vegetarian

Le Commensal (12-4 avenue McGill College, 514/871-1480, 11:30 A.M.–10 P.M. daily, by plate weight $9–15) is an excellent choice for vegetarians or anyone wanting a healthy meal. It's set up buffet-style, and you load your plate with beans, chickpeas, tofu, and other veggie goodies and then get it weighed once you get to the cashier—so go easy on the vegetable lasagna. Also keep some space for the delicious desserts.

Casual

Although Schwartz's on the Main gets all the attention, it was Benjamin Kravitz and his restaurant, aptly named **(Ben's** (990 boulevard de Maisonneuve), who can take the credit for bringing his Lithuanian smoked-meat recipe to Montréal. An institution since 1908, Ben's glory also lies in its décor: faded pictures of B-list actors that cover the walls, '50s-style tables, counters, and dishes and, of course, waiters who seem to have been on staff since the restaurant opened. Just down on Sainte-Catherine is another smoked-meat institution,

Reuben's (1116 rue Saint-Catherine Ouest, 514/866-1029). It may not have the history of Ben's (it opened only in 1976), but many Montrealers have come to consider the restaurant's large storefront window with its jars of pickles and peppers as a landmark. Inside, red booths and friendly waitresses serve the necessary smoked meat and fixings. Both Ben's and Rueben's are late-night places, but probably the most popular after-clubbing spot, especially for students, is **Basha** (930 rue Sainte-Catherine Ouest, 2nd floor, 514/866-4272, 11 A.M.–midnight Sun.–Thurs. and 11 A.M.–1 A.M. Fri. and Sat., mains $8–10), which serves tasty, cheap Lebanese food, including kebabs served with hummus and *shish taouk,* marinated chicken grilled on a spit and shaved into thin pieces.

Bistro

Inside the Musée des Beaux-Arts de Montréal's (**Café des Beaux-Arts** (1384 rue Sherbrooke Ouest, 11:30 A.M.–2 P.M. Tues.–Sun., 6–9 P.M. Wed., table d'hôte $17–21, mains $15–20), you'll find a refined but warm setting: yellow walls with pictures of Hitchcock, big windows, and white-linen-covered tables. Not your typical museum restaurant, this one features upscale contemporary and French food by well-known Montréal chef Richard Bastien. Now that we've got the museum covered, how about the theater? **Le Café du Nouveau Monde** (84 rue Sainte-Catherine Ouest, 514/866-8669, mains $15–20), in the Théâtre du Nouveau Monde, is a popular spot for people attending an evening play. After 8 P.M., however, when they've all hightailed it out of there, the restaurant becomes a tranquil place where you can get French fare such as duck, veal medallions, and excellent apple pie. The new sleek and all-white **Café Daylight Factory** (1030 rue Saint-Alexandre, 514/871-4774, 8 A.M.–4 P.M. Mon.–Wed. and 8 A.M.–11 P.M. Thurs.–Fri., mains $7–15), just south of rue de la Gauchetière, is a popular spot for the *5 à 7* (happy hour) crowd, in this case young multimedia workers. The kitchen serves good sandwiches, panini, salads, and a daily main at very reasonable prices.

French

A Montréal institution, **Alexandre** (1454 rue Peel, 514/288-5105, daily noon–2 A.M., mains $33–65) has an English-style pub, two dining rooms, and a large terrace. In operation for more than 25 years, the restaurant serves classic French dishes such as duck, rabbit, and veal. But to make sure things don't get staid, the restaurant has a guest chef come in every three months. The oozing chocolate molten cake with a foamy cappuccino is a must for dessert. Alexandre's feminine counterpart is **La Mère Michel** (1209 rue Guy, 514/934-0473, 5:30–10:30 P.M., Mon.–Sat., mains $25–40), which is housed on the mezzanine of a Victorian-style, three-floor centennial home. The chef, Micheline Delbuguet, nicknamed la Mère Michel, is one of the first female chefs in Québec. The buffalo tournedos in pepper sauce and the Grand Marnier soufflé for dessert are house specialties. For $47, the restaurant also offers a *menu des grands espaces* (wide-open spaces menu), prepared with a special focus on Québec products. You may not expect much from **Le Mas des Oliviers** (1216 rue Bishop, 514/861-6733, noon–3 P.M. and 6–11 P.M. Mon.–Fri., 5:30–11 P.M. Sat., and 5:30–10 P.M. Sun., mains $24–68, table d'hôte $23–37) when you lay eyes on it from the outside, but this restaurant serves some of the best steak *frites* around. Attracting a business and politico crowd, the restaurant is frequently crowded, but the food, wine menu, and charming wait staff is well worth it. It's pricey, but **Les Caprices de Nicolas** (2072 rue Drummond, 514/282-9790, 6–10 P.M. daily, mains $35–39) is the place to go for a sophisticated gourmet feast and to be doted on. Luxury rules here and it shows in the tuxedoed waiters, the *amuse-gueules* (appetizers), the full-time sommelier, and one of the finest menus in town, featuring caribou, venison, quail, and an incredible after-dinner cheese. It has a beautiful interior garden too.

Contemporary

Rumor has it that businessmen fly in from New York to eat lunch at chef Normand Laprise's famous table. The legendary and highly expensive **Toqué!** (900 Place Jean-Paul Riopelle, 514/499-2084, 11:30 A.M.–2 P.M. and 5:30–10:30 P.M.Tues.–Fri. and 5:30–10:30 P.M. Sat., mains $45–77, six-course tasting menu $81–91) is considered by many to be the city's best restaurant, although some would argue that the place lost some cachet when it moved from its rue Saint-Denis location to downtown. Its modern and ingredients-focused cuisine still gets rave reviews and plenty of crowds, so make sure that you reserve if you plan to eat here. The café is open for lunch every day except Monday and on Wednesday nights for dinner.

Chinese

Although the pink tablecloths and gray-mauve carpet may not be appetizing, **L'Orchidée de Chine** (2017 rue Peel, 514/287-1878, noon–2:30 P.M. and 5:30–10:30 P.M. Mon.–Thurs., noon–2:30 P.M. and 5:30–11 P.M. Fri. and 5:30–11 P.M. Sat., mains $22–31) has an excellent menu. Ingredients are fresh and there is an emphasis on flavor, especially when it comes to the orange chicken and the beef stir-fry. Don't be shy to ask for combinations that are not on the menu. **Mr. Ma** (1 place Ville-Marie, 11:30 A.M.–10:30 P.M. Mon.–Thurs., 11:30 A.M.–11 P.M. Fri., 5–11 P.M. Sat.) is always on hand to welcome guests into his Szechuan restaurant. The décor is simple. The food is aromatic and fresh. House specialties include fish, lobster, and duck. Parking in Place Ville-Marie next door is free after 5:30 P.M. **Zen** (1050 rue Sherbrooke Ouest, 514/499-0801, 11:30 A.M.–2:30 P.M. and 5:30–10 P.M. daily, except Sat. 5:30–11:30 P.M., mains $24–38, table d'hôte $32) is another good choice. It's in the basement of the Omni Hotel, and its duck pancakes, yes, you read correctly, are divine! To savor all the flavors, try its tasting menu of 40 Asian specialties. For dim sum, try **Ruby Rouge** (1008 rue Clark, 514/390-8828, www.restaurantrubyrouge.com, 9 A.M.–11 P.M. daily), a huge Chinatown banquet hall that may be lacking in cozy atmosphere but that makes up for it with fresh ingredients and great service.

Vietnamese

In Chinatown, Vietnamese restaurant **Pho Bac** (1016 boulevard Saint-Laurent, 514/393-8116, 10 A.M.–10 P.M., mains $5–8) is one of the area's best-kept secrets and is said to prepare the best *tonkinoises* (Tonkinese) soups in town. But for the best *banh mi* sandwich (sautéed veggies, cilantro, hot pepper, and pork on a baguette) try **Cao Thang** (1082 boulevard Saint-Laurent, 514/392-0097). The restaurant also carries packed spring rolls, pork buns, and a variety of rice dishes.

Japanese

For good sushi and sashimi, head to **⟨ Katsura** (2170 rue de la Montagne, 514/849-1172, 11:30 A.M.–2:30 P.M. and 5:30–10 P.M. Mon–Thurs., 11:30 A.M.–2:30 P.M. and 5:30–11 P.M. Fri., 5:30–11 P.M. Sat., and 5:30–9:30 P.M. Sun., mains $23–42, table d'hôte $34–45), where the clientele is glamorous and the setting is sleek. There's also **Sho-Dan** (2029 rue Metcalfe, 514/987-9987, 11:30 A.M.–2:30 P.M. and 5–10:30 P.M. Mon.–Fri. and 5–10:30 P.M. Sat., mains $22–40), which features a variety of sushi dishes and several teriyaki and tempura options for nonsushi eaters. The atmosphere is soothing except during the very busy lunch hours. Try the delicious sushi pizza.

Italian

The two-floor **⟨ Bocca d'Oro** (1448 rue Saint-Mathieu, noon–midnight Mon.–Sat., table d'hôte $22–30) serves fresh pasta dishes from the southwest of Italy. Some of the chef's specialties include the veal *escalope* and the lemon sauce and shrimp and avocado *taglioni*. At the end of your meal, you'll receive a bowl of walnuts to crack open and munch on. **Da Vinci's** (1180 rue Bishop, 514/874-2001, 11:30 A.M.–midnight Mon.–Fri., 5 P.M.–midnight Sat, mains $20–48, table d'hôte $32–42) is the preferred restaurant of professional hockey players and many other stars, judging by the pictures hanging on the walls. Its traditional Italian cuisine focuses on fresh pastas and meats.

WESTMOUNT AND OUTREMONT

It's nothing fancy, but Westmount's **Restaurant Claremont** (5032 rue Sherbrooke Ouest, 514/483-5881, www.claremontcafe.ca, 11:30 A.M.–11 P.M. daily), a favorite local hangout, has a warm atmosphere, an eclectic menu with everything from burgers to mussels and fries to yellowfin tuna, and a great nighttime scene with live music and stellar cocktails.

In Outremont, you'll find the famous **Lester's Deli** (1057 avenue Bernard Ouest, 514/213-1313 or 866/537-8377, www.lestersdeli.com, 9 A.M.–9 P.M. Mon.–Fri., 9 A.M.–8 P.M. Sat., mains $5–11), said to serve the finest smoked meat in Montréal. Serving all kinds of smoked-meat sandwich combos, the place will also fix you up with a vacuum-sealed package of your own if you want to take some home. One of avenue Bernard's other famous restaurants, **La Moulerie** (1249 avenue Bernard Ouest, 514/273-8132, 11:30 A.M.–11:30 P.M. Mon.–Fri., 10 A.M.–11 P.M. Sat.–Sun.), is known for its delicious, fragrant plates of mussels in various spice sauces: Italian, Indian, Thai, and Catalan are just some. Montréal's favorite upscale ice-cream shop is **Le Bilboquet** (1311 avenue Bernard, 514/276-0414, 7:30 A.M.–midnight daily Apr.–Sept., 7:30 A.M.–10 P.M. daily Oct.–Dec. and mid-Mar.–late Mar.). Expect to wait in a line on hot summer days, but you won't mind when you get a taste of the handmade ice cream (maple taffy, vanilla with brownie chunks) and sorbets (lychee, grapefruit, mango-raspberry). For the most French atmosphere of Montréal French bistros, try **Chez Lévesque** (1030 avenue Laurier Ouest, 514/279-7355, 8 A.M.–midnight Mon.–Fri. and 10:30 A.M.–midnight Sat.–Sun., table d'hôte $20–30), where a variety of French media types like to hang out. The menu features classic French items such as bouillabaisse, lamb, and foie gras.

MONTRÉAL

QUARTIER LATIN AND PLATEAU MONT-ROYAL

Food Shops

La Vieille Europe (3855 boulevard Saint-Laurent, 514/842-5773, 7:30 A.M.–6 P.M. Mon.–Wed., 7:30 A.M.–9 P.M. Thurs.–Fri., 7:30 A.M.–5 P.M. Sat.–Sun.) is a gourmet paradise. This little food bazaar is filled with delicious European products such as cheese, fine meats, and cookies. Even if you don't want to buy anything, it's worth walking in simply for the aromas that will hit you as soon as you step in the store. Over on Saint-Denis, **Le Festin de Babette** (4085 rue Saint-Denis, 514/849-0214, 10 A.M.–midnight Mon.–Sat. and 11 A.M.–10 P.M. Sun.) is a pretty little gourmet food boutique specializing in chocolates, coffees, teas, olive oil, and soft-serve ice cream in a variety of novel flavors such as Yucatan (mango, strawberry, and pepper) and Cholita (ginger and banana).

Cafés

Although you can find many outlets of the **Brûlerie Saint-Denis** (3967 rue Saint-Denis, 514/286-9159, 8 A.M.–11 P.M. Mon.–Thurs., 8 A.M.–11 P.M. Fri.–Sat., 9 A.M.–11 P.M. Sun., $7–12) across Montréal, this location is the original, responsible for the chain's success. With its own roasted coffee—which can be smelled from a block away—straightforward sandwiches, and cozy atmosphere, this is a good place to stop for a shopping break, especially in cooler weather. Named after its two owners, **Aux Deux Marie** (4329 rue Saint-Denis, 514/844-7246, 8 A.M.–11 P.M. daily, mains $10) has a terrace, the perfect vantage point from which to observe Montrealers strolling down rue Saint-Denis. Pizzas, sandwiches, burgers, and salads are the typical fare. Intellectual types and artists meet at **Café Rico** (969 rue Rachel Est, 514/529-1321, 10 A.M.–6 P.M. Mon.–Wed., 10 A.M.–7 P.M. Thurs.–Fri., 10 A.M.–6 P.M. Sat., $4–6, cash only) to linger, discuss, and debate. This café attracts a socially conscious crowd that appreciates its socially conscious ways: The place doesn't only sell fair-trade coffee, but also fair-trade jam, sugar, nuts,

© JENNIFER EDWARDS

Schwartz's, Montréal's shrine to smoked meat

and more. Unapologetically laid-back, the bohemian **(Café Santropol** (3990 rue Saint-Urbain, 514/842-3110, mains $6–9) has been a favorite student hangout since its inception in the 1970s. Famed for its triple-layer sandwiches, including Saint Urbain Corner, a sandwich featuring cottage cheese, honey, nuts, and olives, Santropol is also renowned for its terrace—an urban oasis complete with a fish pond. If you're a fan of homemade soup and sandwiches, be sure to check out **(Soupe Soup** (80 rue Duluth Est, 514/380-0880, 10:30 A.M.–9 P.M. Mon.–Fri., mains $4.50–7.50), a casual neighborhood spot with different hot and cold soups served each day, depending on the ingredients in season. The creamy, cold, and smooth vichysoisse, with droplets of oil and balsamic vinegar, is to die for.

Brunch

With unique characteristics such as a TV installed on the bathroom floor, a funky mural, and a kitchen at the front of the restaurant, not to mention its stellar breakfasts,

L'Avenue (922 avenue du Mont-Royal Est, 514/523-8780, 7 A.M.–11 P.M. Mon.–Sat., 7 A.M.–10 P.M. Sun.) has become the coolest place in town on weekend mornings and early afternoons. From enormous fruit plates to pancakes and eggs, L'Avenue has great brunch options and very generous portions, which may explain why so many are willing to put up with the absurdly long lines on the weekends. Another brunch landmark, also known for its weekend lines, is ■ **Beauty's** (93 avenue du Mont-Royal, 514/849-8883, 7 A.M.–4 P.M. Mon.–Fri., 7 A.M.–5 P.M. Sat., and 8 A.M.–5 P.M. Sun., mains $4–8). This 1950s-style diner serves the requisite bagels, pancakes, waffles, and hash browns. The food is good, but the real reason people come here is the atmosphere: the blue booths, free coffee refills, and Hymie and Larry, the father-and-son team running the place.

Landmarks

You wouldn't take anyone here on a first date, but the **Montréal Pool Room** (1200 boulevard Saint-Laurent, open until 3 A.M. daily, mains $3–7), in the grimiest section of Saint-Laurent, serves the best fries and steamies (a steamed hot dog, pronounced "steem-AY") in the city. Although this spot, which dates to 1912, doesn't have a pool table anymore, it is still a great late-night chow down. The legendary ■ **Schwartz's** (3895 boulevard Saint-Laurent, 514/842-4813, 8 A.M.–12:30 A.M. Sun.–Thurs., 8 A.M.–1:30 A.M. Fri., 8 A.M.–2:30 A.M. Sat.) is probably Montréal's best-known eatery. Known and treasured for its smoked-meat sandwiches, old, no-nonsense waiters, and décor that has hardly changed since the restaurant first opened in 1927, Schwartz's is not the place to go for a leisurely lunch. You'll probably have to wait in line and then once you get in, you'll be seated wherever there is room, even if that means sharing another person's table. But sample the daily smoked meat, fresh rye bread, and fries and you'll leave a happy person.

If you're tempted to try Québec's favorite junk food, poutine, get yourself to **La Banquise** (994 rue Rachel Est, 514/525-2415,

24 hours daily, mains $5–15), an unpretentious and friendly place that offers more than 15 varieties of the gravy-fries-cheese curd mixture, as well as more classical meals, such as lasagna and burgers. The place is packed at 3 a.m. when the bars close. For the best burgers in town, head to ■ **La Paryse** (302 rue Ontario Est, 514/842-2040, 11 A.M.–11 P.M. Mon.–Fri., noon–10 P.M. Sat., and noon–9 P.M. Sun., mains $8), a pleasant retro-style joint with burgers that come in classic form, tofu, or dressed up with mushrooms, mayo, and hot mustard. The Yukon gold, handcut fries are terrific. Success hasn't changed the working class–style **La Binerie Mont-Royal** (367 avenue du Mont-Royal Est, 514/285-9078, 6 A.M.–8 P.M. Mon.–Fri. 7:30 A.M.–3 P.M. Sat.–Sun., mains $7–12), a Montréal mainstay for more than 60 years. The place, known for its good-for-your heart beans, is still crammed and the original family still owns it. Beyond the beans, the place serves other Québécois classics such as tourtière (meat pie), pea soup, and pudding chômeur (a pudding popular during the Depression). While it may not have been here long enough to be deemed a landmark, **Patati Patata** (4177 boulevard Saint-Laurent, 514/844-0216, 9 A.M.–11 P.M. Mon.–Fri. and 11 A.M.–11 P.M. Sat.–Sun., mains $4–7) is so beloved for its casual friendly feel and great ambience that it's hard to imagine a time when it didn't occupy the tiny corner space at Saint-Laurent and Rachel. Burgers (tofu, fish, and meat), poutine, fish and chips, and roast beef with gravy are the house specialties, which you can enjoy at the small counter or one of the few tiny tables.

French

A delicious Plateau secret, **Vents du Sud** (323 rue Roy Est, 514/281-9913, 5:30–10 P.M. Wed.–Sun., table d'hôte $15–22) is a sunny BYOW restaurant with images of fishing villages painted on the walls, a menu with French and Spanish dishes, and a focus on seafood, of course. You'll see chef Gérard Couret making the rounds at least a couple of times a night. He's the one with

MONTRÉAL

the big moustache. Thankfully, few things have changed at the classic **(L'Express** (3927 rue Saint-Denis, 514/845-5333, 8 A.M.–1 A.M. Mon., 8 A.M.–2 A.M. Tues.–Fri., 10 A.M.–2 A.M. Sat.–Sun., mains $13–22) since it opened 50 years ago. With its long bar, black and white tiled floor, and wait staff decked out in white shirts with the sleeves rolled up, L'Express is the epitome of the charming French bistro. As you wait for your tartar or duck à l'orange, a basket of bread and a jar of tiny pickles are placed on your table to help tide you over. Reservations are essential. The tiny and intimate BYOW spot **(Le P'tit Plateau** (330 rue Marie-Anne Est, 514/282-6342, 5:30 P.M.–midnight Tues.–Sat., table d'hôte $25) may have a casual neighborhood feel, but it's known for its stellar French cuisine, including foie gras and confit *de canard* (duck). There are two sittings per night. The first is between 5:30 and 6:30 P.M., while the second is at 8:30 P.M. The low-key but luxurious **Laloux** (250 avenue des Pins Est, 514/287-9127, lunch 11:30 A.M.–2:30 P.M. Mon.–Fri., dinner 5:30–10:30 P.M. Sun.–Wed., 5:30–11:30 P.M. Thurs.–Sat., table d'hôte $30–50) is an elegant restaurant serving nouvelle cuisine to a sophisticated clientele. If money is no object, come here to sample chef André Besson's signature dishes such as the crab ravioli and red snapper suprême. Creative, but unpretentious, **(Au Pied de Cochon** (536 avenue Duluth Est, 514/281-1114, 5 P.M.–midnight Tues.–Sun.) is known for chef Martin Picard's use of French meats and foie gras in traditional Québécois cuisine such as the legendary foie gras *poutine* or the pig's feet braised in maple syrup. This inventive restaurant is a good bet for the gourmet traveler; just don't forget to reserve. Although **Le Continental** (4169 rue Saint-Denis, 514/845-6842, 6 P.M.–1 A.M. Tues.–Sat. and 6 P.M.–midnight Sun.–Mon., mains $35–45) describes itself as an American bistro, it's a classic French bistro to most. This restaurant hasn't changed much in 20 years, which is a good thing. Its art deco style, complete with columns, collages, and 1950s planes, makes for a cool ambience. Le

Continental's specialty is the lamb shank, served with couscous and ratatouille. The restaurant also serves four new appetizers and main meals each week.

Portuguese and Spanish

It's easy to fall in love with **(Chez Doval** (150 rue Marie-Anne Est, 514/843-3390, noon–11 P.M. daily, mains $10–18). The ambience is authentic, the portions are generous, and the traditional Portuguese food—especially the chicken—is heavenly. The restaurant has two dining rooms, one low-key and the other noisy and raucous. No reservations are taken, so it's best to arrive early. **La Sala Rosa** (4848 boulevard Saint-Laurent, 514/844-4227, 5 P.M.–11 P.M. Tues.–Sun. and 10 A.M.–3 P.M. Sat.–Sun., mains $12–17) is a relaxed and unpretentious hangout, frequented by a young artsy crowd. This Spanish restaurant is the perfect complement to the Casa del Popolo bar just across the street (in fact they are owned by the same people). The tapas and the fish of the day are good choices.

Thai

Even the most carnivorous will enjoy a meal at Thai vegetarian restaurant **ChuChaï** (4088 rue Saint-Denis, 514/843-4194, 11 A.M.–10 P.M. Mon.–Wed., 11 A.M.–11 P.M. Thurs.–Sat., and 11 A.M.–9 P.M. Sun., mains $15–20). First of all, the design of the place is open and minimalist with a brick wall, metal tables, and rare wood finishes. Then there's the food: colorful, spicy Thai dishes with soy products that successfully simulate chicken and beef. Go for the basil and coconut "chicken." Although the ornate décor of mounted elephant heads and statues of dancers may be a tad overwhelming, **(Red Thai** (3550 boulevard Saint-Laurent, 514/289-0998, 11 A.M.–3 P.M. amd 5 P.M.–midnight Tues.–Fri. and 5 P.M.–midnight Sat.–Mon., mains $12–29) has some of the best traditional Thai food in the city. Fragrant soups, crispy imperial rolls, spicy red curry, *pad thai,* and homemade coconut ice cream make for a succulent meal. The wait staff is attentive and friendly.

THE VILLAGE

La Strega du Village (1477 rue Sainte-Catherine Est, 514/523-6000, 11:30 A.M.–midnight Mon.–Fri., 5 P.M.–midnight Sat.–Sun., mains $7–20) is perfect for those on a budget craving Italian food. Clients can mix and match from a variety of pastas and sauces. The restaurant, with its red walls and candlelight atmosphere, has a clientèle consisting mainly of male couples. **Club Sandwich** (1578 rue Sainte-Catherine Est, 514/523-4679, open 24 hours daily, mains $8–15) is the happening spot for partiers who want to fill up on greasy food after a night of clubbing. This chrome, art deco deli that "never sleeps" serves generous helpings 365 days a year. ☖ **Élla Grill** (1237 rue Amherst, 514/523-5553, 5:30 P.M.–midnight Tues.–Sun., mains $11–26) is authentic Greek food at its best. Owner Annie Pellas serves grilled foods and fish amid a pristine white décor. Clients can choose from a wide array of tempting appetizers before digging into a plate of some of the restaurant's specialties, including lamb, filet mignon, and chicken. The service is always friendly and attentive. **Saloon Café** (1333 rue Sainte-Catherine Est, 514/522-1333, 11:30 A.M.–11 P.M. Mon.–Fri., 10 A.M.–midnight Sat.–Sun., mains $15–20) is a local institution in the Gay Village. With a laid-back ambience and funky style, this restaurant is perfect for those eating in a hurry, as well as for those who want to sit and knock back a few. There is a large variety of dishes on the menu, varying from North American to Italian, Mexican, and Thai. It also features an impressive vegetarian menu.

MILE END

Montréal's two most famous bagel shops are in Mile End: **Saint-Viateur Bagel** (263 rue Saint-Viateur Ouest, 514/276-8044, open 24 hours daily) and **Fairmount Bagel** (74 rue Fairmount, 514/272-0667, open 24 hours daily) make their chewy, delicious wonders on the spot. Stop by and you'll see long strips of dough being cut and then twisted into rings, placed on wooden boards, and shoveled into a wood oven. Visitors, especially ex-Montrealers now living in Toronto, stock up and buy several plastic bags' worth to freeze upon their return.

LITTLE ITALY

This area's biggest draw is the food. Restaurants here are typically small and quaint, and you can literally hear someone's *nonna* shouting out orders in the kitchen as you await your meal. **Tre Marie** (6934 rue Clark, 514/277-9859, noon–10 P.M. Mon.–Wed., noon–11 P.M. Thurs.–Fri., 5 P.M.–midnight Sat., and noon–9 P.M. Sun., mains $12–20) is a perfect example. Sisters Rosina and Maria Fabrizio run the show at this popular eatery known for its tender veal. Attracting politicians, business types, and restaurant gourmands, **Ristorante Primo and Secondo** (7023 rue Saint-Dominique, 514/908-0838, 11 A.M.–10 P.M. Tues.–Fri. and 6–10 P.M. Sat., mains $18–37) is home to what many consider the best calamari in the city (and in the country as well). Sauces are made from scratch, the risotto is heavenly, and the tiramisu is utterly decadent. Although it's called **Café International** (6714 boulevard Saint-Laurent, 514/495-0067, 11 A.M.–3 P.M. and 6–10 P.M. daily, mains $8–15), the menu here is strictly Italian with a selection of pizza, pasta, risottos, and meat and fish dishes. The food is simple and delicious and is best enjoyed during the summer on the front terrace.

Information and Services

TOURISM INFORMATION

Montréal's main tourist center, Infotouriste (1001 rue du Square-Dorchester, 514/873-2015 or 877/266-5687, www.tourisme-montreal.org, 7 A.M.–8 P.M. daily June–early Sept. and 9 A.M.–6 P.M. early Sept.–June) acts as a tourist information office for the city and the entire province. The busy office at rue Peel and rue Sainte-Catherine operates on the number system: Grab a number when you come in and wait until it's called to speak to one of the bilingual agents. You'll find rows and rows of tourist brochures and booklets on all of the regions of Québec. The office will also help with reservations, tours, car rentals, and currency exchange. And there is Internet access that you can pay for with cash or a credit card.

There is a second office, Old Montréal Infotouriste (174 rue Notre-Dame Est, 877/266-5687, www.vieux.montreal.qc.ca, 9 A.M.–5 P.M. daily Apr.–June, 9 A.M.–7 P.M. daily June–Sept., 9 A.M.–5 P.M. daily Sept.–Nov., 9 A.M.–5 P.M. Wed.–Sun. Nov.–Apr.), right at the top of Place Jacques-Cartier, near Champ-de-Mars metro. You can buy a Montréal Museum Pass here or at participating museums; they enable you to visit 25 area museums during two full days within a span of three consecutive days. Passes cost $20.

EMERGENCY SERVICES

For all emergencies dial 911. If you want to reach the police for a matter that isn't an emergency, call 514/280-2222.

There are eight major hospitals in the city center, including the Hôpital Royal Victoria (687 avenue des Pins Ouest, 514/842-1231), or the Royal Vic as it's locally known, the Hôpital Général de Montréal (1650 rue Cedar, 514/937-6011), and the Jewish General Hospital (3755 Côte Sainte-Catherine, 514/340-8222) which all have emergency rooms. For children, there is the Hôpital de Montréal pour Enfants (2300 rue Tupper, 514/934-4400).

If it isn't an emergency, contact a CLSC (514/527-2361), a government-run, walk-in clinic. There is at least one in every neighborhood throughout Montréal.

CONSULATES

There are almost 100 consulates in the city of Montréal. The U.S. Consulate (1155 rue Saint-Alexandre, 514/398-9695) is just off boulevard René-Lévesque near rue de Bleury. The Consulate General of Great Britain (1000 rue de la Gauchetière Ouest, 514/866-5863) is in the Atrium Le 1000 building between rue Mansfield and rue de la Gauchetière, and the Consulat Général de France (1 place Ville-Marie, 514/878-4385) is located in Place Ville Marie at the foot of avenue McGill College. All the embassies are in Ottawa.

BANKS AND MONEY EXCHANGE

Many banks and money-exchange outlets are in downtown Montréal. Travelers' checks can be cashed at both. Banks accept all types of bank debit cards (Interac, Plus, and Cirrus systems) and credit cards as do stores and restaurants. Many businesses will take American money at par, but rates can vary wildly, so you are best to exchange your money at an established financial institution.

POST OFFICES

You'll find many postal outlets in shopping malls and pharmacies throughout the city. The main post office (1250 rue University, 800/267-1177, 8 A.M.–5:45 P.M. Mon.–Fri.) has bilingual service. Stamps are $0.65 for U.S. destinations and $1.25 for all other international destinations accessible via airplane. You can buy stamps at post offices, postal outlets, and at many convenience stores and grocery stores.

INTERNET

Internet access is available downtown at the Infotouriste center and at Net 24 (2157 rue Mackay, 514/845-9634, 24 hours daily, $5/

hour) and Presse Café (1264 Sainte-Catherine Est, 514/528-9530, 24 hours daily, $5/hour). You'll find some spots in the Plateau area, including **Virus** (3672 boulevard Saint-Laurent, 514/842-1726, 9:30 A.M.–midnight Mon.–Sat. and 11:30 A.M.–10 P.M. Sun., $5/hour) and **Café Planète** (163 rue Mont-Royal Ouest, 514/844-2233, 10 A.M.–midnight daily, $6/hour).

MEDIA
Newspapers and Magazines
If you want to read up on local news, pick up Montréal's English-language daily, **The Gazette.** The paper, founded in 1778, is actually one of the oldest in North America. Canada's two national newspapers, **The Globe and Mail** and the **National Post,** cover major news events across the country and in Québec. For entertainment listings, Montréal is well served with two free English entertainment weeklies, **The Mirror** and **Hour,** which are available on street corners and various establishments as of Thursday morning of every week. Both papers offer information on movies, music, dance, theater, and art happenings throughout the city. If you read French, have a look though **La Presse,** the city's biggest French-language paper, **Le Devoir,** the more intellectual daily, or **Le Journal de Montréal,** the sensationalist one. **Voir** and **Ici** are the French entertainment weeklies.

For a more literary read, pick up a copy of the excellent **Maisonneuve,** a Montréal-based magazine with an eclectic collection of well-written features. It's typically described as a more lighthearted *New Yorker,* which sums it up right.

Radio and TV
There are a number of English-language radio stations in Montréal including the local Canadian Broadcasting Corporation (CBC) stations, Radio One (88.5) for news and cultural programming and Radio Two (93.5) for classical music. There's also CHOM 97.7 for classic rock, MIX 96 for pop tunes, CKUT 90.3, McGill University's anything-goes radio station, and Q92 for everything that's light and breezy. On the AM band is CJAD 800, the talk radio station, and The Team 990, the sports channel.

All the big U.S. networks are picked up in Montréal, but for local programming, turn to CTV (channel 11), CBC (channel 13), or Global (channel 3). All three have local newscasts.

LAUNDRY
Laundry services in the city run from do-it-yourself spots such as **Lavoir Saint-Laurent** (3632 boulevard Saint-Laurent, 514/845-9664) to we-do-it-for-you spots such as **Buanderie du Parc** (3486 avenue du Parc, 514/844-4648), **Buanderie Net-Net** (310 rue Duluth Est, 514/844-8511), and **Lavoir du Village** (3686 rue Saint-Denis, 514/843-5763), which will wash, dry, and fold your clothes.

MONTRÉAL

MONTRÉAL

Getting There

BY AIR

The city's airport, **Montréal-Trudeau International Airport (YUL)** (514/394-7377 or 800/465-1213, www.admtl.com), is 20 km from downtown Montréal in the borough of Dorval on the west island. A cab ride into the city center can take anywhere from 20–45 minutes and will cost about $30. A cheaper option is the convenient L'Aerobus (514/842-2281, adult one-way/return $13/$23, children 5–12 one-way/return $9/$15), which departs every 20 minutes from the airport and runs to the Montréal Central Bus Station and to several downtown hotels.

Most of the major airlines fly into Montréal, but the most scheduled flights are offered by Air Canada (800/630-3299, www.aircanada.ca), which flies out of most Canadian centers and from New York, Chicago, Miami, Tampa, L.A., and San Francisco in the United States. Continental Airlines (800/231-0856, www.continental.com) and Northwest Airlines (800/225-2525 www.nwa.com) also have daily flights to Montréal from New York and Detroit.

BY CAR

There are many roads leading to Montréal. If you are coming from Toronto, there's the trusty 401, the 504-km highway that hits Kingston mid-way where it then jogs along the Saint Lawrence and turns into Route 20 just before you hit the island of Montréal. Coming from the United States, there are a few routes to get to the city. It's 644 km to get to Montréal from New York City. Interstate 87 will take you right to the border and from there, it's only 47 km along Route 15. The 500 km trip from Boston runs along I-91 to the Canadian border before it picks up on Route 55, which then turns into Route 10 though the Eastern Townships to Montréal.

All the highways in and around Montréal are generally in good condition, but can pose challenges in the winter due to ice and snow-storms. For information on road conditions in and around the city, there is a 24-hour hot line available November–April. Call 514/284-2363 within Montréal and 514/636-3248 outside the city.

BY BUS

Buses coming from all over the province, the rest of Canada, and the United States arrive at Station Centrale d'Autobus (505 boulevard de Maisonneuve Est, 514/842-2281) day and night. The major bus line servicing the city is Greyhound (800/661-8747, www.greyhound.com), which has routes from many U.S. and Canadian locations. A trip from Toronto usually takes about eight hours and has upward of seven departures daily. There are daily buses from New York City and Boston to Montréal. Adirondack Trailways (800/858-8555, www.trailwaysny.com) also has about seven daily departures from New York City to Montréal. The bus station is serviced by the Berri-UQAM metro station.

BY TRAIN

VIA Rail (888/842-7245, www.viarail.ca), Canada's national train carrier, services Montréal on the busy Québec City-Windsor corridor. A major hub, the Gare Centrale (935 rue de la Gauchetière Ouest, 514/871-1331) is right downtown near Place Bonaventure. Trains coming from Toronto and points west usually also offer a stop at the Dorval train station on the western part of the island. VIA trains from Toronto can take anywhere from just over four hours to the overnight train's almost nine-hour ride. Service to Québec City takes about three hours.

The Adirondack route offered by Amtrak (800/872-7245, www.amtrak.com) travels daily from New York City's Penn Station to Montréal's Gare Centrale with many stops in between. It's a 10-hour trip. The Gare Centrale is connected via underground tunnel to the Place Bonaventure metro station.

Getting Around

BY CAR

Montréal is a relatively easy city to navigate. However, right turns on red traffic lights are still prohibited (the island of Montréal is the only community in the province that outlaws it) and, depending on the traffic light, you may have to wait a few seconds for a green turning arrow after seeing one that points straight ahead. Otherwise, the rules of the road are fairly similar to those in most North American cities.

Parking in the city can be frustrating, with limited options downtown and parking signs so difficult to understand that many will opt for a parking lot out of frustration. One parking convenience that the city slowly has been putting in place is smart meters, which enable drivers to pay for their numbered spot, take their ticket, and then pay for more time at any other smart meter close to where they are.

BY BUS AND METRO

Montréal's bus and metro are run by the Société de Transport de Montréal (STM) (800 rue de La Gauchetière Ouest, 514/786-4636, www.stcum.qc.ca). A regular adult fare is $2.50 or $11 for a strip of six tickets. One ticket includes a bus or metro ride and the transfers necessary to complete your route up to 90 minutes after it is issued. You can buy tickets at any metro station or at many convenience stores. Visitors to the city can also take advantage of the tourist card, which gives unlimited access to buses and the metro for one day ($8) or three consecutive days ($16).

The city's low-floor, blue and white buses run along 169 daytime and 20 nighttime routes throughout the city, linking to bus terminals and to all the metro stations. To get a route schedule, pick up one of the Planibus pamphlets at any metro station or look it up on the website. You can also call 514/AU-TOBUS (514/288-6287) for times. At night, buses allow women to disembark between stops. Hours of operation are from 5:30 A.M. to

12:15 A.M. or 1:30 A.M., depending on the day of the week and the line. Bicycles are permitted on the first car of the metro daily from 10 A.M. to 3 P.M. and after 7 P.M.

BY TAXI

Montréal's cabs come in a variety of colors, sizes, and states of cleanliness. There are many cab companies from which to choose and the fares are relatively cheap, with a base fee of $2.75 and $1.30 per kilometer. Two of the more established Montréal companies are Diamond Taxi (514/273-6331) and Taxi Coop Montréal (514/725-2667).

RED LIGHT DISTRICT

When most of Québec rescinded its no right turn on red law in 2002, one blogger sarcastically lamented the negative results of the decision: Now that he can turn right on a red light like the rest of Canada, he said, he's lost valuable time to read the newspaper, chow down on fast food, and listen distraction-free to "drive at five" radio shows.

But the bright side is that he and everyone else can continue to indulge these uniquely western pastimes on the Island of Montréal, where it is still illegal to turn right on a red.

Many claim that the red light legislation is but one example of the paradoxical bureaucratic situations that the province is known for. The government claims that having to sit and wait for a red light to turn green is a small price to pay for everyone's safety in the province's busiest, biggest, and most accident-prone city.

Although most Montrealers grumble about Big Brother babysitting, others are starting to think that, with the city's notorious propensity for jaywalking, the continued legislation may not be such a bad idea. Besides, isn't being in a rush what *Toronto* is all about?

OUTAOUAIS

Situated at the southwestern tip of the province, the vast, 33,000-square-km Outaouais (ooh-TA-way) is perhaps Québec's most difficult region to pinpoint. The area, bordered by Abitibi-Témiscamingue, the Laurentians, and the province of Ontario, can be characterized as much by its urban side as by its small, quaint rural towns and massive wilderness.

In many ways, Gatineau, the region's only city, has a lot more in common with its Ontario neighbor, Ottawa, than it does with the rest of the province. Just across the river, its proximity, many government buildings, and shared workforce have ensured a close relationship with the nation's capital. Even other Outaouais towns are anomalies in Québec, thanks to the still-considerable English in-fluence, which led the region to vote overwhelmingly against separation during the 1995 referendum. You'll hear a lot of English spoken here and read it on many a daring shopkeeper's signs.

But just because the region's character isn't particularly easy to define doesn't mean that it can't be adequately savored. In fact, there is something satisfying in the Outaouais's low-key approach to its own promotion. Its main attractions—the Canadian Museum of Civilization, the Château Montebello, and its incredible Parc de la Gatineau—have made it one of the most popular regions in Québec to visit, and its take-me-as-I-am nature, along with its proximity to two major cities, have made it one of the easiest.

© JENNIFER EDWARDS

HIGHLIGHTS

◖ Canadian Museum of Civilization: Amazing architecture and the country's most impressive chronicle of Canadian history is what you'll find at this museum, one of the country's crown jewels (page 104).

◖ MacKenzie King Estate: Passionate about nature himself, Canada's 10th prime minister bequeathed his 231-hectare estate to Canadians so it would remain a natural sanctuary for all to enjoy (page 109).

◖ Hiking in Parc de la Gatineau: Minutes from downtown Gatineau, this 363 sq km oasis of forests and groomed trails, is heaven for hikers (page 109).

◖ Wakefield: This beautiful historical town that lies along the shores of the Rivière Gatineau has great food, shops, music...and lays claim to being the country's last remaining steam train destination (page 112).

◖ Fairmont Le Château Montebello: The world's biggest log cabin is tucked away in among the trees. Enjoy a drink by the fireplace, roam the magnificent grounds, or dine in the posh restaurant (page 114).

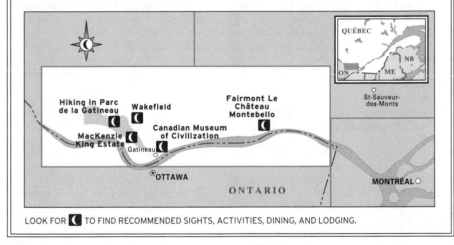

LOOK FOR ◖ TO FIND RECOMMENDED SIGHTS, ACTIVITIES, DINING, AND LODGING.

PLANNING YOUR TIME

If you want to go forth at a leisurely pace, with enough time to visit the attractions of the city of Gatineau and to explore the park and some of the shops and restaurants in the rural towns, plan for at least four days' stay. Luckily, most of Outaouais's attractions are within a short driving distance, so you won't have to spend too much time in the car.

The hub of urban activity, Gatineau has a number of good accommodation choices and makes for a good base from which to explore the surrounding area. Consider staying here your entire visit or, if you prefer

a quiet country escape, Wakefield also has good overnight options.

Take at least one day to explore the attractions throughout the city, including a full afternoon at the **Canadian Museum of Civilization** and an evening's worth of dining at one of the many restaurants in Vieux Hull (Gatineau's downtown core), followed by a wee bit of booty-shaking at one of the city's many nightclubs.

For the next couple of days, explore **Parc de la Gatineau** and stop for an afternoon at the **Mackenzie King Estate.** Intersperse your visits to the park with meals or shopping trips in the two laid-back villages of Chelsea and **Wakefield.**

On your final day, head east along Route 148, following the northern shores of the Ottawa River to the historic village of Montebello. Spend a few hours touring the Manoir Papineau and if you're not already planning to stay at **Le Château Montebello,** then at least consider stopping by for a few hours' visit.

With Ottawa just a stone's throw away from Gatineau, you may be tempted to venture into neighboring Ontario. If you do, and want to fully explore the nation's capital, plan to add at least an extra couple of days to your itinerary. Contact the **National Capital Commission** (613/239-5000 or 800/465-1867, www.canadascapital.gc.ca) for things to see and do.

A car or bike are the best ways to explore the region, but if you're planning to stay in Gatineau, you can take advantage of the steam train do some touring in the nearby town of Wakefield.

HISTORY

Acting as the southern border for the entire Outaouais region, the Ottawa River ("Ottawa" is actually the English translation of Outaouais) was the passage that Samuel de Champlain, Québec City's founder, used in 1613 as he searched for the Northern Sea. Later, many of the Outaouais's rivers were used as primary routes for the fur trade, which saw the French trading with the local Algonquin and in particular, the Outaouak tribe.

But, it wasn't until much later that Outaouais saw its first real influx of European settlers. That moment came in 1800 when

Philemon Wright and a group of Loyalists fled Massachusetts after the American Revolution and made their way to the region around the Ottawa and Gatineau Rivers, first known as Wright's Town and later as Hull. Thinking that the area was ripe for farming, Wright soon discovered the soil's limitations and switched his focus to lumber. Banking on Britain's need for lumber during the Napoleonic Wars, Wright founded a mill and soon was shipping logs across the Atlantic. Other timber mills soon popped up and Wright's Town became known as a major timber-producing area in Canada.

Later the area was further developed by the likes of J. R. Booth and E. B. Eddy who established factories to manufacture lumber products—the latter became the world's largest producer of matches. With this industrialization came new jobs attracting French speakers to the area, which had until that time remained almost exclusively English.

The anomaly in Outaouais's development is the area known as La Petite-Nation, which was parceled off according to the French seigneurial system. Named for the Algonquin tribe that once lived there, the area was given to Bishop François de Laval in 1674 and later passed on to the Séminaire du Québec who didn't take much interest, deeming the spot ill suited to farming. It was only in the early 1800s under the jurisdiction of Montréal lawyer Joseph Papineau, and later, his son Louis-Joseph Papineau, that the region began to prosper and small towns began to crop up.

Gatineau

On January 1, 2002, the former five cities that lined the northern shore of the Ottawa River—Gatineau, Aylmer, Hull, Buckingham, and Masson-Angers—amalgamated to become the city of Gatineau (pop. 229,094), the fifth-largest city in the province. It is not uncommon to hear people refer to the original names of these parts of the new city, especially

in reference to Gatineau's downtown core—still more commonly referred to as Hull.

Once dismissed as a working-class wasteland because of its many factories and lower-income housing, Gatineau (or Hull) also had the dubious reputation of being the preferred drinking location of Ottawa teenagers because of its lower drinking age and somewhat lax

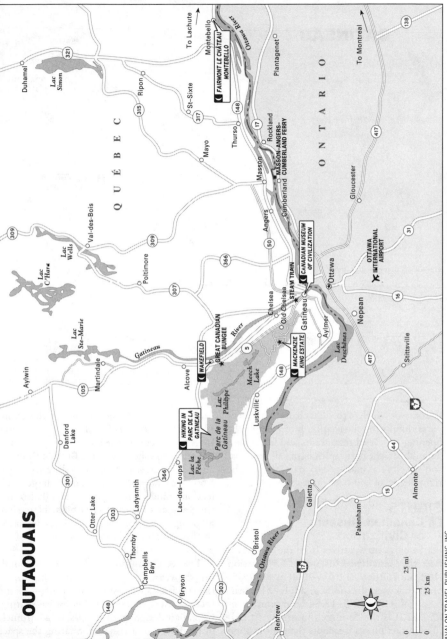

OUTAOUAIS

To Lachute
Montebello
To Montreal
FAIRMONT LE CHÂTEAU MONTEBELLO
Plantagenet
138
Ottawa River
321
Duhamel
Lac Simon
Ripon
St-Sixte
148
17
Rockland
O N T A R I O
315
317
Thurso
Masson
MASSON-ANGERS
CUMBERLAND FERRY
Cumberland
Gloucester
417
Mayo
Val-des-Bois
Angers
50
31
309
Lac Wells
309
366
CANADIAN MUSEUM OF CIVILIZATION
OTTAWA INTERNATIONAL AIRPORT
Lac C'Hara
Poltimore
307
Ottawa
STEAM TRAIN
16
Lac Ste-Marie
Chelsea
Old Chelsea
Nepean
Aylwin
Martindale
Gatineau River
GREAT CANADIAN BUNGEE
Gatineau
Stittsville
105
WAKEFIELD
5
MACKENZIE KING ESTATE
Aylmer
Alcove
Meech Lake
Lac Deschênes
417
Danford Lake
148
HIKING IN PARC DE LA GATINEAU
Luskville
44
301
366
Lac Philippe
Parc de la Gatineau
15
Otter Lake
Ladysmith
Lac la Pêche
Galetta
Almonte
303
Lac-des-Loups
Pakenham
Thornby
Bristol
Campbells Bay
Ottawa River
Bryson
148
303
Renfrew
25 mi
25 km
0
0

Q U É B E C

OUTAOUAIS

© AVALON TRAVEL PUBLISHING, INC.

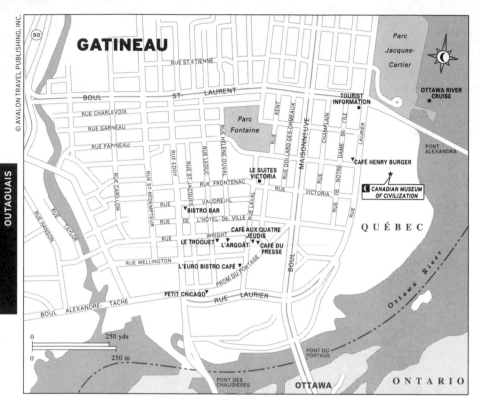

liquor laws. Much of that has changed in recent years thanks to rejuvenation projects and the opening of several restaurants and boutiques. Thankfully, the party spirit hasn't all been lost and the city has managed to maintain just the right degree of laid-back atmosphere.

SIGHTS
⟨ Canadian Museum of Civilization

Half a block up the street from the tourist office, the Canadian Museum of Civilization (100 rue Laurier, 819/776-7000 or 800/555-5621, www.civilization.ca, adults $10, students $6, children 3–12 $4, and families of four $22) is the country's most visited cultural attraction, and, at more than one million square feet, one of the world's largest muse-

ums. Chronicling the history of the country, the museum has four levels, plus its own IMAX theater. On the lower level, you'll find the museum's showpiece, the **Grande Gallerie,** an open room with floor-to-ceiling windows, a forest backdrop, and the world's largest collection of indoor totem poles. You'll also find the **Salle des Premiers Peuples,** a large hall made up of several smaller galleries depicting the history and art of the First Nations of the people of Canada.

The second and fourth levels of the building showcase temporary exhibits highlighting specific aspects of Canadian life—be it a focus on the country's passion for ice-skating, Canadian design in the 1960s, or a chronicle of the East Coast fisheries. Sharing the space with the special exhibits on the second level

OUTAOUAIS

© JENNIFER EDWARDS

Canadian Museum of Civilization

are three permanent fixtures. There are the **Canadian Children's Museum,** an around-the-world series of interactive exhibits, the **Canadian Postal Museum,** a chronicle of the country's social and economic evolution told through stamps, and finally, the massive, 295-seat **IMAX Theatre.**

The third level of the building consists of the **Salle du Canada,** a series of permanent exhibits that trace the entire history of Canada from the arrival of the Norse explorers to the settlement of the West and the Northern Territories.

But there's more to the museum than what's on the inside. Considered one of the country's architectural gems, the building was designed by Albertan architect Douglas Cardinal to reflect the continuous sweeps and curves of the Canadian landscape. Walk around the building to take in all its sides, and then go for a walk around the 24-acre grounds, where you'll catch some good views of both the city of Ottawa and the river.

The museum is open 9 A.M.–6 P.M. Monday–Wednesday and Friday–Sunday and 9 A.M.–

9 P.M. on Thursday May–mid-October. For the rest of the year, it's open 9 A.M.–5 P.M. Tuesday–Wednesday and Friday–Sunday and 9 A.M.–9 P.M. Thursday. Get half-price admission on Sundays and free admission on Thursdays 4–9 P.M. There are additional fees for the IMAX theater, but they are reduced when purchased with the admission to the museum.

Casino du Lac-Leamy

Even if you want nothing to do with a casino, it's hard not to be impressed by the architectural style and sheer massiveness of the Casino du Lac-Leamy (1 boulevard du Casino, 819/772-2100 or 800/665-2274, www.casino-du-lac-leamy.com, 9 A.M.–4 A.M. daily). Surrounded by water and dotted by fountains, the casino possesses more than 1,800 slot machines and more than 60 gaming tables, but it's also part of a massive complex that features a Vegas-style theater, six restaurants, the adjoining 349-room Hilton Hotel, a convention center, and a full-fledged spa. Entrance to the casino is strictly reserved for those 18 years and older but all ages are welcome in the other venues.

Hull-Chelsea-Wakefield Steam Train

Well worth the slightly inflated price, a trip aboard the H. C. W. Steam Train (165 rue Deveault, 819/778-7246 or 800/871-7246, www.steamtrain.ca, adults $39, seniors $36, students $35, children $19, family rate $99), Canada's only remaining steam train, is a great way to take in the Gatineau scenery. Chugging its way through the countryside, the train follows the tracks of the voyages it used to make in the early 1900s. The five-hour round-trip includes a couple of hours to explore Wakefield on your own or with one of the train's tour guides. The train runs May–October with daily service in July and August and late September and October.

Ottawa River Cruise

Mix a little old with the new by navigating the historic Ottawa River aboard the modern *Sea Prince* (613/562-4888, www.ottawariverboat .ca, departs 11 A.M. daily May–Oct., adults $16, seniors $14, children 6–12, $8, family $38). Departing from the Gatineau dock in Parc Jacques-Cartier, the trip takes about an hour and covers many sites, including Rideau Falls, Chaudière Island, and Gatineau village. Buy your ticket in advance at the Museum of Civilization and get both entry into the museum and a boat ticket for $21 adult.

ENTERTAINMENT
Nightlife

After years of attracting youthful partiers, **Place Aubry**, a restored cobblestone courtyard in Gatineau's downtown core, now appeals to a slightly more sophisticated crowd. Bars, open till 2 A.M., really only start swinging around 10 P.M. with the exception of warm summer days, when the patios are jammed with people all day.

For bar options, try the small jazz club **Petit Chicago** (50 promenade du Portage, 819/483-9843, $10 cover charge), whose name is a direct reference to Hull's busy jazz scene during the Prohibition years. The bar has live jazz music on Saturday nights. A more rambunctious choice is the **Bistro Bar** (104 Eddy, 819/772-1806), a popular spot with 30- and 40-something professionals during happy hour and with the younger crowd once the dance floor gets hopping later in the evening. Gatineau's best-kept secret are the Monday and Tuesday night happenings on the beautiful big terrace at **Café Aux Quatre Jeudis** (44 rue Laval, 819/771-9557). Sit outside, with your beer in hand, and once it gets dark enough, you'll be treated to a movie played on a wide outdoor screen. Even if you can't understand the language (most films are in French), it's still fun to soak in the atmosphere and do a little people-watching.

ACCOMMODATIONS

You don't have to spend a fortune to find a good place to stay in Gatineau. There are many good choices that are centrally located.

$50-100

À La Maison Ancestrale (227 rue Laurier, 819/771-0770, $75 d) is a four-room, sans-pomp B&B that is all about the location. It's just down the street from the tourist office and across the street from the Ottawa River at Parc Jacques-Cartier. **Möyfrid's B&B** (43 rue Millar, 819/772-8557, www3.sympatico .ca/moyfrid, $65 d) offers a friendly ambience with three very simple rooms. In the summer, breakfast is served on the deck with a view of the beautiful gardens. Named after the founder of the city of Gatineau, **Couette et Café Le Philémon** (47 rue Dumas, 819/776-0769, www.lephilemon.com, $80–105 d) is a four-star, three-room, modern B&B that is known for its gourmet breakfasts and cute rooftop patio. If you are traveling with children or a group, try the Université du Québec's **(Les Residences Taché** (283 boulevard Alexandre-Taché, 819/595-2393 or 800/567-1283, ext. 2393, $95 d). Comfortable two- to four-bedroom student apartments with kitchenettes are made available to visitors during the summer. Naturally, the décor is bare bones, but you'll be right on the doorstep of Parc de la Gatineau.

$100-150

In the heart of Vieux Hull, **☖ Les Suites Victoria** (1 rue Victoria, 819/777-8899 or 800/567-1079, www.suitesvictoria.com, $90–155 d standard room, $119–195 d suite) is ideally situated for those who want to explore the city on foot. Recently renovated, the hotel's rooms are pleasant enough and come equipped with a kitchenette. **Auberge de la Gare** (205 boulevard Saint-Joseph, 819/778-8085 or 866/778-8085, www.aubergedelagare.ca, $99–145 d) is a 42-room hotel that is a little farther removed from the downtown core. The rooms are clean, if a little drab. A night's stay will get you a continental breakfast and free parking. Make your reservation online seven days before your arrival and save $10.

$150-200

Just west of Parc de la Gatineau is the area's very own "castle," **Château Cartier Relais Resort** (1170 rue Aylmer, 819/778-0000 or 800/807-1088, www.chateaucartier.com, $139–199 d standard room). Offering all the conveniences of a full-service resort, including a health spa, golf course, and tennis courts, the swank 129 rooms are done up in French stylings and offer high-speed wireless Internet. But if you really want to go all out, then make your way to the **Lac Leamy Hilton** (3 boulevard du Casino, 819/790-6444 or 866/488-7888, www.hilton-lacleamy.com, $169–219 d standard room), the casino's adjoining hotel. The ostentatious décor, luxurious rooms, and long list of amenities rival any fine Vegas establishment.

FOOD

With the recent revitalization of the old downtown core, trendy restaurants have been popping up around the tried and true. This area tends to be a zoo during the lunch hour when government workers flock to their favorite local restaurants. Plan to eat a late lunch to avoid the crowds.

Cafés and Bistros

Both the young and the young-at-heart enjoy the bohemian **Le Troquet** (41 rue Laval, 819/776-9595, 11:30 A.M.–2 A.M. daily, mains under $10). The menu features sandwiches and pasta dishes and killer martinis to wash it all down. If you have a sweet tooth, try **☖ L'Euro Bistro Café** (131 promenade du Portage, 819/777-9334, 7:30 A.M.–10 P.M. Tues.–Fri. and 8:30 A.M.–10 P.M. weekends, mains $8–15), where homemade chunky apple cake and banana cake are prepared à la French toast. On Tuesdays and Wednesday evenings its all-you-can-eat mussels and crispy, coated Belgian fries are a local favorite. If you're looking for simple, healthy fare, try **Café du Presse** (161 promenade Portage, 810/770-6006, 7 A.M.–10 P.M. Mon.–Thurs., 7 A.M.–8 P.M. Fri., and 9 A.M.–5 P.M. weekends), a bright, cafeteria-style spot with Internet access and friendly service. You can get a smoothie and a "presswich" for under $10.

French

Next door to Le Troquet is **L'Argoät** (39A rue Laval, 819/771-6170, 11 A.M.–2 P.M. Mon.–Fri. and 5:30–10:30 P.M. Mon.–Sat., mains less than $15), an authentic crêperie brétonne, whose owners pride themselves on having brought the flavor of Bretagne to Gatineau. If you're going to have only one fancy meal in Gatineau, opt for **☖ Café Henry Burger** (69 rue Laurier, 819/777-5646, www.cafeburger.com, 11:30 A.M.–2 P.M. Mon.–Fri. and 5:30–10 P.M. Sat.), a supremely stylish restaurant that has been serving award-winning French cuisine since 1922. Prices are not for the faint at heart (most mains between $25 and $40), but lunch is slightly more manageable (mains less than $20). And if you're planning a romantic soirée, reserve one of the private dining rooms for two upstairs. Reservations required.

INFORMATION
Tourist Information

Make the regional tourist office (103 rue Laurier, 819/778-2222 or 800/265-7822) your first stop when you arrive in Gatineau. You'll find the office easily on the northeast corner of rue Laurier as you descend the Pont Alexandra from Ottawa. The completely bilingual staff will help you navigate your way throughout the entire region. The office is open from 8:30 A.M.–8 P.M. daily June–early September and 8:30 A.M.–5 P.M. Monday–Friday and 9 A.M.–4 P.M. Saturday–Sunday the rest of the year. While you are there, make sure you pick up a Visitor Parking Pass, which will get you free parking at all the metered parking spots in the city.

GETTING THERE
By Car

A car is the most convenient method of transportation with an easy direct route between Montréal and Gatineau. Follow Route 40/417 westbound to Ottawa and once there take Exit 118 to the Macdonald-Cartier Bridge back into Québec. If you prefer a more leisurely route, take Route 17 and cross the Ottawa River via the Masson-Angers-Cumberland Ferry (dock is at the end of Cameron Street, 819/986-8180), which will take you to Route 148 in Québec. The ferry operates 24 hours a day year-round and costs $6.50 per car.

By Bus

The Voyageur bus leaves every hour on the hour 6 A.M.–midnight daily from Montréal Voyageur Bus Terminal (505 boulevard De Maisonneuve Est, 514/843-4231) to the Ottawa Bus Station (265 Catherine Street, 613/238-5900). This trip takes roughly 2.5 hours and costs $37 one-way, $75 return. Once you're in Ottawa, local transit can be taken to Gatineau via downtown Ottawa.

By Train

Another option is the train. VIA Rail has five trains departing daily from Montréal Central Station (895 de la Gauchetière Ouest) to Ottawa Central Station (200 Tremblay Road, 613/244-8289). The trip takes less than two hours. Fares range $28–45 one-way, $56–73 return, depending on advanced booking. From the Ottawa train station take the no. 95 bus to downtown Ottawa, where you can catch one of the Outaouais buses from Wellington or Rideau streets. A cab costs roughly $20.

Parc de la Gatineau

The star attraction of this part of the province is the beloved Parc de la Gatineau. With hundreds of trails, plentiful wildlife, numerous lakes, and easy access from Ottawa and much of the Outaouais region, the park is a favorite weekend escape for locals year-round. The park's forests are home to more than 60 varieties of trees, more than 230 different species of birds, and 54 species of mammals, making a wildlife sighting along any one of the park's paths a common occurrence.

The origins of the park date to 1937, when the Canadian government acquiesced to demands from the Federal Woodlands Preservation League to buy about 10,000 hectares of land to stop clear-cutting in the area. In 1950, the park was further enlarged. Today it spans more than 36,000 hectares and maintains a unique status in the country as the only federal park not managed by Parks Canada.

The obvious, and best, place to begin your park visit is at the **Gatineau Park Visitors Centre** (33 chemin Scott, 819/827-2020 or 800/465-1867, 9 A.M.–6 P.M. daily June–Sept., 9 A.M.–5 P.M. daily Oct.–May). It's only 15 minutes from downtown Gatineau; you can reach the center by heading north on Route 5 to Sortie 12 (Old Chelsea). Turn left onto rue Old Chelsea and follow it for less than a mile until you come to rue Scott. Turn right and the visitors center will be on your left. If you plan to explore any of the park's trails, make sure you pick up a detailed trail map for $4.95.

There's a second seasonal office (10 A.M.–5 P.M. Sat.–Sun. mid–May–Oct.) at the corner of boulevard Gamelin and promenade Gatineau. This spot marks the beginning of the Pioneer Trail, a good 1.3-km introductory hike into the park.

© JENNIFER EDWARDS

MacKenzie King had a thing for ruins.

While there are no fees to enter the park, there is a daily fee of $8 per car from mid-June to early September for access to the parking lots at Lac Meech, Lac Philippe, and Lac La Pêche.

SIGHTS
◖ MacKenzie King Estate

Tucked away in the heart of the park is the 100-year-old MacKenzie King Estate (72 and 75 chemin Barnes, 819/827-2020 or 800/465-1867, 11 A.M.–5 P.M. Mon.–Fri. mid-May–mid-Oct. and 11 A.M.–6 P.M. weekends and holidays, $8 per car). King, Canada's 10th prime minister, was an avid lover of the outdoors as well as a bit of an eccentric. His dynasty began when he bought a small piece of land on Lac Kingsmere in 1903 and built a cottage. Soon he bought up more land and eventually added three more cottages, a year-round residence, elaborate gardens, and a unique collection of restored ruins from Canada and abroad to his 231-hectare estate. When he died in 1950, King's entire Gatineau Hills property was turned over to the people of Canada per

his wishes. The restored estate is now available for public viewing, and, if you're in the mood for a spot of tea and an afternoon nibble, high tea is served at the **Moorside Tearoom** (819/827-3405, $21.95–29.95 for two) 3–5 P.M. on the terrace among the flowers.

Lookouts

For stunning views that don't require any huffing and puffing, make your way atop the Eardley Escarpment found at the very end of the promenade Champlain and you'll witness the meeting point between the Canadian Shield and the Great Lakes. Accessible from mid-May to October, the lookouts get very crowded in the summer, so consider visiting very early in the morning or in the early evening.

RECREATION
◖ Hiking

If hiking's your thing, you've come to the right place. Parc de la Gatineau is home to 165 km of trails, including seven trails that feature interpretation panels, highlighting key natural attractions in the area. For a scenic hike, try the **Lac Pink Trail** as it circles the—not pink, but turquoise—lake set among surrounding cliffs and dense forest. For the more adventurous and physically fit, the **Luskville Falls Trail** offers a challenging climb up the escarpment to the park's largest waterfall—especially beautiful in the spring when it's in full force.

Mountain Biking

First allowed in the park in 1990, mountain biking now has more than 90 km of dedicated trails—although debate still rages regarding the sport's effects on the natural environment. The season runs from mid-May to the end of November on designated trails only. Bike rentals are available at Lac Philippe for $8 per hour or $30 for the day.

Swimming and Other Water Sports

On a hot, sunny day, what could be more divine than a dip in a lake? Swimming is

OUTAOUAIS

THE SECRETS OF MEECH LAKE

In the heart of the southern part of Parc de la Gatineau lies the infamous Meech Lake, named after one of the first settlers in the hills, Reverend Asa Meech. Nearby, on the smaller, more private Harrington Lake, the Canadian government bought land in the 1950s and set up its own version of Camp David, an official country residence for the prime minister of Canada. Some believe it's because of this proximity that Meech Lake was chosen as the location of a series of volatile meetings held in 1987 between the premiers of Canada's 10 provinces and then-Prime Minister Brian Mulroney. The purpose of the discussions was to try to get Québec to agree to the patriation of the Constitution.

Québec's premier, Robert Bourassa, had a list of provisions he wanted put in place to ensure Québec's special status as a "distinct society." Although Brian Mulroney pushed to have Bourassa's provisions met, the controversial accord died within the three-year time limit when Manitoba held out on signing.

Le mouton noir, a riveting documentary film directed by Jacques Godbout, was released in 1992 about Québec's view of the whole affair.

Today there are few signs of the tensions that took place here in the 1980s; in fact, Meech Lake has become so laid-back it's now a favored gathering place of the Ottawa Naturists club.

permitted in three of the park's lakes: Philippe, Meech, and La Pêche. Lifeguards are on duty from 10 A.M.–6 P.M. every day from mid-June to early September. At Philippe and La Pêche, you can rent canoes ($10 per hour, $30 for the day), while single kayaks ($12 per hour) and double kayaks ($16 per hour) are available at Lac Philippe only.

Horseback Riding

At the foot of the Eardley Escarpment on the western edge of the park, this trail has been developed specifically for equestrians. It continues to grow in length and is now close to 25 km long. If you don't happen to have your horse with you, head to **Luskville Falls Ranch** (300 chemin Hotel de Ville, 819/455-2290, June–Oct., one hour $25/two hours $45) for a trail ride.

Bungee Jumping

Who knew that bungee jumping is still alive and well? Just on the outskirts of the park on Route 105 is "The Rock," an old quarry that sees a tremendous amount of action now that **Great Canadian Bungee** (819/459-3714 or 877/828-8170, www.bungee.ca, daily July–Aug., weekends May–June and Sept.–Oct.,

$90 bungee, $30 rip ride) has set up shop. This claims to be Canada's highest bungee jump.

Cross-Country Skiing

During the wintertime, Gatineau Park's 200 km of cross-country ski trails make it one of Québec's best destinations for the sport. Consult the official park trail map or get suggestions from the visitors center staff, who are excellent at recommending trails for every level of expertise. Cross-country skiers must buy a trail-access pass for $9 from one of the 16 parking lots or the visitors center. For ski rentals, head into Chelsea to **Gerry and Isobel's** (14 rue Scott, 819/827-4341) or **Greg Christie's Ski and Cycle Works** (148 chemin Old Chelsea, 819/827-5340), just up the road.

Camping

Camping ($25 tent site) is available at more than 280 campsites, 33 canoe-camping sites, and four winter camping sites. None of the sites has electricity. Reservations are needed and can be made starting in mid-February by calling 819/456-3494 or by mail to Lafleur de la Capitale (Québec),12 chemin Douglas, Chelsea, PQ, J9B 1K4.

GETTING THERE

The only way to get to the park is by car. To get to the park from Gatineau, take Pont MacDonald Cartier, which becomes Route

5. Exit at Old Chelsea and turn left on Chemin Old Chelsea. Then take a right onto Chemin Scott. Follow the signs to the information center.

Vicinity of Parc de la Gatineau

CHELSEA

The small village of Chelsea (pop. 6,500) is the gateway to the park and the choice retreat for a number of artists and ex-Ottawa residents who decided to turn their backs on city life and head for the hills. At once vibrant and laid-back, Chelsea is a great place to stop and pick up a packed lunch before journeying into the park or as an après-hike or ski destination to enjoy a meal and browse the artisan shops that dot the main streets.

Sights

There's no better way to soothe tired muscles after a day of hiking or skiing than with a soak at the outdoor **Le Nordik Scandinavian Spa**

(16 chemin Nordik, 819/827-1111 or 866/575-3700, www.lenordik.com). The area's newly opened adult-only spa is based on a 1,000-year-old Finnish tradition of alternating hot and cold with periods of relaxation for maximizing well-being. Unwind in the sauna, detoxify in the steam bath, lie under the rocky Nordic waterfall or beside two wood-burning fireplaces inside or out. Access to the baths is only $35 or combine it with a massage for $90–135—you'll be totally reenergized in just 2–3 hours without the usual day-at-the-spa expense. Open 10 A.M.–10 P.M. daily year-round, it supplies the towels, bottled water, and a lock. All you have to remember is your bathing suit.

OUTAOUAIS

© JENNIFER EDWARDS

Soak in the sun along Chelsea's main drag.

Food

For such a small town, there is a surprisingly good selection of eateries to choose from. Any hike—big or small—deserves to be rewarded with a homemade ice-cream cone from **La Cigale** (241 chemin Old Chelsea, 819/827-6060, 11 A.M.–10 P.M. daily, early spring–late Oct.). This friendly spot has all kinds of ice-cream flavors, but beware the afternoon lines on sunny days. For soups and gourmet sandwiches, try **Gerry and Isobel's Café and Boutique** (14 rue Scott, 819/827-4341, www.gerryandisobels.com, 9 A.M.–8 P.M. Tues.– Wed., 9 A.M.–9 P.M. Thurs.–Fri., 8 A.M.–9 P.M. Sat., and 8 A.M.–8 P.M. Sun., mains $7–10). Eat on the cottagelike porch or get a picnic lunch packed up to go. Vegetarians, or anyone in the mood for some good healthy food, will want to check out (**Café Soup' Herbe** (168 chemin Old Chelsea, 819/827-7687, 9 A.M.–9 P.M. Tues.–Sat., until 8 P.M. on Sun., mains $8–13) for either its yummy Asian-inspired Red Curry Thai or the hearty Mexican burrito. For finer dining and a cozy atmosphere, there's (**L'Orée du Bois** (15 rue Kingsmere, 819/827-0332, www.oreeduboisrestaurant.com, 5:30–10 P.M. Tues.–Sun., closed Sun. Nov.–Apr., mains $17–23). Tucked away in an old farmhouse, the restaurant serves French and regional cuisine, with a bargain four-course table d'hôte at only $30 per person.

A relatively new arrival on the Chelsea food scene is **Marché Old Chelsea Market** (www.marcheoldchelseamarket.ca, 9 A.M.–2 P.M. Sat. early June–early Oct.). Featuring the wares of local farmers, artisans, bakers, canners, and even musicians, this small but growing market changes locations annually but is always within walking distance of the town center.

Getting There

You can get to Chelsea from Gatineau by taking Pont MacDonald Cartier, which becomes Route 5. Exit at Old Chelsea.

(WAKEFIELD

Stretched out along the most scenic part of the Gatineau River lies the charming little town of Wakefield (pop. 2,000). Founded in 1830 by Irish, English, and Scottish immigrants, the town still has a decidedly Victorian feel thanks to its stately homes, well-preserved shops, quiet side streets, and the fact that English is still the majority language. A number of art galleries, restaurants, bakeries, and cafés line the main drag, River Road. And every day just in time for lunch, you'll be able to witness the picturesque scene of the Hull-Chelsea-Wakefield tourist train pulling into town.

Entertainment

One of the country's very best venues for folk, jazz, and blues music is Wakefield's very own **Black Sheep Inn** (753 chemin Riverside, 819/459-3228, www.theblacksheepinn.com, shows 9 P.M.–midnight, $5–25). Although the décor is nothing to write home about, the venue is renowned for hosting many of the country's best acoustic acts. For musicians, playing on the Black Sheep stage in front of its attentive and critical crowds is actually considered quite a prestigious event. Dress casually and plan on arriving before 8:30 P.M. to ensure you get a seat.

Accommodations

There are a number of good places to stay and eat in Wakefield. Try (**La Grange Country B&B** (37 rue Rockhurst, 819/459-3939, www.lagrangecountryinn.com, $80–130 d) for a bit of pure rural respite. The three rooms in this restored 1898 barn are bright, roomy, and possess a sparse Scandinavian design. There is an adjoining yoga studio, offering ashtanga, kripalu, power yoga, and somayog courses. The owners, a young couple from Toronto, are very accommodating and personable. In the heart of town is **Trois Érables B&B** (801 chemin Riverside, 819/459-1118 or 877/337-2253, www.lestroiserables.com, $119–189 d) a lovely neo-Queen Anne Victorian mansion, which dates to 1896, when it was built for the local doctor.

Converted into an inn in 1980, most of the five rooms still have the elegant estate feel of dark wood furnishings and lacy curtains. The front veranda is a privileged spot to relax. Wakefield's most prized overnight destination, however, is undoubtedly the **(Wakefield Mill Inn** (60 chemin Mill, 819/459-1838 or 888/567-1838, www.wakefieldmill.com, $102–128 per person with breakfast, $139–165 per person with breakfast and table d'hôte dinner). The converted 1838 stone mill, right on La Pêche Falls, has 26 rooms, many with whirlpool bathtubs and fireplaces, a cozy lobby and lounge with fireplace, couches, wood floors and stone walls, and a fine-dining restaurant called **Penstock** (mains $22–28, table d'hôte $38) that serves French and Québécois cuisine.

Food

For casual food options, try the **Wakefield Bakery** (813 chemin Riverside, 819/459-1528, 7 A.M.–7 P.M. daily), which sells sinfully delicious baked goods including to-die-for sausage rolls and cheese-and-onion bread. **(Chez Éric Café** (119 Valley Dr., 819/459-

3747, 9:30 A.M.–5 P.M. Mon., 9:30 A.M.–8 P.M. Wed.–Thurs., and 9:30 A.M.–9 P.M. Sun., specials $8–12) has gourmet vegetarian meals that are so popular they sell out. The one-room dining area can get a bit cramped, so if the weather's good, take your meal to go and sit next to the nearby brook.

Information

In the heart of town, just off Route 105, lies the tourist information center (878 chemin Riverside, 819/459-1709, www.villelapeche.qc.ca, 10 A.M.–6 P.M. Mon.–Thurs. and Sat., 10 A.M.–7 P.M. Friday, and 9 A.M.–5 P.M. Sun. late May–late Aug.). Stop here if you are looking for accommodations, but otherwise, you'll be able to find everything you are looking for.

Getting There

The only way to get directly to Parc de la Gatineau or Chelsea is by car, but there are a couple of other options if you're headed to Wakefield. Voyageur Bus has two departures daily from downtown Gatineau Bus Station (238 boulevard Saint-Joseph,

© JENNIFER EDWARDS

La Cigale, the best ice cream in the Outaouais

OUTAOUAIS

819/771-2442, adults one-way $9, return $17). The trip takes about 45 minutes. And, of course, during the summer and at limited times during the spring and fall, there is the H. C. W Stream Train.

MONTEBELLO

Positioned about halfway between Gatineau and Montréal along Route 148 lies the lovely village of Montebello (pop. 1,093). Unique among the villages in the Outaouais region, Montebello was the sole spot developed according to the French seigneurial system. Called La Petite-Nation after the Algonquin tribe that used to live there, the land was eventually bought by Monseigneur François de Laval in 1674. It was considered ill-suited to agricultural pursuits, and it wasn't until Joseph Papineau, a notary and politician from Montréal, bought the land in 1803 that it started to see an influx of settlers.

Sights

Park at the visitors center and it's a short walk to get to the **Manoir Papineau** (500 rue Notre

Dame, 819/423-6965 or 800/463-6769, www .pc.gc.ca/papineau, adults $7, youth $3.50, and family $17.50). Built in 1850 by prominent Canadian politician Louis-Joseph Papineau, son of Louis Papineau, the manor has been completely restored to its original grandeur by the heritage department of the Canadian government. Reflecting Papineau's refined tastes, the luxurious interiors of the home are open to visitors 10 A.M.– 5 P.M. daily starting in late June–late August, and 10 A.M.–5 P.M. Wednesday–Sunday in the shoulder seasons (mid-May–mid-Oct.). On the grounds, you'll also find the **Papineau Memorial Chapel** (819/423-5681, 10 A.M.– 5 P.M. daily June–Aug.), a small stone chapel where Papineau, his wife, father, and many of his descendants are buried.

◖ Fairmont Le Château Montebello

Another deep source of pride for Outaouais is the spectacular Fairmont Le Château Montebello (392 rue Notre-Dame, 819/423-6341 or 800/441-1414, www.fairmont.com, standard room $199–249 d). An architectural master-

Château Montebello

© JENNIFER EDWARDS

THE WORLD'S LARGEST LOG CABIN

A little bit of Switzerland brought to the forests of rural Québec – that was the thinking behind the massive log masterpiece known as Château Montebello. Inspired by the castles of the Swiss Alps, Swiss-American millionaire Hubert Saddlemire made his dream a reality with the help of Montréal architect Harold Lawson and Finnish master log builder Victor Nymark in 1930. Anxious to have the project finished in time to open during the summer season, Saddlemire was willing to sink in as much money as was required to make it happen.

Work began in March of that year with a team of 3,500 skilled craftsmen and laborers, who often worked around the clock to stick to schedule. The first job was to construct a link from the Montréal-Ottawa train line, so that the logs imported from British Columbia could make it to the site. There were 10,000 giant red cedar logs that went into constructing the Château. Unbelievably, each one had to be cut and set by hand.

In a remarkable engineering triumph, Saddlemire got his wish and his château was completed in just four short months, making headlines around the world. It was initially used as the private retreat of the Seigniory Club, whose hoity-toity membership included the Canadian business elite and politicians such as former Canadian Prime Minister Lester B. Pearson. International members included Juliana of the Netherlands and Princess Grace and Prince Rainier. It officially became the Château Montebello in 1970 when Canada's famous hotel conglomerate, Canadian Pacific Hotels, took it over.

OUTAOUAIS

piece, the star-shaped building was built in a legendary timeframe of less than four months. Constructed of 10,000 red-cedar logs shipped from British Columbia, the building stands as the world's largest log construction. Even if you don't stay here, a short visit is highly recommended. If you're around in the winter, sink back into one of the couches in front of the Château's famous six-sided fireplace with a hot toddy from the lobby bar. If you're around in summer, tour the lovely grounds or buy a day pass to get access to the tennis courts, bikes, and outdoor swimming pool.

Information
As you enter the village, you'll find the visitors center (502A rue Notre-Dame, 819/423-5602, 9 A.M.–7 P.M. daily July–Aug. and 9 A.M.–6 P.M. daily Sept.–June) on your right just past the entrance to the Château Montebello. Housed in the former train station, the cedar-log building is an attraction in itself.

Getting There
To get to Montebello from Montréal, take Route 40, which turns into Highway 417 as you dip into Ontario. About 10 km after the border, take the Hawkesbury Exit, which will lead you to Route 17. Turn right on rue Tupper and follow it to the end. Turn left, then turn right at the first traffic light and cross the bridge. Continue until you hit Route 148 where you'll turn left and eventually pass through the village of Montebello. After the junction of Route 323, you'll see the Château Montebello gates on your left.

If you're coming from Gatineau, take Pont MacDonald-Cartier and then Exit 2 so that you'll be on Route 50 Est toward Gatineau-Montréal. Continue until you come to the rue George Exit. Take it and you'll find yourself on Route 148 Est. Take this road until you get to the main Château Montebello entrance, right before you hit the village of Montebello.

THE LAURENTIANS

As you drive north from Montréal, past the remnants of the city sprawl, the alpine splendor of the 22,000-square-km territory known as the Laurentians (or les Laurentides in French) starts to take shape. Ski hills that seem to spill onto the highway give way to dense forests, gleaming lakes, and picturesque Swiss-flavored towns. This is the Laurentians, the ancient mountain range where Montrealers go when they say they're "headin' up north" or "goin' up to the cottage."

One of Québec's most frequently visited regions, the Laurentians' hilly nature gave rise to some of North America's earliest ski resorts. Today, it contains the highest concentration of skiable hills in North America, including the famed Mont-Tremblant. But the Laurentians aren't just a winter ski desti-

nation. The region's more than 6,000 lakes and rivers are perfect for canoeing, kayaking, or a leisurely swim, its craggy cliffs make for some of the best rock climbing in eastern Canada, and its 200-km former train line, called the Parc Linéaire du P'tit Train du Nord, has been converted into a picturesque, popular multi-purpose route, particularly useful for cyclists.

Although year-round residents and long-time cottagers lament the commercialization of places such as Saint-Sauveur and Mont-Tremblant, two spots that have seen huge amounts of development in recent years, there are still plenty of less touristy towns to explore, such as Morin Heights and Val-David, and many spots where quiet still reigns supreme. The best times to visit the area are in September and early October, once the kids are back in school

© JENNIFER EDWARDS

HIGHLIGHTS

((P'tit Train du Nord: Once used to carry city slickers to the slopes, this former train line is now a fantastic 200-km-long linear park, extending from Saint-Jérôme to Mont-Laurier (page 118).

((Saint-Sauveur Water Slides: Come summer, this town's glistening, winding, sparkling-blue water slides are an oasis of spills and thrills (page 122).

((Val-David: Jocks and artists mingle in this picturesque village that is home to fabulous rock climbing and a unique summertime festival called 1001 Pots (page 129).

((Station Mont Tremblant: Challenging? Maybe. Impressive? Absolutely. The biggest ski hill in the East has a stellar view and more ways to come down the mountain than you can imagine (page 134).

((Parc National du Mont-Tremblant: The province's biggest national park is a mind-boggling 1,510 square km and a prime destination for canoeing and kayaking trips in the summer and snowshoeing or a cross-country ski jaunt in the winter (page 143).

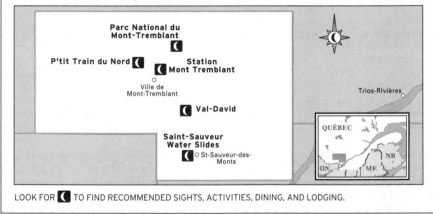

LOOK FOR **((** TO FIND RECOMMENDED SIGHTS, ACTIVITIES, DINING, AND LODGING.

and the fall colors are out, and in January and February before the ski rush that happens during March break.

Official tourist brochures will tell you that the Laurentians begin as soon as you cross the bridge from Laval, but the real Laurentians, those of the mountains, villages, resorts, and lakes, actually start with Saint-Sauveur and extend all the way up to Mont-Tremblant.

PLANNING YOUR TIME

Determining the length of your Laurentians stay depends on the type of trip you want to do. If you're traveling from Montréal, a ski visit or a quiet cottage stay can certainly be done in

the space of a weekend, but it won't give you time to do any additional sightseeing. If you have time for a longer visit, are touring by car, and want to get a true taste of the Laurentian heartland, then plan on at least five days.

Spend a couple of nights in **Saint-Sauveur,** either skiing or water sliding and enjoying the restaurants and shopping in town. Then head off to **Morin Heights** for a wander around the village, a picnic lunch and, if you're feeling the need for relaxation, a soak and massage at the beautifully rustic **Spa Ofuro.** Later in the afternoon, make your way to **Sainte-Adèle** or **Val-David** for dinner and your third night's stay. The next morning venture north to **Sainte-Agathe** and if you're there in summer, idle by **Lac des Sables**. After that it's up to **Tremblant** for two nights. There's no shortage of things to do there, including skiing or hiking, perusing the resort's shops, and making a jaunt up to **Parc National du Mont-Tremblant** for a quick introduction to the rugged, wild heart of the region.

A car is the transportation method of choice to explore the region, permitting you to motor along the autoroute or take the parallel and more leisurely Route 117, which touches on most of the Laurentians' more attractive towns. A car will also permit you to take some of the back roads into cottage country to get a glimpse of how the people who call this place their second home live. But for long-haul cyclists and cross-country skiers, there's also the **Linear Park**, which provides an excellent way to experience the Laurentian outback and many of its towns.

HISTORY

Despite its proximity to the city, settlement of the Laurentians was slow going because its mountainous nature made it ill-suited to farming. It was really only toward the latter half of the 19th century, thanks to the tireless exploration and campaigning by one Curé Antoine Labelle, the parish priest of Saint-Jérôme, that townships began to pop up. Known as the "King of the North," Labelle undertook a massive plan of colonization, hoping to attract his fellow French Catholics to their "promised land" and put an end to any risk of English Protestant expansion.

Labelle's proudest and most significant moment came with the realization of a railway link from Montréal to Saint-Jérôme in 1876. Convincing the government to extend the line north had been a frustrating task, but when Montréal experienced a firewood shortage one winter, the ever-enterprising Labelle organized a wood-collecting team and shipped the load off to the city's poorest families. In thanks, the City of Montréal contributed a cool million dollars to Labelle's train line.

Further expanded to Sainte-Agathe in

1891, a year after Labelle died, the railway line, known as le P'tit Train du Nord, was the beginning of the tourism boom in the Laurentians. Montrealers in search of clean air, scenery, and a little lake swimming started coming up, staying in boardinghouses run by local women. Later, they packed the train with their weekend bags and wooden skis to frolic on the ski hills of Saint-Sauveur, Val-David, Sainte-Agathe, and Mont-Tremblant when skiing became a must-do and must-be-seen-doing activity for the city's fashionable. By the end of the 1920s, the Laurentians had more than 1,600 km of downhill ski trails and by the end of the 1930s, trains were carrying upward of 25,000 skiers a weekend to the slopes.

◖ P'TIT TRAIN DU NORD

Immortalized in song by Québec's great troubadour, Félix Leclerc, le P'tit Train du Nord became a mythical and intangible part of the province's folklore. It was a bittersweet moment for many Quebecers when Curé Labelle's beloved train line closed in 1989 after losing customers to the convenience of the new highways.

Once the tracks, which extended from Saint-Jérôme all the way to Mont Laurier, were lifted, a group of enterprising residents started lobbying the government for a park. Heeding the call, the government converted the old train stations into rest stops, groomed the trails, and officially opened the 200-km **Parc Linéaire du P'tit Train du Nord** (450/224-7007 or 800/561-6673, www.laurentides.com, summer children 17 and under free, adults $5, winter children 17 and under free, adults $7) in 1996. By year-end 1997, the park had already managed to attract more than 1 million people. Today, the park welcomes about 400,000 cyclists per year.

The park is divided into three main sectors that become slightly more challenging and less busy as you climb. The first sector, called **Rivière-du-Nord & Pays-d'en-Haut,** is the shortest, extending only 33 km from Saint-Jérôme to Sainte-Adèle. The **Laurentides**

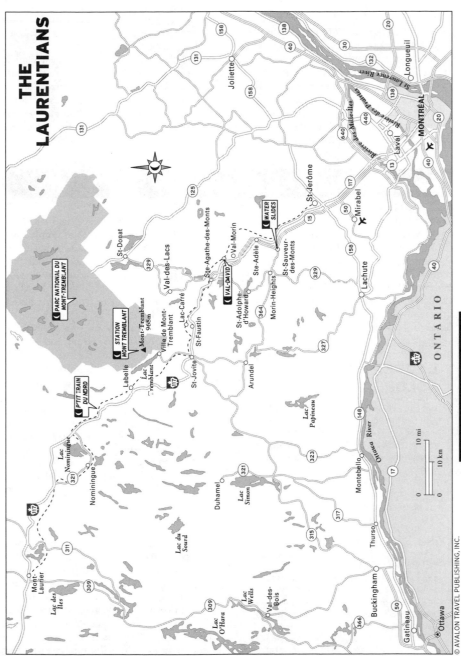

THE LAURENTIANS

PARC NATIONAL DU MONT-TREMBLANT

STATION MONT TREMBLANT

WATER SLIDES

VAL-DAVID

P'TIT TRAIN DU NORD

Joliette

St-Donat

St-Jérôme

Mirabel

Lachute

Val-des-Lacs

Ste-Agathe-des-Monts

Val-Morin

Ste-Adèle

St-Sauveur-des-Monts

Morin-Heights

St-Adolphe-d'Howard

Lac-Carré

St-Faustin

Ville de Mont-Tremblant

Mont-Tremblant 968m

Labelle

Lac Tremblant

St-Jovite

Arundel

Lac Papineau

Lac Nominingue

Nominingue

Duhamel

Lac Simon

Mont-Laurier

Lac des Îles

Lac du Sourd

Val-des-Bois

Lac Wells

Lac O'Hara

Montebello

Thurso

Buckingham

Gatineau

Ottawa

Ottawa River

St. Laurence River

Rivière des Prairies

Rivière des Mille-Îles

MONTRÉAL

Laval

Longueuil

ONTARIO

THE LAURENTIANS

10 mi

0

10 km

0

© AVALON TRAVEL PUBLISHING, INC.

sector is next at 74 km, running from Val-Morin to Labelle. The **Antoine-Labelle** sector from Ville de Rivière-Rouge to Mont Laurier is the longest and most wild at 93 km. The trail is largely flat, but it's still the best way for a cyclist or a cross-country skier to take in the Laurentians. It passes through every major town in the heart of the Laurentians, allowing participants to stop for a stroll, lunch, or a night's sleep. It's also a full-service trail, which means that advance arrangements can be made for overnights, shuttle service, and for hauling your luggage between stops.

If you plan to go for more than just a quick jaunt, pick up the official guide to the park by Association Touristique des Laurentides. It chronicles all the restaurants, bike shops, inns, banks, etc. along the route. You can get the guide at any of the tourist information centers or online at www.laurentides.com.

Saint-Sauveur-des-Monts

Québec skiing was born in Saint-Sauveur (pop. 8,151). Although its first major push came when the ski train pulled into town, it was thanks to an American industrialist named Fred Pabst—he of Milwaukee Brewery fame—who installed the first permanent ski lift on Sauveur's Hill 70 in 1934, that the area really became eastern North America's hot spot for skiing.

LAURENTIAN COLORS

Almost every kid in Canada born after 1951 has drawn a picture using Laurentien (spelled the French way) pencils. Instantly recognizable by the label, which featured a cozy snow-covered cabin with a smoking chimney, set in among the mountains, the multicolored pencils became a must-have item on every student's back-to-school list.

Eventually a fall cabin scene with green, red, and orange foliage was used on the pencil packs so as to better reflect the range of colors inside.

Today's Laurentien products, which now include fancy items such as gel markers and scented pencils, feature the landscape artwork only on the back panel of the package... But you'll still catch adults getting wistful when they catch a glimpse of the Laurentian scene.

Today, with its alpine-meets-Victorian architecture, winding main drag, and dominating silver-spired church, Saint-Sauveur has managed to hang on to its village charm despite the ongoing popularity of its five major ski hills (Mont Saint-Sauveur, Mont Avila, Mont Gabriel, Mont Olympia, and Mont Habitant). A major hangout for the après-ski crowd, Sauveur's rue Principale swarms with people checking out the bars, restaurants, shops, and, of course, each other. Still, it's a magical place at night, with its mounds of snow, buildings decked out in lights, and the golden aura emanating from its hills for nighttime skiing.

Although famed as a ski town, Saint-Sauveur is just as busy during the summer because of its position as the gateway to cottage country and its oasis—or frenzy—of water parks, popular with sweltering families from Montréal. Rue Principale gets fairly choked with traffic, so you are best to leave your car parked and do as much on foot as you can.

SKIING

The Saint-Sauveur Valley, Québec's first major ski destination, is still a great spot for skiing and is less expensive than its showier cousin, Tremblant. While the hills are pretty small in comparison to those in the eastern townships, Sauveur's hills are known for their services, package deals, and great family skiing. With the exception of Mont Habitant, all of the hills (along with Ski

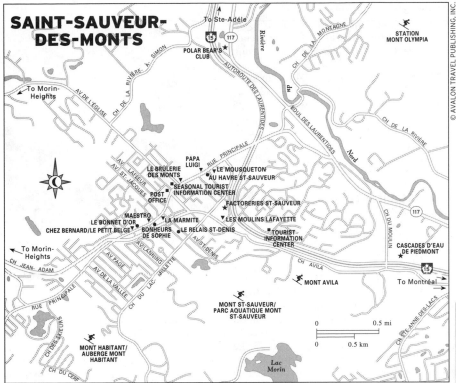

SAINT-SAUVEUR-DES-MONTS

Morin Heights and Ski Mont Gabriel) are owned by MMSI (Mont Saint Sauveur International). All of these are linked by a shuttle and are open 9 A.M.–10:30 P.M. Monday–Friday, 8:30 A.M.–10:30 P.M. on Saturday, and 8:30 A.M.–10 P.M. on Sunday.

Mont Avila

At Mont Avila (500 chemin Avila, 450/227-4671, www.montavila.com, adult weekdays four-hour block/full day $22/$27 and weekends $31/$36, children 6–12 weekdays four-hour block/full day $17/$20 and weekends $22/$25, and students 13–25 weekdays four-hour block/full day $20/$23 and weekends $27/$32), what it's lacking in height, it makes up for in fun. The hill is best known for its **snow park** (www.montsaintsauveursnowpark.com), which

features an Olympic-size half-pipe, 15 tubing runs, two snow-rafting trails, snowshoeing, ice-skating, and a sugar shack. There are a boutique and repair shop on site.

Station Mont Olympia

A good choice for families and beginner skiers, Station Mont Olympia (330 chemin de la Montagne, 450/227-3523, www.montolympia.com, adult weekdays four-hour block/full day $22/$27 and weekends $31/$36, children (6–12) weekdays four-hour block/full day $17/$20 and weekends $22/$25, and students (13–25) weekdays four-hour block/full day $20/$23 and weekends $27/$32) has one of the best ski schools in the province, offering private and group lessons. The mountain has 23 trails with more than half in the beginner category.

Mont Saint-Sauveur

Claiming the longest ski season in Québec, Mont Saint-Sauveur (350 Saint-Denis, 450/227-4671, www.montsaintsauveur.com, adult weekdays four-hour block/full day $33/$38 and weekends $38/$44, children 6–12 weekdays four-hour block/full day $21/$24 and weekends $25/$28, and students 13–25 weekdays four-hour block/full day $28/$32 and weekends $31/$36) also has the Laurentians' most modern lifts with four that are high-capacity. The vertical drop is 213 meters. There are five black diamond runs here.

Mont Habitant

Mont Habitant (12 boulevard des Skieurs, 450/227-2637 or 866/887-2637, www.mont-habitant.com, adult weekdays four-hour block/full day $33/$38 and weekends $38/$44, children 6–12 weekdays four-hour block/full day $22/$26 and weekends $30/$34, and students weekdays four-hour block/full day $17/$22 and weekends $26/$31) is kind of like the neighborhood ski hill. It's small and friendly with only 11 trails and the smallest vertical drop in the valley at 168 meters. But the hill isn't really out to impress as much as it is to prove itself a good place to learn to ski. There are a number of skiing and snowboarding courses on offer for all levels, including introductory private lessons available for $41 per session. There's a snow school on-site and day care. It's open 9 A.M.–10 P.M. Monday–Friday and 8:30 A.M.–10:30 P.M. Saturday–Sunday.

SIGHTS AND RECREATION
◖ Water Slides

In the summertime, Saint-Sauveur turns into water park central with visitors trading in their skis and snowboards for bathing suits and inner tubes. The **Parc Aquatique Mont Saint-Sauveur** (350 rue Saint-Denis, 450/227-4671, www.parcaquatique.com, 10 A.M.–7 P.M. daily June–Sept., admission full day/half day/night children 3–5 $14/$12/$12, 1.39 meters and under $25/$21/$14, 1.40 meters and taller $29/$24/$17) has various slides with names

Mont Habitant

© JENNIFER EDWARDS

such as the Niagara, which has a 35-meter vertical drop, the Twisters, a series of stomach-turning spirals, and the Tandem River, a two-person ride. There are also a wave pool and standard pool for more relaxing soaks. If you're seeking a more adventurous water experience, try the **Cascades d'Eau de Piedmont** (222 chemin des Cascadelles, 450/227-4671, www.cascadesdeau.com, 10 A.M.–4 P.M. mid-June–late June and mid-Aug.–late Aug. and 10 A.M.–7 P.M. daily late June–mid-Aug., admission full day/half day children 3–5 $10/$8, children 6–12 $14/$12, adults $21/$17), which you'll spot from the highway thanks to its giant water faucet. This water park has 16 slides, including the superfast and steep Kamikazes, the Tunnel, which has you sliding in the dark, and a four-person rafting slide.

Polar Bear's Club

If water slides aren't quite your speed, there the Polar Bear's Club (930 boulevard Des Laurentides, 450/227-4616, 11:30 A.M.–9 P.M. daily, admission $25 and up), a Scandinavian-style spa. Sessions usually start with a sauna, then a chilling dip in the Rivière à Simon, followed by a steam bath and another jump in the river. Although it's situated right by the highway, there's enough of a rustic feel to the place to give it the semblance of being more secluded.

Factoreries Saint-Sauveur

If the rural landscape has you yearning for a big-city fix, go to the Factoreries Saint-Sauveur (100 rue Guindon, 450/227-1074, www.factoreries.com, 10 A.M.–6 P.M. Mon.–Wed., 10 A.M.–9 P.M. Thurs.–Fri., and 10 A.M.–5 P.M. Sat.–Sun.), a cluster of outlet stores, including Tommy Hilfiger, Nike, Guess, and Jones of New York, that promise clothing-hounds a savings of 20 percent to 70 percent.

Festival des Arts de Saint-Sauveur

The 10-day **Festival des Arts de Saint-Sauveur** (228 rue Principale, suite 201, 450/227-0427, www.artssaintsauveur.com, tickets $27–52) is one of the biggest and best happenings in the Laurentians come summer. Classical and contemporary dance troupes intermingle with musical groups from all around the world, descending on Saint-Sauveur in late July to early August. There is a competitive aspect to the festival: Choreographers compete for top prize, as do musical composers for dance. Although some shows are free, other require tickets, which you can buy at the kiosk in Filion Park or by phone reservation at 450/227-9935. You can also buy them from the website or at the Big Top two hours before the show.

ACCOMMODATIONS
$50-100

If you're skiing, try the **Auberge Mont Habitant** (12 boulevard des Skieurs, 450/227-2637 or 866/887-2637, $90 d). These aren't the quietest of accommodations, but the rooms are comfortable and have cable TV and kitchenettes. Right on Saint-Sauveur's main drag is 【 **Les Bonheurs de Sophie** (342 rue Principale, 450/227-6116 or 877/227-6116, www.lesbonheursdesophie.com, $85–110 d,

suite $160 d), another great choice that is worth considering for its backyard alone. Pretty gardens surround a round pool with a view of the ski hill in the distance. Rooms are wood-paneled and feel like a cottage.

$100-150

Arguably one of the most charming B&Bs in the province, the cozy 【 **Le Bonnet d'Or** (405 rue Principale, 450/227-9669 or 877/277-9669, www.bbcanada.com/bonnetdor, $100–140) is a true find. Each one of the five bedrooms in this 1888 ancestral home has a private washroom and is tastefully decorated with rustic Victorian style: plush queen-size beds with quilted covers, soft lighting, lace curtains, and period artwork. Wake up in the morning to a gourmet three-course breakfast served in the dining room/salon by the accommodating and discreet owners. Another good B&B option in town is the new **Au Havre Saint-Sauveur** (112 rue Principale, 450/227-9393, www.auhavrestsauveur.com, $100–160 d). There are four rooms and one suite to choose from here. Although the place is so new it lacks that cozy, lived-in feel, the rooms are bright and clean and the hosts accommodating and friendly.

$150-200

With flower gardens, a heated outdoor pool, and a wooded setting, the Victorian **Le Relais Saint-Denis** (61 Saint-Denis, 450/227-4766 or 888/997-4766, www.relaisstdenis.com, $180–200) is a lovely retreat. The selection of rooms is divided between standard rooms (private bath, fireplace) and junior suites (featuring murals with various themes such as nautical, space, nature, and so on, whirlpool baths, and separate living rooms). There's a restaurant on the premises called the Queen Victoria that, thankfully, doesn't serve pot pie but four-course French cuisine.

FOOD
Specialty Food Stores

There may be nowhere to sit at the sumptuous 【 **Chez Bernard** (411 rue Principale,

450/240-0000, 10 A.M.–7 P.M. Mon.–Thurs., 10 A.M.–8 P.M. Fri., 10 A.M.–6 P.M. Sat., 10 A.M.–5 P.M. Sun., take-out mains $6–11), but that shouldn't stop you from sampling the wares. This high-end food store carries all the best Québec cheeses, desserts, jams, pasta sauces, vinaigrettes, and a wide array of individually prepared dishes to go, including lasagna, duck à l'orange, saffron seafood paella, and homemade shepherd's pie. Have a peek in the back of the building at **Le Petit Belge** (411A rue Principale, 450/227-2777, www.lepetitbelge.com) and you'll think you'd made a detour for Belgium. This store carries truffles, cookies, beer, and pralines, as well as CDs, books, and comic strips featuring everyone's favorite Belgian, Tintin.

Cafés

If you're out shopping at the Factoreries, you can take a load off at **Les Moulins Lafayette** (105F rue Guindon, 450/227-7725, 7:30 A.M.–7 P.M. daily, lunch special $6.95), a bakery, deli, pastry shop, and café all rolled into one. Try the daily lunch special, which comes with your choice of a sandwich such as a ham and cheese panini or pork foccacia, salad or soup, and dessert or coffee. The friendly and low-key **(Le Brûlerie des Monts** (197 rue Principale, 6:30 A.M.–close Mon.–Sat., 7 A.M.–close Sun., mains $6–11), right beside the church on the main drag, is the place to go for coffee aficionados. There are more than 100 different ways to drink your java here, from the straightforward to the absolutely decadent. There is also a good selection of salads, panini, sandwiches and soups, and desserts.

Restaurants

The self-proclaimed trendiest restaurant in Saint-Sauveur is **Le Mousqueton** (120 rue Principale, 450/227-4330, 5:30 P.M.–close Tues.–Sat., mains $11–36). Known for its artfully presented wild game (caribou, bison, elk) dishes, its sleek, minimalist décor, and friendly wait staff, this restaurant reflects the personality of its youthful chef Nicolas Ferenczy.

La Marmite

Try local favorite **Papa Luigi** (155 rue Principale, 450/227-5311, 5 P.M.–close daily, table d'hôte $15–44) for seafood, steak, and, of course, a multitude of pasta dishes. There's a surprisingly good wine selection here. The service is friendly and the prices are reasonable. Look for the log cabin on main street and you'll find **La Marmite** (315 rue Principale, 450/227-1554, 5 P.M.–close, mains $20–35), a cozy place with a fireplace, blue and yellow–checked tablecloths, a small bar, and French dishes such as tarragon chicken, seafood puff pastry, salmon, and steak. On Sundays it serves a tropical breakfast. Attractive, youthful wait staff and a clientele of après-skiers make 【 **Maestro** (339 rue Principale, 450/227-2999, 5–11 P.M. Mon. and Wed.–Sun., mains $12–25) a good choice for those wanting to scope the room while eating dinner. The menu features tapas, pasta, steak, lamb, veal, and salmon and a wide selection of wines from all around the world. Try to arrive earlier in the evening, as this place gets packed as the evening wears on. There's nothing remarkable about the décor at 【 **Crêperie à la Gourmandise Bretonne** (396 rue Principale, 450/227-5434, 11:30 A.M.–9 P.M. daily, mains lunch $9–18, dinner $20–25), but this down-home, local favorite serves some of the best crêpes around. You can watch the chef making the crêpes as you wait for a seat in the dining room. There are a huge variety of crêpes to choose from.

INFORMATION AND SERVICES

There is one seasonal tourist office (450/227-2564) that is open in the summertime in Parc Filion on the main drag and a permanent one called the Bureau d'Accueil Touristique de Piedmont/Saint-Sauveur (605 chemin des Frênes, 450/227-3417 or 800/898-2127, 9 A.M.–5 P.M. daily, www.tourismepdh.org) in a cute little chaletlike building.

Les Presses du Monde (195 rue Principale, 450/227-7522) has a selection of English- and French-language newspapers, magazines, and tourist books.

GETTING THERE AND AROUND

It's only about a 45-minute drive from Montréal to Saint-Sauveur via Route 15 north to Exit 58, provided you aren't leaving Montréal on a Friday and returning on a Sunday when all the other Montrealers are. The bus is also a convenient option. It takes only about 1.5 hours and you can catch several daily buses operated by Limocar (514/842-2281, www.limocar.ca, $31 return) that leave from Station Centrale Montréal (505 rue de Maisonneuve Est) and wind up at the Pétro-Canada gas station (91 rue Guindon, 450/227-5446).

MORIN HEIGHTS

The pretty little town of Morin Heights (pop. 2,727), just about 5 km north of Saint-Sauveur, is a peaceful place with a quiet main drag, a wealth of lakes, a major ski hill, and some of the best cross-country skiing in the region. Settled by Irish and Scottish immigrants in 1855, the place became a stronghold of English—still in evidence today. This is also an artist enclave with a large number living in the general vicinity. Studio Morin Heights, a recording studio in town, has hosted many top artists through the years, including the Bee Gees, Céline Dion, the Police, Bryan Adams, David Bowie, Moist, and the Fugees.

Skiing

Ski Morin Heights (231 rue Bennett, 450/227-2020, www.skimorinheights.com, adult weekdays four-hour block/full day $22/$27 and weekends $31/$36, children (6–12) weekdays four-hour block/full day $17/$20 and weekends $22/$25, and students (13–25) weekdays four-hour block/full day $20/$23 and weekends $27/$32) has 23 trails and a 200-meter vertical drop. The hill also offers snowboarding, backcountry telemark skiing, and a wide network of snowshoe trails. A new network of glades covers 10 acres, while expert skiers and beginners alike are sure to enjoy its challenging tabletops, quarter-pipes, bank turns, spines, and more. Day-care service is available to people with a season pass or full-day ticket.

If Saint-Sauveur and Mont-Tremblant are known for their downhill skiing, then Morin Heights is best known as a mecca for cross-country skiers. Just like the P'tit Train du Nord, the **Aerobic Corridor** (winter 450/226-1220 and summer 450/227-3313, adults $7) is a multiuse trail that runs past lakes, streams, and rivers along a former train line. Not as flat or as busy as its cousin, the 60-km pathway, which runs northwest from Morin Heights to Saint-Rémi-d'Amherst, is best suited to inter-mediate-level cyclists and cross-country ski-ers. The welcome center, called the **Centre de Ski de Fond** (50 chemin du Lac-écho), sells tickets and maps and has a waxing room and parking for trail access. In addition to being the starting point to the Aerobic Corridor, the area around Morin Heights lays claim to more than 90 km of backcountry ski trails. Not groomed during the winter, the trails should be used only by more experiences skiers.

Sights and Recreation

Stop in at **Mickey's Store** (834 chemin du Village, 450/226-2401) for a slice of authentic Morin Heights life. Not much has changed inside since the 1960s, except that the store is now run by Mickey's husband (Mickey was a she) and her daughter. If you're not interested in picking up any of the Sorel boots it car-

ries, there's a small coffee bar and launderette on site. Make sure you stop by **Gourmet du Village** (539 chemin du Village, 450/226-7377 or 800/668-2314, www.gourmetduvillage.com) for a selection of gourmet gift products—mostly centered around Christmas, such as cider, hot chocolate and festive drink mixes—made locally in Morin Heights. For a truly Zen experience, get thee to **Spa Ofuro** (777 chemin Saint-Adolphe, 450/226-2442 or 877/884-2442, www.spaofuro.com, 11 A.M.–8 P.M. daily, baths $35), a Japanese-style spa with pagoda-style architecture set among the pines, just off Route 329. There are a sauna, steam bath, and outdoor hot tubs on-site and for the brave, access to the bracingly chilly water. The spa also offers body mas-sages, body sanding, algae wrapping, facials, and pedicures. Now that you've completely re-laxed, get your adrenalin pumping again with **Acro-Nature** (231 rue Bennett, 450/227-2020, www.skimorinheights.com, 10 A.M.–5 P.M. daily July–Aug., 10 A.M.–5 P.M. Sat.–Sun. Sept., and 10 A.M.–4 P.M. Sat.–Sun. Oct., children 8–11 $20, children 12–17 $25, adults $35, families $89). Opened in 2005, Ski Morin Heights's tree-top obstacle course features rope bridges, rickety ladders, and swaying foot bridges. Situated on the edge of the ski trails and accessible only by ski lift, the site offers stunning views.

Central Laurentians

As you head north from Saint-Sauveur you'll reach the Laurentians' most densely popu-lated region, starting with Sainte-Adèle, then the quieter twin "Vals"—Val-Morin and Val-David—and finally, the Laurentians' biggest center, Sainte-Agathe-des-Monts.

SAINTE-ADÈLE

Coming in at a close second for the Lauren-tians' biggest city, Sainte-Adèle (pop. 10,126) actually feels like two separate towns. The downtown core, in the lower part, is a rather unattractive assembly of shops, but take rue

Morin up the hill and you've got estate-lined streets, posh restaurants, attractive B&Bs, and the lovely Lac Rond—a hub of activ-ity during the Sainte-Adèle summer. The birthplace of Claude-Henri Ganon, one of Québec's best-loved authors, Sainte-Adèle was also the setting for his epic 1933 novel, *Un homme et son péché*, a tragic love story between two early settlers and the shrewd and rude town mayor who comes between them. Through the years, the story struck such a chord with Quebecers that it's been turned into a radio drama, a TV series, and

ARE YOU CALLING ME A SÉRAPHIN?

The town of Sainte-Adèle was immortalized in print when its most famous son, Claude-Henri Grignon, sat down to write *Un homme et son péché* in 1933. The book, which is based in a small town strikingly similar to Sainte-Adèle, chronicles the relationship between a stingy and miserable mayor named Séraphin Poudrier, a virtuous but poverty-stricken young woman, and the often-absent man that she loves.

Few books in in the province's history have struck such a chord, enthralling Quebecers with its tragic love story and its gritty portrayal of rural life. (Until then, life in small Québec towns had been depicted as nothing but romantic and rosy).

Sainte-Adèle's residents must have trusted that Grignon knew a thing or two about the dangers of greed and power after writing the novel when they voted him mayor in 1941. The name Séraphin didn't fare so well, though. Once a very popular boys' name, it has virtually disappeared since the book was published. The only time you'll hear it these days is when someone refers to another as "un vrai séraphin," a real penny-pincher in other words.

two films, most notably the 2002 version, starring Québec heartthrob Roy Dupuis.

You'll find the **information center** (1490 rue Saint-Joseph, 450/229-3729 or 800/898-2127) at Exit 67, just off Route 15.

Skiing
If you are here in the winter and want to do some skiing, you can rent ski equipment and use the trails at **Le Chantecler,** which has 23 trails served by eight lifts. Spread out over four hills, Le Chantecler is recognized for its ski school. Some of the trails end right by the main hotel. There's also **Ski Mont Gabriel** (1501 chemin du Mont Gabriel, 450/227-1100, adult weekdays full day $17 and weekends four-hour block/full day $28/$32, children 6–12 week-

days full day $11 and weekends four-hour block/full day $20/$22, and students 13–25 weekdays full day $17 and weekends four-hour block/full day $24/$27). One of the best mogul courses in the Laurentians, Ski Mont Gabriel has hosted a number of World Cup freestyle events. The hill has 18 trails, four of which are classified as extremely difficult.

Sights and Recreation
In the summertime, there's **Super Splash Sainte-Anne** (1791 boulevard Sainte-Adèle, 450/229-2909, www.supersplash.qc.ca, 10 A.M.–7 P.M. June–Aug., children 4–12 $10, adults $17, family of four $49). Although not as massive as some of the water parks near Sauveur, this place can also turn into a zoo on hot, sunny days. In addition to the slides, there are a wave pool, a climbing tower, minigolf, and volleyball nets. If it rains for more than 30 minutes during your visit, you'll get a free pass the next time you go. If you prefer more quiet and relaxation with your water experience, then head to **Station Santé Bagni** (1796 rue des Mélèzes, 450/229-4477 or 866/848-4477, www.spabagni.com, 11 A.M.–9 P.M. daily, $25 for bath access) for a soak in the marine salt swimming pool, a sweat in the Turkish steam bath or Finnish sauna, or if you're brave, a quick jump into the Rivière à Simon. There are also a restaurant and boutique on-site. The **municipal beach** (adults $4, children 5–14 $3) at Lac Rond is a good place to spend an afternoon. At night, you can catch a first-run English-langue movie at **Cinéma Pine Sainte-Adèle** (24 rue Morin, 450/229-7655, adults $10, children $7) or a classical music concert at the **Pavillon des Arts de Sainte-Adèle** (1364 chemin Pierre-Péladeau, 450/229-2586, www.pavillondesarts.com, tickets $25). Once an Anglican chapel, the pavilion is now a year-round concert venue.

Food and Accommodations
Bordered by the woods, ◖ **Aux Dormants du Boisé** (1420 rue du Valais, 450/229-1420 or 877/788-4483, www.auxdormantsduboise.com, rooms $75–85 d) is a

charming, rustic, Québécois-style B&B with three cozy rooms, a big living room downstairs with a stone fireplace, a veranda, outdoor whirlpool tub, beautiful gardens, and a pond. **Hôtel Chantecler** (1474 chemin Chantecler, www.lechantecler.com, 888/916-1616) is a good small hotel with a stellar setting on Lac Rond. While the 215 rooms aren't anything to write home about, they are clean and comfortable. There are also an indoor pool, health center, exercise room, and sauna. One of the best places to stay and dine is **((Auberge La Biche Au Bois** (100 boulevard Sainte-Adèle, 450/229-8064, www.labicheaubois.qc.ca, 6 P.M.–9:30 P.M. Wed.–Sun., table d'hôte $55, rooms $120–130 d with breakfast). This beautiful inn, next to Rivière à Simon, has five rooms that are nicely, but sparsely, decorated. There's a heated outdoor pool. The restaurant is beautiful with exposed wood beams and huge windows overlooking the surrounding forest. The menu includes classic French cuisine such as duck, foie gras, and smoked salmon, with elaborate plate presentation. Another great place to stay is the stunning **((À L'Orée du Bois** (4400 rue des Engoulevents, 450/229-5455, www.aloreedubois.com, rooms $89 d with breakfast). The owners' quarters are separate here, giving the place a more private air. The inside is beautiful with a stone fireplace and wood beam ceiling, comfy chairs, and large windows. There are only four rooms here and one studio apartment, but each is cozy and nicely decorated. The property too is lovely with access to a river, falls, and beautiful gardens.

Situated on Sainte-Adèle's main drag is one of Québec's most highly recognized small hotels and restaurants: **((L'Eau à la Bouche** (3003 boulevard Sainte-Adèle, 450/229-2991, www.leaualabouche.com, 6–9 P.M. daily, mains $35–44, standard room Sun.–Fri. $185 d, Sat. $225 d). It's part of the prestigious Relais and Châteaux circle, but while the hotel is beautiful—each of the 25 rooms has themed décor and is done up in rustic-meets-high-end colors and prints—people really come here for the cooking of chef Anne Desjardins, one of the province's most acclaimed chefs. The menu changes according to the season and fresh ingredients available. Eating here is an expensive endeavor, but if you decide to go all out, do it here. Cooking classes are also offered on-site.

Aux Tourterelles (1141 chemin Chantecler, 450/229-8160, mains $23–33, 5–10 P.M. Mon.–Fri. and 5–10:30 P.M. Sat.–Sun.) is another good choice for ambience and great food that stretches beyond classic French dishes. The place is dark and cozy inside. Try **Café de la Gare** (1000 rue Saint-Georges, 450/229-5886, 10 A.M.–6 P.M. Sat.–Wed., 10 A.M.–8 P.M. Thurs.–Fri., table d'hôte $20–23), a casual café along the P'tit Train du Nord, for world music, croque monsieurs, café au laits, and a selection of delectable fondues made with Québec cheeses for dinner. If you want to experience a typical French bistro, visit **Restaurant Les Délices de Mamie Nature** (996 rue Valiquette, 450/229-7965, 11:30 A.M.–11 P.M. daily May–Oct. and Tues.–Sat. Nov.–May, table d'hôte $16–29). It serves traditional French food such as roast duck with blueberry sauce and veal kidneys with mustard sauce, and Mamie still oversees the operation.

VAL-MORIN

There's not much going on in Val-Morin (pop. 2,286) beyond beautiful scenery and lots of circular breathing. Since 1963, the town has been home to the **Sivananda Ashram Yoga Camp** (673 8ième Avenue, 819/322-3226 or 800/263-9642, www.sivananda.org/camp), one of the longest-running ashrams in the West. Promoting the word of Swami Sivananda, a highly revered yoga master, the volunteer-run camp welcomes both beginners and advanced yoga practitioners. A usual day at the camp consists of rising at 5:30 A.M., followed by meditation, chant, yoga, meals, and karmic exercises—in other words, upkeep chores. People wanting to stay overnight can camp, sleep in the lodge, or bunk in cabins. There are daily drop-in classes ($9), a six-class beginner's course ($79), and four-week-long teacher-training courses ($1,950 if you camp). Another spot in Val-

Morin that ties in nicely with the yoga camp is **Earthshack** (5991 rue Morin, 819/322-7655), a bookstore and café along the main drag that specializes in used books, natural beauty products, fair-trade coffee, and vegetarian meals. There's a pretty municipal beach at **Lac Raymond** for an afternoon swim.

If you're looking for accommodations in the area but aren't big on the communal, yoga existence, you can also try the lovely **Far Hills Inn** (3399 chemin Far Hills, 819/322-2014 or 800/567-6636, www.farhillsinn.com, two nights $256 d, one dinner and two breakfasts inclusive). Surrounded by 500 acres of woodland, this lovely country estate hotel is famous for its ski lodge and 125 km of **cross-country skiing trails** (it's the largest private cross-country ski network in the Laurentians).

⟨ VAL-DAVID

With the P'tit Train du Nord running straight through the village center and many winter cross-country skiers and summer bikers making a stop in town for a meal or a drink, Val-David (pop. 3,800) is much more bustling than its neighbor, Val-Morin. This pretty town, built around the railway line, is an outdoors lover's mecca, with all the hard-body eye candy to match. Also known for its active art community, Val-David saw its first influx of artists when the Butte à Mathieu—the first folk music coffeehouse outside of Montréal—opened in 1959. You'll find the **tourist information center** (2501 rue de l'Église, 819/322-2900, ext. 236, or 888/322-7030, 9 A.M.–7 P.M. daily mid-June–Labor Day and 10 A.M.–4 P.M. daily Sept. 5–June 19) on the main drag.

Sights and Recreation
There's no excuse not do some form of exercise in Val-David. Recognized as eastern Canada's best rock-climbing location, the area immediately surrounding the village possesses more than 500 climbing routes. **Passe Montagne** (1760 Montée 2e rang, 819/322-2123 or 800/465-2123, www.passemontagne.com) is a store with everything a rock climber's heart could desire. It is also a school offering courses varying from day-long beginner lessons ($75 for a group of 3–6 people), two-day excursions

© JENNIFER EDWARDS

THE LAURENTIANS

The P'tit Train du Nord is a favorite of cross-country skiers.

($135), to more advanced offerings. There are also canoeing and kayaking opportunities on the shallow, slow-current Rivière du Nord, a 7.5-km waterway that flows from Val-David to Lac Raymond in Val-Morin. A great way to experience the river is to take advantage of the canoe/bike rental package offered by **Phénix Sport et Aventure** (2444 rue de l'Église, 819/322-1118 or 877/566-1118, www.phenixsport.com). The store will equip you with a canoe to make the trip down the river to Val-Morin and have a bike waiting for you so that you can make your way along the Linear Park back to Val-David. A second company, **Pause Plein Air** (1381 chemin de la Sapinière, 819/322-6880 or 877/422-6880, www.pause-plein-air.com, bike rental adult $7/hour, children $5/hour, bike/canoe package $44) also offers the service along with longer canoe trips. If you're up for hiking, the 15 km of trails at the **Parc Régional Dufresne** (www.leparcdufresne.qc.ca) offer diversified challenges. Operated by the communities of Val-David and Val-Morin, the park offers mountain and valley trails. Dogs are welcome and access is free.

1001 Pots

On the art side, Val-David is well known for its annual festival called 1001 Pots (2435 rue de l'Église, 819/322-6868, www.1001pots.com), the largest exhibition of ceramics in North America. Held for five weeks mid-July–mid-August, the festival is set up on the grounds in the park, with pots—mugs, bowls, tea pots, and so on—scattered absolutely everywhere. More than 100 artists attend the event and are on hand to answer questions and, of course, convince you that you absolutely need that ceramic goblet. Pottery courses are offered to the general public during the week.

Accommodations and Food

If you're thinking of sticking around in Val-David, there are some great places to eat and stay. Tents and trailers are welcome at **Camping Laurentien** (1949 rue Guertin, 819/322-2281, www.campinglaurentien.com, campsite $24), a four-season camping site with an artificial lake three km away from Val-David. A cute, Swiss-style B&B option is **La Maison de Bavière** (1470 Chemin de la Rivière, 819/322-3528 or 866/322-3528, www.maisondebaviere.com, $85–95 rooms d, breakfast inclusive, $125–140 suites d). Situated directly opposite the Rivière du Nord rapids, the B&B's six rooms—named after composers—are bright and spacious. There's 【 **La Sapinière** (1244 chemin La Sapinière, 819/322-2020 or 800/567-6635, www.sapiniere.com, standard room $286–350 d, suites and cottages $336–370 d), a well-known lakeside resort that has played host to many generations of Québec families. It was built by Val-David's first mayor in 1936, and the hotel's history has long been intertwined with the village's. La Sapinière's dining room has long been considered one of the best in the province, offering a delectable selection of French dishes, including rabbit with duck foie gras and venison with port and blueberries. The desserts, made by the full-time pastry chef, are exquisite, so make sure you save room. Far from high-brow, but just as delectable, is the famous 【 **Le Petit Poucet** (1030 route 117, 819/322-2246 or 888/334-2246, 8 A.M.–10 P.M. daily, table d'hôte $20–25), a rustic, checkerboard cloth–type restaurant that has been operating for more than 50 years. Presided over by chef Réjean Campeau, this beloved restaurant features cabane-à-sucre–style Québécois cuisine—meat pie, beans, and the best maple-smoked ham in the country. If you're looking for a big breakfast, choose the Ogre and you'll be presented two eggs, smoked ham, bacon, home-fried potatoes, beans with diced ham, and toast. For something slightly less artery-clogging, try **Le Grand Pa** (2481 rue de l'Église, 819/322-3104, mains $17–20, 11 A.M.–2 P.M. and 5–8 P.M.), a busy restaurant right near the tourist information center. The restaurant serves pasta and pizzas done in the wood-fired oven, along with meaty mains. The best thing about this place is its large terrace, a perfect spot to sit on a sunny afternoon with a pitcher of sangria.

SAINTE-AGATHE-DES-MONTS

Once considered the next Catskills, Sainte-Agathe-des-Monts (pop. 10,350), now the largest town in the Laurentians, was the region's first full-blown tourist resort. Wealthy Montrealers—many from the city's Jewish community—attracted by Lac des Sables and its sandy beach, built their cottages there, spending their summers idling by the lake. Because of its waterfront position and clean mountain air, once believed to be the cure to most illnesses, Sainte-Agathe became home in 1909 to a 12-bed tuberculosis facility named Mount Sinai. By 1939, the small treatment center expanded with demand and ushered in patients from all over. When the tuberculosis threat diminished in the 1950s, the center expanded its reach to treat all kinds of respiratory illnesses. In 1990 Mount Sinai moved to Montréal and is now considered one of the best hospitals for respiratory care.

Despite the idyllic setting, Sainte-Agathe's downtown core is a bit lackluster. It is bustling, but there's a small-town-anywhere feel, making it more of a stop for groceries and other errands than a tourist destination.

To get yourself oriented, drop by the **visitors center** (24 rue Saint-Paul, 819/326-0457 or 800/326-3731, www.sainte-agathe.org, 9 A.M.–8:30 P.M. summer, 9 A.M.–5 P.M. rest of the year) in a very pretty little former train station on the P'tit Train du Nord path.

Sights and Recreation

Beyond the three public beaches, there isn't a huge range of activities in this town. One of the best ways to spend an afternoon is aboard one of the boats operated by **Croisiéres Alouette** (public dock, 819/326-3656, www.croisierealouette.com, $12 adults, $5 children 5–15, daily departures mid-May–late Oct.). A 50-minute cruise around the perimeter of the lake, the *Alouette* features running commentary in French and in English on the historical sites, natural features... and the celebrities who live lakeside. If you want more control over your vessel, there's the **École de Voile de Sainte-Agathe-des-Monts** (public dock, 819/326-2282,

THE LAURENTIANS

Closed for the winter, Théâtre le Patriote welcomes Québec's best talent in the summer.

www.voilesteagathe.com), which offers varying levels of sailing lessons, including private, semiprivate, or small group classes. If
you're looking for a nighttime event, head
out to one of Québec's most treasured play-
houses: **Théâtre le Patriote** (258 rue Saint-
Venant, 819/326-3655 or 888/326-3655,
www.theatrepatriote.com). A simple white
clapboard building, decorated with the occasional fleur-de-lys, the theater is just outside of town on Route 15. Since 1965, it has
brought in some of Québec's best actors and
musicians and continues to do so every summer season.

Accommodations and Food

The best and most well-known campground in the area is called **Parc des
Campeurs** (819/324-0482 or 800/561-7360,
www.parcdescampeurs.com, tent site $24),
but if you're looking for something quiet,
you're best off somewhere else. This campground is massive with 549 campsites, a
restaurant, and numerous family-oriented
activities. **(Auberge Le Saint-Venant**
(234 rue Saint-Venant, 819/326-7937 or
800/697-7937, www.st-venant.com, rooms
$100–150 d) is a beautiful mountainside
B&B with unobstructed views of Lac des
Sables. The bright, spacious rooms are all
tastefully decorated in French Provençal
colors and have their own bathrooms. Also
possessing a good view of the lake, the
(Auberge de la Tour du Lac (173 chemin
Tour du Lac, 819/326-4202 or 800/622-1735,
www.aubergedelatourdulac.com, $100 d)

is a beautiful old century home originally
built by a nurse from New York who believed that there was nothing better than
the clean air of the Laurentians. The foyer,
salon, and wraparound veranda have retained their Victorian authenticity and the
rooms, although a bit on the small side, are
comfortable and clean. Massages are available on-site. The pretty **Auberge Manoir
d'Ivry** (3800 chemin Renaud, 819/321-0858,
www.manoirdivry.com) is right next to the
Linear Park and set in among the trees. Built
by France's count of Ivry in 1903, the inn has
nine guest rooms that are small but charming
and filled with period furniture. Bathrooms
are shared. Situated on the edge of the Rivière
du Nord, **Auberge La Sauvagine** (1592 route
329 Nord, 819/326-7673 or 800/787-7172,
www.lasauvagine.com, table d'hôte $38.50,
rooms $96–116 d weekdays and $116–136 d
weekends) is a good choice if you are looking
to stay put and relax. The inn's eight rooms
are elegant and comfortable, but the real reason people come here is for the food. In an
old chapel, **(La Sauvagine's restaurant**
featured dishes include duck, filet mignon,
and caribou prepared by owner and chef René
Kissler, who's from Belgium. Save room for
the hot-apricot-and-cinnamon mille-feuilles
for dessert. **Del Popolo** (1 rue Principale,
819/326-4422, mains $8–15) has two large
terraces (one downstairs, one upstairs), perfect for sitting out on a hot summer's day. Inside are a bar and dining room area serving
salads, soups, pasta and pizza, and various
meat dishes.

Ville de Mont-Tremblant

There was a time when Mont-Tremblant (pop. 9,000) was just like any other Québec village—there was a cluster of lakeside cabins without running water, a general store, Catholic church, and not much else... beyond a 650-meter mountain. Today Tremblant is a ski resort to rival North America's best, thanks to an enterprising and wealthy American from Philadelphia named Joseph Ryan. Although Ryan's original purpose in visiting the area in 1938 was to do some gold prospecting, he quickly became enamored with the place, especially with the stellar view from the mountain, and he vowed to turn the region into a world-class ski resort.

One year later, he opened the Mont-Tremblant Lodge and enjoyed a steady stream of visitors from Europe and all over North America. More inns opened in the area and the region enjoyed a steady stream of visitors. By the 1980s, however, things had slowed, business was drying up, and innkeepers were setting off for greener pastures.

In 1991, the winds of change started blowing through the region once again when Intrawest, Canada's biggest owner of ski resorts (it also owns Whistler), bought out the Ryan heirs and set out to build eastern Canada's biggest ski resort.

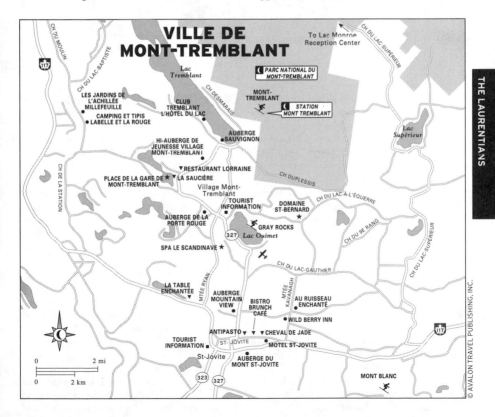

THE LAURENTIANS

© AVALON TRAVEL PUBLISHING, INC.

© JENNIFER EDWARDS

the colorful, steeple-dominated Station Mont Tremblant

To make matters thoroughly confusing, Ville de Mont-Tremblant, the municipal entity, is made up of three principal sectors. The first sector that you'll hit as you head north is **Saint-Jovite,** the administrative center with plenty of shops, restaurants, and bars along its main street, rue de Saint-Jovite. There's the **Village de Mont-Tremblant,** the picturesque old village set on Lac Mercier. And finally, there is **Station Mont Tremblant** (often called "the Resort"), which includes the ski hill and the lego-colored, Disneyesque pedestrian village packed with boutiques, restaurants, bars, and hotels at the base of the mountain.

SKIING

Of course, Tremblant is synonymous with skiing. You'd be forgiven for thinking that there was only one ski hill that matters in the region—the kingpin, Intrawest's Mont-Tremblant, of course—but there are actually two others that share the terrain: the historic Gray Rocks and the feisty Mont Blanc.

🄲 Station Mont Tremblant

Eastern North America's most famed ski resort is without a doubt **Mont Tremblant** (1000 chemin des Voyageurs, 819/681-3000 or 888/736-2526, www.tremblant.ca, 8:30 A.M.–3:30 P.M., adults $64.50, youth 13–17 $48, children 6–12 $37.50). What made this mountain a mammoth is its view—the one that originally convinced Joe Ryan that the place was worthy of a world-class ski resort—and the development dollars poured into it by its owner since 1991, Intrawest. The mountain has 94 runs (17 percent beginner, 33 percent intermediate, and 50 percent expert), a 645-meter vertical drop, and 13 lifts.

The snowboarding is equally impressive, with three different parks and an Olympic super-pipe. There are two different sides to the mountain. The north side, which has the better trail conditions because it gets minimal sun exposure, also features the only spot where you can sit down with your own lunch. The south side covers the most ground and offers a stunning view of the resort and direct access to the pedestrian village. There's a restaurant on the summit called **Le Grand Manitou** (819/681-3000), but if you prefer to bring and eat your own lunch, ski down the north slope to the heated chalet.

There's a free hourlong guided tour of the ski hill that happens twice a day at 9:30 A.M. and at 1:30 P.M. The tour will give you a good orientation of the mountain and resort as well as a rundown on local history. Register at Le Grand Manitou and meet at the summit's trail map.

Gray Rocks

The historic Gray Rocks (2322 rue Labelle, 819/425-2771 or 800/567-6767, www.grayrocks.com, 8:30 A.M.–4 P.M. daily, children 6–17 weekdays full day/half day $18/$18, weekends full day/half day $22/$22, adults weekdays full day/half day $22/$18, weekends full day/half day $27/$23) was the first recreational destination in the area. Today, its ski hill is considered the place to go for families and beginners and those looking for something a little quieter than Tremblant. The resort has a vertical drop of 189 meters and 22 trails (four beginner, 10 intermediate, and eight expert), used predominantly by guests staying at the rambling Gray Rocks Hotel. The ski hill is best known for its Snow Eagle Ski School—considered one of the best in North America—where you can get beginner as well as more advanced lessons in skiing and snowboarding.

Mont Blanc

It's got the second-highest elevation in the Laurentians, 39 trails, and a 300-meter vertical drop, but not the fairytale village, which means that Mont Blanc (1006 route 117, 819/688-2444 or 800/567-6715, www.ski-mont-blanc.com, 8:30 A.M.–4 P.M., children 6–12 weekdays full day/half day $20/$18, weekends full day/half day $23/$20, youth 13–20 weekdays full day/half day $26/$22, weekends full day/half day $31/$26, and adults weekdays full day/half day $29/$24, weekends full day/half day $37/$30) isn't half

as busy as neighboring Tremblant. Considered a skier's ski hill, Mont Blanc has challenging runs (14 difficult, 15 very difficult, and four extreme) and is considered to have one of the region's best offerings for snowboarders, with three dedicated slopes, rails, slides, and boxes. There's a day care on-site.

SIGHTS

To get the best view of the area, take the **Télécabine Panoramique Tremblant** (118 chemin Kandahar, 888/857-8043, 10 A.M.–4:30 P.M. weekends late May–late June, 10 A.M.–5 P.M. daily late June–mid-Oct. including 5 P.M.–9:30 P.M. early July–mid-Aug., adults regular season/fall colors $14/$17, children 6–17 regular season/fall colors $11/$14) all the way up to the summit and climb the 12-meter-high observation tower. You'll be rewarded with a spectacular 360-degree view.

Although it's about the only truly authentic-looking building in the resort, the beautiful, red-roofed **Chapelle Saint-Bernard** (chemin de la Chapelle), commissioned by Joe Ryan and his wife, Mary, is actually an exact replica of a 17th-century chapel once situated on Île d'Orléans. The Ryans, it seems, were so enamoured by an archival photo they found of the original chapel that they had it painstakingly rebuilt. Mass takes place at 11 A.M. every Sunday.

If you're an art fan or interested in local history, then head to **Place de la Gare de Mont-Tremblant** (1886 chemin Principale, 819/429-5529, 10 A.M.–5 P.M. daily except on Tuesdays), situated in the village's old train station, next to the P'tit Train du Nord. Resident artists are set up here and the walls are lined with new works and archival photos that chronicle the development of the mountain.

There are two **public beaches** in the area. One is the **Plage Municipale du lac Mercier** (100 chemin Plouffe) in the village and the other is **Plage de la Station Mont-Tremblant** (chemin de la Chapelle). Both have picnic tables and public washrooms, but the one at Lac Mercier has a lifeguard on duty.

SPORTS AND RECREATION
Centre d'Activités Mont-Tremblant

Right in the middle of the pedestrian village, the Mont-Tremblant Activity Center (Place Saint-Bernard, 819/681-4848, www.tremblantactivities.com, 9 A.M.–5 P.M. daily) acts as the reservations and information center for all the recreational activities, including **rock climbing, mountain biking, rafting, dogsledding, and snowshoeing,** happening at the resort and farther afield. It can be a crazy place with families clamoring for attention, but it's also a good place to get an idea of everything that's on offer. Many of the activities have buses departing and arriving from here.

Hiking

With all the mountain and cross-country trails, there are numerous opportunities for summertime hiking in the area. For trails within the **resort** (866/253-9877), you can either start by the P1 parking lot at the base of the mountain or up at the summit by taking the gondola. Trails vary from easy to difficult with loops at the summit and at the base and various trails that start at the summit and wind down to the pedestrian village. You can also use the extensive trails within the **Domaine Saint-Bernard** (545 chemin Saint-Bernard, 819/425-3588, www.domainesaintbernard.org, entry adults $3, children 17 and under free). Bring your bathing suit along and go for a dip at Lac Raynaud.

Horseback Riding

There are a couple of excellent horseback riding outfits in the Tremblant region. One is the **Equestrian Centre at Gray Rocks** (2322 rue Labelle, 819/425-8886, www.grayrocks.com, 8 A.M.–6 P.M. daily), which takes riders through the beautiful countryside around Sugar Peak ski hill. There are one-hour guided rides for beginners and two-hour trail rides for more experienced riders. The center also offers lessons. The **resort,** not surprisingly, also offers horseback riding at a 1,000-acre ranch about

Gondolas head up Mont-Tremblant.

© JENNIFER EDWARDS

40 minutes away. There are one-hour and two-hour rides around the grounds and it also offers something called the Cattle Round-Up, which is a demonstration and hands-on lesson in corralling cattle. Yee-haw! Sign up at the activity center (place Saint-Bernard, 819/681-4848, www.tremblantactivities.com).

Cross-Country Skiing

Although dominated by its alpine skiing opportunities, there are excellent cross-country skiing opportunities in the Mont-Tremblant region. We can thank Jackrabbit Johannsen for this. He cleared the first trails in the late 1920s, actually a few years before the first downhill trails were cut. Now there's a network of trails totaling 65 km (35 percent easy, 40 percent difficult, and 25 percent very difficult), spread out between the resort and Saint-Jovite.

Heading the cross-country effort is the **Ski de Fond Mont-Tremblant** (539 chemin Saint-Bernard, 819/425-5588, www.skidefondmont-tremblant.com, children 17 and under free, adults $12), an organization that maintains the trails and runs a ski school and the welcome center, at the entrance of the **Domaine Saint-Bernard** (545 chemin Saint-Bernard, 819/425-3588, www.domainesaintbernard.org). There's a rental shop there where you can get skis, boots, and poles, as well as a warm-up lounge and snack bar.

Other Sports and Recreation

You wouldn't think of it as being a summertime event, but it is. The **Alpine Luge** (weekends late May–late June and daily late June–mid-Oct, one ride $10, three rides $19) features nonmotorized carts that race down a 1.4-km course. To get there, you'll have to take the Flying Mile lift. If you've always harbored a secret desire to swing through the trees like Tarzan, you can do it with **Acrobranche** (819/429-9319, www.acrobranche.com, children $23, adults $33, 9:30 A.M.–5:30 P.M. daily, late June–early Sept.). The company will get you decked out not in loincloth, but harness and helmet, give you a lesson, and then set you off on a two-hour, 30-foot-high, platform-

THE LEGEND OF JACKRABBIT

If you spend any time in the Laurentians, chances are you'll quickly hear about Herman Smith Johannsen, or Jackrabbit as he was better known.

Born in Norway in 1875, Johannsen began his career selling construction equipment. His job eventually brought him to Canada, where he sold machinery to the railways. His skiing skills came in handy during the trip as he tried to reach some of the remote settlements in northern Ontario. Some of the Cree people whom he met were so impressed by his dexterity and speed on the two wooden blades that they took to calling him "waupoos," meaning rabbit.

After Johannsen married he settled his family in the West Indies, where he worked as a sales engineer, but it wasn't long before his yearning for snow and skis brought him back north. In 1919, Johannsen set up shop in Montréal, making frequent trips to the Laurentians to explore the backwoods and cut new trails.

He quickly became a mythical figure in the region, especially in the 1930s, when city folk started coming up to the Laurentians to try out the new ski hill. Although Johannsen played a part in the cutting of downhill trails, he later admitted that he would have had no role if he knew that "it would develop into a craze for hill skiing only." Johanssen continued cutting trails in the Laurentians until there was an extensive network set up, including the famed Maple Leaf Trail, which extends from the town of Prévost to Labelle.

Founding a number of ski centers, teaching and officiating at events, and skiing well into his 90s, Johannsen became a legend all over again when he died... at 111 years old.

to-platform swinging expedition through the trees. Children get their own smaller course. On the banks of the Rivière du Diable, about halfway between the village and Saint-Jovite, **Spa La Scandinave** (555 montée

Ryan, 819/425-5524, www.scandinave.com, 10 A.M.–9 P.M. daily, baths $38, hourlong massage $100) pays tribute to things Scandinavian with a Norwegian steam bath, Swedish massages, and a Finnish sauna (let's hope the Danes won't take insult!). The setting is stunning with the spa buildings surrounding the main baths. The resort's **Aquaclub La Source** (819/681-5668, 6 A.M.–8 P.M. Mon.–Fri. and 9 A.M.–8 P.M. weekends early May–mid-June, 6:30 A.M.–9 P.M. Mon.–Fri. and 9 A.M.–9 P.M. weekends mid-June–early Sept., and 6:30 A.M.– 8 P.M. Mon.–Fri. and 9 A.M.–8 P.M. weekends early Sept.–mid-Nov., adult $14, teens 13–17 $12, children 6–12 $9, and children 2–5 $5) is a megacomplex with a fitness center, paddling pools, a main pool, indoor and outdoor whirlpools, a waterfall, and steam baths. It's a good place to bring the kids if you want a break from the ski slope. If you're eager to spend some outdoor time on the water, check out **Les Croisières Mont-Tremblant** (819/425-1045, www.croisierestremblant.com, early June–early Oct., adults $15, children 5–15 $6), which offers a 70-minute boat tour of Lac Tremblant. The 53-foot boat departs from the main dock on Lac Tremblant. There are four departures during the height of the season.

ENTERTAINMENT AND EVENTS
Nightclubs
The legendary **Le P'tit Caribou** (Vieux-Tremblant, 819/681-4500, 10 P.M.–3 A.M.) was voted the "Best Bar in Eastern Canada" by *Ski Canada Magazine,* and judging by the long lines to get in, everyone's aware of it. Although the booming drum and bass and the ski bunny clientele can make any person older than 30 feel ancient, it's still worth a gander. There's also **Bar Café d'Époque** (Vieux-Tremblant, 819/681-4554, 3 P.M.–3 A.M. daily), which features a DJ every night of the week spinning dance, hip hop, and R&B. Finally there's **Le Shack** (3035 chemin de la Chapelle, 819/681-4700), which is a restaurant by day and early evening and a crowded, shoulder room–only bar at night. There's live music on weekends.

Festivals
There are a huge number of festivals and events that the resort puts on all year-round. Probably the most popular event in the region is the annual **Tremblant International Blues Festival** (888/736-2526, www.tremblant.com/bluesfestival). The 10-day event features bigger and lesser-known names from Canada and abroad. Concerts take place on outdoor stages and in some bars all throughout the pedestrian village. One of the best aspects of the festival is the meeting place called L'Aire du Blues, where fans and musicians can rub shoulders, where interviews take place, and where you can pick up most of the recordings from the artists playing at the fest. All outdoor shows are free. Another one of the resort's great musical events is **Les Rythmes Tremblant** (819/681-3000, ext. 46643, www.tremblant.com), a festival that takes place on eight weekends with different musical genres dedicated to each one. There are Latino, folk world music, R&B, and one weekend exclusively dedicated to Canadian music. Concerts outdoors are free. Every April at the beginning of the month, the resort also hosts the **Spin Symposium** (www.tremblant.ca/spin), a 10-day-long event featuring extreme sport competitions and free daily music concerts in Place Saint-Bernard. If you're not a fan of snowboarder culture, stay far, far away.

ACCOMMODATIONS
Saint-Jovite
There are some good accommodation options in Saint-Jovite that are often less expensive than staying on the hill. If you're on a budget or just want to be surrounded by younger folk (many of the resort workers rent a room here by the month), try the **Auberge du Mont Saint-Jovite** (695 rue de la Montagne, 819/429-6225, $20 dorm), an old ski station converted into a youth hostel. Accommodation choices include a dormitory (6–10 beds) or private room (2–5 beds). There's an outdoor swimming pool and a fireplace. Another spot that has good value is **Motel Saint-Jovite** (614 rue Saint-Jovite, 819/425-2761, www.motel-st-jovite.com,

$50 d). A classic motel from the 1950s with the lack of creature comforts to match, there's something charming about it anyway. Even though it's on the main drag, the motel—thanks to its setting amid evergreen trees—is quite serene. Some rooms have kitchenettes. Not far from there is the **Auberge Mountain View** (1177 rue Labelle, 819/425-3429 or 800/561-5122, www.aubergemountainviewinn.com, $65–138 d), which is also a motel. The rooms are no-frills, but this place—with breakfast included in the price—is one of the best values for your buck. About five minutes from the center of town, the lovely 【 **Au Ruisseau Enchanté** (105 chemin du 7e rang, 819/425-7265, www.auruisseauenchante.com, $75 d) has the advantage of beautiful gardens, a babbling brook, and two sunny guest rooms adorned with antiques and beautiful wood work. There's a friendly chocolate Lab on the property. Another quiet inn right on the P'tit Train du Nord Linear Park is **Auberge Gîte le Voyageur** (900 rue Coupal, 819/429-6277, www.bbvoyageur.com, $75–85 d). The rooms aren't very big, but each has its own bathroom and all are bright and nicely decorated. The farmhouse-style dining area and lounge—complete with stone fireplace—is very cozy and a good place to unwind after a ski day. On 12 acres, the extremely picturesque, mansard-roofed 【 **Wild Berry Inn** (855 de la Colline, 819/429-6182, www.wildberryinn.com, $99–139 d) has five spacious rooms, each with its own bathroom. The couple who run this place are extremely hospitable and informative on what to do in the region. There's also a little skating rink in winter.

Village de Mont-Tremblant

In general, the accommodations are a bit more expensive in the village, but they have more an old-time, Québécois authenticity, including numerous inns with fine-dining restaurants. But if you're seeking out a camping spot, check out **Camping et Tipis Labelle et la Rouge** (teepee $60 d, tent $20 d, site $25 d), situated on the Rivière Rouge. This campground offers something unique: teepees and tents already set up and waiting to be rented out with an accompanying Coleman stove and picnic table. You can pitch your own tent too. Canoes and kayaks are available to rent. **HI-Auberge de Jeunesse Village Mont-Tremblant** (2213 chemin du Village, 819/425-6008 or 866/425-6008, www.hostellingtremblant.com) is a friendly, often packed hostel right next to Lac Moore. There aren't only young people staying here, as lots of families opt for its cheaper accommodation and kid-friendly activities. There are dormitories for 4–10 people and private double rooms. Most have full-service dining rooms. Just outside of the village, on the other side of Lac Mercier, is the beautiful 【 **Les Jardins de L'Achillée Millefeuille** (435 chemin des Tulipes, 819/686-9187, www.millefeuille.ca, $95–140 d). Billing itself as a "healthy rest stop," this five-room B&B has a decidedly ecological feel with certified organic meals and a beautiful garden with flowers, herbs, and medicinal plants. If it's available, book yourself into the Lovers' Loft, which is a cute little two-floor chalet right in the middle of the garden. **Auberge de la Porte Rouge** (1874 chemin Principale, 819/425-3505 or 800/665-3505, www.aubergelaporterouge.com, $170 d includes breakfast and dinner) is a cute little roadside and lakeside inn with rooms that have balconies overlooking Lac Mercier. There are rowboats, kayaks, and pedal boats available for rent. And if you're looking for a little more seclusion, there are four fully equipped cottages. Staying at the very tasteful 【 **Auberge Sauvignon** (2723 chemin du Village, 819/425-5466, www.aubergesauvignon.com, $125–190) is a lesson in consummate hospitality. This Swiss-style inn has been in operation since 1939, but it has really started to shine thanks to a recent renovation and the expertise of innkeeper Francine. There are seven simple but cheery rooms with Provençal-type décor and a rustic-style restaurant that serves delicious French bistro-type fare. The well-known **Club Tremblant L'Hôtel du Lac** (121 rue Cuttle, 819/425-2731 or 800/567-8341, www.clubtremblant.com, $220 d includes breakfast and dinner) has 122 suites, all tastefully decorated with wood furniture and earth tones. The place has two restaurants: the pub-style Bistro-sur-le-Lac and the more formal Bar Le Point de Vue. There is also an outddor and indoor swimming pool, a marina, and a full-fledged spa with massages, reflexology, and something called "pressotherapy."

Station Mont Tremblant

Hotels and condos cover the hill, but they all tend to be exorbitantly expensive. But, if you're in town only for the weekend and being able to ski (or walk) right to your hotel door is a top priority, then spring for a room. Before you do, though, check the resort's website (www.tremblant.com) to see what kind of deals it is offering. Packages featuring accommodation and activities are often discounted. Situated between Lac Tremblant and Lac Miroir, **(L'Ermitage du Lac** (150 chemin Cure Deslauriers, 819/681-2222, $190–220 d) is a little quieter and smaller than the other hotels in the pedestrian village. Opened in 2004, it has a modest 69 rooms. There are an outdoor pool, hot tub, and ski valet service. Breakfast is a cold buffet, which you can eat in the lounge or bring up to your room. The mammoth, U-shaped, 314-room **Fairmont Tremblant** (3045 chemin de la Chapelle, 819/681-7000 or 866/540-4415, www.fairmont.com/tremblant, $210–265 d) is probably the resort's most popular hotel. Situated right at the base of the mountain at the ski lift, the hotel has an indoor pool, outdoor hot tub and whirlpools, stean baths, sauna, and fitness room. There are services galore, including day care and recreational reservations, and two restaurants and a cafeteria that is open only during the winter season. **Le Westin Resort and Spa** (100 chemin Kandahar, 819/681-8000 or 800/625-5144, www.starwoodhotels.com/westin, $260 d) is another favored choice for those wanting the big-hotel-on-the-hill experience. The rooms—all one- or two-bedroom—are a bit cramped, but all come equipped with a gas fireplace and have what Westin describes as a "Heavenly Bed." There is a heated outdoor swimming pool and whirlpool and workout room. The hotel's U Restaurant serves sushi and there's a more casual lounge. The resort's only boutique hotel is the **Hotel Quintessence** (3004 chemin de la Chapelle, 819/425 3400 or 866/425-3400, www.hotelquintessence.com, $520–570 d), a five-star, lap of luxury, pay-through-the-nose spot. Suites here come decked out with a beautiful view overlooking the lake, a remote-controlled clawfoot bathtub where you can set the water's temperature and bubble action, a plush king-size bed, and a fireplace, which the concierge will light just before you turn in at night. There are a spa, restaurant, and wine bar, with a 60-foot-long visible wine cellar, on-site.

FOOD
Saint-Jovite

(La Table Enchantée (1842 route 117 Nord, 819/425-7113, 5–9:30 P.M.Tues.–Sat., table d'hôte $19–30) is a cute little restaurant that has been in operation since 1976. Serving Québec-French cuisine, the place is known for rack of lamb, elk medallions, and especially its *cipaille de grand-mère*—a type of extra meaty meat pie with pheasant, rabbit, caribou, veal, and pork. In an ancestral house with a wide veranda is **(Le Cheval de Jade** (688 rue Saint-Jovite, 819/425-3525, 5:30–10 P.M. Thurs.–Tues., mains $26–32, table d'hôte $27–44), a good spot for a romantic dinner. Run by a couple from a small town in France, the restaurant specializes in inventive seafood dishes such as tiger prawns flambéed in tequila, lemon juice, juniper berry, and basil; word has it that the fish used in the Mediterranean bouillabaisse is flown in directly from France. For more casual fare, there's the **Bistro Brunch Café** (816 rue Ouimet, 819/425-8233, 8 A.M.–10 P.M. daily, mains $13–26, table d'hôte $14–24), a laid-back joint with micro-brews, sandwiches, pasta, wood-oven pizzas, and an array of sausages with to-die-for fries. In the winter, there's an ice bar outside. Owned by the same people, **Antipasto** (855 rue Ouimet, 819/425-7580, 11 A.M.–11 P.M. daily, mains $11–25) also serves pizza and pasta. Just a little bit farther down the street, in the old train station, this is the place to sit outside on the terrace and enjoy the street color.

Village de Mont-Tremblant

On the village's main drag, (**La Saucière** (1991 chemin Principale, 819/425-7575, 5–10 P.M.), open only for dinner, is a true French restaurant. It's a quaint spot with delectable dishes such as coq au vin and crêpes. The house specialty, though, are the sauces—which is where the place gets its name. Don't even think of going without a reservation. It's not fine dining by any means, but sometimes you need a **Restaurant Lorraine** (2000 chemin Principale, 819/425-5566, 6 A.M.–10 P.M. daily, mains $6–15) in your life. This no-frills, family-style spot has an extensive menu with big breakfasts, soup and sandwiches, and table d'hôte dinners with decadent, homemade desserts. Lorraine herself is in the kitchen. The (**Auberge Sauvignon** (2723 chemin du Village, 819/425-5466, 6–10 P.M. daily, mains $25–35) has an excellent restaurant that focuses on seafood (mussels, lobster, and scallops) and meat dishes (beef tenderloin, baby-back ribs, and lamb). The service is top-notch and the setting is cozy with big windows overlooking the grounds.

Station Mont Tremblant

There is a huge array of choices at the foot of the hill for fine or casual dining. For a good bistro-type café, try **Au Grain de Café** (promenade Deslauriers, 819/681-4567, 7:30 A.M.–11 P.M. daily, lunch $7), across from the liquor store in Saint-Bernard Plaza, which serves continental breakfasts, soup and sandwich lunches, and several sweets. There are also two high-speed Internet stations that you can use for $3/10 minutes. For pub-style food, there's the excellent (**Microbrasserie La Diable** (3005 chemin Principale, 819/681-4546, 11:30 A.M.–3 A.M. daily, mains $10–20) in a converted, mansard-roofed home. There are six microbrews on the menu, as well as salads, sandwiches, European sausages, hamburgers, and pasta. You can get pizza by the slice

and beer on tap at the very popular **Ya'ooo Pizza Bar** (305 chemin Principale, 819/681-4616, 11 A.M.–3 A.M. daily). **Coco Pazzo** (promenade Deslauriers, 819/681-4774, noon–11 P.M. daily, mains $19–37) has surprisingly authentic Italian cuisine, plus some other meaty dishes, including rack of lamb and grilled veal chop. There's also a separate take-out counter where you can get gourmet deli sandwiches or simple dinner items to go. For French bistro-type food, try the accommodating (**Restaurant les Artistes** (116 chemin Kandahar, 819/681-4606, 5–10 P.M. daily, mains $14–39). A good family spot, the menu straddles the border between casual (pasta, chicken Caesar) and fine dining (filet mignon, lamb) and also includes regular kids' specials. There's a pretty terrace covered with a red awning in summer. And finally, for the finest of fine dining there's the four-diamond (**Aux Truffes** (3035 chemin de la Chapelle, 819/681-4544, 6–10 P.M. daily, mains $32–44), a contemporary French restaurant with some of the most adventurous dishes on the mountain, including various takes on foie gras. If you love crème brulée, you have to try it here; it's served with almond milk and chocolate truffles… How sinful.

INFORMATION AND SERVICES

There are two information centers operated by the Ville de Mont-Tremblant. One tourist office (48 chemin Brébeuf, 819/425-3300, 9 A.M.–5 P.M. daily, wwwtourismemont-tremblant.com) is in the Saint-Jovite district, while the other tourist office is in the village (5080 montée Ryan, 819/425-2434 or 800/322-2932, 9 A.M.–5 P.M. daily, www.tourismemonttremblant.com). The resort's information center (place des Voyageurs, 819/681-3000) has maps, tour information, and anything you need to know about what's going on around the resort.

The only bank in the resort is the Banque Nationale (819/425-8444, 10 A.M.–5 P.M. daily), which has a full-fledged branch for currency exchange, loans, mortgages, and all the other

© JENNIFER EDWARDS

the old train station in Saint-Jovite

usual bank services. It also has an ATM in Place Saint-Bernard. Both Saint-Jovite and Village de Mont-Tremblant have banks.

The *Tremblant Express News* (tremblantexpress.com) is a free bilingual monthly paper servicing the Mont-Tremblant region but distributed throughout the Laurentians. It covers municipal affairs, events, and lifestyle features.

GETTING THERE
By Car
Mont-Tremblant is about 120 km north of Montréal. The drive is pretty simple and will take you about 90 minutes, so long as you don't run into any traffic around the city. From Montréal, take Route 15 Nord toward Sainte-Agathe. You'll see that after Saint-Agathe, the highway merges with Route 117. Continue on 117 to the Saint-Jovite area. If you want to continue to the village or the resort, continue past Saint-Jovite for about five km and then take Exit 119 (Mont-Tremblant–Montée Ryan). Turn right at the first intersection onto

montée Ryan. Go straight. You'll see signs indicating which way to go to the village and which way to the resort

By Bus
There are many buses you can catch to Tremblant from downtown Montréal. Departing from Station Centrale Montréal (505 rue de Maisonneuve Est, 514/842-2281), Limocar (866/700-8899, www.limocar.ca, one-way $26, return $46) has at least a couple of buses running daily to Saint-Jovite (Dépanneur Ultra, 819/425-9224) and the base of the mountain.

By Shuttle
During the winter, you can catch a ride to the resort from Montréal's Trudeau Airport via one of the shuttles operated by Skyport (800/471-1155, www.skyportinternational.com, adults one-way $50, return $95, children one-way $30, return $60), with three departures Monday–Thursday and four Friday–Sunday. Look for the counter in the international arrivals section.

By Air

For people who don't have a lot of time, but who do have a lot of cash, you can now fly directly into the Mont-Tremblant International Airport (877/425-7919, www.mtia.ca), about 30 minutes north of the resort. Flights are offered by Voyager Airlines from Toronto (90 minutes, Thurs., Fri., and Sun., mid-Jan.–late Mar. $289) and New York (80 minutes, Thurs. and Sun., late Dec.–early Apr. $436).

GETTING AROUND
By Car

With pedestrians taking their time, narrow streets, and limited parking, driving around the resort can be a frustrating ordeal, so if you have the option, walk or take one of the shuttles. Many of the hotels offer indoor parking, but you'll have to pay around $20/day for the privilege. There are a series of parking lots at the base of the hill and the closer you get to the pedestrian village, the more expensive they become.

By Shuttle

There's a shuttle for people staying at the resort that will get you from your hotel to Place des Voyageurs at the base of the mountain and another that will bring you to the same spot from each of the parking lots. A detailed schedule is available at the information center.

By Bus

Ville de Mont-Tremblant offers bus service (819/425-8441, www.ccdemonttremblant.com) between the resort, the village, and Saint-Jovite for the stellar price of $1. From May to December buses leave every hour between roughly 6 A.M. and 1 A.M. and every 30 minutes between mid-June to late August. You can get a schedule at any of the information centers.

◖ PARC NATIONAL DU MONT-TREMBLANT

The incredibly beautiful Parc National du Mont-Tremblant (chemin du Lac-Supérieur, 819/688-2281 or 800/665-6527, www.sepaq.com,

adults $3.50, children 6–17 $1.50) has the honor of being Québec's first provincial park and its largest. At 1,510 square km, the park is divided into three sectors: **La Diable** to the southwest is right next to the ski station and hence the most crowded, **la Pimbina** is in the middle, and **de l'Assomption,** the least busy, sits to the east. The park possesses 120 km of trails and more than 20 campgrounds. Its forest reserves of sugar maple are huge, but Parc du Mont-Tremblant is really about the water: 400 lakes, six rivers, three waterfalls. With so many lakes and river systems, it is one of North America's best destinations for canoe-camping excursions. That doesn't mean that you won't want to visit the park once the water is frozen over. It actually makes for a very pleasant side trip to a downhill ski trip, as there are a number of cross-country ski and snowshoe trails, including the beautiful Lac des Femmes trail, a 2.7-km loop.

If you want a few more creature comforts than staying in a campground affords (tent sites $19), the park has an impressive array of huts (no electricity or running water, $21 per person) and cabins (running water and electricity or propane, $60–92 d) for rent. All are along a lake or river and equipped with a woodstove and firewood. And if you want more creature comforts, the village, ski station, and Saint-Jovite are just a quick drive away.

Canoeing

With all of its waterways, Parc National du Mont Tremblant has become a favored destination for day-trip canoeing and longer excursions. Rivière Assomption is 15 km within the park's boundaries and has a wide range of rapids from easy to difficult. Rivière la Diable is 45 km and is the most popular water route to explore the park. In case the rapids are looking just a tad too creepy, both rivers have portages that bypass them. Canoes can be rented at all three visitors centers.

Hiking

Hikers are extremely well served in the park with over 120 km of trails—many of which climb up to stellar viewpoints, like the 5-km round-trip la Roche, or brush by scenic waterfalls, like the 10-km la Chute-aux-Rats. Trails range from very easy and brief (under 1 km) to those that are much more difficult and long (just over 15 km). The easy hikes begin right next to the visitors centers.

Those who want to do longer hikes can choose from intermediate to difficult trails that range from an afternoon stroll to a five-day foray. There are sleeping huts available along the trails.

Cross-Country Skiing

With a vast network of well-groomed trails, the park is one of the favored destinations for Québec's serious cross-country skiers, but can be just as pleasant for those who are beginners or who are interested in a leisurely session. La Diable sector offers 10 loops that make a total of 53 km and range from easy to expert. La Pimbina has seven loops that add up to 33 km and have a similar range of difficulty.

As with canoeing and hiking, longer cross-country trips can be arranged via the more than 100 km worth of backcountry trails. But, backcountry really means just that: These trails aren't groomed or patrolled. They do, mind you, have overnight huts that are spaced out so that a range of 9–21 km can be done each day. The Diable and Pimbina visitors centers both rent cross-country skis and provide a waxing service.

Information and Services

For information and to register, you can visit the main reception center, Lac Monroe Reception Center (mid-May–mid-Oct. and mid-Dec.–late Mar.) in the Diable sector, which also has showers, a launderette, and a convenience store and snack bar open during the summer. There's also the Saint-Donat Information Kiosk (mid-May–mid-Oct.) in the Pimbina sector, which has a nature boutique and items such as wood and ice for sale. Both of these centers have equipment rentals, including canoes, rowboats, kayaks and pedal boats, bikes, cross-country skis, and snowshoes. There are also two smaller summertime-only information centers—Saint-Côme Information Kiosk (mid-May–mid-Oct.) and La Cachée Information Kiosk (mid-June–early Sept.)— in the L'Assomption sector and La Cachée, respectively.

THE EASTERN TOWNSHIPS

It's only an hour's drive from Montréal, and yet somehow once you've set foot in this vast southern corner of the province, it feels as if you've already slipped into New England. True, the Eastern Townships do share a 300-km border with Vermont, New Hampshire, and Maine and possess many of their best natural characteristics, such as fertile lands, lush green hills, and sparkling lakes, but the commonalities are not just a case of shared geography. They strike in the preponderance of English names—Stanbridge East, Cookshire, North Hatley—the fine Victorian, Georgian, Queen Anne, and Second Empire architecture, and most remarkably, in the fact that the Catholic Church's steeple is not the sole one rising from many a town's core.

The settlement of the region by 40,000 British Loyalists who fled the American colonies when they declared independence, combined with the later infiltration and predominance of French-speaking Quebecers, has created a riveting juxtaposition in the land known as the "Garden of Québec." It's one where you may be served a table d'hôte meal of classic French cuisine in a stately and polished Victorian inn once belonging to a founding Loyalist family or where high tea and scones are served by Madame *en français*. Add six major ski hills into the mix and you've got a much sought-after destination, especially for Montrealers who appreciate that a little rural respite is so close at hand.

Looking at a map, it's easy to find the

HIGHLIGHTS

◖ Cycling la Route Verte: Two-wheel it along this major network of designated biking roads that span the north, middle, and south of the region (page 150).

◖ Ski Bromont: Grab your gloves and goggles in the winter and your mountain bike in the summer and head for the hill (page 151).

◖ Dunham: Head to this hub of the Townships' nascent wine region and explore some of the wineries and nearby quiet, quaint towns (page 154).

◖ Knowlton: Admire the lovely Victorian architecture, shop for antiques, and sample the world-famous Lac Brome duck in the region's most British-feeling town (page 156).

◖ Saint-Benoît-du-Lac Abbey: Fill up on blue cheese and cider while listening to soothing Gregorian chants (page 165).

◖ Parc de la Gorge Coaticook: Traverse the world's longest suspension bridge while gazing over farmers' fields and the Green Mountains of Vermont (page 174).

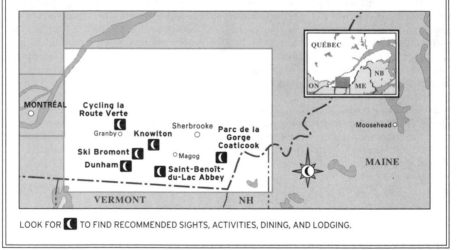

LOOK FOR **◖** TO FIND RECOMMENDED SIGHTS, ACTIVITIES, DINING, AND LODGING.

Townships' tangle of roads a bit daunting (the region has the most dense network of secondary roads in the province), but there are really no wrong turns here. Get lost on a dirt road and you may come across an old covered bridge, a weather-beaten, oxblood-red round barn, a sun-soaked green valley of farmers' fields, or a lost village that seems desolate except for a busy bakery that serves killer chocolate croissants. These roadside pleasantries and the fact that some form of civilization is never too far away have turned the Townships into one of the most coveted destinations for cycling trips and languorous drives.

PLANNING YOUR TIME

To get a good feel for the Townships' heritage, the hidden treasures of its rural roads, and the many recreational pursuits on offer, plan to stay for at least six days. This amount of time should allow for some leisurely driving and exploration, a hike, ski, or a short boat ride along one of the lakes, and the opportunity to sample some meals in the region's most praiseworthy restaurants.

Consider making **Knowlton** your base for the first three nights. Reserve a full day to explore the town's shops, restaurants, and museums and those of neighboring Sutton. On

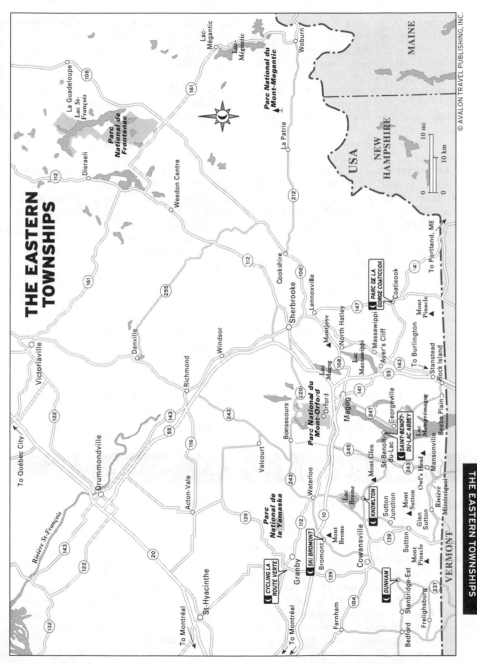

THE EASTERN TOWNSHIPS

MAINE

NEW HAMPSHIRE

USA

VERMONT

To Portland, ME

To Burlington

To Québec City

To Montréal

To Montréal

La Guadeloupe

Lac St-François

Parc National de Frontenac

Disraeli

Lac-Mégantic

Lac-Mégantic

Parc National du Mont-Mégantic

La Patrie

Woburn

Weedon Centre

Cookshire

Sherbrooke

Lennoxville

Coaticook

Mont Pinacle

PARC DE LA GORGE COATICOOK

North Hatley

Montjoye

Massawippi

Ayer's Cliff

Stanstead

Rock Island

Lac Massawippi

Lac Magog

Lac Memphremagog

Beebe Plain

Georgeville

SAINT-BENOÎT-DU-LAC ABBEY

St-Benoît-du-Lac

Mansonville

Owl's Head

Rivière Mississiquoi

Magog

Orford

Parc National du Mont-Orford

Mont Glen

Bonsecours

Windsor

Danville

Richmond

Victoriaville

Drummondville

Acton-Vale

Valcourt

Waterloo

Lac Brome

KNOWLTON

Sutton Junction

Mont Sutton

Glen Sutton

Sutton

Mont Pinacle

Cowansville

DUNHAM

Stanbridge-Est

Freligshburg

Bedford

Farnham

Parc National de la Yamaska

Granby

Bromont

Mont Brome

SKI BROMONT

CYCLING LA ROUTE VERTE

St-Hyacinthe

Rivière St-François

THE EASTERN TOWNSHIPS

108
161
112
161
255
112
108
147
143
55
141
247
245
243
20
122
143
243
116
55
143
243
10
112
139
139
104
237
139
20
122
132

10 mi

10 km

day two tour the **wineries** and small, scenic towns in and around Dunham, and take the third day to **hike, snowboard** or **ski** the mountains of Bromont, Sutton, Owl's Head, or Mont Glen.

Head a little bit farther east for the next three nights and choose a spot in or near Magog or North Hatley. Here, you'll want to spend at least half a day in **Mont Orford,** perusing the park's walking and ski trails or taking in a classical concert at the **Centre d'Arts Orford,** and the second half going for a jaunt up to the **J. Armand Bombardier Museum** in Valcourt and back down for a drive along **Lac Memphrémagog** to the **Saint-Benoît-du-Lac Abbey.** Spend the second day leisurely drinking in the scenery of North Hatley and then head down to the **Parc de la Gorge Coaticook** for a stroll along the park's hiking trails, extension bridge, and a climb up to one of its observation towers. On your last day consider a heritage walk and museum tour in **Sherbrooke** and then a nighttime talk on the stars in **Parc National du Mont-Mégantic.**

A car or a bicycle are musts for anyone wanting a full picture of the region, but beware that locals tend to bomb along these roads at high speeds and don't have much patience for tourists who stop in the middle of the road for a picture. If you are planning a cycling tour,

pick up one of the *Cycling the Eastern Townships* brochures available on order at www.easterntownships.org or at one of the region's local tourist offices.

HISTORY

During the War of Independence (1776–1782) Americans wanting to stay loyal to the British crown first settled the area now known as the Eastern Townships. Canada, a member of the British Empire, welcomed these accomplished farmers, merchants, and industrialists into the fold and granted them vast plots of land according to the British township system instead of the French seigneuries' characteristic long, narrow plots.

Loyalists were then joined by a wave of Irish and Scottish immigrants (and to a lesser extent, Dutch, Polish, and German), but it was only in the latter half of the 1800s, during the Industrial Revolution, that French Canadians, seeking land and jobs, moved south from the Laurentians into the Eastern Townships. Their influence was quick to take hold and within the span of two generations they became the majority population. Today, French speakers account for 94 percent of the population and despite efforts to make their home region's name more French-sounding by calling it Estrie, Cantons-de-l'Est, a direct translation of Eastern Townships has stuck.

Granby-Bromont

Although it doesn't quite feel like you've entered the Townships when you suddenly find yourself in the bustling, zoo-famous town of Granby, you just need to head a little bit farther south to its sister town, Bromont, to start feeling the true Townships pace. Things are a little bit more leisurely in this region and as you head south of Bromont toward the vineyards and past the beautifully quiet small towns of Bedford, Stanbridge East, and Frelighsburg, toward the border. The life is easy here.

GRANBY

Sprawling and unremarkable, Granby (pop. 45,223) is the second-largest city in the Eastern Townships and the first place that most visitors encounter as they enter the region from Montréal. Although it's often bypassed in favor of more typical Township fare, there are some worthwhile attractions here, especially if you're traveling with kids.

Sights and Recreation

There aren't too many born-and-bred Quebecers

who haven't made at least one childhood school trip to the **Granby Zoo** (525 rue Saint-Hubert, 450/372-9113 or 877/472-6299, www.zoodegranby.com), the province's biggest zoo with more than 1,000 animals, including anacondas, snow leopards, wallabies, and Siberian tigers. The zoo gained notoriety a few years back with its proposal to build a "dolphinarium," a swim-with-the-dolphins type of exhibit that had animal activists seeing red, including a particularly irate Brigitte Bardot. Caving into international pressure, the zoo eventually shelved the plan.

Beyond the animal exhibits, there's a water park on-site called **Amazoo** that boasts a warm-water wave pool and a meandering inner-tube watercourse. The entire complex is open 10 A.M.–5 P.M. daily late May–late June and 10 A.M.–7 P.M. daily late June–late August. During the beginning of September, only the zoo area remains open 10 A.M.–5 P.M., and then from mid-September to mid-October the zoo is open weekends only 10 A.M.–5 P.M. Admission, including access to the water park, is $24 for adults, $18 for children 5–12, and $11 for children 2–4. If you don't get your fill of feathered friends at the Granby Zoo, the **Exotic Birds Zoo and Refuge** (2699 route 139, Roxton-Pond, 450/375-6118, www.zooicare.com, 10 A.M.– 5 P.M. daily June–Sept., adults $12, children $7.50, families—two adults and two children—$35) is just the ticket. More than 450 birds of 150 varieties are housed here both temporarily and permanently and kept in outdoor aviaries, set up along a one-km-long path. For something a little quieter and more laid-back, go for a walk along one of the trails at the **Centre d'Interprétation de la Nature du Lac Boivin** (700 rue Drummond, 450/375-3861, 8:30 A.M.–4:30 P.M. Mon.–Fri., 9 A.M.–5 P.M. Sat.–Sun., admission free), a conservation area with four hiking paths that together extend over 10 km and include two observation towers.

The lovely little **Parc National de la Yamaska** (1780 boulevard David-Bouchard, 450/776-7182 or 800/665-6527, www.sepaq .com, entry adults $3.50, children 6–17 $1.50, family—two adults and two children—$7)

ROLLING ON THE ROUTE

Extending from the Outaouais region all the way to Gaspésie, the province's biking network called **La Route Verte** accounts for 3,000 km of roads and is considered the largest in North America. The route is the result of longtime efforts by Vélo Québec, the province's main cycling organization, which in 1992, during the year of its 25th anniversary, decided it was finally time to take its plan to the provincial government. It took three years for a final confirmation, but in 1995, the Québec government announced that it would contribute $88.5 million over 10 years to build the network.

The Eastern Townships section of the route has the widest network. There are seven routes: the Montérégiade (orchards and markets), the Estriade (good for families), the Campagnarde (rugged and quiet), the Montagnarde (mountainous), the Réseau (cyclable), Les Grandes-Fourches (dams and a copper mine), the Cantonnière (British charm), and the Corridors Verts d'Asbestos (pastoral and hilly).

If you spot a little sign with a bicycle on it that says "Bienvenue cyclistes!" along any of these routes, you'll know that you've come to a bike-friendly establishment that has a secure lock-up for bikes, tools for minor repairs and, if it's a restaurant, high-carb foods and lots of fruit and veggies.

You can get a Carte Vélo (cycling map) at any of the tourist offices in the Townships. These maps indicate all the routes, highlighting all the essentials and fun stuff to see and do along them.

at the foot of the Appalachians is centered around the sparkling Choinière Reservoir, a 4.75-square-km lake that is filled to the brim come summer with swimmers, sailboarders, canoeists, and just about every other type of water-sport lover. Surrounding the reservoir are fields and forests rich in varied tree and plant species and 18 km of hiking trails from which to explore them.

THE EASTERN TOWNSHIPS

Cycling la Route Verte

With two major Route Verte (www.routeverte.com) cycling paths, the Montérégiade and Estriade, cycling is a big deal in this part of the Townships. The 25-km, half-paved, half-gravel **Montérégiade Trail** follows the old CN train line that extends from the Vélo Gare in Granby's Parc Boivin to Farnham, passing by apple orchards and along the Rivière Yamaska. All in all, it's a peaceful, relatively flat ride, permitting you to see far ahead.

Heading east from the Vélo Gare is the entirely paved, 21-km **Estriade Trail.** Extending from Granby to Waterloo, the Estriade is considered a good cycling path for families because traffic is minimal and there are plenty of picnic tables and options for bathroom breaks. If you're looking to rent some wheels, head over to **Vélo Gare** (71 rue Denison Est, 450/777-4438, www.velogare.com, $8 per hour, $22 for four hours or $30 per day), in town just on the edge of Lac Boivin. There's a great selection of bikes, trail bikes, and inline skates on-site and a friendly, knowledgeable staff to help you find what you're looking for.

Festival International de la Chanson

If you're in town in late summer check out the Festival International de la Chanson (450/375-7555 or 888/375-3424, www.ficg.qc.ca), an 18-day event at the Théâtre Palace that features some of Québec's best new performers competing for top honors in three categories: best group, best interpretation, and best songwriter. Past winners have gone on to become some of the province's best-loved musicians, including Linda Lemay, Luc De Larochellière, and Jean Leloup.

Accommodations

Many big, built-up campgrounds are around Granby, but if your tastes veer toward the quieter side, check out the campground at **Parc National de la Yamaska** (tent sites $22). There are more than 100 sites available year-round. Not far from the park is the equally low-key **Camping La Rivière du**

Passant (330 8e rang Ouest, 450/539-3835, tent sites $19–24, mid-May–mid-Sept.). This 75-site campground is situated right next to a river (there's nothing like the sounds of rushing water to lull you to sleep) and has laundry facilities and a convenience store on-site. Situated on Lac Boivin, just off the Estriade bike path, the raspberry-colored B&B **Une Fleur au Bord de l'Eau** (90 rue Drummond, 450/776-1141 or 888/375-1747, www.clubtrs.ca/fleurvtg, $65–70 d shared bath, $75–85 d private bath) is a lovely spot with creeping vines, luscious gardens, and a swimming pool. Rooms are comfortable and bright. You'd never guess that you were in the middle of town at **Le Campagnard** (146 rue Denison Ouest, 450/777-0245 or 450/770-1424, www.campagnard.ca, $100–300 d), a rambling, old century home that has five quaint bedrooms, plus a backyard with two rentable chalets, an outdoor shower, two ponds, and a fire pit. If you're traveling with a family or a group, your best choice is the **Auberge du Zoo** (347 rue Bourget Ouest, 450/378-6161 or 888/882-5252, www.aubergeduzoo.com, $75–85 d., $20 per extra adult, $10 per extra child), you guessed it, right next to the Granby Zoo. This place has a common playroom for kids and four nicely decorated suites, each with two bedrooms. Although it's far from chic, the **Hôtel le Castel de l'Estrie** (901 rue Principale, 450/378-9071 or 800/363-8953, www.castel.qc.ca, $85–123 d) has comfortable hotel rooms at decent prices and is right downtown. There are a pub, café, and restaurant on the premises, as well as a decent-size outdoor heated swimming pool.

Food

If the mood strikes for a good ol' plate of spaghetti, try the aptly named **La Casa du Spaghetti** (604 rue Principale, 450/372-3848, www.casagranby.com, 11 A.M.–10 P.M. Sun.–Thurs. and 11 A.M.–11 P.M. Fri.–Sat., mains $10–25), a cozy restaurant with more than 20 types of pasta dishes and 31 different wood-burning-oven pizzas. Come summer, the restaurant has a nice covered patio with a view onto Parc Pelletier. If you're a fondue fan, look for the blue building that houses **((La Closerie des Lilas** (21 rue Court, 450/375-3597, 5 P.M.–closing Wed.–Sun., table d'hôte $23–32) and sample one of its 15 fondue varieties, including Bourguignonne, Swiss, Italian, and Danish blue cheese, as well as a handful of classic chocolate dessert fondues. Situated on a quiet street in an understated house is **((Faucheux** (53-2 rue Dufferin, 450/777-2320, www.restaurantfaucheux.com, 11:30 A.M.–1:30 P.M. Tues. and 11:30 A.M.–1:30 P.M. and 6–9 P.M. Wed.–Sat., table d'hôte $26–40), one of the most well-reputed tables in the Townships. Named after the head chef, Faucheux specializes in superb seafood dishes such as shrimp ravioli and scallop pie with ginger sauce and meaty mains such as filet mignon and veal with duck foie gras. **La Maison Chez Nous** (847 rue Mountain, 450/372-2991, 5–10 P.M. Wed.–Sun., table d'hôte $29–42), just outside Granby on the road to Bromont, is a local favorite, so designated for its warm atmosphere and regional Québec specialty dishes such as maple-smoked duck and pheasant supreme.

Information

If you plan to travel farther into the Townships, look for the regional Granby-Bromont Tourism Office (100 rue du Tourisme, 450/375-8774 or 866/472-6292, www.granby-bromont.com, 8:30 A.M.–7:30 P.M. daily June–Sept., 9 A.M.–5 P.M. daily Oct.–May) just off Route 10 at Exit 68 to get stocked up on maps and accommodation information. If you're thinking of poking around Granby, visit the local tourist office (111 rue Denison Est, 450/372-7056 or 800/567-7273, 8:30 A.M.–7:30 P.M. daily during summer).

Getting There

To get to Granby from Montréal, take Autoroute 10 Est and get off at Exit 68.

BROMONT

Wide boulevards and grand old manors may lend Bromont (pop. 5,473) an air of permanence and Old World charm, but it's actually one of Québec's youngest towns. Founded in 1964 by the entrepreneurial Désourdy family, Bromont quickly became known as a major sporting center because of its busy ski hill and its selection as the site of the 1976 Montréal Olympics equestrian events. More recently Bromont has become the province's hot spot for mountain biking, hosting many international events. If high adrenalin isn't your thing, spend a quiet afternoon strolling down beautiful Shefford Street and check out its old Victorian manors, boutiques, restaurants, and terraces.

((Ski Bromont

With a vertical drop of 405 meters, Ski Bromont (150 rue Champlain, 450/534-2200 or 866/276-6668, www.skibromont.com, adult day/night $44/$33, student day/night $34/$27, children 6–13 day and night $26) may be on the smaller side of the Townships' major ski mountains, but it's become the darling of Montrealers who love the fact that its nighttime skiing allows them to get in a few runs after work. In the summertime, Ski Bromont is still bustling with activity thanks to its **water park** (10 A.M.–5 P.M. daily early–late June, 10 A.M.–6:30 P.M. late June–late Aug., adults $28, children $23, children 3–5 $13, 50 percent off after 3 P.M.), a series of massive water slides with lines to match. The hill is also a major center for **mountain biking** (10 A.M.–5 P.M. early May–early June, 10 A.M.–5 P.M. early–late June and late Aug.–late Oct., and 10 A.M.–6:30 P.M. late June–late Aug., adults (13 or over) $10, children 6–12 $5, or adults $28, children $23 for access to trails with chairlifts), encompassing more than 100 km of easy and expert trails—all accessible by chairlift to the summit or via the gravel path around the base. Check out **Sports Bromont** (58 boulevard de Bromont, 450/534-5858) for skiing, snowboarding, and mountain-biking equipment and rentals.

Sights

Brush up on your chocolate facts and sample some of the wares at **Bromont's Chocolate**

Museum (679 rue Shefford, 450/534-3893, www.bromont.com/chocolat, 9:30 A.M.–6 P.M. Mon.–Fri. and 8:30 A.M.–5:30 P.M. Sat.–Sun.), a tiny museum that chronicles the sweet stuff's origins, the way in which it's made, and some of the world's biggest chocolatiers. Once you've sufficiently worked up your sweet tooth, head straight to the gift shop and drool over the chocolate products made on-site. With more than 1,000 vendors, the outdoor **Bromont Flea Market** (16 rue Lafontaine, 450/534-0440 or 514/875-5500, 9 A.M.–5 P.M. Sat.–Sun. May–Nov.) is the biggest in the Townships. Although roaming the aisles can get quite harried on a sunny day at the height of the summer, it's a good excuse to brush up on your bargaining chops and dig around for some potential treasures. A bar, two restaurants, and an ice-cream stand are also on the grounds.

Horseback Riding

With its legacy as the location of choice for all the equestrian events during the 1976 Montréal Olympics, Bromont has kept up its reputation as a world-renowned equestrian destination, and there's an ample supply of outfitters to prove it. Two of the best are **Centre Équestre Bromont** (100 rue Laprairie, 450/534-0787, www.centreequestrebromont.com, group lesson $30/hour each, semiprivate lesson for two people $40, private lesson $60/hour), where you can take English riding lessons at the original site of the Olympic events and current home of the International Bromont, one of Canada's premiere riding events, and **Équitation Lombart** (374 boulevard Pierre-Laporte, 450/534-2084, www.motelbromont.com/lombart, 9 A.M.–6 P.M. Apr.–Oct., $20/hour), an English and Western-style riding center with access to trails on 250 acres of forested land.

Accommodations

Situated right off La Villageoise bike path on the site of an old train station, (**(Camping Vélo 2000** (1 boulevard de Bromont, 450/776-3864, www.campingvelo2000.ca, tent sites $20/day, $120/week) is a favored spot for cyclists. With only 50 sites—most of them wooded—the campground offers privacy and a quiet stay. There are a laundry and a snack bar on-site. There's also the expansive **Camping Parc Bromont** (24 rue Lafontaine, 450/534-2712, www.campingbromont.com, tent sites $25), which has 190 sites in addition to a swimming pool, walking trails, and miniature golf. Tucked away in the woods is the rustic-meets-zen (**(Casa Bromont** (1208 rue Shefford, 450/534-2429, www.casabromont.com, $80–95 d), a deluxe B&B with three beautiful, minimalist rooms: The Zen, The Sahara, and Green Dream. Each room has its own bathroom and unique character. There is also the deluxe Bali Suite with its own kitchen, DVD, washer/dryer, and private entrance. It sleeps four. Outside, there are lovely gardens along with a four-season hot tub. Another great B&B choice is the regal **La Dolce Vita** (142 chemin Compton, 450/534-2771, www.ladolcevitabb.com, $90–100 d includes breakfast), directly on Le Vieux Village golf course. The four rooms here all have a private bathroom and plush beds with goose-down duvets. There are also a fireplace and pool table for low-key, après-ski soirées. With mountain views and treed surroundings, **Hôtel Le Menhir** (125 boulevard de Bromont, 450/534-3790 or 800/461-3790, www.quebecweb.com/hotelle-menhir, standard $98 d, kitchenette $108, deluxe $140), a small hotel with 41 rooms, some with whirlpool bath and fireplace, is a good choice for those who simply want to stay put and relax. There are an indoor swimming pool, sauna, and whirlpool on-site and a busy bar.

Food

L'Étrier (547 rue Shefford, 450/534-3562, mains $14–30) is a cozy, friendly place in an old Victorian home on the Yamaska River. Menu items include steak, salmon, and filet mignon and there's live jazz music Friday to Sunday during the summer. The luxurious Château Bromont's (**(La Trattoria** (95 rue de Montmorency, 450/534-4882, 6:30 A.M.–10 P.M. daily, table d'hôte $25) restaurant is a lovely, low-key spot with a patio overlooking the golf course and Mont Bromont in the distance. The restaurant serves Italian fare, including pasta and pizza straight from the wood-burning oven.

Information

Tourism Granby-Bromont (15 boulevard de Bromont, 450/534-2006 or 877/276-6668, www.granby-bromont.com, 10 A.M.–6 P.M. daily June–Sept., 9 A.M.–5 P.M. daily Oct.–May), the local tourist office, is right in the center of town.

Getting There

To get to Bromont from Montréal or Granby, take Autoroute 10 Est and get off at Exit 78.

THE WINE ROUTE

The wine scene here may still be in its infancy compared to Canada's more mature industries in British Columbia and Ontario, but Townships vintners are determined to make a go of the advantages they possess: sandy, rocky soil and a microclimate conducive to grape-growing. Every fall, in a measure to ward off killer frosts, vines are hilled (covered in mounds of earth) to protect them from plummeting temperatures. Some go so far as to rent helicopters or wind machines to stir up the air so no frost forms on the vines.

Although you'll find the concentration of wineries centered around Dunham, the official 68-km Wine Route actually encompasses a number of pretty towns and is a route well worth taking even if you have no interest in wine.

Farnham and Vicinity

There's not much going on in Farnham (pop. 7,924), a quiet town on the banks of the Yamaska River, but the small park in the center of town called **Centre de la Nature de Farnham** (rue Yamaska Est, 450/293-3178, ext. 309, admission free) makes for a good picnic stop. You may also want to check out what is happening at **La Petite Église de Farnham** (401 rue Saint-Joseph, 450/293-7779, www.petiteeglise.com), a lovely old Presbyterian church, now a community concert hall with regular shows featuring music from Dixieland to folk to classical and regular children's shows. As you head south from Farnham along Route 235 is the beautiful hamlet of Mystic. Keep an eye out for the **Wallbridge Barn,** a red, 12-sided construction with a conical roof

A ROUND-BARN RAISING

While driving along an Eastern Townships side road, you may come across a curious sight. A strange concoction made out of wood that slightly resembles a flying saucer, these are the round barns, some of the region's most mysterious and photographed sites.

First conjured by the industrious Shakers – an offshoot of the Quakers – popular legend has it that the barns were devised so that the devil couldn't hide in the corners. Likely closer to the truth, but not nearly as riveting, is the fact that a circular barn could house more animals and facilitate feeding and cleanup. Cattle were kept on the ground floor and oriented toward a center feeding station, while the upper floor was reserved for storage.

Dairy farmers who lived close to the American border were the first to champion the round barns in the Townships. The tradition continued until the early 1900s, when the round revolution was abandoned for an easier, less exacting construction. By the 1960s many of the existing structures had fallen into disrepair, burned down, or were demolished. It's only been in the past 25 years that the Heritage Department has taken measures to preserve the buildings.

If you're interested in round-barn gazing, just remember that many are privately owned and in use, so view them from the road. Here are a few to watch for: Austin (rue Fisher), Mansonville (rue Principale), West Brome (rue Scott), and Barnston (rue Baldwin Mills).

THE EASTERN TOWNSHIPS

and 12 mows. Constructed by the eccentric, but entrepreneurial, Alexander Wallbride, at one point the barn featured a rotating floor that would position loaded wagons in front of the appropriate mows so that the crops could be unloaded.

Stanbridge East

One of the prettiest towns in the region, Stanbridge East (pop. 900) was founded in 1801 and born out of the construction of a grain mill on Rivière des Brochets (formerly known as Pikes River). The town is still a major farming and horticulture center and there are several fine examples of 19th-century architecture. Visit the **Musée Missisquoi** (2 rue River, 450/248-3153, www.missisquoimuseum.ca, 10 A.M.–5 P.M. daily late May–early Oct., adults $3.50, children $1) and peruse the collection of Loyalist artifacts, including the red coat worn by pioneer Hendrick TenEyck during the American Revolution and the 500 hand-carved miniatures crafted by Canadian Customs agent Charles Millard and his wife. Also run by the museum is Hodge's Store, an old general store with contents dating to World War II. If you like your surroundings lush, check out **Les Jardins d'Eau de la Vallée de Dunham** (140 route 202, 450/248-7008, www.afleurdeau.qc.ca, 9 A.M.–5 P.M. daily June–Aug., 10 A.M.–4 P.M. daily Sept.–Oct., adults $8, children 12–18 $5, children 6–11 $3, family $20), an aquatic gardening center and park with flower-lined trails, a butterfly garden, and a two-km forest trail.

Frelighsburg

Surrounded by apple orchards at the foot of Mont Pinacle, the town of Frelighsburg (pop. 1,048) has one of the most beautiful settings in the Townships. With the first wave of immigrants arriving in 1790, Frelighsburgh—named after Abram Frelegh, a Dutch doctor from Albany, New York—quickly became a bustling frontier town thanks to its proximity to the U.S. border. In 1866 and 1870, Frelighsburg was the site of two bizarre uprisings led by the Fenians, Irish Americans who tried

the Musée Missisquoi

to bully England into granting Ireland home rule by holding Lower Canada hostage. Needless to say, the raiders didn't get very far before being turned around and ushered home. Today, the town boasts many fine examples of Anglo-American architecture, including the old Freligh Mill, built by one of Abram's sons, the Catholic and Anglican churches, town hall, and the general store, now known as **Sucreries de l'Érable** (16 rue Principale, 450/298-5181), a spot famous for its desserts, especially its traditional maple pies.

Every Labor Day weekend Frelighsburg becomes the backdrop to **Festiv'Art** (450/298-5630, www.village.frelighsburg.qc.ca/festivart), a large, mostly outdoor art festival featuring more than 100 painters exhibiting on the streets, in the galleries, and even on residents' verandas. The whole town gets involved in the festivities and there are often live-music acts booked into the bars.

◖ Dunham

Heading back north on Route 213, you'll soon come to Dunham (pop. 3,370), the heart of the

© JENNIFER EDWARDS

Frelighsburg's town hall

wine region and one of the very first areas to be settled in the Townships.

Starting off from Dunham, the first winery that you'll come across on Route 202 is **Vignoble Les Trois Clochers** (341 rue Bruce, route 202, 450/295-2034, 10 A.M.–6 P.M. daily late June–Oct., 10 A.M.–5 P.M. Sat.–Sun. Nov.–late June). Known for its seyval blanc and sweet strawberry dessert wine, this winery has a beautiful view of Dunham and its three church steeples—hence the name Les Trois Clochers. Farther down the road is **Domaine de Côtes d'Ardoise** (879 rue Bruce, route 202, 450/295-2020, www.cotesdardoise.com, 9:30 A.M.–6 P.M. daily June–mid-Oct.), the first winery to go into production in the area. Housed in a beautiful old barn, this vineyard produces two red and two white wines and aperitifs. There's a walking trail out back and every summer, there's an outdoor sculpture exhibit with more than 40 pieces by local sculptors. Across the street is **Vignoble Les Blancs Côteaux** (1046 rue Bruce, route 202, 450/295-3503, 10 A.M.–6 P.M. daily May–Nov., 10 A.M.–5 P.M. Wed.–Sun. Dec.–

Apr.), in an old farmhouse. In addition to its wines (seyval blanc and noir, Bacchus and Eona), the winery produces apple cider, jellies, and vinegars. They folks here will prepare a lunch for you if you want to picnic on the property. Finally, there's the **Vignoble de l'Orpailleur** (1086 route 202, 450/295-2763, www.orpailleur.ca, 9 A.M.–6 P.M. daily mid-Apr.–mid-Nov., 10 A.M.–5 P.M. Sat.–Sun. mid-Nov.–mid-Apr.), the granddaddy of the Townships' wineries. Known for its dry white wines, an aperitif called L'Apéridor, and its world-renowned ice wine, the winery also has an museum on-site chronicling the history of winemaking in Québec.

Accommodations

If you're not interested in the **nudist campground** (40 chemin des Bouleaux, 250/298-5372) but still want to spend the night outdoors, there are beautiful sites at ◖ **Camping Écologique de Frelighsburg** (174 route 237 Sud, Frelighsburg 450/298-5259 or 877/298-5259, www.campingquebec.com/frelighsburg, tent site $24) just south of

THE EASTERN TOWNSHIPS

Frelighsburg, about two minutes from the border on the banks of the Rivière aux Brochets. Also on the river, although this time right in the center of Frelighsburg, is the cozy **Au Flâneur** (6 rue de l'Église, Frelighsburg, 450/298-5657 or 800/890-5657, $80–90 d). The B&B's red walls and natural wood trim contribute to a warm, rustic feel, further accentuated by simple guest rooms with antique furniture. Just a little bit out of town, at the foot of Mont Pinacle, you'll find **(La Girondine** (104 route 237 Sud, Frelighsburg, 450/298/5206, www.lagirondine.ca, $80 d), a converted farm owned by two French natives who raise grain-fed ducks. There's a beautiful wide porch here and walking trails though the orchards and the forest. There's also a lovely country restaurant that serves dishes such as rabbit and of course, duck. **(Auberge l'Oeuf**'s (229 chemin Mystic, Mystic, 450/248-7529, $77–87 d) prime location at a quiet intersection in the middle of Mystic makes it a great spot to relax and while away the hours. Housed in a one-time general store, this small inn has five rooms with quilted bedspreads, a chocolatier, and a restaurant. Just outside of Dunham, **Au Temps des Mûres** (2024 chemin Vail, Dunham, 450/266-1319 or 888/708-8050, www.tempsdesmures.qc.ca, $65–80 d), is an authentic Victorian home, where the furniture and décor don't seem to have changed much since the 1800s. There's an odd-looking little pool out back with a wonderful view onto the property's 400 acres.

Food

What a welcome surprise to find **(Le Sainte Jeanne d'Arc** (7 rue River, Stanbridge East, 450/248-0718 or 877/248-0718, www.ste-jeannedarc.com, table d'hôte $24.95–39.95), a medieval restaurant in what used to be Stanbridge East's Catholic church. All meals are cooked on *charbonnades* (little, individualized ceramic pots with grills). Table d'hôte menus include combinations of beef, chicken, and shrimp, or more exotic ostrich, bison, and elk, along with an appetizer, salad, dessert, and coffee. Named after the hotel that used to be housed in this handsome brick building, Dunham's **Bistrot Seeley** (3809 rue Principale, Dunham, 450/295-1512, mains $9–15, table d'hôte $23–27, 5:30–9:30 P.M. Thurs.–Sat. Oct.–May, 11 A.M.–9:30 P.M. Tues.–Sat. May–Oct.) has a terrific, laid-back atmosphere and a wide selection of gourmet pasta dishes and desserts.

Information

If you want to tour the wineries, pay a visit to the tourism information center (3638 rue Principale, 450/295-2273, 10 A.M.–6 P.M. daily mid-May–mid-Aug.) in the municipal library. It'll supply you a wine-route map.

Brome-Sutton

This region has two of the best towns to explore in the Townships: The blue-blooded Knowlton (also known as Lac Brome) and the recreation-rich Sutton. With plenty of antique and fashion shops, cafés and the famous Lac Brome duck, Knowlton is a surprisingly upscale Townships town. Sutton meanwhile, is known for its busy main drag, pretty Victorian inns, and, of course, for its "mont," the excellent Mont Sutton, which is busy year-round with skiers and hikers.

(KNOWLTON

Seven villages surrounding Lac Brome (the lake) amalgamated to form Lac Brome (the municipality) in 1971, with Knowlton as the cultural and commercial heart. This pretty, bustling town named after transplanted Vermonter Colonel Paul Holland Knowlton possesses a certain coolness, not only for its numerous shady trees and lakeside location, but for its blue-blooded grandeur present in its stalwart civic buildings, tidy, boutique-lined streets, and spectacular Victorian manors.

The most Anglo-Saxon of all Townships towns—there's even a Ralph Lauren outlet for those needing their regular fix—Knowlton is also known for its antique shops, great restaurants, and beautiful inns. Perhaps most famous of all, however, is Knowlton's Lac Brome duck. Cultivated by **Brome Lake Ducks** (40 chemin Centre, 450/242-3825, www.bromelakeducks. com, 8 A.M.–5 P.M. Mon.–Fri., 10 A.M.–5 P.M. Sat.–Sun.) since 1912, Canada's oldest and biggest duck-breeding business produces more than two million ducks annually, 9,000 of which get exported every month to places such as Japan. There's a store on-site at the breeding plant where you can buy all kinds of duck cuts fresh or cooked, as well as patés, liver, kebobs, and sausages.

There isn't an opportunity gone by that Knowlton hasn't feted its web-footed friend. Almost all local restaurants serve it, either in traditional ways or in new concoctions, such as duck pizza. There's even **Duckfest** (450/242-2982), a festival that takes place on three weekends in September and October and features everything duck—from tastings to paintings.

Lac Brome's town hall

© JENNIFER EDWARDS

Sights and Recreation

Occupying six buildings, the **Musée Historique du Comté de Brome** (130 rue Lakeside, 450/243-6782, 10 A.M.–4:30 P.M. Mon.–Sat. and 11 A.M.–4:30 P.M. Sun. mid-May–mid-Sept., adults $5, students $3, children $2.50, family $15) chronicles the lives of early settlers in the region. The museum's most famous artifact is the Fokker DVII World War I fighter plane. Used by German troops, the Fokker, which was faster and could climb greater heights than others, helped them dominate the skies. You'll also find an old general store, blacksmith shop, and post office re-created in the old fire hall building. Behind the Knowlton Pub, the English-language productions offered by **Theatre Lac Brome** (9 Mont-Echo, 450/242-2270, www.theatrelacbrome.ca, Tues.–Fri. $22, Sat.

$25, matinees $18) include works by English Canadian playwrights and translations of French Canadian ones.

Accommodations

A sunny, serene feeling permeates ☾ **La Venise Verte** (58 rue Victoria, 450/243-1844, www.laveniseverte.com, $90–105 d), a B&B with a gabled roof and polished wood floors. The four rooms (two with shared bath, two with private bath) are airy, yet warm, and painted in subdued colors. There's also a lovely garden with a swimming pool out back. There's only one bedroom on offer at ☾ **Majuka** (266 chemin Stage Coach, 450/243-1239, www.chez.com/majuka, $115 s or d), a massive log cabin in the woods, but oh, what a room it is. Equipped with two log-frame double beds, a sitting room, and a private washroom with sauna, the room also has a private entrance. Out back, the land slopes to a spring-fed swimming pond and provides a beautiful view of the surrounding area. There isn't much to the 12 rooms in the **Auberge Knowlton** (286 chemin Knowlton, 450/242-

THE EASTERN TOWNSHIPS

6886, aubergeknowlton.ca, $110–130 d), but you can't beat this location right in the center of town. This is the oldest hotel in continuous operation in the Townships; it was once a stagecoach stop on the way to Bolton's Pass that has since been gutted and renovated. Le Relais, the bistro on the main floor, serves a variety of Lac Brome duck dishes and other pub food. Knowlton's other famous historic inn is the **Auberge Lakeview Inn** (50 rue Victoria, 450/243-6183 or 800/661-6183, www.aubergelakeviewinn.com, $126–155 d), also a favored stop for stagecoach passengers, among them past Canadian prime ministers. The rooms here vary from straightforward to deluxe studios, but all are plush and accented with country-Victorian stylings. There's a fine dining restaurant on-site that features a table d'hôte menu, silver serving dishes, and tuxedoed waiters, and a pub called Spencer's known for its spicy duck wings.

Food

(Le Saint-Raphaël (281C chemin Knowlton, 450/243-4168, 10 A.M.–5 P.M. daily summer, 10 A.M.–5 P.M. Sat.–Sun. winter, mains $10–15) is a charming, casual spot with good coffee and sandwiches. This being Knowlton, it serves a tasty duck pizza and a *croque-canard*—Brome Lake duck with cranberry sauce and melted cheese in a grilled tortilla crust. If you have room, sample one of its famous desserts, including a to-die-for carrot cake. Also on the main drag is **(Bistro Knowlton Pub** (267 chemin Knowlton, 450/242-6862, 11:30 A.M.–9 P.M. daily winter and 11:30 A.M.–10 P.M. daily summer, mains $8–18), a busy spot with an outdoor patio and music in the summer. Menu items include sandwiches, quesadillas, and fajitas along with more exotic items such as wild boar sausage. Farther down the road is **Restaurant Papa Spiros** (290 chemin Knowlton, 450/242-2409), an unassuming eatery with simple Italian, Greek, and even Chinese fare. With a lovely terrace overlooking Mill Pond, **Café Inn** (254 chemin Knowlton, 450/243-0069, table d'hôte $19–20) has a simple table d'hôte menu with items such as tuna,

veal, and pork. There's jazz music on Thursday and Saturday nights in the summer.

Shopping

A popular stop for antique-hunters, Knowlton boasts about a dozen good antique shops. Some popular places to stop are **Lawrence Antiques** and the upstairs **Antiquités Aura** (107 chemin Lakeside, 450/243-5556, 11 A.M.–5 P.M. daily), which specializes in rustic furniture items and silver, jewelry, and linen. There's also **Au Coin du Bois** (19 chemin Mont-Echo). **England Hill** (104 Lakeside, 450/243-5303, www.englandhill.com) has an incredible selection of linens, quilts, and duvets. For something a little different, try the local creations of former fashion model Jodi Mallinson by visiting **Agnes and Grace** (3 chemin Mont-Echo). You'll find summer dresses, sun hats, and handbags in bold colors and prints.

Information

You'll find Knowlton's tiny tourist center (696 rue Lakeside, 450/242-2870, 9 A.M.–5 P.M. daily early June–early Sept. and 9 A.M.–5 P.M. weekends early Sept.–mid-Oct.) in the Foster section of town.

Getting There

To get to Knowlton from Montéal, take Autoroute 10 Est and debark at Exit 90. Then take Route 243 about 12 km toward Knowlton (Lac Brome).

SUTTON

Situated at the foot of surrounding mountains, the township of Sutton (pop. 3,366) was first settled, along with its neighboring municipalities, Glen Sutton and Sutton Junction, in 1799. In 1898 a fire decimated the center of town, starting with the lumber mill and continuing to a hotel and railway station. In total 35 buildings were consumed by the fire that night, but fittingly the Baptist and Methodist (now United) churches on Maple Street were spared. A popular destination for its recreational opportunities—hiking, cycling, cross-country skiing, and especially winter skiing at

© JENNIFER EDWARDS

It may be small, but Knowlton has fashion savvy.

Mont Sutton—Sutton attracts a wide array of outdoor enthusiasts and those who just want to wander down the café- and boutique-lined rue Principale.

Sights and Recreation

If you're keen on early communications methods, stop by the **Eberdt Museum of Communications** (30A rue Principale Sud, 450/538-2649, 9:30 A.M.–5 P.M. Thurs.–Sun.) and learn about the technological transformations that the Sutton region experienced in the 19th century as a major link between the cities of Québec and New England. The museum is also the starting point to the town walking tours.

More often called just Sutton Park, **Parc d'Environnement Naturel de Sutton** (450/538-4085, www.parcsutton.com, adults $4, children 6–17 $2, children five and under free, family $10, cabin adults $19, children $17) offers close to 80 km of hiking trails that cover the Sutton Mountains. The park has trails for all levels of hikers, including the pop-

ular Roundtop trail that leads to the summit of Mont Rond and a spectacular view overlooking Vermont's Green Mountains. Two camping areas, Le Nombril and Les Falaises, situated on the Estrie hiking trail, and a cabin called the Refuge are available for overnight stays. If you're around in the spring there are some good sugar shacks to visit around Sutton. Try **Érablière Monique et Robert** (367 chemin Mudgett, 450/538-0181), a small operation that still collects sap in buckets and boils it in wood-burning evaporators. The menu is a bit more upscale here—gone are the traditional pea soup and sugar pie; instead there's maple-flavored cream of rutabaga soup and maple mousse. There are even vegetarian options available. Hiking and cross-country skiing trails are on-site to work off lunch's sugar pie.

Mont Sutton

The European-style Mont Sutton (671 chemin Maple, 450/538-2545 or 866/538-2545, www.montsutton.com, adults $44, students $32, children 6–13 $25) has come a long way since its simple beginnings. Founded in 1962 by Harold Boulanger, a dairy farmer, as a means to keep himself and his employees employed in the wintertime, Mont Sutton was an immediate success. Harold's son, Réal, a passionate skier, was the architect behind the ski hill's runs; he prefered to maintain the natural terrain. Now famous for its 460-meter vertical drop and its glades that run for more than 40 kilometers, the 53 trails have 194 junctions, enabling skiers to zigzag the slopes in a variety of ways. Equipment rentals are available at the huge Sports Experts store at the base of the mountain and there is free shuttle service from town to the ski hill on weekends.

Accommodations

Right in town on the main drag is the **Passiflore Inn** (55 rue Principale Sud, 450/538-5555), a lovely renovated Victorian home with three spacious bedrooms featuring large wood-beam floors, large windows, and queen-size beds. The spacious yard backs onto a river. The inn is open from May to October.

THE EASTERN TOWNSHIPS

Recognized as one of the finest places to stay in Sutton, the **(Auberge le Saint-Amour** (1 rue Pleasant, 450/538-6188 or 888/538-6188, www.auberge-st-amour.com, $85–150 d) is also right in the center of town in a beautifully restored mansion dating to the early 1900s. The eight rooms and one suite all have their own bathrooms and vary in décor: Some are straight-ahead Victorian while others feature a Victorian/art deco mix. Owned by a couple who are both chefs, the inn naturally has a restaurant on the premises that is considered one of the best in Sutton. If the typical Victorian fare doesn't turn your crank, try the alpine-meets-medieval-style **Chevalier Mont Écho** (937 Parmenter, 450/243-5284, www.chevaliermontecho.com, $100–110 d) near Mont Sutton. The beautiful living room of the house is all wood with a graystone fireplace and antiques, while the cozy four bedrooms, all named after different countries, are tastefully decorated with own regional touches. The balcony overlooks the forested valley and mountains. If you love the outdoors, consider staying at **(Au Diable Vert** (169 chemin Staines, 450/538-5639 or 888/779-9090, www.audiablevert.qc.ca, inn $95–110 d, cabin $28 per person, tent site $23 d). This mountain inn with

cabins and campsites is situated at 300 meters and has a property of 200 acres. The gorgeous inn, in a renovated farmhouse, has four rooms that feature antique furniture and gabled ceilings. There's a beautiful dining room with wood-beam ceiling, its own fireplace, and a terrace with a mountain view. Cabins able to accommodate 2–6 people are in a wooded area and have their own woodstoves and two double beds. There are also 30 private campsites with picnic tables and firepits. The inn offers a wide range of activities starting with access to its 12 km of trails, kayaking, fishing, and romantic moonlight-snowshoeing excursions. There are even workshops in mushroom identification and photography.

Food

In a red barn building set back from the street, you can find a welcome taste from the far southeast in the **(International Spice Man** (17D rue Principale, 450/538-3177, 3–7 P.M. Fri., 11 A.M.–7 P.M. Sat., 11 A.M.–1:30 P.M. Sun. during summer), a take-out place with killer Indian food including chicken *madras*, tandoori, and shrimp curry. **Tartinizza** (19 rue Principale Nord, 450/538-5067, mains $9–14) serves good thin-crust pizzas, pasta dishes,

---

CHOWING DOWN AT LA CABANE

If Quebecers permit themselves one massive indulgence a year, it usually takes place when the sap starts running in the spring time. Sap, you see, means maple syrup, and maple syrup means its time to go to the *cabane à sucre* where a wealth of traditional Québec indulgences await. Here is a sampling of what you may find:

- **Glazed ham:** roasted ham cooked in maple syrup

- **Pea soup:** a thick soup made from yellow peas

- **Beans:** brown beans that usually come with small pieces of pork

- *Oreilles de crisse* **(Christ's ears):** very crunchy pork rinds

- *Œuf dans le syrop* **(egg in the syrup):** poached eggs cooked in water infused with maple syrup

- *Pets de sœur* **(nun's farts):** tiny cinnamon rolls glazed with maple sugar

- *Tourtière* **(meat pie):** Québec's classic dish is a pie made with a combination of pork, ground beef, onions, and spices

- **Sugar pie:** a super sweet brown sugar pie

- *La tire* **(maple taffy):** hot maple syrup taffy poured over a mound of snow, then wound around a popsicle stick

and desserts. Although the **Auberge des Appalaches** (234 chemin Maple, 450/538-5799 or 877/533-5799, www.auberge-appalaches.com) is nothing to look at from the exterior, there is a terrific dining room and lounge made cozy with a wood-burning fireplace. Dishes vary from duck, lamb, and seafood entrées to Chinese and cheese fondues.

Information

You can find the tiny tourist office (11-B rue Principale Sud, 450/538-8455 or 800/565-8455, www.sutton-info.qc.ca, 8:30 A.M.–5 P.M. Mon.–Fri. and 9 A.M.–5 P.M. Sat.–Sun.) on the main drag. You can get information here about the village and rural and church-cemetery walking tours.

Getting There

If you're heading straight to Sutton from Montréal, get off Autoroute 10 at Exit 68 and take Route 139 south all the way to Sutton. To get to Sutton from Knowlton, take Route 104 and then Route 215 south to Sutton.

Memphrémagog

This area, defined by the long Lac Memphrémagog, the bustling town of Magog, and the luminous Mont Orford, is the Townships' busiest. Heading south from Mont Orford, which is just north of Autoroute 10, you'll hit the busy town of Magog, located just south of the 10. Due to the popularity of the park and the lake, Magog's main drag can get clogged in the summertime. Still, it's a fun town with plenty of shops and restaurants, a great microbrewery, and of course, a sparkling lake, known for its recreational pleasures and a curious resident named Mempré.

Getting around the region is easy, but the lake does cut you off from the rest of the Townships somewhat. There are no bridges, so you'll have to make the tour around the lake. To get to Parc National du Mont Orford from Montréal, take Autoroute 10 Est to Exit 118. Follow Route 141 north to the park. To get to Magog, take the same exit, but choose Route 141 going south.

MAGOG-ORFORD

Situated at the north end of Lac Memphrémagog, the bustling town of Magog (pop. 23,405) started off with the much less evocative name of Outlet, given because of its situation near where the lake drains. Born out of the construction of a variety of mills and a dam by the enterprising Ralph Merry III, who arrived in the area in 1797, the town's main industry was log-cutting and -driving. This changed in the first half of the 1800s with the implementation of a stop on the Montréal-Sherbrooke railway line and more significantly, with the arrival of textile mills in 1884. Nowadays, Magog's streets are often crowded and filled with traffic as people make their way to the lovely but crowded beach right in the middle of town, or peruse the many shops and restaurants.

Sights and Recreation

Right in the center of town, **Le Vieux Clocher** (64 rue Merry Nord, 819/847-0470) is a concert hall in a renovated Protestant church from 1887. The small, 400-seater features musical concerts, plays, and comedy acts from many of the province's up-and-coming comedians. Most other activities that can be done right in town focus on the lake. You can take a ride on the *Aquilo 36* (federal wharf, 819/868-4410, half day $55, full day $75), a 36-foot catamaran. Powerboats, Sea-doos, and sailboats can be rented at the **Marina Le Merry Club** (201 rue Merry Sud, 819/843-2728, 8 A.M.–6 P.M. daily mid-Apr.–mid-Oct., powerboats four hours $260, eight hours $425, sailboats four hours $260 or $285, Sea-doos one hour $85–95), a huge complex just beyond the McDonald's. A store on-site sells everything from gumboots to $30,000 sailboats. If you're feeling more

THE EASTERN TOWNSHIPS

© JENNIFER EDWARDS

the Mont Orford ski hill in the summertime

leisurely, climb aboard one of the cruise ships belonging to **Croisières Memphrémagog** (Parc de la Baie de Magog, 819/843-8068 or 888/842-8068, www.croisiere-memphrema-gog.com, 1.75-hour cruise adults $20, children 3–11 $11.50, full-day cruise $75). You can either take a short cruise around the lake or an all-day cruise down to Newport, Vermont.

Parc National du Mont-Orford

The relatively small but multipurpose Parc du Mont-Orford (819/843-9855 or 800/665-6527, entry adults $3.50, children 6–17 $1.50, tent sites $18, huts $17 per person), just north of Magog, is unique in two ways: It has a concert hall, the Centre d'Arts Orford, right at its center and, of course, a very popular ski hill, Mont Orford. If you're up for a more traditional park visit, however, there are a number of activities here to keep you busy. In the winter, there are snowshoeing and cross-country skiing (equipment for both can be rented for $15 for adults and $12 for children) and in the summer there are kayaking and canoeing opportunities on the

park's two lakes, Fraser and Stukely, biking on the Route Verte's La Montagnarde, and more than 80 km of hiking trails. Most of the trails are rated easy, but two exceptions are the Mont-Chauve Loop and the Sentier des Crêtes—the latter offering a superb 360-degree panorama. Stop by the **Le Cerisier Visitors Center** (3321 chemin du Parc) to register for camping, get information on the park, and visit the nature boutique.

Centre d'Arts Orford

The gorgeous setting of the Centre d'Arts Orford (3165 chemin du Parc, 819/843-9871 or 800/567-6155, www.arts-orford.org, tickets $20–30) is just one of the attractions at this internationally renowned chamber music school and performance center. During the summer, the center hosts the Orford Festival, a six-week-long series of classical music concerts, often featuring the talents of visiting professors, and a visual arts exhibit. There are three main buildings at the center—one is in the shape of an organ case, another, a grand piano, and the third, a bass clef.

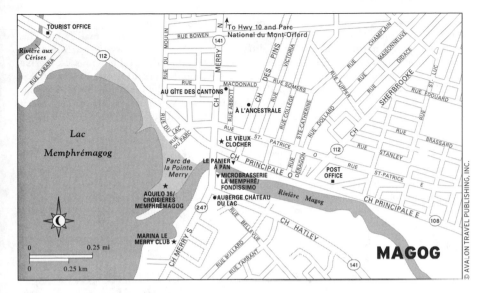

Mont Orford

Tying for first place with Owl's Head in terms of the highest vertical drop in the Townships, Mont Orford's (4380 chemin du Parc, 819/843-6548 or 866/673-6731, www.orford.com, adults $44, students $35, children 6–13 $26) 540-meter drop also makes it the third-highest in Québec. Whereas Sutton is famous for its twisty, tight-corner glades, Orford's 230 acres of skiable land is best known for its speedy cruising runs. In addition to the two quads, Orford recently installed a unique, odd-looking hybrid lift that features a closed-to-the-elements gondola for those wanting to warm up as they head up the mountain and an open-air chair for the no-nonsense skiers who want to keep their skis on their feet and not loose any time.

Accommodations

There is no shortage of places to stay in Magog and closer to Orford. In addition to the two campgrounds in Parc National du Mont-Orford, there's the **Auberge du Centre d'Arts Orford** (3165 chemin du Parc, 819/843-9871 or 800/567-6155, www.arts-orford.org, $35–50 d) right on the arts center's grounds. A member of Hostelling International, this youth hostel is made up of 19 cottages and three pavilions with dorm-style rooms. In July and August, the pavilions are taken over by students and only the cottages are available... just as well since the dorm rooms are on the dingy side. Kitchen facilities are shared and rooms in pavilions have private bathrooms. The very pretty and bright home belonging to **Au Gîte des Cantons** (516 rue MacDonald, 819/868-6644 or 877/906-6644) has five airy rooms (three with queen-size beds, one with twin beds, and one deluxe room with TV and a private bathroom). Walk into the very cozy **À l'Ancestrale** (200 rue Abbott, 819/847-5555 or 888/847-5507, www.ancestrale.qc.ca, $85–105 d, $10 less during the week), in the center of Magog on a quiet street, and you'll feel immediately at ease in the living room equipped with Persian carpet, fireplace, and piano. The B&B has four spacious rooms with large windows and views onto the treed garden. Try the **Auberge Château du Lac** (85 rue Merry Sud, 819/868-1666 or 888/948-1666, www.aubergechateaudulac.com, $95–135 d), an elegant, renovated, three-floor mansion dating to 1864, for peaceful rooms

© AVALON TRAVEL PUBLISHING, INC.

THE EASTERN TOWNSHIPS

decorated in a French Empire style with modern amenities such as TV, air-conditioning, and high-speed Internet access. There's also a fine dining room here with French cuisine and five-, seven-, or nine-course meals. The **Hôtel Chéribourg** (2603 chemin du Parc, 819/843-3308 or 800/567-6132, www.cheribourg.com, $127–226) is a full-on resort hotel at the foot of Mont Orford on Rivière Cherry. Rooms here are comfortable, yet predictable with standard hotel comforters and industrial carpeting. There's a fitness room on-site with a sauna, whirlpools, and indoor and outdoor swimming pools, and spa services, including all types of massages and wraps from seaweed to peat moss to chocolate.

Food

For baked bread, pastries, and chocolates, visit **Le Panier à Pain** (382 rue Principale Ouest, Magog, 819/868-6602, or 2253 chemin du Parc, Orford, 819/847-1352, www.panierapain.com). There's also a café on-site that serves healthy sandwiches, soups, crêpes, and salads and will prepare a boxed lunch for trips into the park. In a century house, the charming 【 **Microbrasserie La Memphré** (12 rue Merry Sud, 819/843-3405, 11:30 A.M.–close Mon.–Fri., noon–close Sat.–Sun.) serves nachos, panini, burgers, and pasta with your choice of six locally brewed beers. In back of the microbrewery is the charming **Fondissimo** (10 rue Merry Sud, 819/843-8999, 5 P.M.–close daily, mains $16 and up), a fondue spot with a lovely outdoor patio. Bring your own wine. One of the most coveted tables in Magog is at 【 **Les Toits Bleus** (1321 chemin Gendron, 819/847-0988 or 888/847-0988, www.toitsbleus.com, 4–6-course meal $30.50–41), a French restaurant set in an old 1854 farmhouse on an actual working farm. Drive up to the house and see sheep grazing and ducks in the pond and an organic garden where all the meals' fresh produce is picked. Enter the building right through the kitchen and choose from a four- to six-course meal with mains consisting of lamb, duck, chicken, or fish. There is a large addition

built on to the old house, but if you can try to grab a table in the cozy small room. This is also a bring-your-own-wine establishment. The Orford landmark known as **La Merise** (2329 chemin du Parc Orford, 819/843-6288, 5 P.M.–close daily) is notable for its numerous paintings of Victorian ladies painted by one of the owners and for its simple, yet pleasurable, entrées of pasta, fish, duck, or pork.

Information

You'll find the main tourist office (55 rue Cabana, 819/843-2744 or 800/267-2744, www.tourisme-memphremagog.com, 8:30 A.M.–8 P.M. daily late June–early Sept., 9 A.M.–5 P.M. Sat.–Thurs. and 9 A.M.–7 P.M. Fri. early Sept.–June) just outside of the downtown core off Route 112.

NORTH FROM ORFORD
Mine Cristal Québec

In Bonsecours, Mine Cristal Québec (430 11e rang, 450/535-6550, www.crystalsanctuary.com, 10:30 A.M.–5 P.M. Sat.–Sun. June and Sept., 10:30 A.M.–5 P.M. daily July–Aug., tours adults $7, students $6, children five and younger free, family $24) is the only quartz crystal mine in Canada and probably the only mine with New Age leanings. The site offers visitors a guided tour of the open-mine pit with an overview of crystal-mining technology, history, and a focus on their healing powers. If you're there, don't miss one of the 45-minute crystal symphonies offered on instruments made entirely of crystal.

Valcourt

Although Valcourt (pop. 3,383) may seem nondescript for those on a quick drive-through, it has actually been the home to two of Québec's biggest newsmakers. On one side there is the ingenious inventor Joseph-Armand Bombardier, who put Valcourt on the map by building the world's first snowmobile (later known as the Ski-doo). To experience the almost mythical stature of the Bombardiers, visit the excellent **J. Armand Bombardier Museum** (1001 avenue J.-A.-Bombardier, 450/532-5300, www.museebombardier.com, 10 A.M.–5 P.M. daily May–early Sept., 10 A.M.–5 P.M. Tues.–Sun. early Sept.–May, $7 adults, $5 students, children under five free, family $15), where through a film and exhibits, you'll find out about the relentless fire that drove the young Joseph-Armand Bombardier to create and perfect the vehicle that would help bridge isolated Québec communities in wintertime. Valcourt's other famous son is one of Québec's most notorious human curiosities, Rael, the leader of the 50,000-strong worldwide cult whose headquarters are in Valcourt. Believing that aliens created humankind though genetic engineering, the Raelians, through their company, Clonaid, are threatening to create the first human clone. Although the cult used to operate a museum called UFOLand that was once open to the public, the museum has since shut down.

LAKE MEMPHRÉMAGOG
(Saint-Benoît-du-Lac Abbey

The most popular visitor destination in the area is the beautifully situated Saint-Benoît-du-Lac (pop. 51). Functioning much like a mini-Vatican, Saint-Benoît-du-Lac is actually a municipality in itself with the sprawling and somewhat austere Saint-Benoît-du-Lac Abbey (819/843-4080, www.st-benoit-du-lac.com, 5 A.M.–9 P.M. daily) as its centerpiece. Founded in 1912 as a result of the exile of 40 Benedictine monks from France, the abbey welcomes busloads of tourists who are welcome to stroll the halls, attend one of the daily Masses, and peruse the wares in the basement store where the monks' famous apple cider and cheeses, including the celebrated blue cheese, Ermite, are sold. The abbey is also known for its Gregorian chanting, which can be heard three times daily and furthermore on CD. A bilingual exhibit focusing on the history of the abbey and chronicling a typical monastic day (report for duty at 5:05 A.M.) lines the wall. For those wanting an extended contemplative stay, there is a guesthouse for men (819/843-4080) and one for women (819/843-2340) on-site.

Owl's Head
Named after a departed Abenaki chief, whose profile in repose resembled the mountain's

Saint-Benoît-du-Lac is like a mini-Vatican.

© JENNIFER EDWARDS

THE EASTERN TOWNSHIPS

THE MYSTERY OF MEMPHRÉ

You've almost certainly heard talk of Scotland's Loch Ness and possibly about Lake Champlain's Champ or Lake Okanagan's Ogopogo, but did you know that deep in the waters of Lac Memphrémagog lies a monster to rival them all? His name is Memphré, and if you're one of the chosen few, he may just decide to rise and introduce himself.

One of the first written accounts of this lake creature dates to an 1867 issue of the *Stanstead Journal* in which the writer matter-of-factly states that "a strange animal, something of a sea serpent...exists in Lake Memphrémagog." Since that point, there have been well over 200 sightings recorded, many of them describing a 20- to 70-foot-long green, black, or brown monster that resembles the shape of a plesiosaur (a warm-blooded, aquatic reptile with a long neck, elongated body, and four fins, said to have roamed the waters during the Jurassic period).

An impressive recent claim occurred in July 1996, when a group of four people said that they watched Memphré for more than a minute. The group claimed that the creature they saw measured about 20 feet long, had a multitude of humps, and swam between their boat and the shore. Earlier in the day, another group of people about 10 miles away reported a similar sighting.

Today, the International Dracontology Society of Lac Memphrémagog is busy keeping tabs on the whereabouts of Memphré and there has even been a lookout set up in Magog dedicated to the lake creature. If you want to keep up-to-date on the most recent recorded sightings, visit the society's website at www.memphre.com.

---

contours, Owl's Head (www.owlshead.com, adults $36, students $29, children 6–13 $24) is known as the Townships' family ski resort. Tied with Mont Orford for the highest vertical drop in the region, it has 43 trails that are evenly classed between beginner, intermediate, and advanced. Many trails boast a spectacular view of Lac Memphrémagog and, on a good day, you can even see Mont Orford to the north. Often considered less busy than the other ski hills in the region, it has a ski and snowboarding school on-site (one hour, one person $37, one hour, two people $56.50). If you're looking for a little après-ski nibble, skip the cafeteria and head to **Owl's Bread** (299A rue Principale, Mansonville, 450/292-3088, 10 A.M.–5:30 P.M. Wed.–Thurs., 10 A.M.–9 P.M. Fri., 8 A.M.–9 P.M. Sat., 8:30 A.M.–5:30 P.M. Sun., lunch mains $6–16, dinner mains $15–27, www.owlsbread.com), a lovely little bakery and restaurant on the main drag in Mansonville. You can indulge in cakes, pies, pastries and croissants, and gourmet sandwiches, and for dinner there's a menu with French cuisine such as caribou, duck, and deer.

Georgeville

On the eastern side of the lake, sleepy Georgeville (pop. 998), named in honor of George III, is where the upper classes come to retreat and relax. Known for its Greek Revival–style homes, old churches, and beautiful surrounding scenery, the town was captured on film in Denys Arcand's *Decline of the American Empire.* Once a busy stop for ferryboats from Newport and from Knowlton's Landing, Georgeville has seen much busier days. For a visitor, there's not much to do here but soak in the quiet village atmosphere and the beautiful view of the lake and Saint-Benoît-du-Lac Abbey from the public wharf. Even if you're not planning to stay, you'll want to have a quick look at the ultra-plush **Auberge Georgeville** (71 chemin Channel, 819/843-8683 or 888/843-8686, www.aubergegeorgeville.com, $235–365 d includes breakfast and dinner). Dating to 1889, it is the oldest continually operating inn in all of Canada. The restaurant is open for breakfast and dinner, a five-course grand affair with items such as caribou-mousse crostini, duck foie gras, and grilled deer with cranberry chutney.

Stanstead

You can't get much closer to a border town than Stanstead (pop. 3,162). Just opposite Derby Line, Vermont, the international border runs right through this town, formed in 1995 when the villages of Stanstead Plain, Beebe Plain, and Rock Island amalgamated. Settled in the 1790s by New Englanders, Stanstead became residence to many well-to-do families and a bustling economy thanks to its designation as the final Canadian stop on the Montréal–Boston stagecoach line. Later on, it became known as the Granite Capital of Canada thanks to its indigenous gray granite—still a major force behind the local economy. Go for a stroll down stately Dufferin Street and take in the residences, churches, and the **Colby-Curtis Museum** (535 rue Dufferin, 819/876-7322, www.colbycurtis.ca, 10 A.M.–noon and 1–5 P.M. Wed.–Fri., 12:30–4:30 P.M. Sat.–Sun., adults $5, children $2, students $2,

seniors $3, family rate $10, children under six free). Once the home of the Colby family, the museum contains the original furniture, paintings, books, and correspondence and paints a picture of the lives of those who settled and lived in this border town. There's a gorgeous tearoom in the solarium of the house that overlooks the Victorian gardens. There's also the impressive **Haskell Free Library and Opera House** (1 Church St., 819/876-2471, www.haskellopera.org, 10 A.M.–5 P.M. Tues.–Wed, 10 A.M.–5 P.M. Fri.–Sat., 10 A.M.–8 P.M. Thurs.) right on the border. The entrance, main office, and most of the seats in the opera house are in the United States, while the library books and the opera stage are in Canada. Guests do not have to go through customs to set foot in either country, designated by a black line that divides the ground floor. The opera house puts on musicals and plays, and jazz, opera, and classical concerts.

Sherbrooke

It may be a two-university town and the Townships' biggest city, but there's a sense that Sherbrooke (pop. 143,000) still hasn't reached its full potential. While it's true that the downtown core, called Old Sherbrooke, possesses some exceptional architecture, covering movements from the mid-19th century to the 1930s, some good museums, and lovely riverside green space, there's still a feeling of neglect that permeates the place. This is particularly noticeable on Wellington Sud with its arcades and strip bars, and the crumbling buildings that line the Magog gorge. Fortunately, there are several rejuvenation projects in the works, and with the 2002 amalgamation with seven neighboring municipalities, including the leafy, mainly English-speaking Lennoxville, there's hope that good things are in store for the city. Sherbrooke is once more aptly referred to as the "Queen city of the Eastern Townships."

HISTORY

With its situation at the junction of the Magog and Saint-François rivers, Sherbrooke has always been a coveted location, first for the Abenaki who traveled its waterways, and later for American Loyalists who in 1801 built a flour mill and sawmill at the Magog gorge. Officially founded a year later, the town was given its current name in 1818 after Sir John Coape Sherbrooke, the governor-general of Canada. As Sherbrooke quietly expanded, three developments solidified its position as the Townships' financial and industrial center: the building of a regional courthouse in 1823; the arrival of the railroad linking Montréal with Portland, Maine, in 1852; and the opening of the Eastern Townships Bank in 1854. Although principally an English-speaking town in the first half of the 19th century, industrialization quickly brought many French Canadians in search of new land and jobs. Today, Sherbrooke is more than 95 percent French-speaking.

THE EASTERN TOWNSHIPS

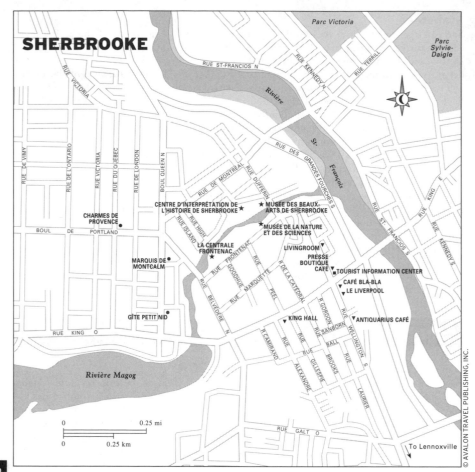

SHERBROOKE

SIGHTS AND RECREATION

Centre d'Interprétation de l'Histoire de Sherbrooke

A good first stop to make is the Centre d'Interprétation de l'Histoire de Sherbrooke (275 rue Dufferin, 819/821-5406, shs.ville. sherbrooke.qc.ca, 9 A.M.–5 P.M. Tues.–Fri., 10 A.M.–5 P.M. Sat.–Sun., late June–early Sept., 9 A.M.–noon and 1–5 P.M. Tues.–Fri., 1–5 P.M. Sat.–Sun., early Sept.–late June, adults $6, children $2). The museum covers more than 200 years of Sherbrooke history told through photos and artifacts. If it's a nice day, be sure to take one of the heritage walks ($10). The center will supply you a tape player and map for either of the two self-guided walks through the Old North Ward and Old Sherbrooke. There's also a two-hour guided theatrical tour that takes place aboard a bus offered on weekends throughout the summer, but only in French.

Musée des Beaux-Arts de Sherbrooke

In the old Eastern Townships Bank, the Musée des Beaux-Arts de Sherbrooke (241 rue Duf-

© JENNIFER EDWARDS

Sherbrooke's Hôtel-de-Ville

ferin, 819/821-2115, mba.ville.sherbrooke. qc.ca, 1–5 P.M. Tues. and Thurs.–Sun., 1–9 P.M. Wed., adults $6, students $5) houses a permanent collection of Eastern Townships, Québécois, and Canadian art from the 19th and 20th centuries, as well as a number of temporary exhibits. The museum also holds a large collection of naïve art.

Musée de la Nature et des Sciences

Although a perpetual lack of funding makes the future of the venerable Musée de la Nature et des Sciences (225 rue Frontenac, 819/564-3200, www.mnes.qc.ca, 10 A.M.–5 P.M. daily late June–early Sept., 10 A.M.–5 P.M. Wed.–Sun. early Sept.–late June, adults $7.50, children 4–17 $5, families (two adults and two children) $20, students $6.75) tenuous at best, it's worth the trip to find out if this excellent museum is open. Dedicated to the human and natural sciences, the museum houses close to 65,000 mammal, reptilian, bird, and insect specimens and specializes in educational and interactive exhibits for kids,

including an exhibit that chronicles the inner workings of a 13-year-old's brain.

Riverside Trail

There are more than 30 km of paths to enjoy along the Riverside Trail (819/821-5893, www.charmes.org), an amalgamation of walking and cycling trails that extend along the Magog and Saint-François rivers. Along the way, you'll go through parks, past Blanchard Beach, down into the Magog River Gorge, and through the Saint-François Marsh. You can stop to visit **La Centrale Frontenac** (395 rue Frontenac, 819/821-5757, 9:30 A.M.–4:30 P.M. Tues.–Sun. late June–early Sept., adults $4, children 7–12 $1.50, students $3, children six and under free, family $8), the oldest operational hydroelectric plant in Québec, to take a tour and find out more about the working of hydroelectricity. There are many points of entry to the trails.

Centre Culturel et du Patrimoine Uplands

In nearby Lennoxville, the main attraction is the Centre Culturel et du Patrimoine

THE EASTERN TOWNSHIPS

Uplands (9 rue Speid, Lennoxville 819/564-0409, www.uplands.ca, 1–4:30 P.M. Tues.–Sun. late June–early Sept., 1–4:30 P.M. Thurs.–Sun. early Sept.–late June, closed Jan.), an 1862 neo-Georgian residence now serving as a museum/community center. Stop by for proper English tea, which is served every afternoon during the summer. You can have your choice of sitting outside on the veranda or inside while enjoying tea, scones, and even cucumber sandwiches with the crusts cut off. The center also features an exhibit room upstairs.

Bishop's University

You'd have to forgive yourself for thinking that you had been beamed to Cambridge or Oxford while visiting the campus of Bishop's University (rue du Collège, Lennoxville). With an air of the well-to-do present in its buildings and well-manicured lawns, Bishop's sits like a fortress in Lennoxville, the Townships' lone English bastion. Founded in 1843 as a liberal arts college by the Anglican bishop of Québec, the school gained university status 10 years later when Queen Victoria pronounced "the said College shall be deemed and taken to be a university." It remained an Anglican institution until 1947, when it was decreed nondenominational. It occupies 500 acres at the confluence of the St. Francis and Massawippi rivers. Stop by the especially beautiful **St. Mark's Chapel** (819/822-9600, ext. 2718, 8:30 A.M.–5:30 P.M. Mon.–Sat., noon–5:30 P.M. Sun.) Modeled after English churches of the 13th-century Tudor period, St. Mark's is typical of the Perpendicular Gothic style, which places emphasis on strong vertical lines and ornate roof vaulting. After a fire nearly gutted the church, it was rebuilt in 1891 with the interior's intricate woodwork crafted from Eastern Townships ash.

ENTERTAINMENT AND EVENTS

Nightlife

Thanks to its university students, Sherbrooke has a small but swinging nightlife. There's the cozy English pub–style **King Hall** (286 rue King Ouest, 819/822-4360), which has a huge selection of international and local beers, as well as pool, table soccer, and darts. If you're keen on a game of pool, head straight for **Le Liverpool** (28 rue Wellington Sud, 819/822-3724, www.liverpool.ca), a pool hall with more than 34 tables and a cigar bar with specimens from around the world. In the summertime there's a large outdoor terrace that fills up quickly. If you're in the mood to shake it with the best of them, try out the huge nightclub **Livingroom** (66 rue Meadow, 819/822-3534, www.livingroom.net). Made up of several rooms, including a cigar lounge, a salon with couches and bookshelves, a dance floor, and five bars, the club features DJs spinning the latest hip-hop tunes.

Theater

Just like its Magog counterpart, Sherbrooke's **Le Vieux Clocher** (1590 rue Galt Ouest, 819/822-2102 or 819/847-4858) is a cabaret-style concert hall in a converted old church that features Québécois musical acts and comedians.

Festivals

Sherbrooke is a festive place throughout the summer with a whole range of public events. For a period of four days in early July, the downtown streets fill up with trapeze artists, jugglers, acrobats, and comedians for the **Fou Rire Labatt Bleue** (819/847-4858, www.fourirelabattbleue.com, tickets $13–28), a comedy festival that features more than 100 performers on stage at the Granada Theatre, the free outdoor stage on Wellington Sud, or on the street. Although most of the main-stage acts perform only in French, many of the buskers perform in English too. After that is the six-day-long **La Fête du Lac des Nations et Les Grands Feux Molson du Canada** (819/569-5888, www.fetedulacdesnations.com, tickets adults $10, children 11–16 $6, children 6–10 $4, children 0–5 free), probably the biggest annual event in the Townships. The festival features a slew of music concerts and a fireworks extravaganza where pyrotechnic companies from all over Canada compete for top prize. In mid-August, there's the **Festival des Traditions du Monde** (819/821-7433, www. ftmf.qc.ca), which features music, dance, food, and crafts from regions around the world.

ACCOMMODATIONS

Options for accommodation in Sherbrooke are surprisingly limited to generic hotel chains or motels. There is a handful of good places, though.

Under $50

There are a few good camping options in and around Sherbrooke. One is **Camping Lac Magog** (7255 chemin Blanchette, 819/864-4401, www.campinglacmagog.ca, tent sites $20), on Lake Magog, about 10 km south of Sherbrooke. Campsites are treed and well maintained. There's also a beach with good swimming. Another option is **Camping Île-Marie** (225 rue Saint-Francis, 819/820-0330, www.campingilemarie.com, tent sites $21) in Lennoxville, on a little island in the middle of the Rivr Saint-François. Check the planned activities calendar, as this place has the potential to get a bit rowdy on weekends, such as the one called Christmas in July.

$50-100

If you're looking to stay on the cheap, try one of the rooms at **Bishop's University Residences** (1800 rue du Collège, Lennoxville, 819/822-9651 or 800/567-2792, ext. 2651, www.ubishops.ca, $32–125 d). Open to the public from mid-May to late August, there are more than 400 simple rooms with single beds and twin beds and 10 apartments with kitchenettes. Access to the sports complex and tennis courts are included. From the student life to the Provence life, there's the popular **◖ Charmes de Provence** (350 rue du Québec, 819/348-1147, www.charmesdeprovence.com, $75 d.), a beautiful Second Empire house painted yellow with blue shutters. The three rooms are decorated in French country style. Another good B&B option is **Gite Petit Nid** (74 boulevard Queen Nord, 819/573-0720, $75–90, www.gitescanada.com/petitnid), which, although it combines an odd assortment of styles and furnishings, is an inviting and cozy spot with a woodstove and four simple rooms with comfortable beds. The more luxurious choice is the **Marquis de Montcalm** (797 rue Montcalm, 819/823-7773, www.marquisdemontcalm.com, $90–100 d), which features three lovely, airy rooms with down duvets, antique lamps, private washrooms, and TV sets with cable.

You won't be knocked out by the décor, but **Le Président** (3535 rue King Ouest, 819/563-2941 or 800/363-2941, www.hotel-le-president.com, $70–80 weekdays, $80–90 weekends) is a good choice for those who want to stay downtown. Rooms either come with two double beds or a king-size bed, and there are a large indoor swimming pool, sauna, and whirlpool on-site.

FOOD
Cafés

The corner café with outdoor patio known as **Café Bla-Bla** (2 rue Wellington Sud, 819/565-1366) may be one of the busiest spots in town, coveted by locals and tourists alike. It serves basic pub fare, including burgers, salads, pasta, pizza, and mussels (Wednesday is all-you-can-eat mussels night). Right across the street is the **Presse Boutique Café** (4 rue Wellington Nord, 819/822-2133), an artsy student hangout that serves a light menu of salads, soups, and sandwiches and hosts a series of film screenings, art exhibits, and literary readings. There's also Internet access on-site.

Pub Food

The oldest microbrewery in Québec is Lennoxville's **◖ Golden Lion Pub and Brewery** (2 rue du Collège, 819/565-1015, www.lionlennoxville.com, 11 A.M.–close Thurs.–Fri., 3 P.M.–close Sat.–Wed.), a popular hangout for Bishop's students and professors. It makes four homemade brews: a blonde, a light bitter, a dark bitter, and an amber. Food tends toward Cajun and Mexican fare with items such as Cajun chicken, quesadillas, fajitas, and nachos. Another microbrewery in the vicinity is the **Le Cartier Café Bistro et le Pub Saint-Malo**

(255 boulevard Jacques-Cartier Sud, 819/821-3311, 9 A.M.–11 P.M. daily). Situated just across the street from the Parc Jacques-Cartier, this place has a beautiful shady outdoor terrace and home brews, mussels, fries, tapas, and burgers on the menu.

Bistro

One of the best restaurants for atmosphere in and around Sherbrooke is the (Antiquarius Café (182 rue Wellington Nord, 819/562-1800, mains $7.50–16), with wood floors, brick walls, and tin ceiling. A restaurant and antique shop, the interior is filled with antique tables and mismatched chairs, and even the walls are covered with various items for sale. It's casual, yet romantic; sit close to the beautiful big window in the front of the restaurant so that you gaze over at the impressive Hotel de Ville across the street. Joni Mitchell plays in the background, and the menu consists prinicipally of panini, salads, pasta dishes, and quiche.

INFORMATION AND SERVICES
Tourist Information

You'll find the tourist office (2964 rue King Ouest, 819/821-1919 or 800/561-8331, www.sdes.ca, 9 A.M.–7 P.M. daily mid-June–mid-Aug., 9 A.M.–5 P.M. Mon.–Sat. and 9 A.M.–3 P.M. Sun. mid-Aug.–mid-June) not too far away from Route 410. The office has all the information you'll need on Sherbrooke and the outlying area. There is also Internet access here.

Newspapers

The only English-language newspaper published in the Townships is Sherbrooke's *The Record* (www.sherbrookerecord.com); it's actually the only English daily published outside of Montréal. You can pick it up in most places.

Banks and Foreign Exchange

Most banks in town are open 10 A.M.–4 P.M. Monday–Wednesday, 10 A.M.–8 P.M. on Thursday, and 10 A.M.–4 P.M. on Friday. Almost all of the bank locations have ATMs that are ac-

cessible 24/7. You'll find the foreign exchange office within the Banque Nationale (3075 boulevard de Portland, 819/563-7832).

GETTING THERE AND AROUND

About 1.5 hours (147 km) from Montréal, Sherbrooke is an easy drive along Route 10. If you're carless, a good alternative is to catch one of the many daily buses run by Limocar (514/842-2281, www.limocar.ca, $5.85 return) that depart Station Centrale Montréal (505 rue de Maisonneuve Est) and wind up just over two hours later at the Terminus de Sherbrooke (80 rue du Dépôt, 819/569-3656). Allô Stop, the ride-sharing service, has offices in both Montréal (4317 rue Saint-Denis, 514/985-3032, www.allostop.com) and Sherbrooke (1204 rue King Ouest, 819/821-3637). The price is about $11 one-way. If you're looking to travel to Lennoxville, there are regular municipal buses (the 2 and the 82) that depart from the bus depot to Bishop's campus. The cost is $2.75.

VICINITY OF SHERBROOKE
North Hatley

On the northern shore of sparkling Lac Massawippi, North Hatley (pop. 812) is blessed with one of the finest natural settings in the Townships. Of course, it also doesn't hurt that the town is dotted with stately old mansions, once the homes of wealthy American vacationers, gourmet restaurants, and beautiful inns. Even Jacques Chirac, the French president, has been charmed by the beauty and spent part of his summer vacation here. If you're here for just a few hours in the summertime, get yourself an ice-cream cone and meander down the boardwalk to the lakeside gazebo. If you're staying for a few days, check out one of the evening shows at **The Piggery Theatre** (215 chemin Simard, 819/842-2431, www.piggery.com). The longest-running English-language theater in Québec, it is in a renovated pig barn and puts on comic plays and musicals.

Just three km north of North Hatley, **Équitation Massawippi** (4700 route 108,

Lac Massawippi at North Hatley

819/842-4249 or 866/942-4249, www.equitationmassawippi.com, one hour $25, two hours $50) offers guided horseback-riding excursions through the nearby forests.

Get a two-hour guided visit of the **Capelton Copper Mine** (800 route 108, 819/346-9545, www.minescapelton.com, 8:30 A.M.–4:30 P.M. daily Apr.–Oct., adults $20.50, children 3–17 $4–17). Originally opened in 1863 to ship copper to the United States for the making of ammunition during the Civil War, the mine hauls tourists equipped with hard hats, jackets, and boots via wagon up Capel Mountain to the entrance of the mineshaft and guides them down about 150 feet for a two-hour tour. Temperatures hover around 9°C, so bring a sweater. For winter visitors, there's downhill skiing at **Montjoye** (4785 chemin Capelton, route 108, 819/842-2447, www.montjoye.qc.ca), a 27-run ski hill that offers night skiing and a snowpark with jumps, rails, and boxes.

There are many reputable accommodation choices in North Hatley and, unfortunately, none of them come cheap. One exception is the **☾ Auberge Le Saint-Amant** (3 chemin Côte Minton, 819/842-1211, www.aubergelesaintamant.com, $150 d includes breakfast and table d'hôte dinner), a cute B&B on top of a gentle slope to the lake. The inn has three simple rooms but is better known for its rustic dining room and French menu. Slightly more expensive and more luxurious is the five-room **☾ Tapioca** (680 rue Sherbrooke, 819/842-2743, www.tapioca.qc.ca, $115–160 d), situated in a white Victorian heritage home. The room names may err on the cutesy side (Praline, Sorbet, Moka, Nougatine, and Mille-Feuilles), but the décor is divine, the beds are plush, and the beautiful grounds make this place a great choice. The exceptionally beautiful, five-star **Manoir Hovey** (575 chemin Hovey, 819/842-2421 or 800/661-2421, www.manoirhovey.com, $145–305 includes breakfast and dinner), once the summer retreat of electricity baron Henry Atkinson, was originally modeled after George Washington's Mount Vernon. Many of its 40 rooms have fireplaces, whirlpool baths, four-poster beds,

© JENNIFER EDWARDS

and balconies with views of the lake. There's a private ice-skating rink set up in the winter and in the summer, a heated pool overlooking the lake. North Hatley's second famous five-star inn is **Auberge Hatley** (325 chemin Virgin, 819/842-2451 or 800/336-2451, www.aubergehatley.com, $145–295 includes breakfast and dinner). A member of the highly exclusive Relais and Chateaux association, the stately gray-shingled, 25-room colonial mansion is perched upon a hill overlooking Lac Massawippi.

If the gourmet dining at the Manoir Hovey and Auberge Hatley are a bit out of your price range, try the more reasonable **❨ Café Massawippi** (3050 chemin Capelton, 819/842-4528, www.cafemassawippi.com, 5:30–10 P.M. daily summer, 6–10 P.M. Wed.–Sat. mid-Oct.–summer, mains $40–48). This tiny place with a casual and colorful atmosphere has a great selection of creative mains, including veal cutlet with pesto and sundried tomato and desserts such as crème brulée with walnuts and caramelized cranberries. There's also the **Pilsen Pub** (55 rue Main, 819/842-2971, www.pilsen.ca, Mon.–Sat. 11:30 A.M.–close, Sun. 11 A.M.–close, mains $10–19, table d'hôte $25–35). You aren't going to get a gourmet meal here, but there are some fine choices in among the pub grub, such as Chinese dumplings, a *fougasse* sandwich, and a warm spinach salad. There's no place better to spend a hot summer's day than on either the lakeside or riverside patios, sipping suds while boats cruise by.

❨ Parc de la Gorge Coaticook

Surrounded by beautiful rolling green hills and valleys, the roads around Coaticook (pop. 9,042) offer some of the most spectacular scenery in all of the Townships. You'll pass by many a dairy farm on your way into town… with more than 300 in the immediate area, Coaticook is considered the dairy capital of Québec. One of the most fascinating natural sites in the Townships is the Parc de la Gorge Coaticook (135 rue Michaud, 819/849-2331, www.gorgedecoaticook.qc.ca), a protected area covering the 50-meter gorge created by the Rivière Coaticook. Extending over the gorge

© JENNIFER EDWARDS

Coaticook: the world's longest suspension bridge

is the impressive suspension bridge, which at a whopping 169 meters is considered the longest in the world. The bridge is just part of 10 km of walking paths that also feature two observation towers, caves, a reproduction native village, and interpretive signs. For mountain bikers, there are 18.5 km of trails appropriate for intermediate to advanced bikers and there's a rustic, yet pretty campground with more than 100 sites (tent sites $24). A second stop to make in town is the **Musée Beaulne** (96 rue de l'Union, 819/849-6560, www.museebeaulne.qc.ca, 10 A.M.–5 P.M. Tues.–Sun. mid-May–mid-Sept., 1–4 P.M. Wed.–Sun. mid-Sept.–mid-May, adults $5, students $2.50, children free, family $10) in the magnificent Château Norton, a 30-room Victorian mansion. The collections cover textiles, fine arts, and local artifacts, many of them belonging to the Norton family.

Parc National du Mont Mégantic

In the vast region of Mégantic known for its rugged scenery, wide-open spaces, and mountains, the impressive Parc National du Mont

Mégantic (189 route du Parc, Notre-Dame-des-Bois, 819/888-2942 or 866/888-2941, www.sepaq.com, entry adults $3.50, children 6–17 $1.50, tent sites $23, huts and tent cabins $21 per person) is about 60 km away from Sherbrooke. There are 50 km of hiking trails here, including challenging hikes to the more than 1,000-meter-high summits of Mont Mégantic and Mont Saint-Joseph—where a tiny red-roofed chapel dating to 1883 still stands and holds Mass on Sundays in July and August. There are only a few primitive campsites here, but there are huts and tent cabins equipped with woodstoves at different spots in the park, including two at the summits. The biggest draw in the park is the spaceship-looking **AstroLab** (www.astrolab.qc.ca, noon–5 P.M. Sat.–Sun. and 8–11 P.M. Sat. mid-May–late June, 10 A.M.–7 P.M. and 8–11 P.M. daily late June–late Aug., noon–5 P.M. Sat.–Sun. and 7:30–10:30 P.M. Sat. late Aug.–mid-Oct., adults $11, students 6–17 $8), an astronomy research and interpretive center that holds a multimedia amphitheater and interpretive exhibits, all to do with the stars, the galaxies, and the universe. Best of all are the nighttime guided tours up to the observation platform. Reservations are necessary.

QUÉBEC CITY

When North Americans set foot in Québec City for the first time, their jaws tend to drop. How could something so beautiful, so majestic… so *old* exist here? Indeed, with its four centuries of history and status as the first permanent settlement in New France, its French flair, and its spectacular split-level setting on the river, there is nothing quite like Québec City to impress the pants off even the most jaded, seen-it-all tourist.

It's a place where window frames, alleyways, and rooftops—things we wouldn't look twice at in other cities—suddenly take on new meaning and beauty. It's also a place where a myriad of monuments, historic attractions, museums, and festivals help us imagine and feel what it was like to be one of the first people to hop the ocean and make the New World a new home.

Recognized for this architectural, cultural, and historical richness, Québec City became the first urban center to be honored as a World Heritage Site by the United Nations in 1985. But in recent years, it's proven that it isn't just about what was. Step up from a cobblestone street and you'll find an ultramodern restaurant with innovative contemporary cuisine, a store with the latest haute fashions, and a boutique hotel with über cool design. The city hasn't only grown up, but it has also grown in size since its 2002 merger with 12 other municipalities. The greater Québec City area is now nearly 100 times its original size, reaching out as far as Île d'Orleans and has a population of 508,000.

Although its winters can be brutal, Québec City is anything but a place that boards up

© JENNIFER EDWARDS

HIGHLIGHTS

Château Frontenac: The 1893 fortress-like hotel nestled on the top of Cap-aux-Diamants has the best view in the city and enough Old World opulence to make you feel like royalty (page 181).

Fortifications of Québec: Explore the city atop the almost five km of walls that once led Charles Dickens to refer to Québec City as the "Gibraltar of America" (page 187).

La Citadelle de Québec: Perched high on Cap-aux-Diamants, the imposing star-shaped battlement is North America's largest military fortification and the home of the Canadian army's Royal 22nd Regiment (page 188).

Place-Royale: Who says North America has no history? This collection of cobblestone streets and centuries-old buildings dates to Champlain's original claim to the spot in 1608 (page 189).

Musée de la Civilisation de Québec: One of the most impressive museums in the province, this museum offers more than 400 years of Québec history to explore and – just

to keep things current – an array of contemporary, innovative, and often daring exhibits (page 190).

Parc des Champs-de-Bataille: Site of the Plains of Abraham, the spot where Québec's most famous battle between English and French took place, this 108-acre green space became Canada's first urban park in 1908 (page 191).

Quartier Saint-Roch: Off the main tourist drag, this rejuvenated neighborhood has a beautiful public garden and a number of hip bars, cafés, and restaurants (page 196).

Basilique Sainte-Anne-de-Beaupré: More than 1.5 million visitors and pilgrims come annually to the church that is said to possess major healing powers (page 215).

Île d'Orléans: The best way to see this scenic island is by bicycle. Two-wheel it along country roads that lazily meander past green fields, produce stands, and more than 600 heritage buildings dating to the time of the first European settlers in the New World (page 216).

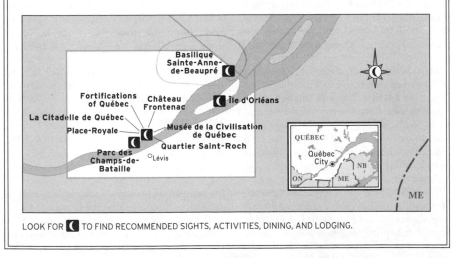

LOOK FOR **(** TO FIND RECOMMENDED SIGHTS, ACTIVITIES, DINING, AND LODGING.

come the cold. In fact, its most famous festival, the Carnaval de Québec, is held during the thermometer depths of February. There is no bad time to visit the city, but the height of summer is definitely the most coveted and there are plenty of tour buses, lines, and no vacancies to prove it.

PLANNING YOUR TIME

There's a lot to absorb in pedestrian-friendly Québec City, so if you want to see it all, give yourself at least a week to avoid blister burnout. Visiting Old Québec can easily take up your full attention for four days—just enough time to get a good handle on the city's historic highlights and sample its restaurants.

Although walking is the only way to really make your way around Old Québec, maps can be hard to follow with tiny streets darting off in all directions, changing names, or ending only to begin somewhere else. Getting lost, though, is part of the adventure, as you never know what will pop up around the corner. Let the looming presence of the Château Frontenac serve as your guide.

Start your Upper Town tour with a visit to the cliff-top **Château Frontenac,** which sits on the site where the city was born. Once you get there, you'll quickly see why the early settlers considered it such a strategic location. Beside the château is the Terrasse-Dufferin, a wide boardwalk with plenty of benches to people-watch and admire the view. From there, head over to the **Fortifications de Québec** and get a guided tour along the tops of the city's old walls. You'll probably be a bit knackered after that, so call it a day and head to the Hotel Clarendon's L'Emprise lounge for a little jazz and a local brew.

Begin day two by exploring the infamous Plains of Abraham at the **Parc des Champs-de-Bataille,** followed by a lunch stop on avenue Cartier. Wander through Upper Town's Saint-Jean-Baptiste neighborhood before stopping for a midafternoon visit to either Parliament Hill, **La Citadelle de Québec,** or the Monastère des Ursulines.

Day three should start with a morning tour

of **Place-Royale,** followed by a visit to Notre-Dames-des-Victoires or to the square's Centre d'Intreprétation. In the afternoon comb the shops that line rue Petit-Champlain and rues Pierre and Saint-Paul. In the evening take the ferry across to the town of Lévis, where you can look back at the city all lit up at night.

Begin day four with a stop at the **Musée de la Civilisation de Québec,** where you could pass most of the day if you were so inclined. Visit the Old Port and stop for a snack at the Vieux-Marché. Continue your walk to Québec's downtown core, **Quartier Saint-Roch,** visit the Jardin Saint-Roch, the local microbrewery, and rue Saint-Joseph. Opt to spend the evening here hitting one of the trendy bars or restaurants.

On day five escape the city and get in touch with the region's rural past. Head out on Route 138 and take the bridge over to **Île d'Orléans.** Tour the island, preferably by bike, while stopping at the historical villages that dot the island's circular route. Overnight here at one of the island's charming B&B or country inns.

Wave goodbye to the island on the morning of day six and take the road up to Québec's famous falls at Parc de la Chute-Montmorency. During the summer, explore both the historical and natural sites along la Route de la Nouvelle-France, including **Basilique Sainte-Anne-de-Beaupré.** In the winter, skip Île d'Orléans and take the ski shuttle from Québec City for a couple of ski days at Station Mont-Sainte-Anne.

HISTORY

French explorer Jacques Cartier was, in 1535, the first European to set his eyes on the land that the local Algonquin called Kebec, meaning "where the river narrows." But it is really his compatriot Samuel de Champlain who is credited with establishing the first permanent settlement in New France when he founded a fur-trading post in 1608 on the site. Although the site had a highly strategic position on the river, the hill that loomed above it made it vulnerable to attacks. So in 1620, Champlain expanded his post to the top of the escarpment

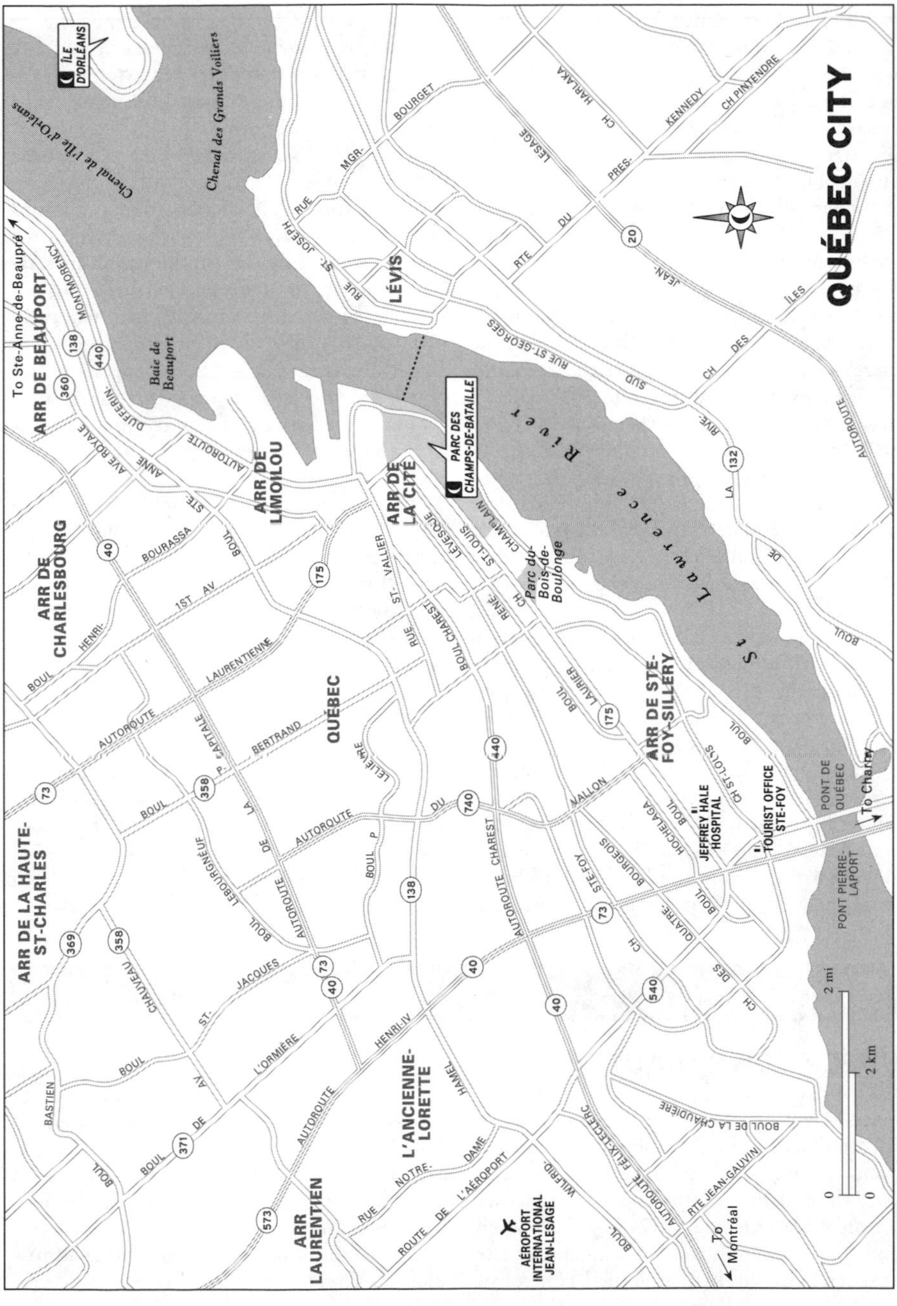

QUÉBEC CITY

To Ste-Anne-de-Beaupré

ÎLE D'ORLÉANS

Chenal de l'Île d'Orléans

Chenal des Grands Voiliers

Baie de Beauport

LÉVIS

St. Lawrence River

ARR DE BEAUPORT

ARR DE LIMOILOU

ARR DE LA CITÉ

PARC DES CHAMPS-DE-BATAILLE

Parc du Bois-de-Boulogne

ARR DE CHARLESBOURG

QUÉBEC

ARR DE STE-FOY-SILLERY

ARR DE LA HAUTE-ST-CHARLES

L'ANCIENNE-LORETTE

ARR LAURENTIEN

JEFFREY HALE HOSPITAL

TOURIST OFFICE STE-FOY

PONT DE QUÉBEC

PONT PIERRE-LAPORT

To Charny

AÉROPORT INTERNATIONAL JEAN-LESAGE

To Montréal

BOULEVARD DE LA CHAUDIÈRE

AUTOROUTE FÉLIX-LECLERC

RTE JEAN-GAUVIN

2 mi

2 km

© AVALON TRAVEL PUBLISHING, INC.

by building Fort Saint-Louis—the site where the Château Frontenac now sits.

Although the colonization of New France began with merchants interested in the lucrative fur trade, it was quickly followed by the arrival of religious orders. In 1639, two orders of nuns were sent to help the efforts of the many priests, already set up in the small city around Fort Saint-Louis. While French settlement grew at a painfully slow pace, English colonies were on the upswing. Recognizing that he would be risking losing any inroads the French had made in the New World to the increasingly aggressive English and Iroquois, King Louis XIV and his cohorts hatched a master plan. For 10 years, between 1663 and 1673, more than 700 women of childbearing years were given an all-expenses-paid trip to New France. Known as Les Filles du Roi or the King's Daughters, these young women, it was hoped, would settle in the colony, and, if all went smashingly well, hook up with a strapping colonist.

French efforts to quietly grow its domain in the area were almost interrupted when in 1690, Sir William Phipps sailed up from Boston, bringing about 30 ships with him in a British effort to take the city. When Phipps met Québec's governor, Comte de Frontenac, and demanded that he surrender the city, Frontenac famously growled, "I have no other answer for your general than the mouths of my cannons and the barrels of my guns!" Thanks to Frontenac's bravado, the British failed to realize that the French actually did not have the army or the infrastructure to back his boast. Frontenac immediately set to work on a massive fortification plan, including the establishment of the city's first defensive walls.

September 13, 1759 was the day of Canada's most notorious and divisive battle. In the night, General James Wolfe and his soldiers climbed the cliff of Cap-aux-Diamants and seized the fort. The next morning on the Plains of Abraham, the British defeated Général Louis-Joseph de Montcalm and his French troops in a battle that only lasted about 20 minutes, but still managed to see both generals killed. Wolfe died just after hearing that the English had won the battle and Montcalm died a few hours after Wolfe, saying: "All the better. I will not see the English in Québec."

The embattled city was again attacked in 1775, this time by American revolutionaries who were swiftly sent on their way home. To defend themselves against future aggressions, the British strengthened the city's fortifications and ultimately built the star-shaped citadel, which came to be known as the Gibraltar of North America, between 1820 and 1850.

With the threat of military attacks over, the city settled into a period of peace and prosperity centered around shipbuilding and the timber trade. During the late 1800s, Montréal took over as Canada's main port, but Québec City retained its role as the province's capital city, where government and tourism are both serious business.

Sights

UPPER TOWN (HAUTE-VILLE)

With its awe-inspiring views of the St. Lawrence River, the Upper Town is largely found within Québec's medieval-looking fortifications, the ones that contained the entire city until the mid-19th century. The walls that we see today were started in 1745 by the French but were not completed till the end of the century after the British gained control of the city in 1759. It is within these confines that Québec's military and religious history is best told. Most attractions have extended hours during the *saison estival,* which means the summer season, roughly from June 24th until Labor Day (the first Monday in September). The rest of the year, all museums are closed on Mondays and offer free admission on Tuesdays.

◖ Château Frontenac

With its green oxidized copper turrets and Scottish brick, the Château Frontenac (1 rue des Carrières, 418/692-3861) reigns majestically over Old Québec. Perched atop Cap-aux-Diamants, on the site that was once the administrative center of New France, this massive hotel with more than 600 rooms made its debut in 1893. It was all thanks to Cornelius Van Horne, the enterprising head of the Canadian Pacific Railway (CPR) who instigated the railway's expansion into the luxury hotel business, including both Château Lake Louise and the Banff Springs Hotel. Van Horne enlisted New York architect Bruce Price, who had also designed Montréal's Windsor Station.

Through the years, the hotel has seen many celebrities breeze through its doors, including Queen Elizabeth, Charles de Gaulle, Alfred Hitchcock, Ronald Reagan, and Charles Lindbergh. The hotel was also the location of the Québec Conferences of World War II, which involved a star-studded political faction, including Franklin D. Roosevelt, Winston Churchill, and Canadian Prime Minister William Lyon Mackenzie King.

Even if you're not staying at the Château Frontenac, it's worthwhile stopping by for a visit. You'll see the lobby, reminiscent of 18th-century Parisian hotels, with vaulted ceilings, chandeliers, and plush carpets, and, if you take the **guided tour** (418/691-2166, www.tourschateau.ca, adults $8, seniors $7.25 and children 6–16 $5.50, tours depart on the hour, 10 A.M.–6 P.M. daily May–mid-Oct. and noon–5 P.M. Sat.–Sun. mid-Oct.–Apr.), you can peek in on rooms such as the Rose Room, the ballroom, and the deluxe presidential suite. Another good option is to attend **afternoon tea** (418/266-3905, 1:30 P.M.–3:30 P.M. Mon.–Sat., $33 per person). It's hardly an inexpensive endeavour, but you'll get to lounge in the luxurious Champlain Restaurant and will be treated to a variety of finger sandwiches, scones, pastries, chocolates, fruit, and tea. Make sure you make a reservation.

© JENNIFER EDWARDS

the mythic Château Frontenac

Terrasse Dufferin

Immediately in front of the Château is the Terrasse Dufferin, an extensive boardwalk providing splendid views of the St. Lawrence. Built at the request of its namesake, Lord Dufferin, Canada's governor-general in 1879, the boardwalk has been enlarged through the years. From this vantage point you can get a better understanding of why the top of Cap-aux-Diamants was such a coveted strategic location for the French. Look to the east and you'll see Île d'Orléans, look directly across and there's the town of Lévis, and to the west you'll see the Pont du Québec, the link between the north shore and the south.

During the summer the boardwalk is a popular spot for street performers and during the winter, those feeling a need for speed can try out **Les Glissades de la Terrasse** (418/692-2955, 11 A.M.–11 P.M. daily late Dec.–mid-Mar., one ride $2), a 250-meter wooden toboggan slide.

The 1985 UNESCO monument that honors Québec City as a World Heritage Site is displayed on the Terrasse, as is a monument

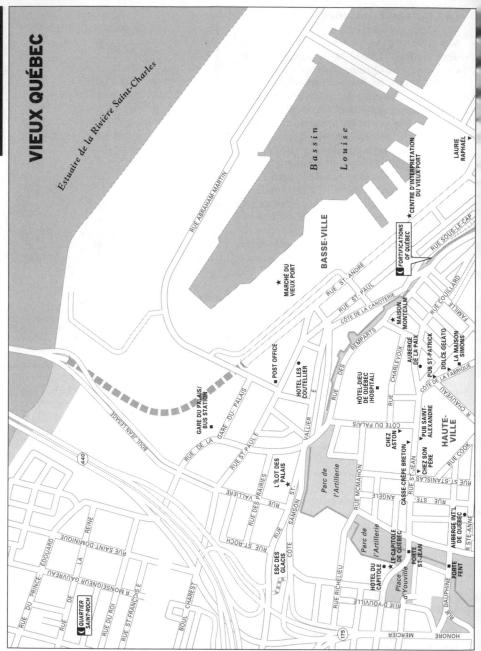

VIEUX QUÉBEC

Estuaire de la Rivière Saint-Charles

RUE ABRAHAM MARTIN

Bassin Louise

★ CENTRE D'INTERPRÉTATION DU VIEUX-PORT

LAURIE RAPHAËL ▼

RUE SOUS-LE-CAP

■ FORTIFICATIONS OF QUÉBEC

BASSE-VILLE

★ MARCHÉ DU VIEUX-PORT

RUE ST-ANDRÉ

RUE ST-PAUL

RUE COUILLARD

FAMILLE ▼

CÔTE DE LA CANOTERIE

★ MAISON MONTCALM

■ POST OFFICE

REMPARTS

RUE DES

RUE CHARLEVOIX

AUBERGE DE LA PAIX

PUB ST-PATRICK

DOLCE GELATO

LA MAISON SIMONS

HÔTEL-DIEU DE QUÉBEC (HOSPITAL) ■

CÔTE DE LA FABRIQUE

HÔTEL LES COUTELLIER ●

CÔTE DU PALAIS

R. CHAUVEAU

PUB SAINT-ALEXANDRE ▼

HAUTE-VILLE

GARE DU PALAIS/ BUS STATION ■

GARE DU PALAIS

CHEZ ASTON ▼

RUE COOK

VALLIER

L'ÎLOT DES PALAIS ●

RUE DE LA

CHEZ SON PÈRE ▼

RUE ST-JEAN

RUE ST-STANISLAS

BOUL. JEAN-LESAGE

RUE ST-PAUL

CASSE-CRÊPE BRETON ●

RUE STE-

Parc de l'Artillerie

RUE MCMAHON

ANGÈLE

RUE ST-

RUE DES PRAIRIES

SAMSON

440

RUE DES VALLIÈRE

RUE ST-ROCH

AUBERGE INT'L DE QUÉBEC ●

RUE REINE

RUE SAINT-DOMINIQUE

LA

COTE

Parc de l'Artillerie

LE CAPITOLE DE QUÉBEC ●

PORTE ST-JEAN

R. STE-ANNE

EDOUARD

R MONSEIGNEUR GAUVREAU

ESC DES GLACIS

HÔTEL DU CAPITOLE ●

Place d'Youville

PORTE FENT ■

RUE DU PRINCE

RUE DE

RUE DU ROI

RUE ST-FRANÇOISE

BOUL. CHAREST

RUE RICHELIEU

RUE D'YOUVILLE

RUE DAUPHINE

■ QUARTIER SAINT-ROCH

175

MERCIER

HONORÉ

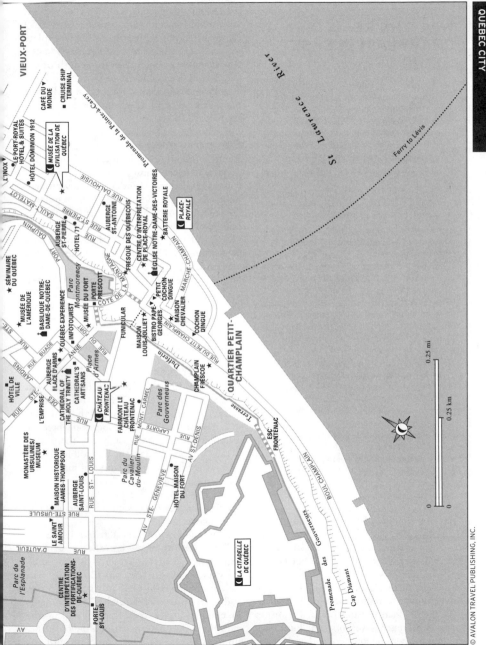

VIEUX-PORT

CAFÉ DU MONDE
■ CRUISE SHIP TERMINAL

LE PORT-ROYAL HOTEL & SUITES
L'INOX
HÔTEL DOMINION 1912
MUSÉE DE LA CIVILISATION DE QUÉBEC

Promenade de la Pointe-à-Carcy

St Lawrence River

Ferry to Lévis

SÉMINAIRE DU QUÉBEC
SAULT-MATELOT
RUE DALHOUSIE
AUBERGE ST-PIERRE
AUBERGE ST-ANTOINE
HÔTEL 71
RUE ST-PIERRE
PLACE-ROYALE
RUE DAUPHIN
RUE ST-PIERRE
FRESQUE DES QUÉBÉCOIS
CENTRE D'INTERPRÉTATION DE PLACE-ROYAL
ÉGLISE NOTRE-DAME-DES-VICTOIRES
BATTERIE ROYALE
RUE MONTAGNE
RUE STE-

MUSÉE DE L'AMÉRIQUE
BASILIQUE NOTRE-DAME-DE-QUÉBEC
Parc Montmorency
QUÉBEC EXPERIENCE
INFOTOURIST
MUSÉE DU FORT
PORTE PRESCOTT
CÔTE DE LA MONTAGNE
PETIT CHAMPLAIN
COCHON DINGUE
MAISON CHEVALIER
MARCHÉ CHAMPLAIN
BISTRO PAPE-GEORGES
COCHON DINGUE

RUE BUADE
AUBERGE PLACE D'ARMES
CATHEDRAL OF THE HOLY TRINITY
CATHEDRAL'S ART SANS
FUNICULAR
MAISON LOUIS-JOLLIET
RUE DU FORT
RUE STE-ANNE
Place d'Armes

HÔTEL DE VILLE
RUE JARDINS
L'EMPRISE
RUE STE-

CHÂTEAU FRONTENAC
FAIRMONT LE CHÂTEAU FRONTENAC
RUE MONT-CARMEL
Parc des Gouverneurs
CHAMPLAIN FRESCOE
QUARTIER PETIT-CHAMPLAIN
RUE DU PETIT CHAMPLAIN
BOUL CHAMPLAIN

MONASTÈRE DES URSULINES/ MUSEUM
MAISON HISTORIQUE JAMES THOMPSON
AUBERGE SAINT-LOUIS
RUE ST-LOUIS
Parc du Cavalier-du-Moulin
AV ST-DENIS
Terrasse Dufferin
ESC FRONTENAC

RUE STE-URSULE
LE SAINT-AMOUR
RUE D'AUTEUIL
AV STE-GENEVIÈVE
HÔTEL MAISON DU FORT

Parc de l'Esplanade
CENTRE D'INTERPRÉTATION DES FORTIFICATIONS-DE-QUÉBEC
PORTE ST-LOUIS
AV

Promenade des Gouverneurs
Cap Diamant

LA CITADELLE DE QUÉBEC

0.25 mi
0.25 km
0
0

© AVALON TRAVEL PUBLISHING, INC.

WILL THE REAL CHAMPLAIN PLEASE STAND UP?

Most Québec City residents would have no problem spotting their city's feisty founder Samuel de Champlain. With a statue on the Terrasse Dufferin, a stoic portrayal in the Fresque des Québécois mural, and loads of portraits on display throughout the city, the goateed, wavy-haired, and droopy-eyed explorer's face has been emblazoned on their brains.

But according to the Champlain Society, an organization that cares for and promotes the country's historical records, the man we all thought to be Champlain is actually Michel Particelli d'Emery, Louis XIII's chief administrator.

So how did Québec's founder come to be confused with the King's tax man? According to the Society, the basis of all the Champlain portraits was a tiny lithograph done by artist Louis C. J. Ducornet. The lithograph in turn is said to be based on a painting done by a Parisian artist named Balthasar Montcornet in 1654.

Missing for ages, the Montcornet painting finally turned up in 1920, found by New France historian Henry Percival Biggar in Paris's Bibliothèque Nationale. It was only then that the true identity of the mustachioed man was revealed.

But with no true portrait of Champlain to go by, Quebecers have decided to stand by the image that they have so long associated with Champlain. Maybe it's the mustache.

to the city's founder, Samuel de Champlain. Dating to 1898, the Champlain monument faces Place d'Armes, the first military parade grounds designed and used by both the French and British regimes.

Just west of the Château is the **Parc des Gouverneurs,** so named because it used to be the site of Château Saint-Louis, a mansion that housed French governors. The huge obelisk monument at the southern end of the park

pays tribute to generals Wolfe and Montcalm, who fought the historic and decisive 1759 Plains of Abraham battle. At the complete west end of the Terrasse is the **Promenade des Gouverneurs,** which runs the length of the Citadel and leads directly to Battlefield Park. The Promenade makes for a great walk, but make sure you still have your energy as there are more than 300 steps.

Place d'Armes

Along with Place Royale in Lower Town, this pretty square plays host to a myriad of outdoor concerts and events. Bordered by government buildings and the old city hall, which today is the home of Québec's Ministry of Finance, the middle of the square is marked by the Monument of Faith, a Gothic-style fountain that pays tribute to the 1615 arrival of the Recollet missionairies, a branch of the Franciscans. Facing the Château Frontenac is the tiny **Musée du Fort** (10 rue Sainte-Anne, 418/692-1759, www.museedufort.com, 9 A.M.–5 P.M. Mon.–Fri., adults $7.50, students $4.50), which features a 25-minute-long sound and light diorama on the city's military history.

Rue du Trésor

Across from Place d'Armes, in the northwest corner, is tiny rue du Trésor (ruedutresor.qc.ca). *Trésor* means treasure and the street was so named because it was the location where the colonists came to grudgingly pay their taxes to the governor. Today, the incredibly narrow laneway is filled with the works of many local artists, all members of the Association des Artistes de la Rue du Trésor, who set up their paintings hoping to get some coinage, just like the old governor.

Halfway down on the left-hand side is a walkway leading to the entrance of **Québec Experience** (8 rue du Trésor, 418/694-4000, www.quebecexperience.com, 10 A.M.–10 P.M. daily mid-May–mid-Oct. and 10 P.M.–5 P.M. mid-Oct.–mid-May, adults $7.50, students $5, children under six free), a 3D multimedia show that offers a lively chronicling of the beginnings of Québec City, complete with wa-

the leafy Hôtel de ville de Québec

terfalls, firing cannons, and talking statues. English showings take place four times a day during the winter season and eight times a day during summer.

Basilique Notre-Dame-de-Québec

Laying claim to the oldest Catholic parish in North America, the Basilique Notre-Dame-de-Québec (20 rue De Buade, 418/694-0665, www.patrimoine-religieux.com, 8 A.M.–4 P.M. Mon.–Fri. and 8 A.M.–6 P.M. Sat.–Sun. Nov.–Apr., and 8 A.M.–5:30 P.M. Mon.–Fri. and 8 A.M.–6 P.M. Sat.–Sun. May–Oct.) sits on the land that once contained the 1633 chapel built under the orders of Samuel de Champlain. Église Notre-Dame-de-la-Paix was then erected in 1647 but fell victim to fire in 1759 during the siege of Québec by the British army. Rebuilt a couple of years later, the church was again destroyed by fire in 1922. The church we see today was reconstructed in 1925 according to the original plans dating to the 17th century.

The inside is thoroughly impressive and grandiose: gold panels, gold altar, gold canopy, not to mention three Casavant organs

and major works of art. In fact, someone was so taken with the paintings that several of them were stolen in recent years. The site also contains a crypt, which contains more than 900 people buried between 1654 and 1898, including bishops and governors of New France. Guided tours of the basilica and the crypt are offered daily.

In the summer, take in **Heavenly Lights** (418/694-4000, 3:30–8:30 P.M. Mon.–Fri. and 6:30–8:30 P.M. Sat.–Sun. May–mid-Oct., adults $7.50, students $5, children under six free), a sound and light show that relates the history of the city and the cathedral.

Séminaire du Québec

Right next door to the basilica is an ornate gateway leading to the courtyard of Québec's fortresslike Séminaire du Québec (1 côte de la Fabrique, 418/692-3981). Founded by Monseigneur François de Laval (New France's first bishop) in 1663, the school was set up to train clergymen in the colony. After the British Conquest, the seminary became a college devoted to classical education, and then in 1852 it became the Université Laval, the first French-language university in North America. Today the university has moved to bigger digs in Sainte-Foy, although fittingly the School of Architecture remains on-site as does a residence for priests.

Musée de l'Amérique Française

Situated in a former student residence of the Séminaire du Québec, the Musée de l'Amérique française (2 côte de la Fabrique, 418/692 2843, www.mcq.org, 9:30 A.M.–5 P.M. daily late June–early Sept. and 10 A.M.–5 P.M. Tues.–Sun. early Sept.–late June, adults $5, students $3, children 12–16 $2, children 11 and under free) is devoted to the history of French America. The oldest museum in Canada, the Musée de l'Amérique française has many fascinating permanent exhibits, including one that chronicles the dispersal of original citizens of New France throughout the United States and another that focuses on the role played by the seminary on Québec society.

There are two special summer-only activities worth mentioning: a behind-the-scenes, 60-minute guided tour into parts of the Séminaire de Québec usually closed to the public and the daytime miniconcerts held in the seminary's pretty little chapel, named the Pavillon François-Ranvoysé, but better known as the *chapelle extérieure.*

Cathedral of the Holy Trinity

King George III ordered the construction of the Cathedral of the Holy Trinity (31 rue des Jardins, 418/692-2193, 10 A.M.–5 P.M. daily late May–late June and Sept.–mid-Oct. and 9 A.M.–8 P.M. daily July–Aug.) in 1804, after the British Conquest. Modeled after London's Saint-Martin-in-the-Fields, it was the first Anglican church built outside the British Isles. You can join a free guided tour to explore the interior of the church, which includes some precious objects—communion silverware, a Bible, and prayer books—donated to the church by George III and the extraordinary 3,058-pipe organ, but it is overall plain and austere (classical Georgian qualities) when compared to the overly ornate décor found in Catholic churches.

the Musée de l'Amérique française, Canada's oldest museum

QUÉBEC CITY

Monastère des Ursulines

Arriving from Tours, France, in 1639, the Ursuline nuns also left their mark in the history books of Québec City. Backed by a benefactor, a determined Marie de L'Incarnation Guyart founded the first Ursuline convent and girls' school in North America in 1641.

About 60 nuns still live at the convent, which remains predominantly off-limits to the public. However, a small museum warrants a visit. **Musée des Ursulines** (12 rue Donnacona, 418/694 0694, www.musee-ursulines. qc.ca, 10 A.M.–noon and 1–5 P.M. Tues.–Sat., 1 –5 P.M. Sun. May–Sept., 1 –4:30 P.M. Tues.– Sun. Sept.–May, adults $5, students $2, children 12 and under free) covers more than 120 years of the nuns' existence, including the educational mission and the steps that the pious women have to go through to become full-fledged nuns. There's also an eclectic collection of art, furniture, and artifacts, including the original document signed by Louis XIII approving the construction of the monastery in New France.

The adjoining **Centre-Marie-de-l'Incarnation** interprets the life and works of the founder of the monastery. Beside the museum, separated by a small laneway, is the lovely little **Chapelle des Ursulines** whose exterior was rebuilt in 1902, but which inside contains some of the original 18th-century woodwork by sculptor Pierre-Noël Levasseur. The chapel has the same opening hours as the museum; however, its doors close at 4:30 P.M. Admission is free.

(Fortifications of Québec

One of Québec City's unique features is the 4.6-km rampart that encircles the old town. Best explored by walking along the top, the walkway, once a simple dirt path used by soldiers to keep watch, has since been lined with interpretation panels that examine the evolution of the city's defense system between the 17th and 19th centuries. Near the Citadel at Porte Saint-Louis—one of the four surviving city gates—is the **Centre d'Interprétation des Fortifications-de-Québec** (100 rue Saint-Louis, 418/648-7016 or 800/463-6769, www.pc.gc.ca/fortifications, 10 A.M.–5 P.M. daily early May–early Oct., $4 adults, $2 students), the interpretive center established after the wall was declared a national historic site in 1957. View a short film, visit the restored **Esplanade Powder Magazine,** a gunpowder storage facility built in 1815, and see models and maps outlining the walls' history. The museum offers informative 90-minute walking tours (June–mid-Oct.) for $10, which includes the cost of admission.

If you would rather go it alone, the best place to start is at the staircase next to the city gate. Continue clockwise along the walls as you pass over Porte Kent, named after Queen Victoria's father, who once called the city home, and Porte Saint-Jean, the oldest gate site, dating to 1693 but rebuilt several times. You'll soon arrive at **Parc de l'Artillerie** (2 rue d'Auteuil, 418/648 4205 or 800/463 6769, www.pc.gc.ca/ artillerie, 10 A.M.–5 P.M. daily Apr.-early Oct., $4 adults, $2 students), a national historic site and home to **Dauphine Redoubt,** a unique white roughcast building with massive buttresses that was built by the French to defend the city from attack in 1712. It became the barracks for British officers after the siege, and in 1871 it was turned into a munitions factory, which closed in 1964. The park also is home to the **Arsenal Foundry,** now an interpretive center with an authentic 19th-century model of the city, and the **Officers' Quarters,** the old residences of the officers and their families, which have been restored to their 1830s splendor. Two additional exhibits on the site—one on antique toys and another titled *Les Dames de Soie,* an economuseum for silk dolls—are also worth checking out.

Farther along, the walls are lowered as you follow rue des Remparts, passing **Maison Montcalm** (45–51 rue des Remparts), home to the Marquis de Montcalm from 1758 to 1759, until the Battle of the Plains of Abraham. You'll then come to **Parc Montmorency,** once the site of North America's first cemetery north of Mexico, now a park where stands a statue of Sir Georges Étienne Cartier, one of the fathers of Confederation. Cross over the final gate, the Porte Prescott, before returning up the staircase to the **Terrasse Dufferin.** Just past the Château Frontenac at the end of rue Mont-Carmel you will find the quiet, often-overlooked **Parc du Cavalier-du-Moulin,** where part of the first true fortification, surrounding what was in 1693 a much smaller city, can still be seen. The wall continues, hugging the cliff side below the Citadel along the **Promenade des Gouverneurs.**

❈ La Citadelle de Québec

Perched on the highest point in Québec City, the impressive star-shaped fortress known as La Citadelle (côte de la Citadelle, 418/694-2815, www.lacitadelle.qc.ca, adults $8, students $7, and children 17 and under $4.50) was initiated by the French but abandoned when France failed to provide the coin necessary to get the job done. The British slowly took over the job once they gained control after the Conquest, but they only began in earnest under threat of American attack.

Under the direction of Lieutenant Colonel Elias Walker Durnford, construction began on the outer walls in 1820 and was completed only 30 years later. Spanning 37 acres, the Citadel is still an active military base, home to the Royal 22nd Regiment or the "Van-Doos," the only francophone unit of the Canadian Army. The only way to visit is by taking a one-hour guided tour, which focuses on the lives of the soldiers in the 19th century and includes visits to the two on-site museums. Tours run daily year-round.

The Citadel is also the site of the **Residence of the Governor-General of Canada** (418/694-2815, 10 A.M.–4 P.M. daily late May–late June, 11 A.M.–4 P.M. daily late June–early Sept., and 10 A.M.–4 P.M. Sat.–Sun. early Sept.–late Oct.), a secondary home, after Rideau Hall, to all governors general since 1872. The home is a showcase of Canadian art, featuring paintings by artists such as Jean-Paul Riopelle and a stellar collection of Inuit art. An hourlong guided tour is offered.

During the summer, two traditional ceremonies are held. There's the 10 A.M. **Changing of the Guard,** which features a parade of the regimental band in full red getup and the Citadel's mascot, "Batisse," the regimental goat, said to have royal bloodlines tracing back to a herd belonging to the Shah of Persia. The pomp continues on Friday, Saturday, and Sunday nights at 7 P.M. between July 1st and the last Sunday in August, when the regiment performs **The Retreat** as part of the flag-lowering ceremonies.

LOWER TOWN (BASSE-VILLE)

Encompassing the city's vital beginnings in Place-Royale and the Quartier Petit-Champlain, Old Québec's Lower Town is a narrow strip of land between the St. Lawrence and the cliff. It is here that Samuel de Champlain built a primitive trading post called L'Abitation when he first arrived in 1608, making it the oldest area in the city. The Old Port, which was once the busiest port in North America, complete with shipbuilding yards and warehouses, is now a collection of government buildings, shops, and boutique hotels.

Quartier du Petit-Champlain

With its maze of narrow laneways and cobblestone streets, Québec's original commercial district, Quartier du Petit-Champlain (www.quartierpetitchamplain.com), directly below Terasse Dufferin, is only accessible by foot. Ascending the Cap-aux-Diamants escarpment via côte de la Montagne is Québec's most famous staircase, **Escalier Casse-cou** (Breakneck Stairs in English). Linking Lower Town with Upper Town, this staircase first appeared on a city plan in 1660. Take a moment to climb the stairs and linger at the top as you set your eyes on **rue Petit-Champlain** with its length of colorful signs and flower baskets and throngs of people. Houses began to appear along this path starting in the 17th century, eventually elevating the path to laneway status. Today the homes have been converted into artisan shops and boutiques, some tacky, some not.

Below the staircase, you'll see Maison Louis-

© JENNIFER EDWARDS

the always-bustling rue Petit-Champlain

Jolliet, the historical 1683 home of Louis Jolliet, the French explorer credited with the discovery of the Mississippi River, who lived here until his death in 1700. Today, the house serves as the boarding point for the **Funicular** (16 rue Petit-Champlain, 418/692-1132, www.funiculaire-Québec.com, 7:30 A.M.–11:30 P.M. daily, $1.50), a high-tech cable car that will carry you swiftly to Dufferin Terrace at the top of the cliff. Farther down the street, past the Théâtre Petit Champlain, which regularly hosts French musical acts, is a tiny parkette called **Parc Félix-Leclerc,** named after the famous Québécois singer-songwriter. At the end of the street is one of the city's handful of trompe-l'oeil murals, the *La Fresque du Petit-Champlain.* This one, which looks as though the bricks have been blown off the side of a house, shows scenes from the neighborhood over time. You'll spot shipbuilders and the well-loved Père Frédéric on the first floor, and rooms from the Neptune Inn, including many local historical figures and the passionate embrace between Lord Nelson, a British officer, and his love, a Québécoise, on the second. The third floor is split between

a scene from the Conquest bombings and one spotlighting the neighborly spirit of the people who lived here. The attic scene is symbolic of new immigrants.

Just off the larger rue Champlain, you'll find the **Maison Chevalier** (50 rue du Marché-Champlain, 418/643-2158, www.mcq.org), an old stone house built for shipowner Jean-Baptiste Chevalier. Restored in 1959 and again in 2005, the house is a museum dedicated to chronicling the daily lives of the merchants of New France. The visit is free.

Place-Royale

The beautiful, immaculately restored Place-Royale is where it all began. This is where, in 1608, Samuel de Champlain founded the first permanent French settlement in North America. Later, the area became known as Place du Marché (market square), and quickly became the center of trade in New France with wealthy merchants' homes being erected along the perimeter. The square's name was changed to Place-Royale when a bust of Louis XIV was erected in the middle.

Later, in the last half of the 1700s, when the city fell under British rule, Place-Royale became a center for shipbuilding, fur trading, and logging activities and continued to flourish until 1860, when Montréal surpassed Québec City as the port city of choice. The once-vibrant square became forlorn and decrepit until 1959, when a budding nationalist pride saw to it that the area was restored to its former glory. Now, the square is the center of summertime outdoor activities and during **Les Fêtes de la Nouvelle France,** it is transformed again into the market square it was in days of old.

Make a stop at the **Centre d'Interprétation de Place-Royale** (27 rue Notre-Dame, 418/646-3167, www.mcq.org, 9:30 A.M.–5 P.M. daily late June–early Sept. and 10 A.M.–5 P.M. Tues.–Sun. early Sept.–late June, adults $4, students $3, children 12–16 $2), opened in 1999 on the site of the former Hazeur and Smith houses after they burned down in 1990. The museum explores more than 400 years of history with artifacts, stories, and photos of this historic site. Skip the amateurish multimedia show and head to the three floors of permanent exhibits that take you through the lives of the sailors and merchants of Place-Royale. Departing from the center is a free 45-minute guided tour held daily in English at 10 A.M. and 2:45 P.M. during the summer. This outside tour will give you an in-depth look into New France life during the 17th century.

Built on the foundations of Champlain's original trading post in 1688, **Église Notre-Dame-des-Victoires** (32 rue Sous-le-Fort, 418/692-1650, 9 A.M.–4:30 P.M. daily except during services) is a simple little stone church that may be the oldest existing church in North America, although no one has been able to prove it. The name stems from two French victories against the British (and the Church is supposed to be impartial…). In the summer there are guided tours of the interior.

A couple of other sites worth exploring are just off the square. At the end of the rue Sous-le-Fort, you'll find **Batterie Royale,** the first fort to protect the Lower Town from enemy attacks; it was built by Frontenac in 1691. The Royal Battery gunner is in attendance during the summer, giving instructions on how a cannon is fired. And just beyond the square, at the end of côte de la Montagne, is **Parc de la cetière** with its old house foundations and the especially impressive *Fresque des Québécois,* a mural that encompasses many of the city's historical and cultural figures. It was created to seamlessly blend in to the surroundings, and you'll spot Cartier, Champlain, Lord Dufferin, Félix Leclerc, Marie de l'Incarnation, and many others.

Old Port

The Old Port has seen many changes in the last 400 years. From its humble beginnings when European settlers first arrived to its status as one of the world's most important ports with more than 1,600 ships passing through in 1863, Québec City's Old Port is now a modern port with a blooming tourist trade.

The entire port area between Place-Royale and the entrance of Bassin Louise is known as **Point-à-Carcy,** where a boardwalk extends the length, making it the only place to stroll along the St. Lawrence. Cyclists can follow the **Corridor du Littoral** that links up to the port and ride it as far out as the Chutes Montmorency with exceptional views of the river along the way. Bikes can be rented right on site from **Cyclo Services** (160 quai Andre, 418/692-4052 or 877/692-4050, 9 A.M.–9 P.M. Mon.–Sat. and 9 A.M.–6 P.M. Sun., $20 per day), which also offers a wide variety of bike tours in and around the city.

Those looking to learn more about Québec's seafaring days will want to visit Parks Canada's **Centre d'Interprétation du Vieux Port** (100 quai Saint-Andre, 418/648-3300 or 800/463-6779, www.pc.gc.ca, 10 A.M.–5 P.M. daily early May–early Sept., noon–4 P.M. early Sept.–early May, adults $4, youth $2)—although rumor had it that its days may be numbered. Surrounded by marinas on either side, the **Marché du Vieux Port** (160 quai Saint André, 418/692-2517, 8 A.M.–6 P.M. daily) was revived in the 1980s. Today more than 50 vendors are on hand selling fresh produce, meats, and cheeses that come from the surrounding rural areas of Île d'Orléans and Sainte-Anne-de-Beaupré.

Boat Cruises

Two good cruising options leave from Pier 19 at 180 rue Dalhousie in the Bassin Louise of the Old Port. **Les Croisières Le Coudrier** (418/692 0107 or 888/600 5554, www.croisierescoudrier.qc.ca, adults $24.95, children 6–16 $10) offers a guided 90-minute cruise aboard a typical sightseeing ship five times daily. **Le Groupe Dufour** (418/692-0222 or 800/463-5250, www.dufour.ca, adults $25, seniors, $23, child $10) runs its beautifully restored 1928 wooden schooner, the *Marie-Clarisse,* all the way up to the Québec bridge.

◖ Musée de la Civilisation de Québec

Québec City's largest museum (85 rue Dalhousie, 418/643-2158 or 866/710-8031, www.mcq.org, 9:30 A.M.–6:30 P.M. daily late

June–early Sept., 10 A.M.–5 P.M. Tues.–Sun. early Sept.–late June, adults $8, students $5, children 12–16 $3) is one of the finest in the province. Designed by architect Moshe Safdie (he of Montréal's Habitat '67), the museum's exterior has a sleek limestone façade. The museum has two permanent exhibits: *People of Québec… Then and Now,* which focuses on life in the province of Québec through the last 400 years, and **Encounter with the First Nations,** an exhibit that goes far beyond the folklore and clichés of Native American life to relive the realities of those who first called the land that became Québec home. Many of the museum's temporary exhibits emphasize interactivity and fun, such as a recent one exploring the workings of the body and another focusing on the symbolic power of money.

L'Îlot des Palais

Québec had a palace—in fact it had two. On this site in 1685 the first palace was built for Jean Talon, the king's *intendant,* a representative from France who oversaw the financial affairs of the colony. A fire destroyed this one in 1713 and a second one was built facing the spot where the first one stood. All that remains today are the Voûtes du Palais, the vaults of the palace, which are one of the key archaeological sites in the city. The adjoining **Centre d'Interprétation Archeologique** (8 rue Vallière, 418/641-6173, 10 A.M.–5 P.M. daily late June–early Sept., adults $3, students $2, children free) has an exhibit on what life was like at the palace as well as samples of the many artifacts that have been uncovered in the last 15 years on the site. Unfortunately, the exhibits include only a limited English explanation.

BEYOND THE WALLS

There is plenty to explore just beyond the walls of Old Québec that will give you a deeper understanding of the city and its denizens. There are more historic sights, of course, but there are also hip neighborhoods such as the Quartier Saint Jean-Baptiste and the Quartier Saint-Roch.

◖ Parc des Champs-de-Bataille

Immediately outside the walls, you'll find the 250-acre Parc des Champs-de-Bataille (www.ccbn-nbc.gc.ca), which is to Québec City what Central Park is to New York—a huge, scenic oasis in the middle of the city. Created in 1908 to commemorate the 300th anniversary of the foundation of Québec and the Battle of the Plains of Abraham, the decisive confrontation of 1759 that saw the British defeat the French and take control of what would later be called Canada. Funny to think that the Plains got their name from such peaceful origins—they were the fields where a farmer by the name of Abraham Martin used to bring his cows to graze every morning.

Begin your tour at the **Discovery Pavilion** (835 avenue Wilfred-Laurier, 418/648 4071, www.ccbn-nbc.gc.ca, 8:30 A.M.–5:30 P.M. daily late June–early Sept., 8:30 A.M.–5 P.M. daily Jan.–late Mar., and 8:30 A.M.–5:30 P.M. Mon.–Fri. and 9 A.M.–5 P.M. Sat. and 10 A.M.–5 P.M. Sun. the rest of the year, entry all sites adults $10, teens $8, children free), the park's official reception center, which has a large diorama of the site, displays on the battles, and a historical multimedia exhibition called Canada Odyssey. Then you can knowledgeably meander through the park on your own or take the guided tour aboard **Abraham's Bus** (10:30 A.M.–5 P.M. late June–early Sept).

The park is also home to the beautiful **Joan of Arc Garden.** A sunken, rectangular garden that combines French and British styles, it was created around and named after the statue of the stoic Joan of Arc, donated to the park by an American couple wanting to pay tribute to the bravery of the soldiers who died during the 1759 battle. Horticulturalists can consult Info-Plant, a computerized terminal in the gardens, for information on all the species planted there.

Get a more in-depth look at the Battle of the Plains of Abraham through a multimedia presentation at the **Battlefields Park Interpretation Centre** (1 rue Wolfe-Montcalm, 418/648-5941, 10 A.M.–5 P.M. daily, closed Mondays mid-Oct.–late May, adults

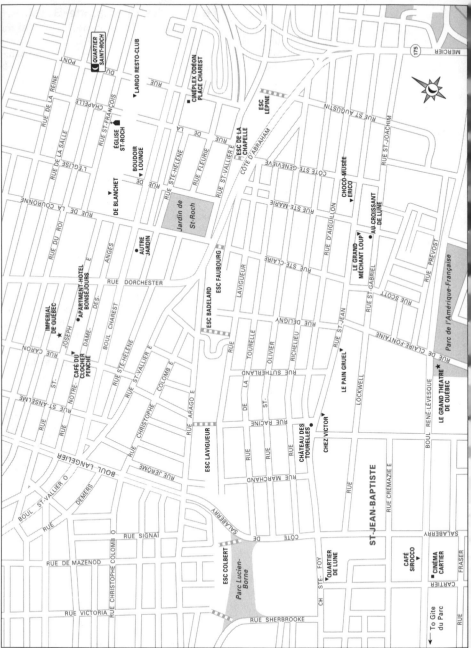

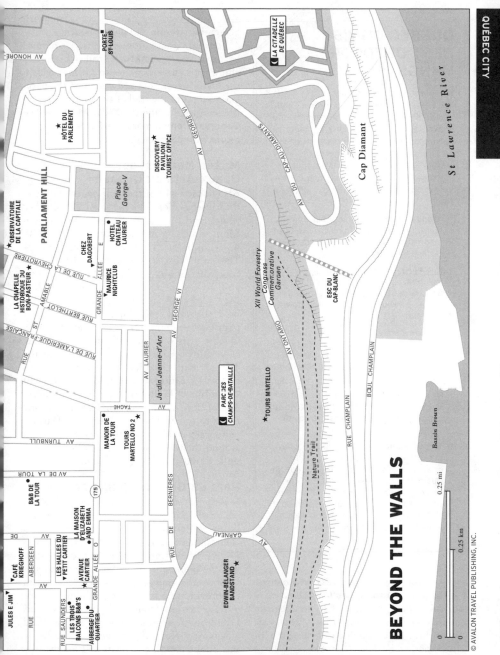

BEYOND THE WALLS

Map labels:

- LA CITADELLE DE QUÉBEC ★
- PORTE ST-LOUIS
- AV HONORE
- HÔTEL DU PARLEMENT ★
- PARLIAMENT HILL
- OBSERVATOIRE DE LA CAPITALE ★
- DISCOVERY PAVILION/ TOURIST OFFICE ★
- Place George-V
- LA CHAPELLE HISTORIQUE DU BON-PASTEUR ★
- RUE DE LA CHEVROTIÈRE
- CHEZ DAGOBERT ▼
- HÔTEL CHÂTEAU LAURIER ●
- GRANDE ALLÉE E
- ST AMABLE
- RUE BERTHELOT
- MAURICE NIGHTCLUB ▼
- RUE DE L'AMÉRIQUE-FRANÇAISE
- AV GEORGE VI
- AV GEORGE VI
- AV CAP-DIAMANTS
- XII World Forestry Congress
- Commemorative Garden
- ESC DU CAP-BLANC
- Cap Diamant
- St Lawrence River
- AV DU CAP-DIAMANT
- AV LAURIER
- Jardin Jeanne-d'Arc
- PARC DES CHAMPS-DE-BATAILLE ◀
- TOURS MARTELLO ★
- AV ONTARIO
- Nature Trail
- RUE CHAMPLAIN
- BD CHAMPLAIN
- Bassin Brown
- MANOIR DE LA TOUR ●
- TOURS MARTELLO NO 2 ★
- AV TACHE
- AV TURNBULL
- AV DE LA TOUR
- B&B DE LA TOUR ●
- (175)
- RUE DE BERNIÈRES
- AV GARNEAU
- EDWIN-BÉLANGER BANDSTAND ★
- CAFÉ KRIEGHOFF ▼
- ABERDEEN
- AV DE
- LES HALLES DU PETIT CARTIER ▼
- AVENUE CARTIER
- LA MAISON D'ELIZABETH AND EMMA ●
- GRANDE ALLÉE O
- JULES E JIM ▼
- RUE
- AV
- RUE SAUNDERS
- LES TROIS BALCONS B&B'S ●
- AUBERGE DU QUARTIER ●

0.25 mi
0.25 km
0

© AVALON TRAVEL PUBLISHING, INC.

QUÉBEC CITY'S BEST OUTDOOR HANGS

When warm weather finally arrives, Québec City suddenly wakes up to the sounds of clinking wine glasses, menu recitals, and conversation as restaurants compete to see who can open their terraces the fastest. Overnight it seems, the once-lonely streets become hot spots for outdoor dining, lingering, and people-watching. For the best in open air, try some of the following places:

- **Grande Allée:** Here, every bar and restaurant (even fast food places like Chez Aston and McDonalds) have terraces directly on the street.

- **Rue Petit-Champlain:** If you like watching up close, the restaurants that line the Breakneck Staircase here see throngs of people walking by – and up and down – on a sunny afternoon.

- **Avenue Cartier:** For more local watching, find a spot on one of the busy terraces that line this avenue. Pub Java has just a few tables, while Café Krieghoff has a large raised patio.

- **Rue de l'Église:** This new pedestrian street in Saint Roch is where to go to mingle with the business crowd for a scintillating 5 à 7.

- **Terrasse Dufferin:** Although you'll have to bring your own snacks, this is hands down the best place to be outside in Québec City. No matter what the time of day, regardless of the season or weather, you'll see lovers, hear buskers, and spot visitors from all over the world walk by. And then there's that view.

a weekend mystery dinner, complete with Scotch-barley soup and plum pudding.

For more exploration of the park's natural beauty, there's the **nature trail,** which runs along Cap-aux-Diamants to Gilmour Hill, the Plains' most untamed corner of the park. Gain access to the trail at the top of the Cap Blanc stairs through the **XII World Forestry Congress Commemorative Garden,** an arboretum with 28 species of trees.

Musée National des Beaux Arts du Québec

Also housed within the confines of the park, the Musée National des Beaux Arts du Québec (Battlefield Park accessible by avenue Wolfe-Montcalm, 418/643-2150 or 866/220-2150, www.mnba.qc.ca, 10 A.M.–6 P.M. Thurs.–Tues. and 10 A.M.–9 P.M. Wed. June–early Sept., 10 A.M.–5 P.M. Thurs.–Sun. and Tues. and 10 A.M.–9 P.M. Wed. early Sept.–late May, adults $10, students $5, and children $3) holds the world's most important collection of paintings, sculpture, sketches, and photos by Québec artists, including Jean-Paul Riopelle, Marc-Aurèle Fortin, and Jean-Paul Lemieux. The permanent collection spans six rooms and was recently joined by the **Brousseau Collection of Inuit Art,** an exceptional collection of Inuit carvings dating from prehistoric times to today. The art gallery also features temporary exhibits highlighting artists from around the world, such as Pablo Picasso, Camille Claudel, and Auguste Rodin.

Parc du Bois-de-Coulonge

A little farther out beyond Battlefields Park, where the Grande Allée changes to Saint-Louis, is **Parc du Bois-de-Coulonge** (1215 chemin Saint-Louis, 418/528-0773, 6 A.M.–11 P.M., free entrance). This 24-hectare estate was the home of the lieutenant governors of Québec (the king or queen's representative in the province) up until 1966, although its origins can be traced to property owned by Louis D'Ailleboust, sieur de Coulonge and the third governor of Nouvelle France in 1653. Today this public park has gardens and noteworthy

$5, teens $4, children free), set in the old jail. You can also visit the **Tours Martello,** two of four towers built in Québec City to safeguard against American invasion. Tour Martello no. 1 has a three-floor exhibit chronicling the life of a soldier, while Tour Martello no. 2 hosts

restored historic buildings all scattered along forest paths, and it is a good spot in the city to bring a picnic of go for a jog.

Parliament Hill

As you exit Porte Saint-Louis, the **Hôtel du Parlement** (1045 rue des Parlementaires, 418/643-7239, www.assnat.qc.ca, 9 A.M.–4:30 P.M. Mon.–Fri. and 10 A.M.–4:30 P.M. Sat.–Sun. and holidays, late June–early Sept., 9 A.M.–4:30 P.M. Mon.–Fri. early Sept.–late June) will loom on the left-hand side. This impressive Second Empire–style building was built by architect Eugène-ÉtienneTaché beginning in 1877 and completed in 1886. Today, the building is home to Québec's National Assembly, which has 125 provincial representatives. The light on the crown at the top of the central tower is illuminated when the house is in session (the joke around town, of course, is that it is so rarely lit).

Stand directly in front of the building and you'll see 22 bronze statues that pay tribute to prominent figures in Québec history, along with interpretation panels that detail the achievements of each. It's a good minihistory lesson. There's also a free half-hour guided tour of the interior chambers. Enter through door no. 3, at the southeast corner near the Grande Allée. When you're done, wander along the **Promenade des Premiers Ministres,** an outdoor museum on the boulevard René-Lévesque side with statues of the province's leaders since 1867. Just around the corner at the **Observatoire de la Capitale** (1037 de La Chevrotière, 888/497-4322, www.observatoirecapitale.org, 10 A.M.–5 P.M. daily late June–mid-Oct., closed Mondays the rest of the year, adults $5, students $4, children free), you can climb to the 31st floor of the concrete Marie-Guyart office tower, the tallest building in Québec, to get a bird's-eye view of the city.

Grande Allée

Originally a country road leading to the historic chemin du Roy that first linked Québec City to Montréal in 1734, Grande Allée is still a major artery leading in and out of the city, with a row of touristy restaurants and nightclubs in fancy 19th-century Victorian-style

MEET YOU AT THE FRESCO

Saint-Roch may now be the coolest hood in Québec City, but at one point it possessed a pocket that most residents wished would miraculously disappear: Two overpasses from Québec's Autoroute Dufferin-Montmorency – a highway that stopped dead right at Cap-aux-Diamants due to bad planning – hung over the neighborhood, sheltering nothing more than an eyesore.

It was only once a group of artists went in to see what they could do with the wasteland that the area's potential was discovered as fertile ground. The group painted over the grey cement pillars with beautiful, lush scenes of brilliant color and turned the wasteland into a jewel.

As you walk through Québec City, you'll notice other works of fresco fabulousness, among them, of course, are the two most famous: the Fresque des Québécois in Place Royale and the Fresque du Petit-Champlain along the street of the same name. Created by a collective of artists entitled Murale Création, these frescoes are part of what Québec City hopes will one day become a major fresco tourist circuit.

Another favorite is Bibliothèque Gabrielle-Roy (350 rue Saint-Joseph Est). Also located in the Saint-Roch neighborhood, this fresco displays 20 literary quotes from authors who loved Québec, including Rudyard Kipling and Anne Hébert. It's a quick walk from the highway pillars. There's also Hôtel-Dieu de Québec (11 côte du Palais corner rue Saint-Jean). North America's oldest hospital now has its past unveiled on the walls of its teaching compound. This illustrated chronicle of the history of one of Québec's major medical landmarks is outstanding.

town houses. After it changes from east to west, it meets **Avenue Cartier,** named in honor of Sir Georges-Étienne Cartier, the voice of the French Canadian people in the mid-1800s. Today this street is a popular local hangout and shopping street where residents come to pick up fresh fruit and veggies, meet friends on the terraces of restaurants and bars that line the street, or shop in trendy boutiques.

Quartier Saint Jean-Baptiste

To the north of Grande Allée is the Quartier Saint Jean-Baptiste, perched on a hillside overlooking the city's downtown core between avenue Honoré-Mercier in the east to avenue de Salaberry in the west. This neighborhood is another residential spot just outside the walls with a handful of hip, affordable restaurants and shops scattered along popular rue Saint-Jean. This sector is easily accessible by exiting the Upper Town by the Porte Saint-Jean along rue Saint-Jean at Place D'Youville.

🅲 Quartier Saint-Roch

There are five staircases (and one elevator) that are accessible off rue Saint-Réal at the northern edge of Quartier Saint-Jean-Baptiste that link it to Quartier Saint-Roch. Once a thriving financial sector, the neighborhood quickly sank into a state of desolation after World War II when businesses and residents hightailed it out of the city center and settled in the 'burbs. In the last 10 years, however, Saint-Roch has become cool again, with artists moving in and substantial government dollars spent in an effort to polish up the 'hood and bring it back to its glory days.

In the center of the neighborhood, you'll find the **Jardin Saint Roch,** a major symbol of the revitalization of the area. The garden is small but impressive with a calming waterfall and Cap-aux-Diamants as its backdrop. Restored buildings, trendy shops, and restaurants now line rue Saint-Joseph Est between rue du Pont and rue du Caron. The 1917 **Théâtre Impérial de Québec** (252 rue Saint-Joseph Est, 418/523-3131), with its distinctive white façade, can be found on this strip as can the **Théâtre de la Bordée** (315 rue Saint-Joseph Est, 418/694-9721). Almost next store is the community's library, which hosts an array of artistic and cultural events. And farther down the way is the pretty **Église Saint-Roch** (590 rue Saint-Joseph Est, 418/524-3577), the neighborhood's first church, dating to 1829. With a little imagination, you'd think you were almost looking at a miniature version of Montréal's Basilique Notre-Dame.

Entertainment and Events

Québec City is bustling at night. The rowdier crowds flock to the clubs on the Grande Allée, while those looking for a quieter pint find the right hangouts in the pubs and bars on rue Saint-Jean and avenue Cartier. Saint Roch is emerging as the newest hot spot for trendy bars and nightclubs. Locals flock here after work to enjoy the cocktail hour, or the *5 à 7* as it's known in Québec. There's no cover charge at most places (unless otherwise noted) and most bars and clubs stay open until 3 A.M.

Pick up a copy of *Québec Chronicle Telegraph,* the only English-language publication that lists the weekly entertainment listings, at the Infotourist center (12 rue Sainte-Anne). Another publication with cultural listings is the monthly *Québec Scope Magazine,* which has some bilingual sections and is available free in most hotels. For readers fluent in French, *Voir* is the most extensive weekly arts and entertainment guide in the city and is distributed widely in restaurants and shops and on street corners.

BARS AND LOUNGES

With the best view of the St. Lawrence hands down, the Château Frontenac's upscale **Saint-**

Laurent Bar and Lounge (1 rue des Carrières, 418/692-3861, 11:30 A.M.–1:30 A.M. daily) exudes an old-money atmosphere without being too pretentious. There's a piano player on hand at happy hour. The other lounges worth checking out are attached to Québec's swanky boutique hotels in the Old Port. **Le 48** (48 rue Saint-Paul, 418/694-4448), the new bohemian-type lounge at Le Port-Royal Hotel and Suites, has a beautiful terrace, while the sleek main floor lounge in the **Hôtel Dominion 1912** (126 rue Saint-Pierre, 418/692-2224) serves martinis and a wide selection of wine.

If you are near the avenue Cartier in the evening, a local favorite is the small neighborhood bar **Jules et Jim** (1060 avenue Cartier, 418/524-9570, 3 P.M.–3 A.M. daily), which has been around since 1978 (along with some of the clients). The bar gets its name from the popular '60s French film and is decked out in film paraphernalia. There are 50 varieties of scotch on hand as well as a number of Hollywood film books to leaf through. When you just need to rock out, there's **Quartier de Lune** (799 avenue Cartier, 418/523-4011, www.quartierdelune.com, 2 P.M.–3 A.M. daily), which blasts classic rock music Wednesday to Sunday, starting at 9 P.M. The place attracts all ages but generally those 30-plus who know the lyrics to *Smoke on the Water.*

One of the latest posh places to open in trendy Saint-Roch is the very stylish **Boudoir Lounge** (441 rue de L'Eglise, 418/524-2777, www.boudoirlounge.com, 3 P.M.–3 A.M. daily). With wood and leather furnishings and two DJs who spin both dance and world-music tunes, the place has a relaxed, worldly feel. Close by is **Mo Taverne Urbaine** (810 boulevard Charest Est, 418/266-0221, www.motaverneurbaine.com, 11:30 A.M.–3 A.M. daily), a happening place that caters to a hip 20-to-30 crowd looking to boogie on Friday and Saturday nights. There are a tapas menu and four tables where you can pour beer from your very own tap. So far, it is also the only nonsmoking bar in Québec, so breathe.

NIGHTCLUBS

The Grand Allée is *the* place to go clubbing. **Chez Dagobert** (600 Grande-Allée Est, 418/522-0393, www.dagobert.ca, 9 P.M.–3 A.M. daily), or "Dag" as it is better known around town, is the spot where the young and well-dressed set (no jeans or sneakers) shake their booties. Free concerts are held daily at 11 P.M. and 1:30 A.M. on the first floor and vary between pop-rock, alternative, and tribute bands. One floor up is the mega–dance floor, where the crowd grooves to the sounds of six different house DJs. If you want to avoid the lineups in summer, show up before 10 P.M. and even earlier on weekends. Anyone older than 25 will feel more at home directly across the street at **Maurice Nightclub** (575 Grande-Allée Est, 418/647-2000, www.mauricenightclub.com, 9 P.M.–3 A.M. daily, $4 cover charge Fri. and Sat. nights). This ultramodern club features a different DJ every night. Should your feet or ears need a break, escape to **Charlotte's Lounge** upstairs or to the first floor Cigar Lounge, where you can puff away to your heart's content. Its restaurant, **Voodoo Grill,** is next door and will satisfy any late-night cravings.

LIVE MUSIC

Québec City is known for its *boîte à chansons,* which typically means a small hole-in-the-wall establishment where singers belt out traditional Québécois-style folk tunes. **Chez Son Père** (24 rue Saint-Stanislas, 418/692-5308, 8 P.M.–3 A.M. daily) is a well-known spot with a festive laid-back atmosphere. Go on a Friday or Saturday night when popular local folkies inevitably lead the crowd in a sing-along or two. In the Quartier Petit Champlain there's **Bistro Pape-Georges** (8 rue du Cul-de-Sac, 418/692-1320), which comes alive after 10 P.M. on weekends with jovial folk music. The rest of the time, it's a casual wine bar where you can pair a fine vintage with a savory local cheese. Best known for its lively Celtic musicians, **Pub Saint-Patrick** (1200 rue Saint-Jean, 418/694-0618, 11:30 A.M.–2 A.M. daily) is Québec's lone authentic Irish pub. Things get hopping downstairs on

QUÉBEC CITY

Friday and Saturday starting at 9:30 P.M. in the pub's 18th-century stone vaulted cellars, creating a rustic Gothic feel more commonly found in Europe. Classical-music enthusiasts should check out what is on the bill at **La Chapelle Historique du Bon-Pasteur** (1080 de la Chevrotière, 418/522-6221, $8–15), not far from Le Grand Théâtre de Québec. This 19th-century church is the perfect place to listen to chamber and baroque music, classical guitar, choral music, and a variety of classical performers all year long.

Summer brings with it free outdoor concerts at the **Edwin-Bélanger Bandstand** (418/648-4050, www.ccbn-nbc.gc.ca, mid–June to the end of August, $5 parking) in the middle of Parc des Champs-de-Bataille, adding a cultural twist to this historic site with rhythms from the four corners of the world. Bring a blanket and stretch out on the grass, Thursday to Sunday starting at 8 P.M.

JAZZ

If you are in the mood for some jazz, Québec City's oldest hotel, the Hotel Clarendon, built in art deco and art nouveau styles, attracts local and internationally known musicians to its own highly regarded jazz club, **L'Emprise** (57 rue Sainte-Anne, 418/692-2480, beginning at 9:30 P.M. daily). This 1920s-style lounge seems to be hidden away except to people in the know. Thursday, Friday, and Saturday nights are becoming popular at Saint Roch's **Largo Resto-Club** (634 rue Saint-Joseph Est, 418/529-3111, www.largorestoclub.com), when it hosts jazz dinner concerts starting at 7:30 P.M. Those looking to combine some soothing sounds with some creative Mediterranean cuisine accented *à la Italien* will want to make reservations.

THEATER, MUSIC, AND DANCE

Canada's oldest symphony, the Québec Symphony Orchestra, and l'Opéra de Québec call **Le Grand Theatre de Québec** (296 boulevard René-Lévesque Est, 418/643-8131, www.grandtheatre.qc.ca) home. It is here that some of the region's best music, dance, and theater are performed. **Le Capitole de Québec** (972 rue Saint-Jean, 418/694-4444 or 800/261-9903, www.lecapitole.com) hosts a musical that runs all year and cabaret shows that change with every season. Its restored 1903 theater provides a gorgeous backdrop. A more intimate venue is **Impérial de Québec** (252 rue Saint-Joseph, 418/523-3131 or 877/523-3131. www.imperialdeQuébec.com), where touring pop and rock bands set down to perform.

CINEMAS

Most films in Québec City are shown in French or in English with French subtitles. The closest first-run theater is downtown at **Cinéplex Odéon Place Charest** (500 du Pont, 418/529-9745). You can catch art-house and foreign flicks at **Cinéma Cartier** (1019 avenue Cartier, 418/522-1011, www.cinemacartier.com).

FESTIVALS

With a history such as Québec's, it's only natural that it should have a number of festivals to commemorate it. While the city's most famous festival, the Carnaval de Québec, draws most of the spotlight, there are a number of other festivals taking place throughout the year that also warrant a special trip.

Carnaval de Québec

Québec City's biggest festival, Carnaval de Québec (290 rue Joly, 418/523-4540 or 866/422-7628, www.carnaval.qc.ca, general admission $7), is the world's third-largest carnival after the one in Rio and New Orleans's Mardi Gras. But what those other festivals don't have going for them is snow…plenty of it! During the festival, held from the end of January to the middle of February, Québec City is transformed into a gigantic snow globe, complete with an ice palace, ice slides, and an oversize snowman called Bonhomme, the Carnaval mascot, sporting a goofy grin and a red hat and sash.

Although the first Québec City carnival took place in 1894, as a way for residents to mix, mingle, be merry, and get the sin out of their systems before Lent, it was held only periodically during the next 60 years because of wars and economic hardship. In 1954, the carnival was reborn by a local group of businesspeople and has since grown into the world's biggest winter event.

Activities during the two-week-long festival include parades, canoe races across the partially frozen St. Lawrence, an international ice-carving competition, dog sled races and, for the particularly insane, the snow bath—an opportunity to strip down to your bathing suit, roll around in a snow bank, and prove…I'm not quite sure what.

Even if you do have your proper winter wear, things, can, of course, get chilly. Dress warmly (extra socks and long underwear) and do what the locals do, have a swig of "caribou," a potent, ruby-colored drink that mixes red wine, whisky, and maple syrup. With a few shots, maybe you'll even opt for the snow bath!

Festival d'Été de Québec

The city comes alive with the sound of music for Carnaval's summertime counterpart, the Festival d'Été de Québec (226 rue Saint-Joseph Est, 418/529-5200 or 888/992-5200, www .infofestival.com, general admission $20). Held for 11 days at the beginning of July, the festival features musical acts covering all genres from Québec, Canada, and abroad. Shows—usually numbering about 200—take place at 10 different venues all over the city, both indoors and out. There are plenty of family-oriented concerts, too.

Les Grands Feux Loto-Québec

For three weeks' worth of Wednesdays and Saturdays at the end of July and beginning of August, Les Grands Feux Loto-Québec (156 rue Saint-Paul, 418/523-3389 or 888/934-3473, www.quebecfireworks.com, general admission before June 30 $8, from July 1 $12) lights up the skies over Montmorency Falls—a stunning setting and natural amphitheater. A "pyromusical" competition between five countries, the fireworks shows are all choreographed to classical music. A shuttle service is available from town.

Place Royale gets turned into an old market square during Les Fêtes de la Nouvelle France.

© JENNIFER EDWARDS

Les Fêtes de la Nouvelle France

To experience Les Fêtes de la Nouvelle France (5 rue Cul-de-Sac, 418/694-3311 or 866/391-3383, www.nouvellefrance.qc.ca, entrance to all 10 sites $7) is like being trapped—well, enjoyably enveloped is more like it—in an 18th-century time warp. For five days in early August, minstrels roam the streets, peasant women scurry around with baskets, and seigneurs in waistcoats bow in welcome as you walk by. But the impressive thing about this festival is that it's not at all stuffy like so many other heritage festivals can be. It's as much an event for locals as for tourists, and a huge number of Québec City residents take full part, volunteering, dressing up, and performing.

Place Royale is transformed into a market square, where theatrical and musical concerts and—later at night—folk dancing take place. One of the many highlights of the festival are the parades led by the Giants—huge effigies depicting historical or mythical figures.

Festival de Cinéma des 3 Amériques

With an inordinate amount of film festivals in Montréal, it was about time that Québec City got its own. The Festival de Cinéma des 3 Amériques (www.festival-inm.com, individual tickets $8, passport $40) is one that locals can take pride in. Taking place for five days at the end of March and extending into early April, the festival takes place in several theaters throughout town, screening more than 100 feature-length and short films from America south, central, and north. There are also round-table discussions with filmmakers and awards given out in 10 different categories.

Shopping

During the summertime shops here always seem to be open. There are no official hours as many shopkeepers set their own depending on the weather and the number of people milling about on the street. During the winter, however, shops usually close by 5:30 P.M. except during Carnaval.

UPPER TOWN (HAUTE-VILLE)
La Maison Simons

Québec's answer to Macy's, La Maison Simons (20 côte de la Fabrique, 418/692-3630, www.simons.ca, 9:30 A.M.–9 P.M. Mon.–Sat., noon–5 P.M. Sun.) has been in business since 1840 and is one of the oldest department stores in the city. The store offers fashionable clothing for men and women, linens, and accessories. Its original location was on rue Saint-Jean but after a fire destroyed the building, the store moved to its present location on côte de la Fabrique. There are two other locations in the city at Place Sainte-Foy and Galeries de la Capitale, two large shopping complexes in the city's suburbs.

Cathedral's Artisans

Artisans set up colorful wooden booths in the Cathedral of the Holy Trinity Park along rue Sainte-Anne near Château Frontenac to sell their wares from mid-June to the beginning of September, from 11 A.M.–10 P.M. daily. There are more than 15 booths, sporting everything from jewelry to pottery to scarves.

© JENNIFER EDWARDS

Québec City's favorite department store, La Maison Simons

Rue du Trésor

Across from Place d'Armes between rue Sainte-Anne and rue Buade, the tiny little rue du Trésor (www.ruedutresor.qc.ca) is lined with the works of dedicated local artists throughout the year, sun or snow. Founded in the 1960s by fine-arts students, this open-air gallery has become a must-see for tourists and a good place to pick up an inexpensive lithograph of the city or a pricier original work of art. Make sure you bargain to get the best deal.

Rue Saint-Jean

One of the busiest shopping streets for tourists and nontourists is rue Saint-Jean. You'll find magazine, music, and bookstores here as well as the **Marché Richlieu,** a small grocery store that sells both beer and wine on top of the regular grocery fare. There are many souvenir shops (mostly of the tacky variety) and familiar Canadian clothing and shoe stores such as Jacob, Le Château, and Aldo. Once rue Saint-Jean ventures outside the wall, you'll encounter more local shops, including North America's oldest grocery store **J. A. Moisan** (699 rue Saint-Jean, 418/522-0685, www.jamoisan.com, 9 A.M.– 10 P.M. daily), which opened its doors in 1871.

LOWER TOWN (BASSE-VILLE)

Lower Town has plenty of souvenir shops, many of them stocked with high-quality items from local artisans. Go for a stroll along rue Petit-Champlain or head out to the Antiques District.

Rue Petit-Champlain

The oldest-known commercial street in North America, rue Petit-Champlain (418/692-2613, www.quartierpetitchamplain.com) is known for its boutiques and artisan shops. There are a few cheesy souvenirs, but overall the merchandise is high quality, with prices to match. There are a number of art galleries on the street that showcase local and international artists, including **Le Portal** and **Studio d'Art Georgette Pihay,** both at no. 53, while farther down at no. 91 Dominique Huot sells her unique silk paintings at **La Soierie Huo.** At no. 84 you can satisfy your sweet tooth with a sample or two from the **Confiserie Madame Gigi** or take home some colorful kitchenware from **Pot en Ciel** at no. 27. **Pauline Pelletier** has some exquisite jewelry at no. 38 and if you have a thing for gold, **Louis Perrier** at no. 48 has been designing pieces that combine pearls and precious stones for 50 years.

strolling the Lower Town

Antiques District

Head to the rue Saint-Paul and rue Saint-Pierre area, better known as the Antiques District, to browse a cluster of 20 or so quality antique and furniture stores. Here you'll find books, prints, chairs, tables, plates, and lamps from the Victorian and art deco eras as well as traditional Québécois stylings. The number of high-end art galleries is on the rise, meaning that prices are too, but it's still worth a gander. Two definitely worth stopping by are **Boutique aux Mémoires Antiquités** (105 rue Saint-Paul, 418/692-2180, 9 A.M.–5 P.M. daily Mon.–Sat.) for lamps, desks, plates, and utensils, and **Rendez-Vous du Collectionneur** (123 rue Saint-Paul, 418/692-3099), which carries an array of lamps, toys (you can never have enough Dinky Toys!), dolls, and cool trinkets.

Accommodations

For the most part, hotels will offer breakfast—usually a continental one, but a few spoil with a full à la carte selection. There is an extra fee for parking at most hotels.

UPPER TOWN

Because of its proximity to everything, Upper Town is the most sought-after area to stay. You don't have to drain your bank account to find something affordable and quaint, especially if you visit sometime from November to the end of April (except during Carnaval in February).

$50-100

Two youth hostels are within the Upper Town. There's the newly renovated and enlarged ◖ **Auberge International de Québec** (19 rue Sainte-Ursule, 418/694-0755, www.aubergeinternationaledequebec.com, dorm $29, private rooms $69 d without bath, $79 d with bath, deduct $4 for members), which features very clean and airy rooms with bunk beds. The hostel, on a residential street, was honored with a prestigious tourism award in 2005 for best lodging (50–149 room category) in the region. There are plenty of mix-and-mingle activities with guided tours of the city and weekly Friday night pub crawls. Not too far away, just off rue Saint-Jean where it ends at côte de la Fabrique, is **Auberge de la Paix** (31 rue Couillard, 418/694-0735, www.aubergedelapaix.com, $20 per person including breakfast, bedding $3 extra), a more rustic-feeling spot with a great outdoor courtyard and rooms with wooden beds. The staff is very friendly and helpful. Both hostels are sought-after spots, so be sure to reserve well in advance. For B&B options, try centrally located **La Maison Historique James Thompson** (47 rue Sainte-Ursule, 418/694-9042, www.bedandbreakfastQuébec.com, $85–100 d), a historic house dating to 1793 that was the home of the last surviving member of the battalion that fought in the 1759 war. It has three simply decorated rooms and comes with a full breakfast, including your choice of wild blueberry pancakes, French toast, eggs, or waffles.

$100-150

Don't be fooled by the classic 1830s exterior of the **Auberge Saint-Louis** (48 rue Saint-Louis, 418/692-2424 or 888/692-4105, www.aubergestlouis.ca, $90–140 d with full breakfast). Inside, the 27 smallish rooms have a distinctively modern feel, done up in gray and beige tones with simple furnishings. Included with the price of the room is a hot breakfast (eggs and bacon, French toast, pancakes with sausage, or for a healthier option, cereal with fruit salad) served before 10:30 A.M. at the **Petit Château** restaurant just up the street from the hotel. Tucked away on a quieter street behind the Château Frontenac is one of Québec City's best-kept secrets, the ◖ **Hôtel Maison du Fort** (21 avenue Sainte-Geneviève, 418/692-4375 or 888/203-4375, www.hotelmaisondufort.com,

$100–200 d). This 1851 Georgian-style home has nine colorful rooms that are elegant and warm. The smaller rooms are good value and suit a couple nicely. Marielle Roy, the friendly owner, makes no secret of having two beloved resident cats so those with allergies should steer clear. You'll also find warm, well-appointed rooms at **Auberge Place d'Armes** (24 rue Sainte-Anne, 418/694-9485, www.aubergeplacedarmes.com, $90–145 d, continental breakfast an additional $5 per person), also within view of Château Frontenac, on the popular pedestrian-only street of Sainte-Anne. Recently renovated, the 19th-century brick walls—on display in most rooms—have been well preserved. Unwind on the outdoor terrace of the hotel's restaurant Pain Béni for some good people-watching or try the more intimate courtyard setting for drinks and dinner.

Over $200

The 1903 Théâtre Le Capitole underwent major restoration in the early '90s, adding the full-fledged **Hôtel du Capitole** (972 rue Saint-Jean, 418/694-9930 or 800/363-4040, www.lecapitole.com, $189–259 d) to its playlist. In keeping with a theatrical theme, the 40 rooms are flamboyantly decorated in art deco style with vivid blue and red furniture positioned against white walls and bedding. Nothing says staying in style quite like a night or two at the famous (**Fairmont Le Château Frontenac** (1 rue des Carrieres, 418/692-3861 or 800/441-1414, www.fairmont.com, $229–459 d). This 618 room, four-star hotel is pure luxury with first-class amenities and service—the staff are known to treat you like royalty. If you are going to splurge on a stay at the Château, you most certainly will want a room with a view, one that overlooks the St. Lawrence River. Prices for these rooms start at $329 (anything less are the smaller lower-level rooms; most overlook the busy and noisy courtyard, not exactly the setting for a romantic *séjour!*) For those for whom money is no object, there are the four Fairmont Gold floors with their own private elevators and concierge—a hotel within the hotel. Fine dinner can be enjoyed in the award-

winning Le Champlain dining room but for those looking for something a little less hoity-toity, Le Café de la Terrasse has a spectacular view of the river and won't put a serious dent in your wallet.

LOWER TOWN

In the last 10 years, the Old Port's tired old warehouses have seen huge changes. Millions of dollars have gone into converting them into the city's largest cluster of boutique hotels. If style, cushiness, and cachet are on your list of wants, then stay somewhere here.

WHEN HOTEL FREEZES OVER

Québec's most popular winter choice since its inaugural year in 2000 remains the **Ice Hôtel Québec** (143 route Duchesnay, Pavillon l'Aigle, 418/875-4522 or 877/505-0423, www.icehotel-canada.com, $199-900 d). With only two ice hotels in North America – the other is in Alaska – novelty seekers can't stay away.

The Ice Hotel covers an area of 30,000 sq. ft, although no two years are ever the same inside. Ice Hotel Québec is usually open January-April. Anyone planning to go should book well in advance and read the preparation guide on the hotel's website before arriving. If the thought of sleeping here doesn't excite you, opt for the guided tour to see what all the hype is about. It's a tad pricy at $14 for a 30-minute tour, but you really are paying to see something unique. Led by ice carvers, the tour takes you through the icy halls to all the hot spots – the wedding chapel (yes and people do use it!), the cinema, the exhibit rooms and art galleries, and a guest room or two. They save the best for last with a stop at the **ABSOLUT ice bar** where even the vodka is served in square ice glasses – no ice cubes required. The Ice Hotel is only 30 minutes west of downtown Québec City off Autoroute 40, exit 295 at the Station Touristique Duchesnay.

$150-200

Everything about the **(Hôtel Les Coutellier** (253 rue Saint-Paul, 418/692-9696 or 888/523-9696, www.hoteldescoutellier.com, $165–185 d) is "charmant," including the price. This hotel could easily be four star—rooms have a classic boutique feel and warmth to them. The Coutellier family pride themselves on paying attention to the little details. You'll find fresh fruit in the lobby, a basket of breakfast goodies with hand-written weather report delivered to your door, robes awaiting your arrival, and an umbrella in all of their 24 rooms. Adjoined to the hotel is the **Môss Bistro** with its classic Belgian fare. It's best known for its 14 variety of mussels served in three different ways—with cheese, with sauce, or in a casserole. Sit outside on the flower-filled terrace or send down for a cheese plate and wine to be enjoyed in your room for just $20. Once the location of the first fire-insurance company in Canada, the building that now houses the **Auberge Saint-Pierre** (79 rue Saint-Pierre, 418/694-7981 or 888/268-1017, www.auberge .qc.ca, $149–219 d) dates to 1821. Here you will find 31 rooms (plus 10 more expensive suites) accented with warm colors, new wood floors, and old stone and brick walls. You'll feel safe going to the washrooms, knowing that they were once safes. Included in your room price is a full gourmet breakfast. Go for the to-die-for crêpes Florentine stuffed with cheese and spinach. The owners also run the hotel next door, the logically named **Hôtel 71** (71 rue Saint-Pierre, 418/692-1171 or 888/692-1171, www.hotel71.ca, $175–250 d), an elegant boutique-style hotel that rivals all the others found in this area in price and décor.

Over $200

Probably the most stylish of stays in Québec City is at the beautiful **(Auberge Saint-Antoine** (8 rue Saint-Antoine, 418/692-2211 or 888/692-2211, www.saint-antoine. com, $149–369 d). The Price family, a Welsh family with long roots in Québec, in 1990 bought the site, an old collection of homes and warehouses dating to the early 18th

century. The first phase of the Auberge was opened in 1992 and a series of renovations since have added more rooms and unearthed some major artifacts, now displayed in common areas and in the rooms. The décor is sleek but warm with queen or king-size beds, plush chairs, and large windows with a view overlooking the port or the inner courtyard. And there are two restaurants on-site: Panache, with an authentic setting of stone walls and wood beams, and Café Artefact, a sleeker, more modern atmosphere. **Le Port-Royal Hôtel and Suites** (144 rue Sainte-Pierre, 418/692-2777 or 866/417-2777, www .hotelportroyalsuites.com, $175–345 d breakfast included) is one of the newest hotels to hit Québec City and this one does it with a bang. Transformed from a warehouse of a local hardware store, this all-suites urban-style hotel is decked out in modern attire in tones of beige, gray, and taupe. Each suite is uniquely designed and they all are equipped to accommodate four adults comfortably with both a bed and a sofa bed, complete kitchen appliances with dishes and utensils, and adequate storage space, making it a great deal for friends or families traveling together. The beautiful **(Hôtel Dôminion 1912** (126 rue Saint-Pierre, 418/692-2224 or 888/833-5253, www.hoteldominion.com, $169–325 d), part of the Germain group of boutique hotels, is situated in a stately 1921 warehouse building. The 60 spacious rooms feature modern design with calming tones of beige and brown and windows that overlook either the port or Old Québec. Beds are big, soft, and heaped with pillows. A continental breakfast is served in the lobby.

BEYOND THE WALLS

The Quartier Saint Jean-Baptiste, especially in and around avenue Cartier, is good spot to find a B&B to spend your nights in Québec City. Saint-Roch and Grande Allée have their fair share of affordable hotels, too. You won't be right in the thick of things, but you'll remain close enough to Old Québec to be able to walk to everything.

$50-100

At the end of a quiet street, **B&B de la Tour** (1080 avenue de la Tour, 418/525-8775, www.bbdelatour.com, $70–80 d) has four brightly colored rooms decorated with a mishmash of furniture and two bathrooms to share. A little farther along past avenue Cartier is the **Gîte du Parc** (345 rue Fraser, 418/683-8603, www.Québecweb.com/giteduparc, $70–85 d), a nearly 100-year-old home. It has three no-frill but comfortable rooms with one complete bathroom to share among them. The owner of **Les Trois Balcons B&B** (130 rue Saunders, 418/525-5611, www.troisbalcons.qc.ca, $75–95d) is a designer who has personally created a classy home with English touches found throughout the three first-rate rooms (two have private bathrooms). A charming home throughout, **Au Croissant de Lune** (594 rue Saint-Gabriel, 418/522-6366, $77–82 d) has a great location on a street that runs parallel to popular rue Saint-Jean outside the walls in Quartier Saint-Jean-Baptiste. The three rooms have shared washroom facilities and are decorated with just the right balance between romance and style. Directly on rue Saint Jean a little farther down is another great find, **Château des Tourelles** (212 rue Saint-Jean, 418/647-9136 or 866/346-9136, www.chateaudestourelles.qc.ca, $95 d), with five spacious yet minimally decorated rooms; the owners won an award for its restoration. Check out the amazing views from the rooftop patio and breakfast served in the dinning room promises not to disappoint.

$100-150

Manoir de la Tour (385 Grande-Allée Est, 866/625-6276, www.hotelmanoirdelatour.com, $100–120 d with continental breakfast) is a grand old mansion, conveniently situated within walking distance of both the walled city and rue Cartier with the Plains of Abraham literally at your backyard. With 14 simply decorated rooms, this no-frills inn was recently renovated and in the last year has

acquired new owners who continue to make improvements. Its sister hotel, **Auberge du Quartier** (170 Grande-Allée Ouest, 800/782-9441, www.aubergeduquartier.com) is just down the street and offers a similar experience at similar prices; however, the rooms tend to be smaller and Internet access is available for a fee. **La Maison d'Elizabeth and Emma** (10 Grande-Allée Ouest, 418/647-0880, www.bb-canada.com/699.html, $100–120 d) is an intimate B&B with three elegant and spacious rooms, all with private baths. A unique concept hotel, **Autre Jardin** (365 boulevard Charest Est, 418/523-1790 or 877/747-0447, www.autrejardin.com, $120–135 d including breakfast buffet), whose name is derived from its proximity to the Jardin Saint-Roch, funds the nonprofit organization Tiers-Monde. The 27 rooms have a worldly feel to them, decorated with touches of fair-trade products handmade by its members' cooperatives. The staff is extremely accommodating. Just down the block on Saint-Roch's fashionable rue Saint-Joseph is the **Apartment-Hôtel Bonséjours** (237 rue Saint-Joseph Est, 418/380-8080 or 866/892-8080, www.bonsejours.com, $115–225). The 14 one- or two-bedroom apartments are fully equipped with kitchen, dining room, living room, and bathroom. Décor is Québec-style, with bold prints, wood accents, and black lacquered furniture.

$150-200

At the beginning of the lively Grande Allee, **Hôtel Château Laurier** (1220 Place-George-V Ouest, 418/522-8108 or 800/463-4453, www.vieuxQuébec.com/laurier, $149–239 d) is an attractive, mostly modern, 154-standard-room hotel whose higher-floor rooms (fourth floor and up) overlook the Plains of Abraham. Make sure you request a room in the newer section—old-section rooms are very small, and most important, tend to be noisier because of proximity to the busy street. There is a convenience store connected to the hotel stocked with all essentials, including beer, wine, and snacks.

Food

UPPER TOWN

Although the cuisine options are diversifying, French still rules. Try to steer clear of the tourist traps in the vicinity of the Château Frontenac and along rue Saint-Louis. They charge top dollar and will have you surrounded by people from every other place in the world but Québec.

Gelato

When the temperature soars, stop at the divine **Dolce Gelato** (50 côte de la Fabrique, 418/692-3100, 9:30 A.M.–10 P.M. daily, dish $3–5), where flavorsome gelato and sorbet are the main menu. Opt for the large dish as the portions are not overly generous. For $2.95, enjoy the specialty, a skewer of fruit (pineapple, melon, and strawberries) dipped in milk chocolate.

Fast Food

Just off rue Saint-Jean at Côte de Palais is Québec's fast-food version of homecooked meals, **(Chez Ashton** (54 rue Côte du Palais, 418/692-3055, 11 A.M.–4 A.M. Sun.–Thurs.,11 A.M.–4:30 A.M. Fri.–Sat., *poutine* $3–9). Locals claim it is the best spot in the old city for *poutine*. The fries are smothered in a rich gravy and topped with bite-size pieces of cheese curd. There are plenty of variations for the more adventurous.

Bistros

If you are in the mood for something different, try the tiny **(Casse-Crêpe Breton** (1136 rue Saint-Jean, 418/692-0438, 7 A.M.–midnight daily, crêpe specials $5–8, cash only), an inexpensive but savory place to sample crêpes. There are plenty of specials on the menu, including the good-value Special no. 4, which comes with *potage* (soup), usually of a creamy nature, a three-ingredient crêpe, salad, and a beverage for $7.95. Seating is limited and lunch hour brings lines that can extend out the door and down the street, so you're best to stop by after 1 P.M.

Pub Fare

Right down the street from Casse-Crêpe Breton is the well-known watering hole **Pub Saint-Alexandre** (1087 rue Saint-Jean,

POUTINE PERFECTION

As the cliché goes, to truly get to know a place, you must try the local delicacies. In Québec, you could sample sweet maple syrup or a delicious, savory tourtière (meat pie), but nothing comes closer to a Quebecer's heart than *poutine*.

The fast-food staple consisting of French fries, gravy, and cheese curds can be found all over the province, from the high-end Montréal restaurant Au Pied de Cochon, where it's served with foie gras, to any street-side joint between Gatineau and Gaspé.

There is controversy over who initially created this sinfully delicious concoction, but there is no doubt that it originated in the Bois-Francs region (whether it's Victoriaville or Drummondville, we may never know).

Any true poutine-lover would advise against trying the comfort food classic at a chain restaurant, save for one found in and around Québec City called Chez Ashton. Founded in the late 1960s, Ashton bases its success on variations of the poutine theme. So, if you consider yourself the experimental visitor, try some of the famous spin-offs like La Galvaude (*poutine* with chicken and green peas) or Le Dulton (*poutine* with sizzling ground beef). As tradition obliges, any poutine is best eaten at night, after a long string of bar-hopping around town. Lucky for you, there is a Chez Aston on rue Saint-Jean, and for more select partiers, you'll also find one on Grande Allée.

418/694-0015, www.pubstalexandre.com, 11 A.M.–3 A.M. daily), renowned for its collection of 200 beers from around the world, with 20 on tap. The menu serves pub fare with a twist; try the chicken supreme with beer and maple sauce or tempura shrimp with a kick of rum. It's known for its boisterous atmosphere, and live music can be heard throughout the week.

French

Tucked away in a quiet little residential street is one of Québec City's finest restaurants, **Le Saint Amour** (48 rue Sainte-Ursule, 418/694-0667, www.saint-amour.com, 11:30 A.M.–2:30 P.M. and 5:30–11 P.M. Mon.–Fri, dinner-only served Sat.–Sun., mains $20–35). The creation of award-winning chef Jean-Luc Boulay, this place is all about the foie gras. Foie Gras Façon Saint Amour allows you to share four different combinations, including a melt-in-your-mouth foie gras crème brûlée, and a number of artistic garnishes. If you are out on a date, ask to reserve a seat in the romantic garden room, made airy and bright by the high glass ceiling.

LOWER TOWN

As in the Upper Town area, there are many good restaurants in the vicinity.

Market

A little country comes to the heart of the city at the **Vieux Marché du Port** (160 quai Saint André, 418/692-2517, 8 A.M.–6 P.M. daily Thurs.–Sun. Jan.–mid Mar.), a food market where 650,000 visitors shop annually. When it is in full swing, there are more than 50 producers and growers on hand selling fruit and veggies, seafood, regional meats, cheeses, and drinks of all sorts. It's a great place to put together a picnic, but make sure you arrive early so that you miss all the lunchtime crowds.

Cafés

The tiny **Petit Cochon Dingue** (6 rue Cul-du-Sac, 418/694-0303, 7:30 A.M.–10 P.M. daily, $2–7) is the only patisserie in the immediate vicinity. This café offers pastries, raisin buns, and breads as well as sandwiches, panini, and *tortière*. Try the homemade minidoughnuts for a modest $0.58 each.

French

Local favorite **Cochon Dingue** (46 boulevard Champlain, 418/692-2013, www.cochondingue. com, 8 A.M.–11 P.M. Mon.–Fri. and 8 A.M.–midnight Sat.–Sun., mains $10–15), or as it is known in English, the Crazy Pig, is a colorful, traditional bistro serving French home cooking. Specialties include steak *frites,* flaky quiches, and many great seafood choices, including a creamy lobster Alfredo linguine. Have a slice of pie with cheese and fresh strawberries for dessert. A Parisian bistro with a nautical flair, **Café du Monde** (84 rue Dalhousie, 418/692-4455, www.lecafedumonde.com, 11:30 A.M.–11 P.M. Mon.–Fri. and 9:30 A.M.–11 P.M. Sat.–Sun., mains $15–25) is along the promenade de la Pointe-à-Carcy on the St. Lawrence River. The menu is limited, but what the café does make it does well. The house specialty is a gourmet trio of *moules et frites* (mussels and fries) done à la Provençale, à la Madagascar, and à la *marinière* (a combination of white wine, seafood, and onions). The portion is big enough for two. Try the scrumptious chocolate profiteroles, a doughy pastry filled with creamy chocolate mousse for dessert.

Contemporary

For a culinary experience that oozes sophistication, try **Laurie Raphaël** (117 Dalhousie, 418/692-4555, www.laurieraphael.com, 6–10:30 P.M. Tues.–Sat., mains $32–45), one of city's finest restaurants. The menu showcases typical French fare such as duck, quail, and pigeon, all made with seasonal local products. Dinner is served on custom-made tableware designed by a local artisan, which you can of course buy in the adjoining boutique.

BEYOND THE WALLS

Rue Saint-Jean beyond the walls offers some great, eclectic local eats as do avenue Cartier and rue Saint-Joseph Est in Quartier

Saint-Roch. The Grande Allée, however, is a better spot for a late-afternoon drink but notorious for its overpriced menus.

Speciality Shops

A great little find is **Les Halles du Petit Cartier** (1191 avenue Cartier, 418/524-3682, 9 A.M.–7 P.M. Mon.–Wed., 9 A.M.–9 P.M. Thurs.–Fri., 9 A.M.–6 P.M. Sat.–Sun., some coffee shops open as early as 7 A.M.), a small indoor market square complete with drugstore, a butcher for deli meats and cheese, a corner store to pick up some local Québec ale or wine, and a grocery store, **Le Jardin Mobile,** at the back for fresh fruit and veggies. There are also a mini–food court, where you might pick up a coffee or a light lunch of soup and sandwiches, and a fabulous patisserie, **Artisan Eric Borderon,** with excellent pastries—not to be missed is the *pain chocolat.* If you are looking to grab a quick bite, **de Blanchet** (435 rue Saint-Joseph Est, 418/525-9779, 10 A.M.–5:30 P.M. Mon.–Wed., 10 A.M.–9 P.M. Thurs.–Fri., 9:30 A.M.–5 P.M. Sat., and noon–5 P.M. Sun., sandwich $4.50–5.50) is a deli and store that doles out a variety of gourmet sandwiches without the gourmet prices. Le Thai is popular with chicken, carrots, and bok choy served à la sweet and sour; top it off with a *morceau* of some local cheese and a refreshing Clearly Canadian, a sparkling water in fruity flavors such as strawberry, melon, or blackberry. Skip the baked goods; you can find better elsewhere.

Snacks

Lick-your-fingers yummy, **Choco-Musée Erico** (634 rue Saint-Jean, 418/524-2122, www .chocomusee.com, 9 A.M.–5:30 P.M. Mon.–Wed., 9 A.M.–9 P.M. Thurs.–Fri., 10 A.M.–5:30 P.M. Sat., and 11 A.M.–5:30 P.M. Sun., treats $1–5) is Québec's own museum shop dedicated to the sweet stuff. Learn about the origins of chocolate-making while indulging in a truffle, a brownie, or a sure bet, the cookie of the day. During the summer cool off with a sample of homemade ice cream, gelato, or frozen yogurt.

Bakeries

If you are looking for an exceptional local bakery, look no further than **(Le Pain Gruel** (375 rue Saint-Jean, 418/522-7246, 6:30 A.M.–6:30 P.M. Tues.–Fri., 6:30 A.M.–5 P.M. Sat., bread $2–4). Known throughout the region for itsorganic flours, it offers an assortment of handmade artisan breads and pastries every day. Visit on Wednesdays or Saturdays to taste the choco-cranberry bread, or for something less sweet try Thursday for the popular cheese bread, made with parmesan and cheddar. Come early for day-old breads at 25 percent off the original price.

Microbrewery

More off the beaten track, **La Barberie** (310 rue Saint-Roch, 418/522-4373, www .labarberie.com, noon–1 A.M. daily) is best visited in the afternoon when tourists drop by to sample a pint or two. The most popular way is the "Galopin" sampler, a spinning wooden holder of six-ounce fluted glasses. For $12.50, taste eight different beers that are listed behind the bar. But don't go if you are hungry; it serves only beer.

Cafés

Along rue Saint-Jean as you exit the walls, you'll find an excellent spot to enjoy a soup that eats like a meal at **Le Grand Méchant Loup** (585 rue Saint-Jean, 418/524-7832, 11 A.M.–9 P.M., till 11 P.M. in the summer, closed Mon., soups $6–8). Try the famous gazpacho and minestrone or its more exotic take on chicken noodle soup, chicken *tonkinoise,* and then top it off with one of the homemade desserts. If you are looking for an original creation, the chef's Grasshopper Mousse, served with mint, marshmallows, and chocolate pieces, is lipsmacking, or for something more decadent, the chocolate cake baked with chocolate pieces sprinkled throughout is served warm so they melt in your mouth. **(Chez Victor** (145 rue Saint-Jean, 418/529-7702, 11:30 A.M.–10 P.M. daily, burgers $10–12) is a cozy café with exposed brick walls recently featured in *The New York Times,* best known for its burgers of both a meat and a meatless variety. Try Le Raf-finé, which comes dressed with cream cheese, bacon, sautéed mushrooms, and onions on top of all the regular fixings. For an additional $1.50, opt for the Viande Bio (organic beef) for an even healthier and tastier meal. Vegetarians will go crazy for Le Tofu burger. With a half pot of sangria to share, two can dine for just over $30. A favorite local neighborhood hangout, **Café Krieghoff** (1089 avenue Cartier, 418/522-3711, wwwcafekrieghoff.qc.ca, 7 A.M.–11:30 P.M. daily, table d'hôte after 5 P.M., $18–20) attracts a devoted clientele made up of artists, university students, politicians, and tourists. Claude's crew serves a different daily special for lunch with soup, quiche, or something along these lines and coffee for $10–13. Because it has been in business for more than 28 years, it is constantly changing to keep with the times. A fresh new menu item is the chicken salad topped with grilled peppercorn chicken and served with a duck and ginger dressing.

Contemporary

A funky new spot to unwind is on the rooftop patio at the **Café Sirocco** (64 boulevard René-Lévesque Ouest, 418/529-6868, www .cafesirocco.com, 11 A.M.–3 P.M. and 5–11 P.M. daily, with breakfast served starting at 9 A.M. Sat.–Sun., tapas $2–5), whose décor and cuisine is inspired by the grand cafés of southern Europe. Owner Carole Surgant prides herself on the large selection of tapas (little bite-size appetizers), including grilled fish, fried calamari, bruschetta, and souvlakia. And it has an equally large list of specialty and classic martinis, more than 30 at last count. Drop by for the *5 à 7* when the tapas are half price.

French

A little farther down rue Saintt-Joseph, the spot for brunch on the weekend is classy 【 **Café du Clocher Penché** (203 rue Saint-Joseph Est, 418/640-0597, 11:30 A.M.–10 P.M. Mon.–Fri., 8:30 A.M.–10 P.M. Sat.–Sun., brunch $13). It is served as a table d'hôte that begins with fruit and yogurt and coffee and finishes with a wide assortment of yummy main dishes, including L'Abbé Chamel, a large waffle with poached egg, ham, and mushrooms smothered in a creamy béchamel sauce (the French equivalent to hollandaise sauce), or the chef's latest creation laid out in the menu each week. Lunch is served the rest of the week and dinner every night.

Information and Services

TOURISM INFORMATION

If you are looking for information on any part of the province, one of Québec's two provincial tourism offices is in Old Québec, just across the street from the Château. Infotouriste (12 rue Sainte-Anne, 877/BONJOUR—877/266-5687, www.bonjourQuébec.com, 8:30 A.M.–7:30 P.M. daily late June–early Sept., 9 A.M.–5 P.M. early Sept.–late June) is the place to go for brochures or to ask questions on any place or activity in the province. It's very busy place, though, so expect a line if you need to speak to one of the information officers.

Québec City's own tourist office, l'Office du Tourisme de Québec (835 avenue Wilfred-Laurier, 418/641-6290, www.quebecregion. com, 8:30 A.M.–7:30 P.M. daily late June–early Sept., 8:30 A.M.–6:30 P.M. daily early Sept.–mid-Oct., 9 A.M.–5 P.M. Mon.–Sat. and 10 A.M.–4 P.M. Sun. rest of the year), is just outside the walls in La Maison de la Découverte. The office's friendly and bilingual staff can help you in person or over the phone. It has a secondary office (3300 avenue des Hôtels) in Sainte-Foy, directly off autoroute Henri-IV immediately after you cross the Pont Pierre Laporte. You'll see the big question mark. Both offices have the same telephone number and same hours of operation.

During the summer in Old Québec you'll see people riding around on blue mopeds with question marks displayed on them. These are the city's mobile tourism information staff, a nifty little service provided by the tourism board to help you with any questions... such as where the nearest public washroom is.

EMERGENCY SERVICES

For all emergencies dial 911. For advice on medical matters, you can call Info-Santé (418/648-2626) 24 hours a day. Hospitals in the area that have 24-hour emergency service include Hôtel-Dieu de Québec (11 côte du Palais, 418/691-5151), within the walls of Old Québec, and Jeffrey Hale Hospital (1250 chemin Sainte-Foy, 418/683-4471), farther out in the district of Sainte-Foy.

If it isn't an emergency, a better option is to visit a CLSC (a government-run, walk-in clinic) where the waits are usually not as long. There's a CLSC (55 chemin Sainte-Foy, 418/641-2572, noon–8 P.M. Mon.–Fri. and 9 A.M.–noon Sat.–Sun.) at the end of rue Saint-Jean where it becomes chemin Sainte-Foy.

Québec's Provincial Police force, known as the Sûreté du Québec or simply, the SQ, can be reached in Québec City at 310/4141 or *4141 on your cell phone. For nonemergencies, call 418/623-6262.

CONSULATES

You can find the U.S. Consulate (2 Place Terrasse-Dufferin, 418/692-2095) right on the Terrasse Dufferin and the French Consulate (25 rue Saint-Louis, 418/694-2294) not too far away. Both are within easy walking distance of the Château Frontenac. The British Consulate (700-1150 Claire-Fontaine, 418/521-3000) can be found in the Complexe Saint-Amable near Québec's Grand Theatre.

BANKS AND MONEY EXCHANGE

Generally, all main branch banks and *caisse populaires* (credit unions) will exchange foreign currency and offer the best rates. During the summer, they have extended hours, includ-

ing weekends. Directly on rue Sainte-Anne, across from the Château Frontenac, is the Caisse Populaire Desjardins du Vieux-Québec (19 rue des Jardins, 418/522-6806, 9 A.M.–6 P.M. daily mid-May–mid-Oct., 10 A.M.–3 P.M. Mon.–Wed. and Fri. and 10 A.M.–6 P.M. Thurs. mid-Oct.–mid-May), which has a separate money exchange area and ATMs. It also has an ATM on the bottom level of the Château Frontenac, which is accessible by its own outside door. The Banque Nationale (1199 rue Saint-Jean, 418/647-6988, 9 A.M.–5 P.M. Mon.–Fri. and 10:30 A.M.–6 P.M. Sat.–Sun.), situated where côte de la Fabrique meets rue Saint-Jean, has extended summer hours until 8 P.M. in July and August. There is also a money exchange bureau at the Infotourist office (12 rue Sainte-Anne, 8:30 A.M.–7:30 P.M. daily late June–early Sept., 9 A.M.–5 P.M. early Sept.–late June) or Transchange International (43 rue de Buade, 418/694-6906, 8 A.M.–10 P.M. daily May–Oct., 9 A.M.–5 P.M. Mon.–Wed. and Thurs.–Fri. 9 A.M.–9 P.M. Oct.–May) around the corner in les Promenades du Vieux-Québec on the ground floor.

LIBRARIES

The libraries of Old Québec are worth a visit regardless of whether you are looking for books. On a tiny street up from La Porte Kent, you'll find the Bibliothèque Vieux-Québec (37 rue Sainte-Angèle, 418/641-6797, noon–8 P.M. Tues. and Thurs., noon–5 P.M. Wed. and Fri., 1 P.M.–5 P.M. Sat.–Sun.) in the old Wesley Methodist Church. On rue Saint-Jean at rue Saint-Augustin is the more historic Bibliothèque Saint-Jean-Baptiste (755 rue Saint-Jean, 418/641-6798, noon–5 P.M. Tues. and Thurs.–Fri., noon–8:30 P.M. Wed., and 1 P.M.–5 P.M. Sat.–Sun.), also housed within a church, although this time an old Anglican one.

BOOKS, MAGAZINES, AND NEWSPAPERS

Bookstores that carry a good selection of English books are generally found in the larger malls outside the main city center. Try Archambault (2452 boulevard Laurier, 418/653-

2387) for a variety of English-language Québec-focused travel books and La Maison Anglaise (2600 boulevard Laurier, 418/654-9523) for a wider selection of books. The two major dailies in the city—*Le Soleil* and *Le Journal de Québec*—are, of course, in French. The *Montreal Gazette,* the *Globe and Mail,* and other English-language foreign newspapers and magazines can be found at La Maison Internationale de la Presse (1050 rue Saint-Jean, 418/694-1511, 7 A.M.–11 P.M. daily).

POST OFFICES

The main post office (300 rue Saint-Paul, 418/694-6175) is in the Old Port next to the train station. However, Canada's oldest post office, opened in 1837, is inside the walls (5 rue du Fort, 418/694-6102) down the hill from the Château Frontenac. All post offices are open 8 A.M.–5:45 P.M. Monday–Friday.

INTERNET

Most hotels offer some form of Internet service, so check with the front desk. Other options include Centre Internet (52 côte du Palais, 418/692-3359, 10 A.M.–9:30 P.M. daily, $2.50/20 minutes or $6.75/hour), right beside Chez Aston off rue Saint-Jean, and Cybarcafé (359 rue Saint-Joseph, 418/529-5301, open 24 hours, $6/hour), in the Quartier Saint-Roch.

LAUNDRY

If you have managed to pack light, you may be in need of laundry services at some point in your stay. Try Lavoir Sainte-Ursule (17B avenue Sainte-Ursule, 9 A.M.–9 P.M. Mon.–Sat. and 9 A.M.–6 P.M. Sun.), which is within the walls, and Lavoir la Lavandière (625 rue Saint-Jean, 418/523-0345, 8 A.M.–9 P.M. Mon.–Fri., 8 A.M.–8 P.M. Sat., and 9 A.M.–6 P.M. Sun.), which is just outside them.

Getting There and Around

GETTING THERE
By Air
Québec City's Jean Lesage International Airport (YQB) (418/640-2700, www.aeroportdequebec.com) is 19 km northwest of downtown on the border of Sainte-Foy and Ancien-Lorette. Getting a taxi to take you downtown will run you in the neighborhood of $24–28. To fly directly to Québec City, your best bet is to go with Air Canada (800/630-3299, www.aircanada.ca). Most flights to the city will stop in Montréal, where you will most likely have to switch to a smaller aircraft. In addition to Air Canada, Continental Airlines (800/231-0856, www.continental.com) and Northwest Airlines (800/225-2525 www.nwa.com) have daily flights to Montréal from New York and Detroit.

By Train
Traveling by train is probably the nicest way to arrive in Québec City. Situated in Lower Town, Québec's train station, called the Gare du Palais (450 rue de la Gare-du-Palais), is a gorgeous building dating to 1915. Completely renovated a few years ago, its appearance has placed it among the top heritage train stations in Canada.

VIA Rail (888/842-7245, www.viarail.ca) provides direct three-hour service from Montréal four times daily with connections from Toronto and Western Canada. VIA passengers arriving from Atlantic Canada and the Gaspé Peninsula will arrive in the Gare de Charny on the south shore unless a ticket is booked all the way through to Québec City, in which case you'll be transported via minivan to the Gare du Palais. For American visitors, Amtrak (800/872-7245, www.amtrak.com) goes only as far as Montréal. Once there you can hop on a VIA train to take you directly to Québec City. Your entire trip, though, can be booked directly through Amtrak.

The Gare du Palais also houses the city's main bus depot, two popular restaurants, a candy shop, a magazine shop, lockers, and

© JENNIFER EDWARDS

Gare du Palais, Québec City's train station

an ATM. It is a short walk from here to most hotels, but if you prefer to take a cab, there will be some ready and waiting in front of the station.

By Bus

Next to the train station is the city's main long-distance bus depot, the Terminus d'Autobus de la Gare du Palais (320 rue Abraham-Martin, 418/525-3000). Greyhound (Canada 800/661-8747 or U.S. 800/231-2222, www.greyhound.ca) links cities across Canada and the United States with Montréal's main bus station and from there, passengers can board an Orléans Express (888/999-3977, www.orleansexpress.com) bus for a 3.25-hour express ride to Québec City. There are buses leaving Montréal every hour on the hour between 6 A.M.–8 P.M. with additional evening service at 9:30 P.M., 10:30 P.M., and 12:15 A.M. Return fares are $62 for adults, $53 for students, $38 for children 5–12, and free for children under six (taxes extra).

If you fly into Montréal's Trudeau Airport, you can also catch an Orléans Express bus to

the main bus terminal in Québec City for $60 one-way and $94 return. There are four daily eastbound buses from Montréal and five westbound buses from Québec City.

By Car

Québec City is easily accessible by car from the rest of Canada as well as the northeastern United States. Route 401, part of the Trans-Canada highway that travels from coast to coast, links eastern Ontario to the province of Québec. For those who live in the United States, Montréal is only about 60 km north of the state line of Vermont, accessible by I-87.

Once you reach Montréal, you have two principal options: the fast route or the scenic one. If you want to get to Québec City as quickly as possible, then follow the bland Route 20, which runs along the south shore, right into the suburb of Sainte-Foy. The slightly slower highway but definitely the more scenic one is Route 40, which runs along the north shore through Trois-Rivières and brings you directly into the heart of Old Québec. Both these highways have older companion roads: Route 20 has Route 132 and Route 40 has Route 138, which skirt along the sides of the river.

For those driving from the east, Highway 2 from the south or Highway 11 from the north via New Brunswick both join to Route 20. I-91 and I-93 from Hartford and Boston also link to Route 20 at Drummondville, about halfway between Montréal and Québec City. U.S. 201 from Portland, Maine, represents part of the Kennebec-Chaudière International Corridor linking it directly with Canadian highways that head directly to Québec City. If you are traveling in the winter, check the road conditions by calling 418/648-7766.

By Boat

Le Groupe Dufour (418/692-0222 or 800/463-5250, www.dufour.ca, adults $79–99, children $40–50) offers a catamaran ride from Montréal all the way to Québec. The trip lasts about 5.5 hours and includes a meal. You can catch a ride back the next day.

The little ferry (877/787-7483, www.traversiers.gouv.qc.ca, adults $2.50, children 5–11 $1.75, car with driver $5.60) that runs between the town of Lévis and Québec City lasts only about 10 minutes, but the view of the city skyline it affords makes it a great option. In high season the ferry runs from 6 A.M. until 2 A.M.

GETTING AROUND
By Bus
The most central place to catch a city bus is at the hub across from Place d'Youville beside le Théâtre de la Capitale, but you will find the main city bus station (225 boulevard Charest, 418/627-2511, ticket $2.50, day pass $5.65) not too far away in Saint-Roch. Contact it directly for specific route information.

By Taxi
A few reliable taxi companies in town include Taxi Coop Québec (418/525-5191) and Taxi Québec (418/525-8123).

By Walking Tour
You can go it alone, but taking one of the city's excellent walking tours will help you gain better perspective and let you in on a few of the hidden gems that you may not ordinarily be made aware of. Parks Canada offers an excellent 90-minute tour of Old Québec titled Québec, Fortified City (100 rue Saint-Louis, 418/648-7016, www.parkscanada.gc.ca/fortifi-cations, adults $10, children $5, or family $20 includes admission to center), which begins at the Frontenac Kiosk, the green pavilion at the beginning of the Dufferin Terrace. English tours are led daily at 1:30 P.M. and 3 P.M. from June to mid-October, with an additional tour held at 10 A.M. from June 25th to the last weekend in August. There are also the Corporation du Patrimoine et du Tourisme Religieux de Québec (20 rue de Buade, 418/694-0665, www.patrimoine-religieux.com, $8), which runs tours throughout the city that focus on the city's religious heritage, and the Québec City Tourist Bureau (835 avenue Wilfred-Laurier, 418/641-6290, $10 for one, $15 to share), which rents out audio CD tours so that you can go about at your own pace.

By Carriage
Although more and more cities are offering carriage rides, there is something authentic and true to form about seeing Old Québec in this manner. The calèches are generally ready and waiting in Place d'Armes beside the Château Frontenac and at the Porte Saint-Louis. Otherwise, you can call Calèches du Vieux-Québec (418/683-9222) or **Calèches de Nouvelle-France** (418/692-0068) directly and arrange for pickup from a specific location. The cost is usually around $75 and the tour typically lasts between 45 and 60 minutes.

East of Québec City

CÔTE DE BEAUPRÉ
A great day trip from Québec City, the Côte de Beaupré means the coast of "beautiful meadow," which is what Jacques Cartier is said to have said out loud of it as he sailed past in 1535. This pretty much sums up this region that follows the St. Lawrence just east of Québec City. Farms dating to the seigneurial system still dot the landscape, their narrow parcels of land jutting down toward the river, as do the ancestral homes of English and French families whose roots go back to the early days of colonization.

To explore the area, follow avenue Royale, also known as Route 360, also known as the **Route de la Nouvelle France.** The 50-km route, marked by signs bearing the coat of arms of New France, leads past the momentous Montmorency Falls through the tiny villages of Château Richer, Saint-Anne-du-Beaupré, and Saint-Joachim. Farther to the northeast is Mont Sainte-Anne, one of the province's most popular places to ski.

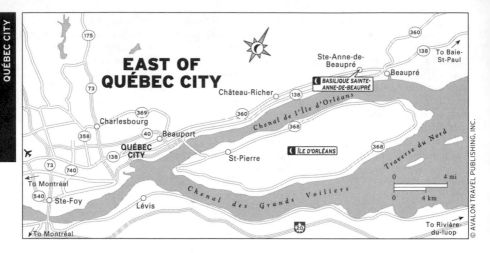

EAST OF
QUÉBEC CITY

© AVALON TRAVEL PUBLISHING, INC.

Parc de la Chute-Montmorency

Just a 15-minute drive from Québec is the Parc de la Chute-Montmorency (2490 avenue Royale, 418/663-3330, www.sepaq.com, parking $8.50 Apr.–Oct., rest of the year free), centered around the dramatic 83-meter plunge that the Rivière Montmorency makes when it meets the St. Lawrence; the Montmorency Falls were named in honor of the viceroy of New France, the duc de Montmorency. As locals love to point out, the falls are about 1.5 times higher than Niagara Falls. Although the impression isn't quite the same, the falls here are still worth a look, especially in springtime when the gorged river rushes through at a rate of 125,000 liters per second.

On the grounds is the **Manoir Montmorency,** reconstructed after a severe fire in 1993. Originally built in 1781, the manor was once the house of the Duke of Kent, father to Queen Victoria. Today the manor houses the park's interpretation center as well as a fine dining restaurant with famous Sunday brunches, best enjoyed while sitting on the outdoor terrace that overlooks the falls. On the east side of the falls is the **Wolfe House and Redoubt** where British General Wolfe set up headquarters before the infamous Plains of Abraham assault against the French in 1759.

The park also contains a network of walk-ways, bridges, and a close-to-500-step stairwell, along with a more leisurely cable car that heads right to the top of the falls. The cost is $8 for adults and $4.75 for children 6–16 round-trip.

Le Moulin du Petit Pré

Just beyond the falls on the left-hand side of the road is the Moulin du Petit Pré (7007 avenue Royale, 418/824-7007, www.moulin-petitpre.com, 10 A.M.–5 P.M. daily late June–early Sept. and Sat.–Sun. May–late June and early Sept.–mid-Oct., adults $6, children 6–12 $2), the first commercial mill in New France, built in 1695 beside the pretty Rivière Petit Pré. The mill has a working waterwheel and grindstone, but of much more interest are the samplings of the fruit liqueurs and the savory and sweet crêpes offered on site.

Centre d'Interprétation de la Côte de Beaupré

The Centre d'Interprétation de la Côte de Beaupré (7976 avenue Royale, 418/824-3677, 10 A.M.–5 P.M. daily mid-May–mid-Oct., 10 A.M.–4:30 P.M. Mon.–Fri. mid-Oct.–mid-May, adults $5, students $4) is a quiet museum in an old converted convent. The center tells the history of the area through exhibits and walking tours through the historic center of Château-Richer. Tours take place throughout the summer with English ones offered three times a week.

Musée de l'Abeille

Dip down to Route 138 to take in the cute Musée de l'Abeille (8862 boulevard Sainte-Anne, 418/824-4411, www.musee-abeille.com, 9 A.M.–6 P.M. daily late June–early Sept. and 9 A.M.–5 P.M. daily early Sept.–late June), or the Bee Museum in English. Part of Québec's network of economuseums, this one covers everything you could want to know about bees and our relationship to them. You can witness the beekeeper in action, sample honeys from around the world, and of course, shop in the gift shop stocked with honey, beeswax candles, bee-shaped candies, and everything else bee-related that you can imagine.

◖ Basilique Sainte-Anne-de-Beaupré

With all the parking lots, motels, tour buses, and cheap souvenir shops, you'll get a strong whiff of commercialism, instead of spiritualism, as you approach Basilique Sainte-Anne-de-Beaupré (10018 chemin Royale, 418/827-3781, www.ssadb.qc.ca, 7 A.M.–9 P.M. daily May–early Sept. and 7 A.M.–9 P.M. daily early Sept.–May). But even the greatest nonbeliever will find it tough not to be somewhat impressed by the impact that this church has had on so many. North America's first pilgrimage site and magnet to more than an astonishing 1.5 million visitors every year, the Basilique Sainte-Anne-de-Beaupré, a shrine to Sainte Anne, the mother of Mary, has been said to be working miracles for more than 300 years.

The incident that kick-started the shrine's reputation happened when the original wooden church that used to stand on the site was being built in 1658. A local man who was suffering from rheumatism reportedly placed three stones on the foundation and was soon completely healed. Word of the miracle quickly spread, and the church became an instant pilgrimage site said to cure countless people of whatever ailed them.

Today, the Gothic basilica, which actually only dates to 1922 (a fire wiped out the first stone church, which was built in 1876), displays many of the crutches and canes left behind. You'll also see beautiful stained-glass windows, mosaics, and statues. There are guided tours in the summer.

Réserve Nationale de Faune du Cap Tourmente

At the end of Route 360 is Réserve Nationale de Faune du Cap Tourmente (570 chemin du Cap-Tourmente, Saint-Joachim, 418/827-4591, 8:30 A.M.–5 P.M. daily mid-Apr.–late Oct., 8:30 A.M.–4 P.M. Sat.–Sun. early Jan.–mid Mar., adults $6, students $5), a wetland area home to more than 300 species of migratory birds, including droves of greater snow geese that touch down in the area in the spring and fall. The reserve also has 20 km of hiking trails, including La Falaise, a challenging four-km route that leads up the escarpment and gives way to a spectacular view of the surrounding area.

Mont-Sainte-Anne

The sizeable Mont-Sainte-Anne (2000 boulevard Beau Pré, 418/827-4561, www.mont-sainte-anne.com, day passes adults $50, seniors/students $40, children 7–13 $26), which reaches 800 meters and has an impressive 625-meter vertical drop, is one of the province's busiest ski hills. Known for its many expert runs, Sainte-Anne has hosted many a World Cup event. Recently the mountain invested big bucks in snow-making machinery, including 285 snow guns, ensuring a longer than normal ski season (mid-November–end of April).

In addition to the ski runs, 17 of which are lit up at night, the mountain has a half-pipe for snowboarding, cross-country trails, and a ski school.

During the summer, Sainte-Anne has a stellar network of walking trails and mountain-biking trails, including two extreme zones, obstacle courses designed by someone who goes by the suspect name of "Dangerous Dan." The

Mountain Bike World Cup, held in late June, has been held here since 1990.

During winter, the best way to get to Mont-Sainte-Anne from Québec City is the **Winter and Ski Shuttle** (418/525-5191), a taxi service that runs both on schedule and on request. The shuttle's regular service is in operation seven days a week from mid-November to the end of April (or whenever the ski season ends). The three daily scheduled pickups are from participating hotels in Old Québec.

Information

You can get all the tourist information you need from the bureaus in Québec City or else you can visit the new seasonal tourist information center (3 rue de la Seigneurie, 418/824-3439, 9 A.M.–7 P.M. daily late June–early Sept.), opened in the town of Château-Richer, just off rue Huot between avenue Royale and Route 138. The staff is knowledgeable and bilingual.

☕ ÎLE D'ORLÉANS

Mansard-roofed homes, farms, soaring-steeple churches, chocolatiers, and an abundance of roadside fruit and veggie stands make up the incredibly scenic landscape of Île d'Orléans (pop. 7,000). The exclusive Association of the Most Beautiful Villages in Québec has awarded three of its villages (Saint-Jean, Sainte-Pétronille, and Saint-Laurent) with the "most beautiful" distinction, while it is well known that the island has long been a major muse to many Québécois artists, most notably its famous residents the legendary folk singer Félix Leclerc and painter Clarence Gagnon. Although Île d'Orléans is only a 15-minute drive east of downtown Québec City, it feels like a major time-travel trip backward to a simpler, more poetic era.

Quite appropriately, the 34-km island was first named Minigo, which means "the Enchantress," by the Algonquin people. But when Jacques Cartier happened upon it in 1535, he spotted many vines and thought that it was better served by the name "Island of Bacchus." Neither name stuck. In 1536, Cartier—perhaps in a move to garner favor for his explo-

ration costs—renamed the island after the duc d'Orléans, the son of the French king.

Hearing of the island's fertile conditions, the first European residents began arriving at the beginning of the 17th century. The island's many well-preserved mansard-roofed homes make it one of the best examples of traditional Québec architecture, which led the government to declare the entire island a national historic site in 1970.

Today, Île d'Orléans, divided into six sectors (Saint-Pierre, Sainte-Pétronille, Saint-Laurent, Saint-Jean, Saint-François, and Sainte-Famille), has built a strong economy on farming—it's Québec City's major supplier of fruit and veggies—and tourism. It is such a popular summertime destination for weekend getaways that its bridge is often choked with traffic. One of the island's best offerings is its supremely bike-friendly 67-km highway, which does the tour of the island, passing through many villages.

Manors

The beautiful **Manoir Mauvide-Genest** (1451 chemin Royal, Saint-Jean, 418/829-2630, www.manoirmauvidegenest.ca, 10 A.M.–5 P.M. daily May–Oct., adults $5, children under 12 $2), which dates to 1734, is today a museum that chronicles the trials and tribulations of the first settlers by focusing on the home's first residents: Jean Mauvide, a young naval surgeon who came to Île d'Orléans in 1721, and his wife, Anne-Marie Genest. The manor also has a fine dining restaurant called the Restaurant du Manoir. Over in Sainte-Famille, there are two old manors worth seeing. Built in 1625, the **Maison Drouin** (4700 chemin Royal, Sainte-Famille, 418/829-0330, 10 A.M.–6 P.M. daily late June–mid-Aug., 1 P.M.–5 P.M. Sat.–Sun. mid-Aug.–late Oct., $2) is one of the oldest houses on the island. Although it was inhabited until 1984, the house has never been modernized. You can tour the tiny white home with the extremely sloping roof and feel blessed for modern conveniences. West of there is the **Maison de Nos Aïeux** (3907 chemin Royal, Sainte-Famille, 418/829-0330, 10 A.M.–

6 P.M. daily late June–mid-Aug., 1–5 P.M. Sat.–Sun. mid-Aug.–late Oct.). Once an old presbytery, this house honors the just more than 300 founding families of the island with an exhibit on the lives of the early inhabitants and genealogical records for those wanting to trace their island roots.

Churches

The lovely **Église Sainte-Famille** (3915 chemin Royal) was built in 1749 and is unique for its five alcoves fitted with statues and its three steeples with bells, two of which were added in 1803. Inside, the ornate furnishings have been the result of many artisans's work, including the impressive vaulted ceiling designed by Louis-Bazile David in 1812. The oldest church on the island, and it is claimed, in the entire province, is **Église Saint-Pierre** (1249 chemin Royal, 418/828-9824), built in 1717. Despite a dramatically sloping roof, the exterior of the church is simple. Inside things get a little bit more fancy with its golden neoclassical décor. The church is also home to La Corporation des Artisans, who sell their handiwork—knitting, weaving, quilting, and pottery—there 9 A.M.–6 A.M. daily, May–October. In the beautiful village of Sainte-Pétronille sits the rather sober **Église Sainte-Pétronille** (chemin de l'Église, 418/828-1410), designed by the interestingly named Joseph-Ferdinand Peachy. Positioned on the top of a hill, the church turns itself into a chamber music concert venue on Thursday nights in the summer. The acoustics, of course, are superb.

Agritourism

There's a reason the island is known as a haven for foodies. With chocolate makers, a cheese factory, vineyards, and cideries, not to mention the many fruit and veggie producers, Île d'Orléans is packed with good eats. Some of the best stops include **Vinaigrerie et Cidrerie Domaine Steinbach** (2205 chemin Royal, Saint-Pierre, 418/828-0000, www.domaines-teinbach.com, 10 A.M.–7 P.M. daily May–Oct., free admission), an organic farm with an interpretation center where you can sip cider and

munch on duck pâté. **Les Fromages de l'Isle d'Orléans** (4696 chemin Royal, Sainte-Famille, 418/829-0177, 10 A.M.–6 P.M. daily late June–early Sept. and Sat.–Sun. early Sept.–Oct.) has revived the art of making "cheese d'isle," the first cheese made in North America. To sample the local wines, try **Vignoble de Sainte-Pétronille** (1A chemin du Bout-de-l'Île, Sainte-Pétronille, 418/828-9554, 10 A.M.–6 P.M. daily May–mid-Oct. and Sat.–Sun. mid-Oct.–mid-May), right near the bridge, for its white, red, and rosé wines. There's also **Cassis de l'Isle Ensorceleuse Monna et Filles** (721 chemin Royal, Saint-Pierre, 418/828-2525, 10 A.M.–6 P.M. daily June–Oct.), which also produces a few wines but is famous for its sweet and smooth black current liqueur. Chocolate and ice cream lovers should stop by **Chocolaterie de l'Île d'Orléans** (160 chemin Royal, Sainte Sainte-Pétronille, 418/828-2250) for its array of homemade Belgian and French-influenced chocolates and selection of ice cream, including the popular "L'Érable" made with the island's maple syrup, and fresh-fruit sorbet. There's a nice terrace for you to take time to enjoy your two scoops.

Espace Felix-Leclerc

The big impressive barn near the island's bridge is Espace Félix-Leclerc (682 chemin Royal, 418/828-1682, www.felixleclerc.com, 9 A.M.–6 P.M. daily spring–summer, 9 A.M.–5 P.M. Tues.–Sun. fall–winter, adults $5, students $3.50), a coffeehouse and museum devoted to the life and times of Québec's most famous poet and songwriter, and Île d'Orlé resident, Félix Leclerc. The museum features a multimedia exhibit chronicling Leclerc's life with photos, audio, and video. There is also a recreation of Leclerc's old work space. The center also hosts nighttime concerts featuring a variety of upcoming and well-known Québec performers. Pick up one of Leclerc's CDs and have a listen as you tour the island.

Cycling

You can cycle the entire scenic loop around the island's edge or just a section if you're not

AND LECLERC PLAYS ON

Saying that Québec's most beloved and influential singer-songwriter, Félix Leclerc, who died in 1988, still has a hold on the hearts and imaginations of the people who live here is a wee bit of an understatement.

The spirit of the charismatic and mystical wordsmith who so perfectly captured the essence of Québec's landscape, people, and sentiments still looms large over almost every pocket of the province. Leclerc has at least a few schools, concert halls, and libraries named after him, along with at least four parks and a multitude of streets in towns big and small. There's also "Les Félix," Québec's version of the Grammies, handed out every year to the province's best musicians and a statue in Montréal's Parc Lafontaine.

But nowhere is Leclerc's presence felt as strongly as on Île d'Orléans, the place where the busy performer, who spent much of his time traveling back and forth between Europe and Canada, came to relax, be quiet, and observe. Now the island is home to L'Espace Félix-Leclerc, a busy museum chronicling the songwriter's life and a performance space run by Leclerc's daughter.

But not all Leclerc homages have come off smelling like roses. When Radio-Canada (the French counterpart to the CBC) broadcast a miniseries chronicling the life of Leclerc in 2005, Quebecers were left holding their noses instead. Outraged by a portrayal that made the revered Leclerc into a kitschy, flaky caricature, Leclerc's family and fans were quick to denounce the film. As one reviewer from Le Nouvel Observateur put it, "With one luminescent horse and three swamp zombies, you'd think you were watching outtakes from Michael Jackson's Thriller." The lesson learned? Don't mess with Québec's best.

up to the full challenge. Bikes can be rented from two spots on the island. One is in Saint-Laurent from **Écolocyclo** (1979 chemin Royal, 418/828-0370, 9 A.M.–7 P.M. Thurs.–Mon. mid-May–late June and early Sept.–mid-Oct. and 9 A.M.–7 P.M. daily July–early Sept.), while the other is in Saint Pierre from **Auberge le Vieux-Presbytère** (1247 avenue Monseigneur d'Esgly, 418/828-9723, hour $6, three hours $15, full day $25). Pick up a biking brochure that outlines the four bike tour options from the island's information center.

Accommodations

There are plenty of accommodation choices on the isle, although in the height of summer, things can get booked up quickly. A good camping option is **(Camping Île d'Orléans** (357 chemin Royal, Saint-François, 418/829-2953 or 888/829-2953, www.campingiledorleans.com, tent site $27–39), which recently won an award for best camping spot in the region. Situated in the far southeastern corner of the island in Saint-François, the campground

has 140 mostly shady spots. The coveted sites by the river are often crowded and noisy, so consider staying in the Section du Haut Boisé. Although it has limited privacy, it's your best bet for a quieter stay. The two-story century home **Gîte au Toit Bleu** (3879 chemin Royal, Sainte-Famille, 418/829-1078, $67–92 d) has a beautiful view overlooking the river on the north side of the island. The five rooms, done up in rich earthy tones, come with or without private bath. Over in Saint-Pierre is **(Gîte Isle de Bacchus** (1071 chemin Royal, Saint-Pierre, 418/828-9562, www.isledebacchus.com, $75–90 d), a B&B and winery where you can pretend that you live on a vineyard estate. The four rooms are sunny and cheerful. Try to book the L'Oiseau du Paradis room. It's got the third floor all to itself and great angled ceilings. **La Dauphinelle B&B** (216 chemin du Bout-de-l'Île, Sainte-Pétronille, 418/828-1487 or 866/828-1487, $130 d) is the former summer house of a retired colonel of the British army. Built in 1895, it has kept its Victorian authenticity with antique furniture, floral patterns, and claw-foot bath-tubs. Although a bit pricey for a B&B, the beautiful rooms, salon, and front porch, along with the orange-flavored pancakes, make it worthwhile. As for inns on the island, one of the best is 🄲 **Auberge La Goeliche** (22 chemin du Quai, Sainte-Pétronille, 418/828-2248 or 888/511-2248, www.goeliche.ca, $169–207 d). Right on the St. Lawrence, with a great view of Québec City, the inn dates back only a few years; it was reconstructed after fire consumed the original, which dated to 1895. There are 16 rooms, each with their own décor (some are a little dubious). The restaurant has fine French food and there's a nice swimming pool.

Food

Restaurant menus tend to change with the seasons, featuring whatever fruit, veggies, and meat are most plentiful. All places have extended hours during the summer with most either closed or reducing their hours starting in September or October. The setting in an old 18th-century mill certainly adds some cachet to the 🄲 **Moulin de Saint-Laurent** (754 chemin Royal, 418/829-3888 or 888/629-3888, www.moulinstlaurent.qc.ca, mains $12–25). Thick stone wall interiors with wood beams and hanging copper pots and pans make for a cozy setting, but if you're there on a nice summer day, opt for a seat on the terrace instead, which overlooks a waterfall. The food features a range of regional cuisine, including glazed duck salad and filet mignon. There's live music on Sunday nights. Some of the interpretive historic manors on the island also have exceptional restaurants, such as the **Restaurant Manoir Mauvide-Genest** (1451 chemin Royal, 418/829-2630, 5–8 P.M. Tues.–Sun. May–Dec., table d'hôte $30–40). The chef serves an inspired menu with dishes influenced by the early days of New France. The house specialties are smoked dishes such as duck à l'érable (or maple duck). What's a French island without a café au lait and croissant? **La Boulange** (2001 chemin Royal, 418/829-3162, 7:30 A.M.–6 P.M. Mon.–Sat.

and 7:30 A.M.–5 P.M. Sun. mid-June–mid-Sept., limited days rest of year, $2–5) sets the scene with not only the golden flaky ones but also with hearty breads, gourmet pizzas, and sandwiches. At **La Crêpe Cochonne** (3963 chemin Royal, 418/829-3656, 10 A.M.–9 P.M. Mon.–Fri., 8 A.M.–9 P.M. Sat.–Sun. May–Oct., table d'hôte $14–17), you put the thought power into guessing which combination of fixings will taste best. The restaurant's table d'hôte is a bargain. It includes, on top of your main dish, soup, a dessert crêpe, and coffee or tea.

Information

The island has a permanent tourist information center (490 côte du Pont, 418/828-9411 or 866/941-9411, www.iledorleans.com, 8:30 A.M.–7:30 P.M. Sun.–Thurs., 8:30 A.M.–8 P.M. Fri.–Sat. late June–early Sept., 9 A.M.–5 P.M. daily except 10 A.M.–4 P.M. Sat.–Sun. Nov.–Apr.) immediately on your right as you disembark the bridge. The center has maps of the island, including one for biking, and rents audio tour tapes and CDs that you can listen to in your car while you do the tour. The cost is $11.50 for a daylong rental.

Getting There and Around

If you're driving from Old Québec, take auto-route Dufferin-Montmorency, Route 440, to the bridge, which is no more than a 10-minute drive. The bridge will take you directly to Route 368, also known as the chemin Royal, which circles the island. If you'd rather approach by water, every day throughout the summer Croisières Le Coudrier (Pier 19 at 180 rue Dalhousie, 418/692-0107 or 888/600-5554, www.croisierescoudrier.qc.ca) departs Québec City at 9 A.M. arriving at Saint-Laurent on Île d'Orléans at 9:30 A.M. The return boat leaves the island at 4 P.M. If you want to combine the trip with a bike rental to tour around, the cost is $52 for adults, $49 for students, and $35 for children. And if you're feeling unenthusiastic about the hills, you can always, for $20 extra, rent an electric bike—a regular bike with a motor attached to it.

CHARLEVOIX

Less than an hour away from Québec City, the Charlevoix region—6,000 square km that cover the north shore of the St. Lawrence River from the ski slopes of Le Massif to the banks of the Saguenay—is one of the province's most resplendent.

With a rich architectural heritage, diverse flora and fauna, and a unique geography caused by a 15 billion-ton meteorite that crashed to the earth 350 million years ago, Charlevoix's natural and cultural charms have not been lost on the rest of the world. In 1988, the region won the distinction of being the first populated UNESCO World Biosphere Reserve, instilling a huge sense of pride in its 30,000 residents and restricting large-scale development.

Although it's Canada's oldest tourist destination, it's Quebecers themselves who love coming to Charlevoix. With scenes that inspired the province's famous landscape artists such as Clarence Gagnon and René Richard, charming, mansard-roofed inns that are centuries old, and foods—fine cheeses, lamb, veal, and unique fruit and vegetables—all cultivated and prepared on Charlevoix soil, this is where Quebecers come to find out where they came from. For the rest of us, Charlevoix yields a merciful lack of tacky tourist traps and an insightful glimpse into the cultural and historical heart of Québec.

To get the region into perspective, think of it as divided into three distinct characters. There are the farms, charming villages, and towns interspersed along the coast that offer great dining, scores of inns and B&Bs, and an array of cultural sites and shops. There's the backcoun-

HIGHLIGHTS

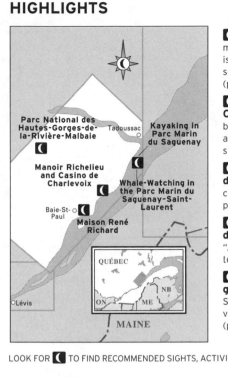

CHARLEVOIX

◖ Maison René Richard: Roaming the many art galleries of historic Baie-Saint-Paul is a highlight, and this former home of landscape painter René Richard is one of the best (page 225).

◖ Manoir Richelieu and Casino de Charlevoix: Stop by for high tea or a highball in one of the bars of this majestic château, and then try your luck at the neighboring casino (page 232).

◖ Parc National des Hautes-Gorges-de-la-Rivière-Malbaie: Explore the soaring cliffs and sunken gorges of this new provincial park in Charlevoix's hinterland (page 234).

◖ Whale-Watching in the Parc Marin du Saguenay-Saint-Laurent: "Ooh!" and "Ahhh!" at the mighty residents of these waters aboard a cruise ship or kayak (page 240).

◖ Kayaking in Parc Marin du Saguenay: Soak in magnificent views of the Saguenay Fjord, some of the most stunning views in the province from the seat, of a kayak (page 241).

LOOK FOR **◖** TO FIND RECOMMENDED SIGHTS, ACTIVITIES, DINING, AND LODGING.

try—a vast, rugged landscape of lakes, mountains, and boreal forest where adventure seekers go to test their mettle. And finally, heading toward the region's eastern border and a bit beyond will bring you to the bountiful waters and prime whale-watching, kayaking, and hiking opportunities of the Saguenay Fjord.

PLANNING YOUR TIME

Plan for at least a week's stay in the region if you want to move at a fairly leisurely pace. Only 100 km away from Québec City, you'll find that **Baie-Saint-Paul** works well as a base from which to explore the immediate area and is a good introduction to Charlevoix's cultural scene. Spend at least a couple of nights so that you can explore the museums, galleries, and

restaurants in town and make a jaunt up to **Parc National des Grands-Jardins,** the 300 square km park of tundra and taiga frequented by caribou, for a day hike.

Follow that up with a day's exploration of the historic villages of Les Éboulements and Saint-Joseph-de-la-Rive and the pastoral Isle-aux-Coudres, and either head back to Baie-Saint-Paul for the night or consider moving to an inn on the island.

You'll want a couple of nights' stay in the historic resort destination of **La Malbaie,** about 48 km from Baie-Saint-Paul. Take one day to unhurriedly explore town, gaze at the St. Lawrence from the windows of Bar La Brise in the **Fairmont Manoir Richelieu,** and build up your slot-machine muscle at the **casino.** Spend

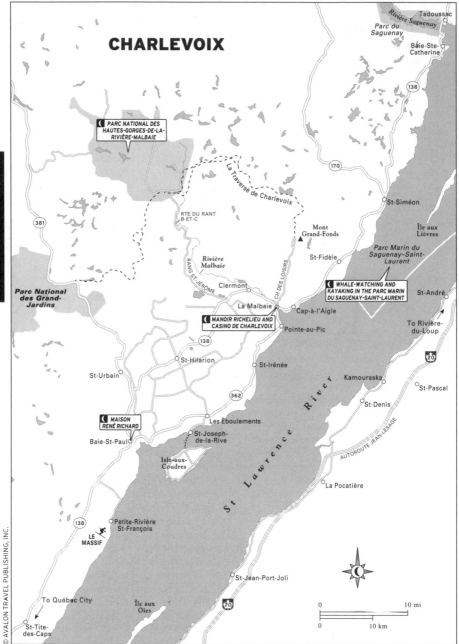

CHARLEVOIX

Tadoussac

Rivière Saguenay

Parc du Saguenay

Baie-Ste-Catherine

138

(**PARC NATIONAL DES HAUTES-GORGES-DE-LA-RIVIÈRE-MALBAIE**

170

La Traverse de Charlevoix

St-Siméon

381

RTE DU RANT B-ET-C

Mont Grand-Fonds

Île aux Lièvres

RANG ST-JÉRÔME

Rivière Malbaie

St-Fidèle

Parc Marin du Saguenay–Saint-Laurent

Clermont

CH DES LOISIRS

(**WHALE-WATCHING AND KAYAKING IN THE PARC MARIN DU SAGUENAY-SAINT-LAURENT**

St-André

Parc National des Grand-Jardins

La Malbaie

Cap-à-l'Aigle

To Rivière-du-Loup

(**MANOIR RICHELIEU AND CASINO DE CHARLEVOIX**

Pointe-au-Pic

138

20

St-Hilarion

St-Irénée

St-Urbain

Kamouraska

St-Pascal

362

St-Denis

(**MAISON RENÉ RICHARD**

Les Éboulements

AUTOROUTE JEAN-LESAGE

St-Joseph-de-la-Rive

Baie-St-Paul

Isle-aux-Coudres

St Lawrence River

La Pocatière

138

Petite-Rivière-St-François

LE MASSIF

St-Jean-Port-Joli

To Québec City

Île aux Oies

20

0   10 mi

0   10 km

St-Tite-des-Caps

the second day working off the sins of the first by hiking, kayaking, or white-water rafting in **Parc National des Hautes-Gorges-de-la-Rivière-Malbaie.**

You'll need a full afternoon to drive to Baie-Sainte-Catherine or take the ferry to Tadoussac and take a **whale-watching** tour. Exploring the museums, cafés, and shops of Tadoussac, and kayaking or hiking in the **Parc Marin du Saguenay-Saint-Laurent** and the **Parc du Saguenay** will tag on at least another couple of days to your itinerary.

Touring the region by car is the best way to go. You'll be able to visit the smaller villages, stop off at farmers markets and scenic lookouts, explore the back roads, and head up to the parks. Cycling is also an option, although you'd have to be a glutton for extremely hilly conditions. Otherwise, buses run from Québec City and hit all the major towns along Route 138, including Baie-Saint-Paul, La Malbaie, and Tadoussac.

HISTORY

Although it's one of the oldest areas in Québec, Charlevoix wasn't an immediate hit with the colonists. Named after François-Xavier Charlevoix, a Jesuit priest and New France's first historian, the land was first divided into *seigneuries* (feudal properties) in 1675, but with its many hills and valleys, it was considered too much of an agricultural challenge. Eventually, the area's residents adapted to their surroundings and began farming, fishing, logging, and shipbuilding, but with no through road, Charlevoix remained somewhat cut off from the rest of the world.

Things changed in 1800 when two Scottish seigneurs named John Nairne and Malcolm Fraser were granted land in the Malbaie area after the British Conquest against the French. In awe of the beauty of their new surroundings, the two started inviting friends and family from Montréal, Québec City, and from as far away as Scotland and England. Word spread quickly about the hunting, fishing, and fresh, sea air and soon other families in the area were opening their doors to accommodate the overflow.

With access to Charlevoix still restricted to water by the start of the 20th century, wealthy visitors started cruising the St. Lawrence aboard giant steamships—coined "floating palaces"—to get there. This era was known as Charlevoix's "belle époque," a time when the region was considered one of the most fashionable and desirable places to spend the summer.

Beyond a tourism renaissance, the Charlevoix of today is known for one more fact, this one far less palatable. Through the 1980s, scientists discovered that Charlevoix and the neighboring Saguenay–Lac-Saint-Jean region were home to a number of rare genetic diseases. These newly discovered disorders, such as Andermann Syndrome and Leigh's Syndrome, were found to be unique to or in highest concentration in these two regions. A background of big families, isolation, and a small gene pool contributed to the diseases' proliferation and concentration. Geneticists from all over the world now come to Charlevoix and Saguenay–Lac-Saint-Jean to study hereditary genetic defects, but don't expect to read about it in the tourist brochures.

Baie-Saint-Paul

Dubbed "SoHo with snow," Baie-Saint-Paul (pop. 7,380) has the highest concentration of art galleries in the country and is the cultural heart of the Charlevoix region. Many of Québec's notable painters, including Clarence Gagnon, Jean-Paul Lemieux, and René Richard, spent time here, drawn by the mountains, sea, pastoral scene, and a supposed "quality of light" said to be unique to the place. Although there are some good attractions in Baie-Saint-Paul, you'll find that the most memorable experience lies simply in roaming the streets. The main drag of rue Saint-Jean-Baptiste has many centuries-old mansard-roofed buildings converted into art galleries, inns, restaurants, and cafés, lending the place an air of small-town sophistication. But take a stroll down rue Saint-Joseph, a residential street that skirts the Gouffre River, and you'll get a true sense of the Baie-Saint-Paul of yesteryear that inspired so many painters.

SIGHTS
Centre d'Art and Centre d'Exposition de Baie-Saint-Paul

An ode to the town that inspired so many painters, the Centre d'Art de Baie-Saint-Paul (4 rue Ambroise-Fafard, 418/435-3681) hosts a permanent exposition of almost 20 Charlevoix painters. The center also has a gallery and a weaving workshop. It's open from 10 A.M.–5 P.M. daily April–late June and September–October, 10 A.M.–6 P.M. daily June–August, and 10 A.M.–5 P.M. Wednesday–Sunday November–March. Admission is free. Just up the street, you'll find the architecturally impressive Centre d'Exposition (23 rue Ambroise-Fafard, 418/435-3681) with three floors of contemporary and modern art. The center is open 10 A.M.–5 P.M. daily late September–late June and 10 A.M.–6 P.M. daily late June–August. Adults pay $3, students and seniors $2, and children under 12 get in free.

the restaurant and shop-lined rue Saint-Jean-Baptiste

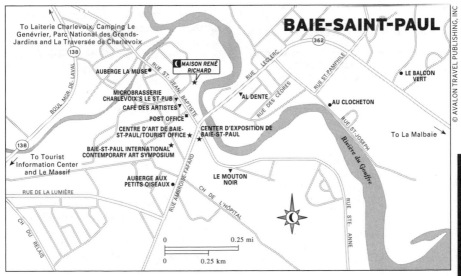

Baie-Saint-Paul International Contemporary Art Symposium

Every year during the month of August about 10 jury-selected, up-and-coming artists from Canada, Europe, and Asia descend on the Luc et Marie Claude Arena (11 rue Forget, 418/435-3681, noon–6 P.M., admission free) for the International Contemporary Art Symposium. While the artists chip away in their respective art forms including painting, photography, and digital media, the public is free to walk around, watch the progression of their work, and ask questions. Every Friday at 2 P.M., the artists take turns conducting more formal presentations.

☾ Maison René Richard

This gallery/museum (58 rue Saint-Jean-Baptiste, 418/435-5571, 10 A.M.–6 P.M. daily, admission free) was once the home of René Richard, a favorite Québécois painter known for his landscapes of the region. The Swiss-born, one-time trapper moved into the house when he married the daughter of the family who lived there and who were already accustomed to inviting artists such as Clarence Gagnon and Jean-Paul Lemieux into their home.

The rustic and folksy charm of the place has been preserved by Richard's nephew and his wife who live on-site (notice the sink and toothbrushes in one of the gallery rooms) and offer bilingual tours of the house and impassioned lessons in Québec art history.

Laiterie Charlevoix-Économusée du Fromage

Every day before 11 A.M., you can watch the traditional way cheese was made in this factory (1167 boulevard Mgr. De Laval, 418/435-2184) dating to 1948 and still owned by the Labbé family. Head upstairs for bilingual displays, old photos, machinery, and other paraphernalia, documenting the glory days of cheese-making. Many fine Charlevoix cheeses are sold here, including one of Canada's finest: Le Migneron, a unique soft cheese noted for its nutty, buttery flavor. The Laiterie is open 8 A.M.–7 P.M. daily late June–early September and 8 A.M.–5:30 P.M. Monday–Friday and 9 A.M.–5 P.M. Saturday–Sunday early September–late June. Admission is free.

RECREATION
Le Massif

Hugging the water, the scenic, tiny town of

CIRQUE DU SOLEIL

Landscape painting is not the only art form to rise from the streets of Baie-Saint-Paul. The Cirque du Soleil, one of the most successful live-entertainment companies of all time, has its roots here too. Formed in the early 1980s by a group of dexterous street performers who called themselves Le Club des Talons Hauts (the High Heels Club), the troupe juggled, breathed fire, and walked on stilts (hence the name) every year during the town fair. It didn't take long before the enterprising group, led by current Cirque president Guy Laliberté, took to the road with shows all over the province and the rest of the country. By the time Cirque du Soleil somersaulted into the United States in 1987, its show's mix of audacious acrobats, death-defying trapeze artists, and precocious tumblers and jugglers became the hottest ticket around. Today, the troupe from Baie-Saint-Paul has parlayed its creativity into revenues of $500 million and nine working shows around the world.

With proven international success out of the way and a fatter wallet, at least one of Cirque's members has come home to roost. Daniel Gauthier, previous Cirque du Soleil president and cofounder, bought Le Massif ski hill in 2002, promising to complete work on the Canadian National Alpine Training Centre and expand Le Massif into an international, yet true-to-its-roots, destination.

Petite-Rivière-Saint-François (pop. 750) has the distinction of being the oldest in Charlevoix, but it is probably best known as the gateway to Le Massif (418/632-5876 or 877/536-2774, www.lemassif.com, day passes adults $45, students $36, children 7–16 $26), the highest ski mountain in Québec at 770 meters. With an impressive annual snowfall of six meters, 42 runs varying from easy to extremely difficult, and five lifts (three quads, one double, and one surface), this ski resort is starting to steal some of the thunder from neighboring Mont-Sainte-Anne. From the summit, the views of the St. Lawrence are exhilarating, as is the feeling that

you might just ski down the slope right on into the river. Two cafeterias, the Mer et Monts restaurant, and one pub and one bistro-style food court are on hand for a little midday or après-ski nosh. Skiing season typically starts in mid-December and lasts to mid-April.

Parc National des Grands-Jardins

Wide-open spaces and a subarctic environment characterize the 310-square-km Parc National des Grands-Jardins (866/702-9202, www.sepaq.com, adults $3.50, youth 6–17 $1.50, tent sites $19, shelters $20 d), just 42 km north of Baie-Saint-Paul. Black spruce, tundra, and taiga dominate the landscape here, making it a suitable home for a small herd of about 80 caribou that were reintroduced to the area starting in 1969. The park also boasts one of the best views in the region atop the 980-meter-high Mont du Lac des Cygnes. The three-hour moderate-to-difficult hike up the mountain concludes with an outstanding panoramic view that showcases the full effect of the meteorite crater that defines the region around Baie-Saint-Paul. There are other easier hiking trails extending 2–8 km and lake canoeing and kayaking.

The park's visitors center, **Centre d'Accueil Thomas-Fortin** (route 381 at Km 31, 418/890-6527 or 866/702-9292, ext. 4, late May–mid-Oct.), is the place to go for fishing and camping permits and more information about the park.

La Traversée de Charlevoix

The longest and most challenging hiking trail in Québec is La Traversée de Charlevoix (418/639-2284, www.charlevoix.net/traverse), an exhilarating 100 km of wild, vista-filled backcountry extending from the Parc National des Grands-Jardins to the Parc du Mont Grand-Fonds. Not for the faint of heart, the trail assumes that you can hike or ski about 15–20 km per day by placing six overnight stopovers that far away from each other. Trail accommodations include log cabins suitable for 4–8 people and cottages for up to 15. These are sold in six-night bundles for $132 (cabin) and $173 (cottage). For groups, food and luggage transportation is available

the pretty Auberge La Muse

© JENNIFER EDWARDS

from cottage to cottage, as is car transportation from departure point to finish line.

ACCOMMODATIONS
Under $50

Although accommodation tends toward the pricey in Baie-Saint-Paul, **Le Balcon Vert** (22 côte du Balcon Vert, 418/435-5587, www.balconvert.charlevoix.net, mid-May–mid-Oct., tent site $18, shared cabin $20 per person, private cabin or room $47 d), just two km outside of town up a soaring slope, is a terrific alternative. Welcoming, relaxed, and self-contained, the hostel has a restaurant, bar, and cafeteria. There's also entertainment every weekend—from live music to readings to theater. No wonder so many people find it hard to leave.

The enormous, family-oriented campground of **Camping Le Genévrier** (1175 boulevard Mgr-De Laval, 418/435-6520 or 877/435-6520, www.genevrier.com, tent site $34, chalet $130 d), three km away from Baie-Saint-Paul, includes almost 400 camping sites and more than 30 private chalets. With a beach, minigolf, volleyball, tennis, and paddleboats, this spot should have more than enough activities to keep children busy. The real gems here however, are the 15 km of biking trails that follow the Rivière de la Mare.

$50-100

Along the lovely and historic rue Saint-Joseph, the intimate **Au Clocheton** (50 rue Saint-Joseph, 418/435-3393 or 877/435-3393, www.auclocheton.com, $70–100 d) is a charming, four-room B&B run by the Robins, a mother-daughter team. The old Victorian building dates to 1897 when the town welder *(forgeron)* called it home and built himself a bell turret *(clocheton).* Today, it's common to walk in and be greeted by the heavenly smell of some baked treasure created by the elder Madame Robin.

In a peaceful setting, just across the street from the Petites Franciscaines de Marie convent, **Auberge Aux Petits Oiseaux** (30 rue Ambroise-Fafard, 418/435-3888 or 877/435-3888, www.quebecweb.com/oiseaux, $85–110), an attractive brick inn close to the downtown core, actually feels further removed. The inn has seven rooms, named and modeled after different art forms. There are La Musique, Le Cinéma, La Littérature, and the priceless La Bande Déssinée (the cartoon strip), which is adorned with Tintin illustrations.

$100-150

Five km away from the center of town, **Auberge La Corbière** (188 Cap-aux-Corbeaux Nord, 418/435-2533 or 800/471-2533, www.lacorbiere.com, $79–149 d), with its view of the St. Lawrence and Isle-aux-Coudres, is a good choice for those wanting peaceful surroundings above all else. The home dates to the late 1700s and, with its newer pavilion, possesses 10 antique-filled rooms, some with shared washroom. The pièce de résistance is the all-season outdoor hot tub in back of the house.

The serene, yellow Victorian house nestled behind four giant maple trees on Baie-Saint-Paul's main drag is home to **Auberge La Muse** (39 rue Saint-Jean-Baptiste, 418/435-6839 or 800/841-6839, www.lamuse.com, $90–180 d), an elegant French Provençal-style inn that offers every luxury package imaginable including ski, golf, spa, and whale-watching excursions. The inn also has a well-reputed dining room with a Japanese chef who prepares a variety of regional foods and his own particular specialty… sushi à la Charlevoix.

$150-200

If there's one place that dominates Baie-Saint-Paul's accommodation scene—in terms of both size and popularity—it's **【 La Maison Otis** (23 rue Saint-Jean-Baptiste, 418/435-2255 or 800/267-2254, www.maisonotis.com). Perched right in the center of town, the inn consists of an old manor, which dates to the mid-1800s, and two connecting pavilions. The relaxed lobby has the feel of an alpine chalet with its low lighting, couches, fireplace, and bar, while the rooms, although a bit cramped, are tastefully decorated and furnished. The PC Plan (lodging and breakfast), sold only Mondays and Tuesdays during high season, ranges from $110–235 d. The MAP plan (lodging, breakfast, and dinner) is in effect every day, ranging from $208–325 d.

FOOD

As the hub of the Route des Saveurs, Baie-Saint-Paul has no shortage of excellent restaurants. There are only a few worthwhile lower-priced options, but you'll be tempted to spend a little more anyway to sample some of the terrific à la carte and four- or five-serving table d'hôte menus.

The **【 Microbrasserie Charlevoix's Le Saint-Pub** (2 rue Racine, 418/240-2332, www.quebecweb.com/microbrasserie, 11:30 A.M.–midnight daily, kitchen closes 9:30 P.M., mains $10–30) is a lively spot and a must for all beer lovers. Order the microbrew sampler ($4.50) and get four ministeins of beer that vary from blonde ("tastes like a wheat field after rain") to a nutty brown ale called "Bootlegger." Many dishes incorporate regional products and some, natch, are made with beer.

Doing its best to live up to its bohemian name, the **Café des Artistes** (25 rue Saint-Jean-Baptiste, 418/435-5585, 9 A.M.–midnight daily, mains $8.50–12) is an intimate little spot with local art and a back wall covered with marker musings that vary from the profound to the absurd. Tasty European thin-crust pizzas shaped in a square are popular, while panini and mussels round out the menu. There are patios in front and back.

A local favorite, **【 Le Mouton Noir** (43 rue Sainte-Anne, 418/240-3030, 11:30 A.M.–3:30 P.M. and 5:30–10 P.M. daily, five-course meal $28–42) is situated near the quay with a large outdoor patio overlooking the Gouffre River. French cuisine with local specialties including Charlevoix veal, cheese, vegetables, and wild mushrooms are on the menu.

Nondescript from the outside, **Al Dente** (30 rue Leclerc, 418/435-6695, www.aldente-charlevoix.com, 10 A.M.–9 P.M. daily, mains $7–14) serves fresh pasta made on-site. With room for only 20 seated customers inside, things can get a little cozy until the patio opens out back come summer. Pasta dishes using local products such as linguini with sauce made from Migneron cheese and cannelloni made with veal are tasty choices.

If you want to pull out all the stops and impress your date, try the gourmet dining room at ⟨ **La Maison Otis** (23 rue Saint-Jean-Baptiste, 418/435-2255, two seatings at 6 P.M. and 8 P.M. daily, five-course table d'hôte $42.95). Presided over by Chef Bernard Tapin, the menu includes original items such as caribou and stingray. For the full romantic effect, start with a cocktail at the lobby bar or on the terrace and then move into the dining room— preferably the older section at the front of the building—and choose a table next to a window overlooking the street.

INFORMATION AND SERVICES
Tourist Information
Stop in at the visitors center on Route 138, just before you get to town. Called the Maison du Tourisme de Baie-Saint-Paul (444 boulevard Mgr-De Laval/route 138, 418/435-4160), the center has lots of useful information on restaurants, attractions, and accommodations and an incredible view of the surrounding area from its balcony. The doors are open 8:30 A.M.–7 P.M. daily mid-June–late September and 8:30 A.M.–4 P.M. daily late September–mid-June.

A second, smaller, seasonal tourist office is right downtown in the Centre d'Art Baie-Saint-Paul (4 rue Ambroise-Fafard, 418/435-3681, 10 A.M.–6 P.M. Tues. –Sun. June–Sept.).

GETTING THERE
By Car
If you're traveling by car from Québec City, take Route 138 eastbound to get to Baie-Saint-Paul. The trip is an enjoyable and fast 100 kilometers.

By Bus
Intercar (888/861-4592, www.intercar.qc.ca) runs three daily bus trips, with an extra trip on Friday, from Québec City's Gare du Palais (320 rue Abraham-Martin, 418/525-3000) to Baie-Saint-Paul's bus station (Restaurant La Grignote, 2 route de l'Équerre, 418/435-6569). The bus ride takes just over an hour and costs $17.50 one-way, $28 return.

ISLE-AUX-COUDRES
The serene, 16-km-long Isle-aux-Coudres (pop. 1,350) was discovered by French explorer Jacques Cartier in 1535 and named after its many hazelnut trees, *couldres* in French. Although only a short, 15-minute ferry ride away from the mainland, in many ways the island seems much more remote. The feeling likely stems back to the first settlers who arrived here in 1720. Without the luxury of traveling back and forth to the mainland, they became a largely self-sufficient lot, growing all their own food and hunting beluga whales to make boots from the skin and lamp oil from the fat. Today, tourism has become the central force behind the economy and yet, beyond a few sights and some great cycling, there aren't too many diversions here. But that's probably the way most people like it.

Sights
Before heading over to the island, spend a bit of time in **Saint-Joseph-de-la-Rive** (pop. 200), the tiny village nestled between the

one of two old windmills at Les Moulins de l'Isle-aux-Coudres

CHARLEVOIX

© JENNIFER EDWARDS

hillside and the ferry. Stop off at **Papeterie Saint-Gilles** (304 rue Félix-Antoine-Savard, 418/635-2430 or 866/635-2430, www .papeteriesaintgilles.com, 8–11:30 A.M. and 1–5 P.M. Mon.–Fri. and 9 A.M.–5 P.M. Sat.–Sun., admission free), a beautiful museum and workshop dedicated to papermaking. Founded in 1965, this paper place specializes in making fine cotton paper laced with flowers and leaves from the region. Today, artisans still make paper the 17th-century way and you can watch them in action. Across the street, in an old schooner shipyard, the **Musée Maritime de Charlevoix** (305 rue de l'Église, 418/635-1131, www.museemaritime-charlevoix.com, adults $3, children 15 and under free) covers Charlevoix's maritime history through displays, navigation equipment, and tours of schooners onsite. The museum is open 9 A.M.–5 P.M. daily during the height of the summer (late June–early Sept.). In early summer (mid-May–late June) and in the fall (early Sept.–early Oct.), it's open 9 A.M.–4 P.M. Monday–Friday and 11 A.M.–4 P.M. Saturday–Sunday. Only a few steps away, **Les Santons de Charlevoix** (303 rue de l'Église, 418/635-2521, www .quebecweb.com/santons, 10 A.M.–5:30 P.M. mid-May–mid-Oct.) is the perfect place to wean your aunt from her collection of souvenir spoons. Open the door and you'll find hundreds of tiny, clay figurines depicting scenes from the nativity, traditional Québécois characters, and famous Charlevoix people and buildings.

Once on the island, head to the picturesque **Les Moulins de l'Isle-aux-Coudres** (36 chemin du Moulin, 418/438-2184, www.charlevoix.qc.ca/moulins, 9 A.M.–6:30 P.M. daily mid-June–mid-Aug., adults $5, children 6–18 $3, children five and under free). Dating to the mid-1800s, the working pair of mills—one water, the other wind—were built by the Seminary of Québec to grind wheat and buckwheat into flour and feed a population that often struggled through the long, cold winters. You can buy bread made with both types of flour in the gift shop.

Cycling

With a 26-km road that circles the island, cycling is by far the best way to take in the place. Islanders suggest doing the route counterclockwise, so that the winds and terrain work in your favor. **Vélo Coudres** (2926 chemin des Coudriers, 418/438-2118 or 877/438-2118, www.charlevoix.qc.ca/velocoudres) is Isle-aux-Coudres's prime rental spot, offering mountain, touring, and all sorts of other bikes, including funny-looking side-by-side tandems and canopy-covered quadricycles perfect for a leisurely family trip. It's five km from the ferry landing, and a free shuttle will take you to the shop. Prices range from $6 per hour or $21 per day for a mountain bike and $42 per hour or $147 per day for the jumbo quadricycle that accommodates six adults and two children.

Accommodations and Food

If you're considering staying overnight, try **Camping Sylvie** (1275 chemin des Coudriers, 418/438-2420, tent sites $12–20, cabins $40–60 d). With its 42 sites and five clean, yet barebones cabins, it's a good choice for campers and especially families. There are a beach and an artificial lake with canoes and paddleboats for rent. There's also the fun-loving **Crapet Soleil** (1064 chemin des Coudriers, 418/438-1010, www.crapetsoleil.com, rooms $15 per person, cabins $40–50), an inn/bistro/concert venue that caters to a youthful, lively crowd. Touring Québec musicians play in the bar and although rooms tend toward the bland, at $15 per person, who's complaining? In the summertime, the bistro serves fine Québec beers on tap along with inexpensive gourmet pizzas and homemade fish and nut burgers. Not far from the ferry landing, **Un Petit Coin de Paradis** (1021 chemin des Coudriers, 418/438-2979 or 877/438-2979, rooms $80 d) has modern, comfortable cabins on a wooded lot. Each green-roofed cabin has two bedrooms that can accommodate up to six people. Finally, there's the luxurious (**Cap-aux-Pierres Hotel** (444 chemin La Baleine, 418/438-2711 or 888/222-3308, www.hotelcapauxpierres.com, rooms $109 d and up), which was once the ancestral home of local hotel magnates the Dufour family. The Dufours raised 17 children here, eventually turning the kids' rooms into guest rooms as they flew the coop. The hotel's La Lucarne Restaurant has regional cuisine with a seafood bend and is known for its Sunday brunches, which go for $10.95.

Information

You'll find the tourist office (1024 chemin des Coudriers, 418/438-2930, www.charlevoix.qc.ca/isle-aux-coudres) near the ferry dock. There is one bank on the island with an ATM. It's the Caisse Populaire Desjardins de L'Isle-aux-Coudres (29 chemin de la Traverse, 418/438-2555 or 888/430-2555).

Getting There

If time isn't of the essence, take the longer route from Baie-Saint-Paul by taking Route 362 to Les Éboulements and then heading down the sleep slope to Saint-Joseph-de-la-Rive. You'll get a stunning view of the village, the quay, and Isle-aux-Coudres.

The ferry (418/438-2743 or 877/787-7438) makes daily runs between Saint-Joseph-de-la-Rive and the island during the summer from 7 A.M.–11:30 P.M. It departs every 30 minutes from 9 A.M.–5 P.M.; otherwise it departs every hour. The ride lasts about 15 minutes and is free.

Les Éboulements

For all its small-town serenity, the picturesque hillside town of Les Éboulements (pop. 1,040) has seen a lot of action in its day. Its name, which means "landslide" in English, attests to the big earthquake that washed away part of the nearby coast in 1663. It was also the point of impact of the 15 billion-ton meteorite crash that occurred more than 350 years ago. Today it is arguably one of the prettiest villages in all of Québec, offering a spectacular view of the St. Lawrence River and a mountainside dotted with farms and historic homes. Visit the **Moulin Banal** (157 rue Principale, 418/635-2239, 10 A.M.–5 P.M. mid-June–early Sept., adults $3, children 12

LA ROUTE DES SAVEURS

Everyone who sets foot in Québec's fine-dining mecca should plan to gain at least a couple of pounds. With the region's well-refined history of hospitality and diverse array of local products, which include raw-milk cheeses, chocolate, emu, pheasant, lamb, cider, and organic fruit and vegetables, Charlevoix has become a place to eat and eat well.

Seizing the tourism potential, an alliance of food producers and chefs created La Route des Saveurs (The Flavor Trail), a thread of accredited establishments in the region that either produce local foods or prepare it. Following the trail isn't only about great food, mind you; it offers a cultural and historical snapshot of the region, created through visits of family-run farms, old mills, and cheese factories. Pick up the brochure titled "Circuit de la route des saveurs/Charlevoix Flavour Trail" at any Charlevoix tourist information center for a foldout map with descriptions and locations of each establishment or visit www.terroircharlevoix.com.

and under free), a functioning mill dating to 1790 that sits atop a 30-meter waterfall and possesses its original machinery. At the other end of town, **La Ferme Éboulemontaise** (350 rang Saint-Godefroy, 418/635-2682, www.agneausaveurscharlevoix.com) is a sheep and organic vegetable farm. You can get a tour of the site or meander along two hiking trails, one five km, the other three km, that start from the farm. Ever tried a blue potato or a yellow beet? Here's your chance. Sample these oddities and 70 varieties of fruit and veggies at **Les Jardins du Centre** (91 rang Centre, 418/635-2710), a family-run farm open for picnics and group tastings.

Saint-Irénée

Another beautiful hillside village, Saint-Irénée (pop. 697) is best known for **Le Domaine**

Forget (5 Saint-Antoine, 418/452-8111, www.domaineforget.com), a music and dance academy that attracts more than 600 international students annually. Just off Route 362, the 60-hectare site originally contained three separate residences, one of which was owned by Rodolphe Forget, a member of Parliament and successful local businessman. The properties were merged in 1945 to accommodate a Catholic girls' school, and then in 1974, a nonprofit music collective took it over and started to offer music classes. Now, in addition to the school, the Domaine Forget offers an annual summertime festival (June–Aug.) featuring a who's who of European and North American classical and jazz masters. Tickets range $21–34 and you can buy them by calling 418/452-3535, ext. 800, or 888/336-7438. If you're around on a weekend, drop by the Domaine Forget's famous Sunday brunch and dine to the sounds of a live music ensemble. Brunch is

$26.75 for adults and $12.75 for children 6–12 (taxes and tip included). Many area inns offer partnering packages including accommodation and concert tickets.

Another stop to make in Saint-Irénée is the **Ateliers DeBlois** (1131 Terrebonne/route 362, 418/452-3229, 9 A.M.–6 P.M. daily, May–Nov.), which consists of a grouping of artists' studios all huddled together. The shining star here is the "factory outlet" of **Les Bas de Julie** (800/650-3558, www.basdejulie.com), a tiny shop featuring multitudes of colorful, striped wool socks. According to Julie, she is continuing a tradition started by a little Charlevoix craft shop whose own striped socks, known as "Murray Bay Socks," became a hit with American tourists. When the Duke of Windsor came to visit the summer home of some friends in the late 1950s, he bought a pair of his own and was later photographed wearing them in *Time* magazine.

La Malbaie

The area now referred to as La Malbaie (pop. 9,334) is the result of the 1999 amalgamation of five municipalities: La Malbaie–Pointe-au-Pic and Sainte-Agnès on the west side of the Malbaie River and Rivière Malbaie, Cap-à-l'Aigle, and Saint-Fidèle on the east side.

According to legend, La Malbaie, the birthplace of Canada's resort industry, was not as hospitable to Samuel de Champlain, the first European explorer to land here in 1608. Anchored in the bay for a night's rest, it was come morning that Champlain realized that the bay had completely emptied overnight. Belligerent about having to wait until later in the day to depart, he scribbled *Ah! La malle bayes* in his notes, which loosely translates to "Oh! What a bad bay." Although the name stuck, the sentiment didn't. After a couple of Scottish seigneurs started inviting family and friends to enjoy the clean, sea air in the early 1800s, it didn't take long for word to spread of the area's curative powers. By the

time the romantic era was in full swing, ships filled with urban bourgeoisie from New York, Toronto, and Montréal chugged up the St. Lawrence in eager anticipation of reaching that same "bad bay."

Although Malbaie's commercial sector lacks yesterday's charm, Pointe-au-Pic proper still has the overwhelming feel of that golden era. Buildings such as the Manoir Richelieu and many of the original summer residences built along the chemin de Falaises, including the one that used to belong to U.S. President Howard Taft, are a testament to what a beautiful piece of land and lots of money can do.

SIGHTS AND RECREATION
◖ Manoir Richelieu and Casino de Charlevoix
Built in response to the area's popularity as a resort destination, the magnificent and imposing Le Manoir Richelieu (181 rue Richelieu, 418/665-3703 or 800/441-1414, www

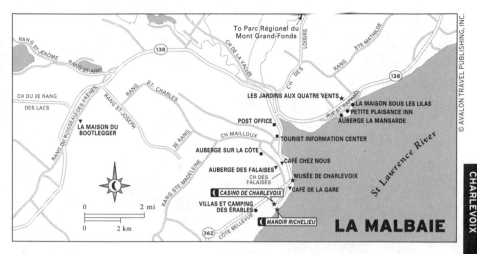

© AVALON TRAVEL PUBLISHING, INC.

CHARLEVOIX

.fairmont.com) was first opened in 1899. Destroyed by fire in 1928, the second Manoir Richelieu opened its doors only a year later. The Norman-style château, with its towers and turrets, passed through many hands and met varying levels of success until Canadian Pacific (later Fairmont Hotels) took it over and, in 1999, gave it a $140 million facelift. If you're visiting during the day, stop by the Bar La Brise for a drink. Just off the lobby, the bar has huge windows overlooking the St. Lawrence, deep wicker chairs, and a sunny terrace, perfect for whiling away the afternoon hours.

Although the Casino de Charlevoix (183 rue Richelieu, 418/665-5300 or 800/665-2274, www.casino-de-charlevoix.com) is the region's number one tourist destination, there's something a tad jarring about the sound of 780 cha-ching-ing slot machines in the midst of this peaceful town. Still, it's worth a stop to witness some of the high-stakes playing at the roulette wheel and poker tables even if you're not in the mood to gamble. The casino doors are open 10 A.M.–2 A.M. Sunday–Thursday and 10 A.M.–3 A.M. Friday–Saturday during the height of summer (late June–early Sept.). It's open 11 A.M.–1 A.M. Sunday–Thursday and 11 A.M.–3 A.M. Friday–Saturday in early summer (mid-May–late June) and fall (Sept.–late Oct.), and finally,

11 A.M.–midnight Sunday–Thursday and 11 A.M.–3 A.M. Friday–Saturday during the winter season (late Oct.–early May).

Musée de Charlevoix

The excellent, but small, Musée de Charlevoix (10 chemin du Havre, 418/665-4411, www .museedecharlevoix.qc.ca, 9 A.M.–5 P.M. daily mid-June–early Sept., 10 A.M.–5 P.M. Tues.–Fri. and 1–5 P.M. Sat.–Sun. late Sept.–June, adults $5, students $4, family—two adults and two children—$11, children 11 and under free) offers a complete cultural history of the region told through photographs, displays, and a focus on folk art, a significant form of artistic expression in the area. Displays are in French and English.

Les Jardins aux Quatre Vents

What began as a family hobby garden turned into a sprawling, all-consuming passion for Francis H. Cabot, the green-thumbed American behind Les Quatre Vents (The Four Winds). Situated in the Cap-à-l'Aigle sector, the gardens, which have been deemed by many as North America's most magnificent, are sprawled out over 20 acres and encompass 22 smaller gardens, each with its own theme. Sadly, this oasis remains largely inaccessible to the general public. It's open only four Saturdays

CHARLEVOIX

© CHARLES ROBERGE

a quiet section of the Rivière Malbaie

during the summer, and tickets go on sale in December of the previous year on a first-come, first-served basis and sell like hotcakes. Try your luck by getting in touch with the Centre Écologique de Port-au-Saumon (418/434-2209, www.cepas.qc.ca, tickets $25).

(Parc National des Hautes-Gorges-de-la-Rivière-Malbaie

It took an agonizingly long time for the Québec government to officially welcome Parc National des Hautes-Gorges-de-la-Rivière-Malbaie (4 rue Maisonneuve, 418/439-1227 or 800/665-6527, www.sepaq.com, mid-May–mid-Oct., adults $3.50, children 6–17 $1.50, children under five free) into the provincial park fold. When it finally did in 2000, this 225-square-km park, made up of some of the highest cliffs east of the Rockies, deep-cut valleys, waterfalls, and the meandering Malbaie River, may well have become its most spectacular member.

Lucky for us, the infant park's wily charms still remain somewhat undiscovered. For expe-

rienced outdoor enthusiasts there are canoeing, kayaking, rock-climbing, and mountain-biking opportunities, as well as the challenging hike to the summit of the 770-meter Acropole des Draveurs, a mountaintop with a stunning view of the Malbaie River valley. Some easier hikes and a glass-top riverboat that cruises the Malbaie River (adults $25, children 6–17 $15, children six and under free) service the more leisurely crowd. You'll find the park entrance and the **Félix-Antoine-Savard Visitors Center** about 45 km north of La Malbaie on Route 138. There are three campgrounds in the park. Le Pin Blanc has showers and toilets, while Le Cran and the campground situated in the Équerre sector have primitive sites with outhouses only. Tent sites are $19 (wild camping) or $24 (regular camping, however, none of the sites have service). Kayaks can be rented for $12 per hour, $24 for a half day, and $34 for a full day. Canoes can be rented for $11 per hour, $23 for a half day, and $32 for a full day. Bikes are $11 per hour, $19 for a half day, and $27 for a full day.

White-Water Rafting
Prove your might by riding the rapids of the Malbaie River on one of the many summertime rafting trips organized by **Descente Malbaie** (316 rue Principale, 418/439-2265, www.descentemalbaie.com). This outfit, in Saint-Aimé-des-Lacs, lets you choose between a half-day rafting trip for $49, a daylong excursion that combines rafting and fishing for $149, and two half days of rafting and one night of camping for $199.

Parc Régional du Mont Grand-Fonds
Although not quite as dazzling as Le Massif, the Parc Régional du Mont Grand-Fonds' (418/665-0095 or 877/665-0095, www.montgrandfonds.com, cross-country adults $12, students $10, downhill adults $31, children 6–15 $21, children under six free) ski hill, with its 335-meter drop and 14 trails, is nothing to sneeze at. The gem here is the 160 km worth of cross-country skiing trails that run the gamut from easy to very difficult. Snowboarding is also popular and an on-site ski and snowboarding school offers lessons for beginners. Private courses are $30 per person per hour and $50 for two people per hour. Five-hour clinics are $120 and $60 per additional person.

ACCOMMODATIONS
Under $50
About three km away from the casino, the small hilltop **Villas et Camping des Érables** (69 rang Terrebonne, 418/665-4212, June–Sept., www.campingdeserables.com, tent sites $19) is the most centrally located campground in La Malbaie. Many of the 30 grassy tent sites afford superb views of the St. Lawrence 750 feet below.

$50-100
Cap à l'Aigle's ◖ **La Maison sous les Lilas** (649 Saint Raphaël, 418/665-8076, rooms $75–95 d) is worth staying just for its scented gardens and picturesque gazebo. With quilt-covered beds, antique furniture, three old stone fireplaces, and only four guest rooms, this century home is the essence of Victorian charm.

Another choice in the Cap à l'Aigle sector is **Auberge la Mansarde** (87 rue Saint Raphaël, 418/665-2750 or 888/577-2750, www.aubergelamansarde.com, rooms with shared bath $75–78 d, regular rooms $85–100 d). The lovely gardens and apple trees in the backyard make it a good choice for people who like the idea of staying put on the veranda and gazing over the grounds. The rooms are all tastefully decorated in French-country stylings such as plaid and floral prints and rustic antique furniture.

$100-150
The family-run **Petite Plaisance Inn** (310 rue Saint-Raphaël, 418/665-2653 or 877/665-2653, www.quebecweb.com/petiteplaisance, $110 d includes continental breakfast) is not quite the lap of luxury, but with its six simple, clean rooms, interesting assortment of antiques, and good dining room, it's a great choice for those on a budget. This is especially so when you factor in that breakfast and dinner for two into the room rate for an extra $55. Rooms have a shared bathroom.

The award-winning ◖ **Auberge des Falaises** (250 chemin des Falaises, 418/665-3731 or 800/386-3731, www.aubergedesfalaises.com, rooms MAP $110 d, suites $145 d) has two types of accommodation: there are the main inn's pleasant yet straightforward rooms and there are the adjacent pavilion's plush junior suites with fireplace and whirlpool bath. Many types of packages are offered, including honeymoon, casino, whale-watching, and golf.

Over $200
Auberge sur la Côte's (205 chemin des Falaises, 418/665-3972 or 800/853-3972, www.charlevoix.qc.ca/surlacote, room rates of $225–291 d include breakfast and supper) big, yellow, cheery estate with creeping vines and a sprawling lawn sloping toward the St. Lawrence is a hospitable place run by a friendly couple who live on-site. The inn has 12 cushy

rooms, some with their own fireplaces, and two villas for bigger groups.

It will cost you a pretty penny, but it's hard to pass up a night's stay at Charlevoix's landmark hotel. The ((**Manoir Richelieu** (181 rue Richelieu, 418/665-3703 or 800/441-1414, www.fairmont.com, rooms start at $190 d) has everything you'd expect from a luxury resort. There are the health club, the spa, and saltwater swimming pools, not to mention the three restaurants, cigar room, tea salon, and the very friendly and accommodating staff. But with 405 guest rooms and a constant wave of name-tagged seniors being unloaded from enormous tour buses, the place can start to feel a tad impersonal. Rooms tend to be small, but they are all nicely furnished and possess views of the St. Lawrence or the gardens out back.

FOOD

The sunny, 1950s-inspired ((**Café Chez Nous** (1075 rue Richelieu, 418/665-3080, 7 A.M.–9 P.M. daily, mains $6–12) is a great choice for brunch and lunchtime fare. With a large veranda ideal for people-watching, a wide variety of coffees, and a menu featuring breakfast variations on eggs Benny and lunchtime panini and that French classic made from ham and melted cheese, *croque-monsieur,* this is a great spot to while away an hour or two.

Another good casual dining spot popular with families is **Café de la Gare** (100 chemin du Havre, 418/665-4272, 11:30 A.M.–midnight daily, mains $9–15), right across from the Pointe-au-Pic pier. Main dishes include pasta, chicken, steak *frites,* and a heaping two-pound plate of mussels served with fries. The outdoor summer patio is heavenly on a calm, sunny day.

Get ready for a megadose of kitsch and limited elbow room at **La Maison du Bootlegger** (110 Ruisseau des Frênes, 418/439-3711, www.maisondubootlegger.com, 6 P.M.–closing Tues.–Sun., table d'hôte with tour and entertainment starts at $30), a popular country road curiosity. The restaurant was once the home of Norrie Sellar, an enterprising American who sought to undermine Prohibition by creating a men's sporting club in the attic and an elaborate maze on the ground floor should the mo-

The Café Chez Nous is the spot for coffee and people-watching.

rality police come a-calling. Today the place has been turned into a museum/restaurant specializing in charcoal-grilled meats.

A local favorite, the dining room at the (**Auberge des Falaises** (250 chemin des Falaises, 418/665-3731 or 800/386-3731, www.aubergedesfalaises.com, 8–10:30 A.M. and 6–9 P.M. daily, five-course table d'hôte $45) has a beautiful view of the St. Lawrence and meaty mains including duck, Charlevoix veal, and deer steak. The restaurant is considered by Tourisme Québec as one of the three best restaurants in the province.

In the beautiful Cap-à-l'Aigle sector of La Malbaie, the dining room of the lovely (**Auberge des Peupliers** (381 Saint-Raphaël, 418/665-4423 or 888/282-3743, www.aubergedespeupliers.com, 6–9:30 P.M. daily, five-course table d'hôte $48) is also regarded by locals as one of the best tables in the area. Known for its adventurous menu, grandma's-house style, and personable wait staff, the restaurant has won numerous awards. If you're a crème brûlée fan, try it here; it comes topped with rhubarb and cardamom.

INFORMATION AND SERVICES
Tourist Information
The busy Maison du Tourisme (495 boulevard de Comporté, 418/665-4454 or 800/667-2276, www.tourisme-charlevoix.com, 8:30 A.M.–9 P.M. daily early June–early Sept.

and 8:30 A.M.–4:30 P.M. early Sept.–early June) services La Malbaie and the entire Charlevoix region. It has the scoop on all the whale-watching excursions and will make reservations for you.

Banks
There are two banks in town, the Banque Nationale Du Canada (316 rue Saint-Etienne, 418/665-6487) and the Caisse Populaire Desjardins (130 rue John-Nairne, 418/665-4443). Both have ATMs open all the time.

GETTING THERE
By Car
If you're driving from Baie-Saint-Paul, you'll have two roads to choose from and a distance of 48 km to cover until you hit La Malbaie. There's the slower, more scenic Route 362 with many diversions along the way or the less spectacular inland Route 138.

By Bus
You can catch an Intercar (888/861-4592, www.intercar.qc.ca) bus from the Gare du Palais in Québec City (320 rue Abraham-Martin, 418/525-3000) to Malbaie for $29 one-way, $47 return or from Baie-Saint-Paul's bus station (2 route de l'Équerre, 418/435-6569) for $8.50 one-way, $14 return. The Mabaie bus stop is at Dépanneur J. E. Otis (46 rue Sainte-Catherine, 418/665-2264), right near the information center.

Tadoussac

It may be a true test of maturity to find out that "Tadoussac" means "breasts" and not snicker a little. Named by the Montagnais because of the many hills that surround it, Tadoussac (pop. 910) was a significant trading center for native peoples even before Jacques Cartier landed here in 1534 and subsequent European settlers established it as Canada's first fur-trading post.

In the latter half of the 19th century, after

trading died down, Tadoussac was rediscovered by wealthy tourists as a favored destination to escape the city's heat. Today, it is considered one of the best places in the world to view whales, and local businesses, with their cruise tickets, tacky T-shirts, inflatable toys, and key chains, do their best to not let you forget it. But even the whale-watching excess can't obscure the fact that this lovely town with its sea salt air and magnificent

Tadoussac with its famous red and white hotel

Petite Chapelle de Tadoussac

Right next door to the landmark Hotel Tadoussac is the tiny Petite Chapelle de Tadoussac (169 rue du Bord-de-l'Eau, 418/235-4324, 9 A.M.–9 P.M. daily mid-June–mid-Oct., adults $2, children $0.50). Built by Jesuits in 1747, it is Canada's oldest wooden church and contains some noteworthy objects, including Jesuit vestments and an 18th-century tabernacle.

Poste de Traite Chauvin

Learn about trade relations between the first European settlers and the Montagnais by dropping by the Poste de Traite Chauvin (157 rue du Bord-de-l'Eau, 418/235-4657,10 A.M.–6 P.M. daily late May–mid-June and early Sept.–mid-Oct., 9 A.M.–8:30 P.M. daily mid-June–early Sept., adults $3, children $2.25), a replica of the country's first trading post, built in 1600 by Pierre Chauvin. Exhibits are only in French, but there are English guidebooks and bilingual tours. If you're feeling adventurous, seal-meat tastings happen Sunday mornings at 11:30.

Musée Maritime de Tadoussac

Schooners, luxury liners, and tall ships… the Musée Maritime de Tadoussac (145 rue du Bateau-Passeur, 418/235-4657, 10 A.M.–4 P.M. mid-June–late Aug., adults $2.50, children $2) chronicles the area's rich maritime past with the help of model ships, photos, and navigation equipment.

Festival de la Chanson de Tadoussac

Every year a throng of people descend on Tadoussac for one of the province's best-loved music festivals. Held during four days in mid-June, well-known musical acts and up-and-comers mostly from Québec play all around town in intimate venues such as the marina, the Protestant chapel, and the youth hostel. For more information or to get tickets call 418/235-2002 or 866/861-4108 or check out the website at www.chansontadoussac.com. Individual concert tickets run from $15–32, a day pass is $10–20 depending on the day of the week, and a full access pass is $130.

surroundings has much more to offer, including a vibrant cultural scene, rich heritage, and a wide variety of outdoor wilderness opportunities.

The town works on a seasonal cycle coinciding with the migration of the whales. You'll find most tourist sites and boat trips operating June–October, but expect a bit of a ghost town November–May.

SIGHTS
Centre d'Interprétation des Mammifères Marins

Run by members of a local whale-research group, the excellent Centre d'Interprétation des Mammifères Marins (108 rue de la Cale-Sèche, 418/235-4701, noon–5 P.M. mid-May–mid-June and late Sept.–mid-Oct., 9 A.M.–8 P.M. mid-June–late Sept., adults $6.25, children 6–12 $3) offers videos, slide shows, and exhibits on the whales of the St. Lawrence, including a collection of skeletons and a chance to listen to whale vocalizations.

A WHALE OF A FEAST

Wouldn't you come a-calling if you were offered one all-you-can-eat buffet after another? It's a no-brainer for 12 species of whale, including minke, blue, fin, humpback, and sperm, who make the trip north to the St. Lawrence Estuary every year and stay from June to October. Thanks to a phenomenon called upwelling that occurs in these waters, whales can ingest the requisite 4 percent of their body weight each day.

An upwelling is a movement of cold, nutrient-rich water from the bottom of the sea to the surface that occurs when currents encounter an obstacle (in this case, a sharp incline of the riverbed around Tadoussac). When the collision occurs, the water has no other place to go but up, bringing with it a motherlode of tiny crustaceans called krill, a whale's food of choice. Only the beluga remains in these waters

year-round. Sadly, their sedentary lifestyle in a home contaminated with agricultural and industrial pollutants has contributed to an alarming decline in their numbers. At the beginning of the 20th century, the estimated number of St. Lawrence beluga whales was near 5,000. Today, that number has dwindled to about 700.

Belugas are nicknamed sea canaries because of their frequent vocalizations, which help them find food and navigate through dark waters; studies are being performed to see if they suffer the effects of noise-inducing whale-watching boats and freighters. Recent government regulations for the Parc Marin du Saguenay–Saint-Laurent have tried to control overeager outfitters by stipulating things such as distance, speed, concentration of boats, and time limits.

CHARLEVOIX

BAIE-SAINTE-CATHERINE

There's not much point going to Baie-Saint-Catherine (pop. 290) if you're not interested in whales. This little town, much like its bigger, more-renowned cousin, Tadoussac, eats, breathes, and sleeps the underwater creatures. Beyond the throngs of tourists lining up for whale-watching expeditions, there is a pretty sand beach here that extends all along the bay. There is also the **Centre d'Interprétation et d'Observation de Pointe-Noire** (route 138, 418/237-4383 or 800/463-6769, 8 A.M.–8 P.M. daily mid-June–early Sept., 9 A.M.–5 P.M. Fri.–Sun. early Sept. –mid-Oct., adults $5, family $12.50) just up from the ferry landing. With an observation deck looking over the confluence of the Saguenay and the St. Lawrence, it offers one of the best vantage points from which to see the whales.

PARC MARIN DU SAGUENAY-SAINT-LAURENT AND PARC DU SAGUENAY

These two parks—one water, one land—encompass two-thirds of the **Saguenay Fjord,** which flows over 150 km from the Rivière Saguenay to the St. Lawrence Estuary. It is the second-longest fjord in North America. Its dramatic cliffs, clear water, and narrowness make it exceptionally scenic while its seals, whales, bird- and fishlife make it biologically rich.

The park also encompasses pockets of land on either side of the fjord. The marine park, called the Parc Marin du Saguenay–Saint-Laurent (418/235-4703 or 800/463-6769, www.sepaq.com) was created by the federal and provincial governments after intense lobbying from environmental groups due to the beluga's dwindling numbers. Covering an expanse of 1,138 square km, including the rich feeding grounds of the St. Lawrence Estuary, the park is home to hundreds of species of marine life, including various types of whale, fish such as capelin and herring, birds, porpoises, and seals.

Back on land, the enormous sand dunes and craggy cliffs of the 282-square-km Parc du Saguenay (418/272-1556 or 800/665-6527, www.sepaq.com, adults $3.50, children 6–17 $1.50) are divided into three distinct sectors:

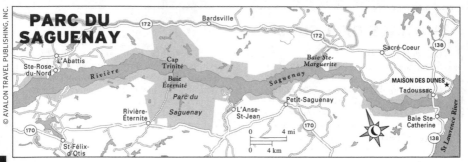

two on the north side of the fjord and one on the south. Each sector has its own characteristics and interpretation center.

Baie-du-Moulin-à-Baude

Known locally as *le désert,* the Baie-du-Moulin-à-Baude sector, about five km north of Tadoussac, is characterized by its plunging marine terraces, commonly referred to as sand dunes. Visit the **Maison des Dunes** (750 chemin du Moulin à Baude, 418/235-4238, June–mid-Oct., adults $3.50, children $1.50) for exhibits on how these terraces took shape and learn about the curious sport of sand skiing.

Baie-Éternité

The Baie-Éternité sector, in the Saguenay region just off Route 170, is dominated by 350-meter cliffs and magnificent views of the fjord. Its visitors center, the **Centre d'Interprétation du Fjord du Saguenay** (June–mid-Oct., adults $3.50, families $7) features exhibits on the formation of the fjord, guest speakers, guided walks, and a fjord flight simulator.

Baie-Sainte-Marguerite

And finally, there's the Baie-Sainte-Marguerite sector, about 10 km west of the village of Sacré-Coeur on Route 172. This sector's **Centre d'Accueil et d'Interprétation** (June–mid-Sept., adults $3.50, families $7) has exhibits focusing on the beluga and an observation point looking over the bay where a beluga pod settles for the summer.

Campgrounds

There are campgrounds with tent sites, huts, and cabins along both sides of the fjord, making the park a prime spot for longer hiking or kayaking trips. One-bedroom cabins are $94 d, and two-bedroom cabins are $164 for up to four people. Huts are $20 per person and tent sites are $18–20.

◖ Whale-Watching

Every year approximately 50 whale-watching boats transport more than 300,000 people to the waters near Tadoussac. If you want to take a cruise, you'll have to first decide how close to the water and how wet you want to get. There's a wide variety of vessels to choose from, including 12-passenger zodiacs to 600-passenger ships. But it's also worth shopping around to find out a few other things, including the expertise of the naturalist aboard, the quality of English spoken, and whether the outfit possesses Marine Park permits. Don't forget to dress warmly, as even at the height of summer, it can cool off considerably out on the water.

Croisières AML (800/563-4643, www .croisieresaml.com, adults $52, children 6–16 $22, two adults and two children $135, seniors $47), the biggest cruise/excursion company in Canada, offers three-hour cruises departing from Baie-Sainte-Catherine and Tadoussac six times a day during high season. In addition to scouting for whales, a short exploration of the Saguenay Fjord is offered. Three-hour and two-hour Zodiac trips

© JENNIFER EDWARDS

waiting for the whales on the Saint Lawrence

are also available, but they are a little bit more expensive than the cruise ships.

Counting a huge single-hull boat, a glass-bottom catamaran, and a Zodiac-type sport boat among its fleet, **Famille Dufour Croisières** (418/692-0222 or 800/463-5250, www.dufour.ca, adults $52, children 6–13 $22) offers two departure times from Baie-Sainte-Catherine and Tadoussac. Cruises last 2.5 hours.

During the height of summer, **Croisières 2001** (418/627-4276 or 800/694-5489, www.croisieres2001.com, adults $52, children 6–16 $22, children five and under free, two adults and 2 children $12) offers three-hour cruises and three departure times from Baie-Sainte-Catherine and Tadoussac aboard the 225-passenger catamaran *Katmar*. An underwater camera shows you what's going on below water.

Kayaking

The best way to take in the marine park is undoubtedly from the seat of a kayak. Rentals, lessons, and excursions are available for the beginner to experienced kayaker. A guided tour is a must for beginners as winds and currents on the fjord can be strong, and the water is frigid.

Tadoussac's **Mer et Monde Ecotours** (405 de la Mer, 418/232-6779 or 866/637-6663, www.mer-et-monde.qc.ca) has half-day ($46) and full-day ($91) whale-watching tours and two- to five-day Saguenay Fjord excursions ($270–695). **Azimut Aventure** in Baie-Sainte-Catherine (185 route 138, 418/237-4477 or 888/843-1110, www.azimutaventure.com) rents kayaks for $40 a day and plans multiple nonguided and guided tours. L'Anse-Saint-Jean's **Fjord en Kayak** (359 rue Saint-Jean-Baptiste, 418/272-3024, www.fjord-en-kayak.ca) organizes guided trips from three hours ($48) to five days ($885).

Hiking

There are more than 100 km of hiking trails in Parc du Saguenay, including everything from 20-minute walks to multiple-day hikes. For those who don't want anything too strenuous, consider the two short trails that depart directly from Tadoussac. There's the relaxed 20-minute **Sentier de la Pointe de l'Islet,** which meanders over to a whale observation point, and there's the 30-minute **Sentier de la Colline de l'Anse à l'Eau,** which culminates in a 360-degree view of town and the surrounding waters. For those wanting more of a challenge, there's the spectacular four-hour **Sentier de la Statue** in the Baie Éternité sector that departs from the interpretation center and heads up the bluffs of Cap Trinité to the statue of Our Lady of the Saguenay. Erected in 1881 by Charles Robitaille, a local man who narrowly missed drowning in the icy waters directly below the cape, the statue stands in honor of the Virgin Mary, who now safeguards all those who pass under her gaze.

If you're looking for something longer than a day hike, try the **Sentier les Caps,** a 24-km trail that departs from Baie Éternité and travels along the fjord and various capes to L'Anse-Saint-Jean. Plan on a three-day trip.

For a complete list of park trails, go to www.sepaq.com.

ACCOMMODATIONS
Under $50
Within walking distance of the ferry, **Camping Tadoussac** (428 rue Bateau-Passeur, 418/235-4501 or 888/868-6666, www.essipit.com, tent site without a view $20, with a view $27.50) has 200 grassy camping spots, which fill up quickly come midsummer. The campground is open early June–mid-October.

One of the liveliest places to stay in Tadoussac is the **◖ International Youth Hostel,** also known as Maison Majorique (158 rue Bateau-Passeur, 418/235-4372, www.fjord-best.com/ajt, dorms members $16, nonmembers $19, doubles $49.50). The laid-back camaraderie at this big, jovial, red-roofed building with a few private rooms, many dorm-style rooms, and a campground has led many a youthful, free-spirited guest to want to put down roots. Breakfast is all-you-can-eat and the three-course dinners are hearty, home-cooked affairs.

$50-100
The recently renovated and centrally located hotel-motel **Le Béluga** (191 des Pionniers, 418/235-4784, www.le-beluga.qc.ca, rooms $89 d) has clean, bright, reasonably priced rooms and the hotel's adjoining Restaurant Auberge du Lac has seafood specials.

Open year-round, **Auberge Maison Gauthier** and its annex, **Les Suites de l'Anse** (159 rue du Bateau-Passeur, 418/235-4525, www.maisongauthier.com, rooms $50, shared room $19 per person), have 12 simple rooms that are comfortable if somewhat sparse. Ideal for families, some rooms have kitchenettes.

The intimate century home called **◖ Maison Hovington** (285 rue des Pionniers, 418/235-4466, www.charlevoix.qc.ca/maisonhovington, May–late Oct. $75–100) has five charming Victorian rooms, each with its own bathroom. The owner, Monsieur Hovington, was born in the house and can give you some insider recommendations on what to do and see in town. Make sure you wake up in time for the killer homemade buffet breakfasts.

Perched atop a hill, the posh B&B **◖ La Maison Harvey Lessard** (16 rue Bellevue, 418/235-4802, www.harveylessard.com, June–late Oct., rooms $89–95, luxury suite $145) has four cozy, nicely furnished rooms with private balconies overlooking the gardens and the St. Lawrence River.

$100-150
Ideal for couples and larger groups, **Domaine des Dunes** (585 chemin du Moulin à Baude, 418/235-4843, www.domainedesdunes.com, cabins $125 d) has 10 self-contained, no-frills chalets that accommodate 2–6 people. Surrounded by birch trees, the setting is lovely summer and winter.

$150-200
The building that is the face of Tadoussac and that fuels so many people's imaginations about the place is a bit of a letdown once you step inside the front doors. Originally built in 1864 as a luxury destination for vacationing

Americans, the sprawling, red and white **Hotel Tadoussac** (165 rue Bord de l'Eau, 418/235-4421 or 800/463-5250, www.hoteltadoussac.com, rooms $149 or $165 with breakfast, or $220 with breakfast and buffet dinner) passed through many hands before it was acquired in 1984 by local hotel entrepreneurs the Dufour family. Cold and unremarkable, the interior is in need of some of yesteryear's sheen. The magnificent exterior and grounds however, are still something to behold.

FOOD
Bistros
Started by two backpackers who came to Tadoussac in 1994 and fell in love with the place, **C Café Bohème** (239 rue des Pionniers, 418/235-1180, 7 A.M.–midnight daily, May–Oct., mains $8–11) is part café, part gallery, and all youthful glow. The menu includes breakfast items such as stuffed waffles and yogurt, and lunch items such as soups, quiche, salads, and panini along with fair-trade coffee. There is also Internet access on-site.

The **C Café du Fjord** (152 rue du Bateau-Passeur, 418/235-4626, 11 A.M.–3 P.M. and 6–11 P.M. daily June–Sept.) is the most rocking place in town. Providing an annual stage for the Festival de la Chanson, this rustic café-bar also serves a solid lineup of Québécois musicians year-round. The buffet includes fish and seafood options, and you can either have your plate weighed or go for the all-you-can-eat dinner for $20.

French
A pricier option is **Restaurant la Bolée** (164 rue Morin, 418/235-4750, June–Sept., $18–

34), which serves crêpes, grilled meats, and seafood dishes. Visit the little bakery and deli downstairs for delicious breads, squares, and other sinful treats.

INFORMATION
Tourist Information
As a launching pad, visit the Maison du Tourisme (197 rue des Pionniers, 418/235-4744 or 866/235-4744, www.tadoussac.com, 8 A.M.–9 P.M. daily June–Aug., 9 A.M.–5 P.M. weekdays Sept.–May). The extremely helpful bilingual staff can help you navigate your way through town and the entire Côte-Nord region.

Bank
There's one Caisse Populaire (187 rue Bord de l'Eau, 418/235-4482) with an ATM.

GETTING THERE
By Ferry
The ferry (Baie Sainte-Catherine dock, 418/235-4395, free) that runs from Baie Sainte-Catherine in the Charlevoix region over to Tadoussac takes only 10 minutes and runs pretty much all day. Between 8 A.M. and 10 P.M., the ferry runs every 20 minutes.

By Bus
Intercar (888/861-4592, www.intercar.qc.ca) has two daily buses (9:45 A.M. and 6 P.M.) that depart Gare du Palais in Québec City (320 rue Abraham-Martin, 418/525-3000) for Tadoussac. The trip takes 3–4 hours and costs $46 one-way, $74 return. The Tadoussac dropoff is at Dépanneur de la Côte (433 route 138, 418/235-4653), right near the information center.

CHARLEVOIX

GASPÉ AND LES ÎLES DE LA MADELEINE

In the language of the Mic-mac, Gaspé means "Land's End" and in the province of Québec, you can't get much farther out than this. With the Gaspé starting nearly 600 km from Montréal, the region is mountains away in actual distance, yes, but in spirit too. Even for Québec's urban dwellers who have never ventured to the Gaspé coast, the region has come to symbolize spaciousness, serenity, and golden light—visions popularized by many postcard and calendar shots of the famous Rocher Percé. It's when you go there that you actually get to *feel* the difference. The fresh and invigorating saltwater air is a dramatic switch from the severe humidity that takes hold of the central part of the province during the summer. And the warmth and casu-alness of the Gaspé people are a refreshing change from the sometimes hurried pace in the rest of the province.

Circling the entire peninsula's 730 km of coast, Route 132 is the only main highway in the region and leads through the tourist towns of Sainte-Anne-des-Monts, Gaspé, and Percé. This makes your touring options refreshingly straightforward: Just take your time and cruise.

Québec's other maritime jewel sits an incredible 215 km away from Gaspé, right in the middle of the Gulf of Saint Lawrence. They are les Îles de la Madeleine (or the Magdalene Islands in English). Although it takes a bit more time and money to get to the islands, their striking red sandstone cliffs, lush green

HIGHLIGHTS

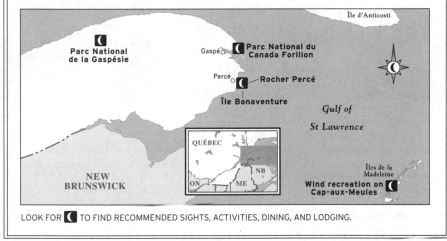

◖ **Parc National de la Gaspésie:** With 25 of the 40 highest peaks in Québec, this park is all about how high you can climb (page 250).

◖ **Parc National du Canada Forillon:** The mountains and the sea make a dramatic meeting in Forillon, located in the eastern most tip of the Peninsula (page 253).

◖ **Île Bonaventure:** Take an early morning boat ride to Île Bonaventure, home to 250,000 birds, including one of the largest communities of northern gannets in the world (page 257).

◖ **Rocher Percé:** At low tide, you can venture out to this mesmerizing mammoth of a rock, which has become the face of the Gaspé (page 258).

◖ **Wind recreation on Cap-aux-Meules:** This Îles-de-la-Madeleine island channels its ever-present gusts into peaceful kite-flying and the more daring buggy coasting and speed sailing (page 265).

LOOK FOR ◖ TO FIND RECOMMENDED SIGHTS, ACTIVITIES, DINING, AND LODGING.

valleys dotted with thick forests, sprawling sand dunes, and ever-present waters give them a uniqueness and magic that are definitely worth the trip.

PLANNING YOUR TIME

Give yourself a week to tour the Gaspé coast and longer if you plan to do some serious camping in any of its parks. Route 132's tour of the peninsula is a fair distance, so try to spread out your travel as much as possible. There are hordes of tourists in July and August, so if you can schedule your travel in June or September, you'll enjoy warm days, off-season prices, and a little bit more elbow room.

As you enter the Gaspé, definitely stop at the incredible **Jardins de Métis** for a few hours—it's a great introduction to the region. Stay for lunch, then venture forth to **Sainte-Anne-des-Monts,** the gateway to the **Parc National de la Gaspésie.** You can either stay in town, or better yet, book yourself a room in the cushy surroundings of the park's popular lodge **Gîte du Mont Albert** for a couple of nights.

On day three, head to the more maritime surroundings of **Parc National du Canada Forillon** and plan to spend a day there, staying either in the park or in Gaspé. Your next day will be spent admiring the region's landmark, the iconic **Rocher Percé** where you'll snap a

© JENNIFER EDWARDS

on the way to Gaspé, a Saint Lawrence River scene

few, or a few dozen, pics. Settle in the village of Percé for a couple of nights so that you can explore town and set out in a boat to explore the **Parc National de L'Île-Bonaventure-et-du-Rocher-Percé.** Your route will next take you west for the last couple of days along the **Baie des Chaleurs** where you can take in some Anglo- and Acadian-flavored historical sights, cool off at the beach, and hike along the great local trails in **Carleton,** the spot where you should consider spending your final night in Gaspé.

Add four extra days if you plan on making the well-worthwhile trip to **Îles de la Madeleine.** Plan on doing some kite flying or other wind activities on **Île du Cap-aux-Meules** on the first day. Explore **Île du Havre-Aubert** and its historic sights on the second. Make day three a trip to the English enclave of **Île d'Entrée,** while saving the magnificent **Île du Havre-aux-Maisons** and some lagoon exploration for final day four. Les Îles' six main islands are linked to one another by Route 199.

HISTORY

Basque fishermen were dipping their fishing poles in the waters of the St. Lawrence long before France's earliest attempts to stake a claim in the New World. It was in 1534 that French explorer, Jacques Cartier officially claimed the land, home to the Mic-mac Indians for more than 2,500 years, for the King of France by doing what he did in several Québec spots, erecting a wooden cross. He set it on the shores of the Baie de Gaspé and on that same voyage came across les Îles de la Madeleine, which he appropriately referred to in his trip journal as "Les Araynes," the latin word for sand.

After Jacques Cartier's initial visit, fishermen from France started trolling the waters surrounding the Gaspé coast every summer, bringing scores of cod back to their homeland. Permanent French settlement in the Gaspé soon began although it suffered a slow start due to a lack of enthusiasm for the extreme landscape and climate and constant threat of attack from the English who started taking an interest in the hearty fish supplies.

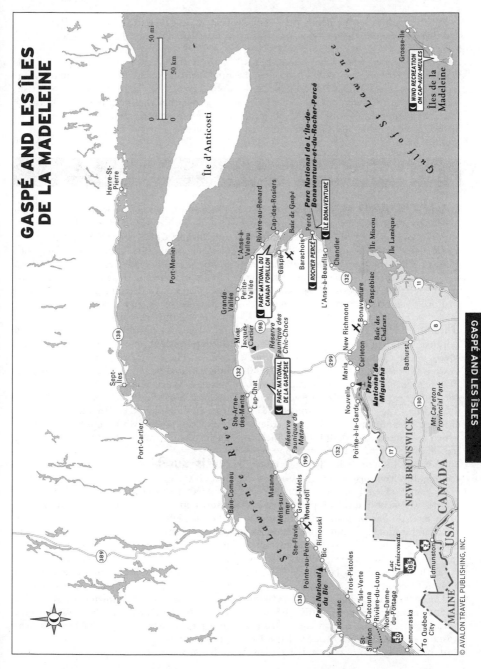

GASPÉ AND LES ÎLES DE LA MADELEINE

Île d'Anticosti

Gulf of St. Lawrence

St. Lawrence River

50 mi

50 km

Havre-St-Pierre

Port-Menier

Sept-Îles

Port-Cartier

Baie-Comeau

Grosse-Île

WIND RECREATION ON CAP-AUX-MEULES

Îles de la Madeleine

Cap-des-Rosiers

Rivière-au-Renard

L'Anse-à-Valleau

Baie de Gaspé

Parc National de L'Île-de-Bonaventure-et-du-Rocher-Percé

ÎLE BONAVENTURE

Percé

ROCHER PERCÉ

Gaspé

Barachois

PARC NATIONAL DU CANADA FORILLON

Grande-Vallée

Petite-Vallée

198

Mont Jacques-Cartier

Réserve Faunique des Chic-Chocs

L'Anse-à-Beaufils

Chandler

Île Miscou

Île Lamèque

132

11

Paspébiac

Bonaventure

PARC NATIONAL DE LA GASPÉSIE

Réserve Faunique de Matane

Ste-Anne-des-Monts

Cap-Chat

132

299

Maria

New Richmond

Carleton

Baie des Chaleurs

Bathurst

8

Matane

Nouvelle

Pointe-à-la-Garde

Parc National de Miguisha

Mt Carleton Provincial Park

130

195

132

17

NEW BRUNSWICK

389

Métis-sur-mer

Grand-Métis

Mont-Joli

Ste-Flavie

Rimouski

Bic

Parc National du Bic

Pointe-au-Père

Trois-Pistoles

L'Isle-Verte

Cacouna

Rivière-du-Loup

Notre-Dame-du-Portage

Lac Témiscouata

Edmundston

CANADA

USA

MAINE

138

St-Siméon

Tadoussac

Kamouraska

To Québec City

20

185

Expelled from their homeland in 1755 by the British because they would not pledge allegiance to the Crown, French-speaking Acadians began to settle along the Baie des Chaleurs, setting up successful logging and fishing businesses. After the British Conquest in 1759, they were joined by English, Irish, and Scottish immigrants and later on by Loyalists who fled the newly formed United States after the American Revolution and settled in places like New Richmond and New Cárlisle.

Today the Gaspé is surprisingly "multicultural" with descendants of the French, Acadian, Loyalist, English, Irish, and Scottish, not to mention the founding Mic-mac, scattered throughout the peninsula and les Îles de la Madeleine.

Gaspé Peninsula

LA MITIS AND MATANE

A gateway to the Gaspé peninsula, the serene Mitis area (the word "mitis" comes from a Mic-mac word meaning "poplar river") encompasses historic resort villages and one of the Gaspé's most well-known landmarks: the Jardins de Métis. Just beyond it is Matane, the first major commercial town in the region.

Jardins de Métis

Located in the pretty, tiny village of Grand Métis, one of Québec's oldest resort destinations, is the spectacular Jardin de Métis (200 Route 132, 418/775-2222, www.jardinsmetis. com, 8:30 A.M.–5 P.M. daily June–Oct., until 6 P.M. July–Aug., adults $14, students $12, children 13 and under free). The gardens, which hold more than 3,000 species including the famous blue Himalayan poppy, have an international reputation for their beauty and highly accomplished design—the result of the remarkable talent and passion of Elsie Reford, who acquired the property from her uncle in 1918. She first started gardening in 1926, and it quickly became an all-consuming pursuit, which she continued for more than 30 years. Today, the gardens are maintained by Les Amis des Jardins de Métis, a non-profit group.

The Reford family home, called **Estevan Lodge,** now houses a museum with temporary exhibits and a permanent display upstairs on the life and times of Elsie Reford, her family, and of course, the gardens.

There is a lookout here with an exceptional view of both rivers. There is also the pleasant **Garden Café,** which serves light meals of salads, soups, and sandwiches along with toothsome homemade desserts. The **Visitors Pavilion** located at the entrance of the gardens, also has a café and a boutique that carries books, seeds, and postcards.

Since 2000, the Jardins de Métis have also played host to the annual **International Garden Festival,** which takes place June–September. The event brings in Canadian and international landscape designers who work onsite to create new, innovative garden designs that you won't find in any backyard. You can have a peek at their creations and attend some of the lectures and workshops that take place during the festival.

Métis-sur-Mer

Just off the main highway, the incredibly scenic Métis-sur-Mer was once a wealthy seaside resort popular with Montréal's English elite who vacationed here every summer. Many of the cedar-shingled summer homes remain, making the village an impressive reminder of the way the bourgeois would spend their summer vacations. Interestingly, there are four churches here, none of them Catholic. There's not much to do in this town beyond making trips to the Jardins de Métis and watching the superb sunsets, but that's probably exactly why people decide to stay.

If you're looking for a quick and easy meal,

visit **Place Petit Miami** (508 rue du Beach, 418/936-3411, mains $3–7), which is easy to find at the intersection of Route 132 and the road that brings you into the village. Try the fried clams, but skip the fried cod. The pretty **Auberge du Grand Fleuve** (131 rue Principale, 418/936-3332, www.auberge-dugrandfleuve.qc.ca, May–mid-Oct., table d'hôte $40, rooms $175–205 d with breakfast and dinner) is a restaurant and inn with a great view of the St. Lawrence. The sunny restaurant serves dishes like braised rabbit, almond-crusted pork, and freshly caught halibut. The hotel is a gold mine for book lovers. There are books everywhere throughout the place, including the 13 no-frills rooms. Try to snag one of the five rooms that overlook the river. With the village lighthouse right in front, **Auberge Métis-sur-Mer** (1301 Route 132, 418/936-3563 or 877/338-3683, www.aubergemetissurmer.qc.ca, June–Sept., $55–60) is another spot with a great view. The standard rooms and handful of rustic cottages won't get any prizes for their décor, but the reason for staying here is really all about the beautiful grounds and the relaxation potential. There's a spa onsite where you can get massages, wraps, manicures, and pedicures. For campers, there's **Camping Annie** (394 Route 132, 418/936-3825, www.campingannie.com, June–Oct., tent site $20). The RV section has the tendency to get overwhelmingly packed, as do the main facilities like the pool, but the tent sites are grassy, nicely wooded, and well maintained.

Matane

The large commercial fishing port of Matane is the area's largest city and the most easterly port of call for the ferries connecting the south shore to the north shore towns of Baie-Comeau and Godbout. It's known more for its naval shipyard and its huge shrimp-processing plant than for its tourist jewels. That said, there is the interesting **Centre d'Observation de la Montée du Saumon de l'Atlantique** (260 avenue Saint-Jérôme, 418/562-7006, 7:30 A.M.–9:30 P.M. daily mid-June–early

Sept., 8 A.M.–8 P.M. daily early Sept.–late Sept., adults $2, children and students free), a center with observation windows that showcase the migration of Atlantic salmon. There are also interpretive panels on the history of the salmon-rich Matane River.

About 40 km south of town is the **Réserve Faunique de Matane** (Route 195, 418/562-3700 or 800/665-6527, www.sepaq.com, tent site $20). The wildlife reserve is known for being packed with all kinds of critters big and small and is your main chance to catch a glimpse of a moose. There are hikes and guided tours to mud flats and peat bogs, favored by the big beasts and a moose interpretation center where you can brush up on all you need to know. The park also has some excellent hiking trails with good views of the surrounding area.

HAUTE-GASPÉSIE

The scenery gets more spectacular as you slowly begin your ascent into **Haute-Gaspésie,** which also signals the beginning of the fabulous Chic-Choc mountain range, the highest mountains in southern Québec. This sector houses the ruggedly beautiful Parc National de la Gaspésie.

Cap-Chat

As you enter Cap-Chat, the landscape is dotted with an almost otherworldly sight. Unless you have traveled through central California, you'll probably be struck by the odd-looking windmill parks that have been constructed in the area to harness a little of that natural blowing action. More than 70 wind turbines exist here, making it one of the largest wind-based energy generating facilities in Canada. The biggest turbine, called Éole, is 110 meters and is actually the tallest vertical axis turbine in the world. And because it holds so much distinction, Cap-Chat has set up the **Éole de Cap-Chat** (Route 132, 418/786-5719, 9 A.M.–5 P.M. daily late June–Sept., adults $10, students $9, children 6–17 $7) interpretive center, which offers a 45-minute guided tour of the interior of the windmill and a video presentation.

As you head out of town, stop at the subtly indicated rest area. There's a nice little trail that begins there and heads down to the beach, where you'll get a great view of the Chic-Chocs.

Sainte-Anne-des-Monts

The town of Sainte-Anne-des-Monts is considered the gateway to the Parc National de Gaspésie. It's the place to stock up on supplies before venturing into the park, but not to do too much else. One worthy stop is the **Centre de Découverte Explorama** (1 rue du Quai, 418/763-2500 or 877/913-2500, www .explorama.org, 9 A.M.–6 P.M. daily mid-June–mid-Oct., adults $10, students $8, children 7–17 $6). The center is an ode to the river with aquariums, exhibits, and talks on underwater St. Lawrence life. It also offers a tour aboard the *Explorama,* a zodiac boat that fits 18 people. Tours leave three times daily.

With its proximity to the park, Sainte-Anne-des-Monts is a good place to overnight if the campgrounds in the park are full. One of the best bets for an inexpensive but comfortable stay is **Auberge Internationale Sainte-Anne-des-Monts** (295 1ère avenue Est, 418/763-7123, www.aubergesgaspesie.com, dorm $24, room $54 with breakfast). Housed in an old school not far from the center of town, the inn/hostel has dormitories and private rooms. There is a decent restaurant onsite and a self-service kitchen, as well as laundry and Internet facilities. Another good choice is the pretty **Auberge la Seigneurie des Monts** (21 1ère avenue Est, 418/763-5308 or 800/903-0206, $85–100 d, includes breakfast), an 1860s historical home peppered with antiques. The couple who purchased the home in 2002 have since added an art gallery, a restaurant, and a tiny museum that tells the story of the home's former occupants, including Sainte-Anne-des-Monts' first mayor and the post office.

In the evening, stop by **Resto-Bar le Vieux Sainte-Anne** (100 1ère avenue Ouest, 418/763-3114) to sit on the terrace overlooking the sea with a local brew. One of the town's more popular bars, it hosts live music in weekends.

◖ PARC NATIONAL DE LA GASPÉSIE

Until 1990, Parc National de la Gaspésie was the Gaspé's best-kept secret. Today, the very thing that made the park somewhat daunting and impenetrable—its 25 summits that reach more than 1,000 meters—is attracting all kinds of hikers, skiers, snowshoers, and those who just like to gaze. This is mainly thanks to the construction of roadways and also to the Gîte du Mont Albert, the park's mountain inn that takes wilderness luxury to new heights. Founded in 1937, the park covers 802 sq km, including two spectacular mountain ranges—the Chic-Chocs and the McGerrigles—and four diverse ecosystems that span deciduous to tundra, something usually only seen in much more northern reaches.

One of the park's biggest claims to fame is that it houses the most southerly species of woodland caribou. Although their numbers are small, they can be spotted from the summit of Mont Albert.

The park has a new and expanded **interpretation center** (1981 Route du Parc, 418/763-7811 or 866/727-2427, www.parksquebec.com, 8 A.M.–10 P.M. daily June–early Sept., 8 A.M.–8 P.M. daily Sept–mid-Oct., 9 A.M.–5 P.M. daily late Dec.–late April, adults $3.50, children 6–17 years $1.50, children under 6 free), located about 25 km from the entrance gates, right next to the Gîte du Mont Albert. If you need some prehike fuel or posthike cool down, you can stop by their **Bistro Piedmount.** They offer good cafeteria-style food and will also pack a lunch for you to take into the hills.

Hiking

There are 140 km of trails to explore that range in length from a no-sweat 1 km to a huff-and-puff 17 km. The **Lac aux Americains** trail in the McGerrigle sector is an easy walk that culminates at the beautiful glacial lake where the setting could easily be the Lake Louise of the east. Probably the toughest and most rewarding trails are the ones that lead up to **Mont Jacques-Cartier,** which is the highest peak in Québec at 1,270 meters, and **Mont Albert,**

REINDEER IN THE PARK?

When one thinks of reindeer, it's often in the context of Christmas – Donner and Blitzen are pulling Santa's sleigh and being led by that funny-looking one with the bright red nose. But Canada has quite a sizeable population of reindeer – here called caribou – including one very special herd in the Gaspé region or more specifically, the Parc National de la Gaspésie.

Hanging out atop the peaks of the Chic-Choc and McGerrigle Mountains (Mont Albert and Mont Jacques-Cartier are the ones where you are most likely to see them grazing) where a subarctic climate and plenty of lichen is found, the Gaspé's woodland caribou herd is the lone surviving population located south of the Saint Lawrence.

But the herd isn't ambling about without a care in the world. The park was created in 1937 with the principal objective of creating a safe and protected place for the isolated caribou to live. These caribou had seen their numbers drop dramatically to about 200 in the 1970s. All logging in the park was halted, and a national recovery plan was put into

place in 1994. Although the caribou's numbers seemed to stabilize in the 1990s, current counts place them at about 140 total.

You'll know a caribou if you spot one. They are typically about one meter high from ground to shoulder, so you can't miss them. Their fur changes color: It's grey in the winter and light brown in the summer. They also sport a veil of creamy fur on their chest and back and under their belly. Both male and female caribou have antlers, but the males' headwear is much larger. When you hear a caribou, you probably would not know that that's what it is. Although they are typically quiet and tend to keep to themselves, when these calm creatures speak up, they are known to let out a kind of snort that you'd much more easily imagine coming from a barnyard pig. Or maybe that's just their way of throwing you off course.

If you do get to see a caribou, consider yourself one of the lucky few. But if you don't, you can always rent the movie *Never Cry Wolf*, where you'll see the full impact of the Arctic's incredible caribou migration... and a naked biologist to boot.

which is a wee bit less daunting at 1,181 meters. The trails take you to the mountains' summits, where the best views of the surrounding area can be had. Thankfully, there is shuttle service provided from the Mont Jacques-Cartier campground (five times daily, adults $5, children 6–17 years $3) to the beginning of the Mont Jacques-Cartier trail, the park's most popular one. Of course you'd want to bring your own, but if you forget to pack your hiking boots or they mysteriously go missing, you can rent a pair from the information center for $13. Raincoats and backpacks are also available.

In the mid-1990s, a group of enthusiastic hikers from Québec, New Brunswick, and Maine got together and asked a poignant question: The Appalachian Mountains don't end at the border, so why should the trail? The answer was a no-brainer: It shouldn't. So, in 1995 the **International Appalachian Trail (IAT)** com-

mittee opened the first Canadian portion of the trail called **Grande Traversée,** which extends 100 km from Mont Jacques-Cartier to Mont Logan. Other bits of the trail followed suit and in 1999, the full Canadian portion of the trail was complete, extending all the way to Cape Gaspé in Parc National Forillon. Many consider La Grande Traversée, however, the IAT's most beautiful region. The full 10-day backcountry trek is for experienced hikers only, although various sections are appropriate for intermediate hikers. A passenger transportation service is available, and there are 14 huts for up to eight persons that can be used along the trail.

Canoeing and Kayaking
Picturesque **Lac Cascapédia** in the western part of the park is where the moose officially hang loose. You can rent a canoe or kayak to

© SUE MOORE

Gîte du Mont Albert

paddle around the four-km-long lake set on the southern side of the Chic-Chocs and see if you can spot the gangly creatures. Prices range $12–22 for 1–4 hours.

Accommodations

There are an abundance of camping sites—220 spread throughout four campgrounds—in the park that range $20–25 per night. Although the sites beside Rivière Sainte-Anne are the most picturesque, the ones at Lac Cascapédia offer a bit more privacy. If you don't want to bother with a tent, there are number of huts available that act almost like mini-hostels in the woods. You rent by the bunk or, if you want to splurge, you can rent out the whole place. They range $21–28 per person.

Of course, the park's absolute gem is the ◖ **Gîte du Mont Albert** (2100 route du Parc, 418/763-2288 or 866/727-2427, closed Nov.– late Dec., $105–148 d, $109–265 cabin). Situated at the foot of Mont Albert, the turret-topped, Swiss-style inn has 48 rooms, 25 chalets, a bar, fine-dining restaurant, pool,

sauna…basically everything you need for a stay in the woods. Surprisingly, the rooms in the inn are pretty basic, so if you can, opt for one of the cabins. This way, you can still use the main inn's facilities, including the beautiful lobby with the huge windows that look out onto the surrounding mountains.

Getting There

By car, take Route 299 from either Sainte-Anne-des-Monts in the north or New Richmond in the south directly to the park. The park provides public transit to the interpretation center from the Sainte-Anne-des-Monts tourism office (96 boul. Sainte-Anne-Ouest, 418/763-7633, adults $5, children 6–17 $3) along Route 132 once daily at 8 A.M. June–September. The return trip leaves the park on the dot at 4:45 P.M.

Réserve Faunique des Chic-Chocs

Adjacent to the Parc National de la Gaspésie and sharing its prized Chic-Choc Mountains, the **Réserve Faunique des Chic-Chocs** (116 rue

Prudent-Cloutier, 418/797-5214 or 800/665-6527) is actually partly surrounded by the park. While the mountains here aren't as high as the ones in the park, they are still impressive, some reaching more than 900 meters. Trout fishing, moose, bear, and small-game hunting are the main activities done here, but people also come to hike. The easy four-km Pics Trail offers a great view of the McGerrigles.

GASPÉ COAST

Like its name implies, this part is classic Gaspé, the one that people think of when they envision the region. With lighthouses, a road that hugs the shore, cliffs, coves, fishing villages, and that famous Rocher Percé, this is the most scenic part of the trip. The region begins with the green **Grande-Vallée,** which has a rest area atop the cape just before you arrive that offers a spectacular panoramic view of the village.

If you're not in too much of a hurry to get into the Parc National du Canada Forillon, have a stop in L'Anse-au-Griffon at the bright-yellow, green-shuttered, 1850s manor once belonging to John LeBoutillier, a cod merchant

and tycoon. Today the **Manoir LeBoutillier** (578 boul. Griffon, 418/892-5150, 9 A.M.–5 P.M. daily June–mid-Oct., adults $7, students $5, children under 12 free) serves as a national historic site. Tours are offered, and there is theater in the summer. The little café has some of the best desserts around. Farther along Route 132, you can't miss (literally and figuratively) the tallest lighthouse in Canada, **Phare de Cap-des-Rosiers** (418/892-557, 10 A.M.–7 P.M. daily late June–late Sept., adults $2.50), which soars up to 34 meters in height. Stop for a photo op outside or climb a ton of stairs inside for an aerial view.

◖ PARC NATIONAL DU CANADA FORILLON

Marking the end of the Appalachian Mountains, Parc National du Canada Forillon (122 boul. de Gaspé, 418/368-5505 or 800/463-6769, www.pc.gc.ca/forillon, adults $6, youth 6–16 $3) located in the northeastern extremity of the peninsula is another must-see in the Gaspé—even if you can only stay for a couple of hours. If the Parc National de la Gaspésie is

the view from Cap-Bon-Ami in Parc National du Canada Forillon

all about the mountains, then this park is all about where the mountains meet the sea. There is a constant interplay here between the rugged and dramatic and the soft and peaceful landscapes. There is also a vast array of wildlife, including fox, coyote, mink, and lynx. Step close to the sea, and you may also see harbor seals, porpoises, and even blue whales.

There are **visitors reception centers** open mid-June–early September at both entrances of the park: l'Anse-au-Griffon in the north and Penouille in the south. However it is in the eastern tip of the park where the majority of the services lie.

Hiking

There are nine trails in the park that mostly range from easy to intermediate. **Les Graves,** considered an intermediate trail but is actually fairly easy, follows the southern shore until it ends with a bang at Cap-Gaspé. This is the end of the road for the Appalachian Mountains and the Forillon peninsula, which dramatically drop off into the gulf. For a bird's-eye view of the landscape, hike the **Mont Saint-Alban** nine-km loop, which leads to an observation tower at 283 meters and has great views of the surrounding sea and cliffs. For something more challenging and mountainous, try **Les Crêtes,** the longest (18 km) and one of the most difficult trails in the park. It's accessed from the visitors center near Fort Péninsule, where there is also a number of wilderness campsites that you can reserve for free.

Camping

The park has three different campgrounds. If you are looking for the privacy of wooded sites, try **Petit-Gaspé** or the semi-wooded sites at **Des-Rosiers,** which also has a pebble beach nearby. The one with the best view is **Cap-Bon-Ami,** which is reserved for tenters only. It's worth crawling out of your sleeping bag early and seeing the sun rise on the cape, the park's most jaw-dropping lookout. Campsites are $21–23, plus the individual park entrance fees. This is a very popular park, so make sure you book well in advance.

GASPÉ

It was here in Gaspé that the wandering Jacques Cartier, first set foot in 1534, on land that what would later become Canada, erected a cross on the shore, and pronounced the land belonged to France. The original cross has, of course, long disappeared, but a commemorative one was erected in its place on the occasion of the 400th anniversary of that first visit. Although Gaspé is the administrative heart of the region, it's not that impressive and often has the feeling of small-town anywhere.

The heart of Gaspé surrounds the Baie de Gaspé, a large natural basin into which three pristine salmon rivers empty. It is here that you will find the **tourism information office** (27 boul. de York Est, 418/368-6335, www.tourismgaspe. org, 8:30 A.M.–8 P.M. Mon.–Fri., 10 A.M.–8 P.M. Sat.–Sun. June–Sept., reduced hours rest of the year), just across the main bridge off Route 198. The tourism office has audio guides that you can rent to go out on a walking tour.

Sights

Located on the very site where Cartier landed, the tiny **Musée de la Gaspésie** (80 boul. Gaspé, 418/368-1534, 9 A.M.–5 P.M. daily late June–mid-Oct., closed Mon. rest of the year, adults $5, students $4, children under 11 free) fittingly has a main exhibit entitled *Jacques Cartier, Embodiment of a Hero,* which explores the impact of the country's most significant early explorer. The museum has other exhibits chronicling Gaspé life. Up the street in a brand new building, the **Centre d'Interprétation Gespeg Micmac** (783 boul. Pointe-Navarre, 418/368-7449 or 866/870-6005, 9 A.M.–5 P.M. daily June–Sept., adults $5, students $4, children 6–12 $2.50) details the lives of the original inhabitants of the area, the Mic-Mac. Guides lead tours of a re-created traditional village where you can learn about how they lived, dressed, ate, and coped with the arrival of the first European settlers.

Accommodations

With students gone in the summer, the **Cégep de la Gaspésie et des Îles Residences** (94 rue Jacques-Cartier, 418/368-2749, www.cgaspesie.qc.ca, $40 d, $77–101 apartments) offers inexpensive, no-frills stays. The apartments are perfect for traveling families, as they can accommodate up to six or eight people comfortably. Although the kitchens have basic appliances, you're out of luck when it comes to kettles, toasters, pots and pans, and utensils. If you prefer a few more creature comforts, try ▐(**Gîte historique l'Émerillon** (192 rue de la Reine, 418/368-3063, $65–80 d.), named after the boat Jacques Cartier arrived on in 1535. The B&B overlooks the Baie de Gaspé, just a block or two down from the main hub of town. There are three small but comfortable rooms here with one shared bath between them, plus one super suite, which comes with private balcony, bathroom, and hot tub. There's also the sweetly named **Gîte Honey's** (4 rue de la Marina, 418/368-3294, May–Oct., $55–60 d), located across the bay right next to the train station. This 1876 house once belonged to the owner's grandmother, but has now been updated with five homey guestrooms with either shared or private bath.

If you are willing to go a little farther afield, ▐(**Auberge Fort-Prével** (2053 boul. Douglas, 418/368-2281 or 888/377-3835, www.sepaq.com, rooms $72–107 d, tent site $27) is located on Route 132 almost mid-way between Gaspé and Percé. Located on the grounds of an old battery built during World War II, the spot is now a mini-resort operated by Québec's provincial park association. The place has all kinds of accommodation options, including rooms in the inn, a motel, campsites, or more expensive cabins. There is also a golf course, a fancy restaurant, a pool, and direct access to the beach. It's open mid-June–mid-September.

Food

Mona of **Restaurant Mona** (1275 boul. de Cap-des-Rosiers, 418/892-5057), the closest restaurant to the park, is known for her famous bouillabaisse. It's so popular that you'll have to make sure you reserve well in advance for a dinner seat. The **Boulangerie Fine Fleur** (3 côte Cartier, 418/368-6116, snacks $2–5) is a

great little bakery with plenty of good to-go items such as croissants, chocolatines, pizzas au gré, and baguettes. One of the best restaurants in the area, ▐(**Café des Artistes** (249 boul. Gaspé, 418/368-2255, www.gaspesie.net/cafedesartistes, 11 A.M.–11 P.M. mid-June–Oct., table d'hôte $30–36) has an award-winning menu and great views overlooking the bay. The pesto-lobster duo and the filet mignon with goat cheese are prized dishes. They have a cute smaller café in town called the **Brûlerie** (101 rue de la Reine, 418/368-3366, 7 A.M.–9:30 P.M. daily, sandwiches $6) with lighter meals, good breakfasts, and fair-trade coffee. On top of their anything-goes menu, **Brise-Bise** (135 rue de la Reine, 418/368-5408, www.brisebise.ca, 11 A.M.–11 P.M. daily) is popular for its nightly live concerts with local and import acts. Try their shrimp fajitas or salmon burger, or simply drink beer with the locals.

PERCÉ

If you're only as good as the company you keep, then this town is magnificent. Although Percé (pop. 3,610) itself is not terribly fascinating, it's close to two famous sights: the Rocher Percé and Île Bonaventure.

The village's seasonal **tourism office** (142 route 132, 418/782-5448, www.rocherperce.com, 8 A.M.–8 P.M. daily July–Aug., reduced hours June and Sept.) is situated in an old house directly on Route 132.

Sights and Recreation

There's some great **scuba diving** to be done in the waters just off Percé, where there are plenty of caverns, coral, and gray seals. **Club Nautique de Percé** (199 route 132, 418/782-5403, www.percenautic.com, late June–early Sept., $95–115) offers full-day excursions for both beginning and experienced divers, led by certified guides. Percé also has some very worthwhile **walking trails** that climb up Mont Sainte-Anne and Mont Blanc, the two mountains that provide the backdrop to the village, or through "la Grotte," the gorge in the middle. You can access them from rue de l'Église at their base, or if you're not too keen on an uphill climb, you can skip the sweat and head straight for the top by the access point from Route des Failles. Naturally these two trails have excellent views of town, the rock, and the island.

Just off Route 132 in l'Anse-à-Beaufils, a pretty fishing community next door to Percé, the **Magasin Général Historique Authentique** (32 rue Bonfils, 418/782-2225, 10 A.M.–5 P.M. daily mid-June–late Sept., adults $6, children $4) has been frozen in time at year 1928. Owned by the Robin, Jones and Whitman Company, which was originally based in the Channel Islands, the store was the town's center of activity and gossip. Today, it acts as an interpretive museum, showcasing wares from the old days. It also has animators who dress up in period costume and recount stories of the local folk and the goings-on at the store.

Accommodations

Beyond the conglomeration of cheap, run-down motels, there are some good and inexpensive accommodation options in town. Remember that Percé is also one of the busiest spots, so book well in advance. Located atop the mountain, **Camping Gargantua** (222 route des Failles, 418/782-2852, June–mid-Oct., $22–26) has stunning views of the bay and Île Bonaventure. The campground has close to 40 wooded sites with a local-fave restaurant on the premises serving up superb French cuisine in a rustic, picturesque setting. Listen for the dinner bell. Situated right in town opposite the Rocher Percé, **(‌ La Maison Rouge** (125 Route 132, 418/782-2227, $69 private room, $20 dorm) is Percé's excellent youth hostel. There are five spacious private rooms to rent in the main house, or you can spend the night in the renovated stable, which has dormitory-style beds spread over three rooms. The people here are very welcoming and accommodating. A little further down the road, **Auberge au Fil des Saisons** (232 route 132, 418/782-2666, www.aubergeperce.com, $45–70 d) offers a bit more comfort and sophistication with its bright, spacious rooms.

Hôtel-Motel Fleur de Lys
© SUE MOORE

Open year-round, the Victorian-style house has a tearoom and a good lounging porch. Farther still is the **(‌ Hôtel-Motel Fleur de Lys** (248 Route 132, 418/782-5380 or 800/399-5380, $65–129), a combination inn/motel that wears its Québec colors proudly. There are only four rooms in the inn, but if you can, try to get one of them. The rooms in the motel are okay, but a little basic. If you arrive by train, the hotel's shuttle will pick you up free of charge. If you would rather a bit more space and independence, consider renting one of the cute little white cottages from **Au Pic de l'Aurore Village** (1 Route 132, 418/782-2151 or 866/882-2151, www.aupicdelaurore.qc.ca, June–Sept., $59–140 triple). Some of the cottages date from the 1930s, and most come with one or two bedrooms, fireplaces, kitchenettes, and TVs.

Food

Call the night before, and the sweet **La Boîte à Lunch** (155 route 132, 418/782-5274, 5:30 A.M.–10 P.M. mid-May–mid-Oct., lunchboxes

$8.50–10.50) will have your lunch all ready the next morning to bring with you on a trip to the island or the hiking trail. Go for either the shrimp or ham-and-cheese sandwich boxed lunch, which will also include homemade banana bread, cheese, an apple, and either a bottle of water or juice. This spot also serves up a mean breakfast of eggs, omelets, or pancakes. One of the first seafood restaurants in the area, (**La Maison du Pêcheur** (155 route 132, 418/782-5331, 11:30 A.M.–10:30 P.M. daily June–Oct., table d'hôte $27–42) remains one of the best. It's all laid-back atmosphere and good fresh-from-the-sea cooking, including seafood pizza, lobster with maple syrup, and the ultimate pig-out meal of lobster, salmon, and scallops. Whatever you do, save room for the sinful "Christine," a Belgian chocolate cake. Downstairs is the **Café de l'Atlantique** (7:30 A.M.–1 A.M. daily July–Aug. only), a good breakfast spot with a must-try dish called "Homardoeuf " for those who like eggs Benny. Nights are also good with nightly acts—mostly folk singers with repertoires of local songs.

PARC NATIONAL DE L'ÎLE-BONAVENTURE-ET-DU-ROCHER-PERCÉ

As its name indicates, the tiny 5.8 sq km Parc National de L'Île-Bonaventure-et-du-Rocher-Percé (4 rue du Quai, 418/782-2240 or 800/665-6527, www.sepaq.com, 9 A.M.–5 P.M. daily late May–mid-Oct., adults $3.50, children 6–17 $1.50) is home to two precious properties: Île Bonaventure and the Rocher Percé.

(Île Bonaventure

This beautiful, craggy island is home to the second-largest colony (behind Scotland) of northern gannets. Their French name, *fou du bassans,* literally means "crazy about diving" and is appropriate given the birds' penchant for 100-km-per-hour dives to catch their prey. Although the tourist brochures will describe the island's heady fragrances of wildflowers and sea salt air, they forgot to mention the potent scent of the gannet's guano. That shouldn't be a deterrent, though, as seeing the spectacle of the birds squawking and jockeying for position is something to behold. During summer, boats

© SUE MOORE

the sole remaining buildings on Île Bonaventure

make the one-hour trip from Percé out to the island where people can hike one of the four trails that lead to the colony.

There's a barrage of boat companies in Percé that offer trips to and around the island. The smaller boats, **Les Traversiers de l'Île** (9 rue du Quai, 418/782-5526 or 866/782-5526) or **Les Bateliers de Percé** (rue du Quai, 418/782-2974 or 877/782-2974) can weave in and out of the coves for some up-close wildlife viewing. If you are prone to seasickness, stick to the larger one, **Les Bateaux de Croisière** (9 rue du Quai, 418/782-2161 or 877/782-2161). Cost is $20 for adults and $6 for children.

Rocher Percé

Famous, beautifully simple Rocher Percé, the 471-meter monolith with a hole through it, has been attracting admirers since the end of the 19th century when wealthy tourists began to build estates on the shores opposite. But it was really only in the 1930s, when Route 132 was completed, that tourism to the site really exploded. The name Percé actually means "pierced," a reference to the rock's distinguishing round hole. Not many people realize that the rock actually had two—the second hole was lost when the rock experienced a small earthquake in June 1845.

As for seeing the Rocher Percé up close, simply wait for the tide to go out (a timetable is available at the visitors center), then weave your way to the edge of the rock. Getting out there can be a slippery affair, so make sure you are wearing solid shoes or boots with treads.

LE BAIE DES CHALEURS

Once you enter the Baie des Chaleurs, the road flattens out and the more populated side of the peninsula begins. The body of water that this section of the Gaspé wraps itself around was given its name—"Baie des Chaleurs" means "bay of warmth"—because of its sheltered warmer waters. You'll hear more English spoken in this part (what do you expect with town names like New Richmond, New Carlisle, and Carleton?), but you'll also experience the influence of other local cultures, including the Aca-

THE ROCK

It may not be as well known as the Blarney Stone, but Québec's own mythic boulder, Rocher Percé has its own story to tell.

The legend begins with a lovely young woman from Normandy named Blanche de Beaumont who set sail for New France in order to join her fiancé. As the ship finally approached the coast of Newfoundland, the lovelorn Blanche was overjoyed to know that she was almost there. But just as quickly, a pirate ship was spotted headed directly for them. The beautiful Blanche was taken prisoner, and the pirate captain vowed that she would immediately become his wife.

As the motley crew gathered for the wedding and the procession started, Blanche bolted for the side of the ship and jumped overboard. Over the next few days, the pirate captain searched the seas for his bride-not-to-be. On one stormy night, the ship approached Rocher Percé. Through the fog, they were able to make out the ghostly figure of a woman sitting on top. It was none other than Blanche de Beaumont. Suddenly, Blanche pointed toward the ship, and a bolt of lighting came down from the skies and turned the vessel into stone. The moral of the story? Beware of getting close to the Rocher Percé on a stormy day.

dians, the Basques, and the Mic-mac. Recently honored with the exclusive title of one of the "Most Beautiful Bays in the World," the Baie de Chaleurs is now part of an elite group of only 30 bays worldwide. The area certainly isn't as spectacular as its northern coast counterparts, but it has a more relaxed nature that is soothing.

Paspébiac and New Carlisle

The French-speaking village of Paspébiac (pop. 3,360) is a worthwhile stop for its **Site Historique du Banc-de-Pêche-de-Paspébiac** (3e rue, route du Quai, 418/752-6229, 9 A.M.–5 P.M. daily June–Sept., adults $5.50, children $4.50). It was on this site in

1767 that Charles Robin established his successful cod processing and exporting business, which shipped products all over the world and made the village the Gaspé's main fishing industry town. Bilingual guided tours will run down the history of the place, and there's dried cod passed around for people to gnaw on. There's also a restaurant on site.

Just a little ways down the road is New Carlisle, the first in a string of English towns. Funnily enough, it was here, in a Loyalist-founded village with plenty of New England-style homes, that Québec's father of independence, René Lévesque, was born. There's not much here to commemorate that fact except for a bit of a funny-looking statue in the park of the miniature Lévesque with outstretched hands. The charismatic leader and heavy smoker would probably have liked the fact that every now and then a cigarette will appear between his statue's fingers.

Bonaventure
The heart of Acadian culture on the bay and one of the most important Acadian towns in the province, **Bonaventure** (pop. 2,780) was founded in 1760 after the expulsion of the Acadians from Nova Scotia. Not surprisingly, the town's main attraction is dedicated to that fact. The **Musée Acadien du Québec** (95 avenue Port-Royal, 418/534-4000, www.museeacadien.com, 9 A.M.–6 P.M. daily late June–early Sept., reduced hours rest of the year, adults $7, children $5) has two permanent exhibits. One, *Une Acadie Québécoise* is on the history of the Acadians from the time they arrived on the continent to their situation in present-day Québec, and the other showcases a miniature scale version of Bonaventure's more interesting heritage buildings. There are five boutiques on site including a glass shop, a regional products shop, and la Maison des Gâteries, an artisan bakery that serves up light lunches and homemade chocolate. If you get into the Acadian spirit and want to sample a traditional meal with a slight Cajun twist, try le Café Acadian beside the Beaubassin Beach. And if you're around on a Wednesday night in the summer,

stop by for Chapeau à Nos Artistes, a free event where local musicians from the Maritimes belt out the traditional tunes.

Another good stop in Bonaventure (actually just a little bit north of town) is the **Grotte de Saint-Elzéar** (198 route de l'Église Nord, 418/534-3905, adults $22). This is actually the oldest cave in Québec at over half a million years old. To see it, you need to take a guided tour and reserve in advance. The weather is cool and humid in the cave, so don't forget to wear your woolies.

New Richmond
Just before you arrive in New Richmond, stop at the municipal rest stop that is on the side of a hill. Many consider this the most breathtaking view of the bay. In terms of town sightseeing, there is not a ton to do and see in New Richmond (pop. 3,750), beyond just taking in its beautiful homes. There is one exception however, it's the **Village Gaspésien de l'Héritage Britannique** (351 boul. Perron Ouest, 418/392-4487, 9 A.M.–5 P.M. mid-June–late Sept.), which focuses on the lives of the Gaspé Loyalists. This beautiful site has more than 20 buildings, which sit on 80 acres of land right at the mouth of the Rivière Grande Cascapédia. There's a school, lighthouse, general store, and more that give an adequate picture into the inner-workings of the stubborn Loyalist clan.

Carleton
The largest town in the area, **Carleton** (pop. 4,050), which is wedged between Mont Saint-Joseph and the bay, could almost be compared to Percé due to all its outdoor activities, pretty setting, and crowded hotels and shops. The public beach here, located right in the center of town, is a local favorite, so be prepared to fight for blanket space in the height of summer. The town's **tourism information center** (629 boul Perron, 418/364-3544, 8 A.M.–8 P.M. late June–early Sept.) is located in the city hall building. If you are interested in some good day hikes, ask them for one of their trail maps, which indicate the more than 30 km of paths called the Carleton-Maria network.

One of the most popular hikes (which you can drive as well) is to the summit of Mont Saint-Joseph (555 meters), where you'll get a stunning view. Up at the top, you also can visit the curious, if somewhat lackluster, **Oratoire Notre-Dame-du-Mont-Saint-Joseph** (837 rue de la Montagne, 418/364-3520, 8 A.M.–8 P.M. daily mid-June–early Sept. and 8 A.M.–5 P.M. daily early Sept.–Oct., adults $4, students $3), which has been a pilgrimage site since 1935.

For a fast nosh, try **Le Cantine** (559 Route 132, 418/364-3113, 9 A.M.–10 P.M. daily, $5–8), located right on the main drag. There are picnic tables set up for you to sit down and enjoy all the fried seafood classics they have on the menu, including clams, scallops, shrimp, and fish. It's so greasy, but so good. The slightly more health conscious should head straight to **Le Boulanger Pâtisserie la Mie Véritable** (578A boul. Perron, 418/364-6662, 7 A.M.–5 P.M. daily July–Sept., reduced hours rest of year, snacks $2–5), a very popular local bakery… and rightly so. This spot has the most deliciously flaky croissants of the cheese, almond, and chocolate varieties.

Parc National de Miguasha

Definitely one of the Baie-des-Chaleurs' most impressive sights is the **Parc National de Miguasha** (231 route Miguasha Ouest, 418/794-2475, www.parcsquebec.com, 9 A.M.–6 P.M. daily June–Sept., reduced hours the rest of the year, adults $3.50, students 6–17 $1.50, children under 6 free). Named a Natural World Heritage site in 1999 by UNESCO, the park is considered the second-most important fossil site in the world because of its 9,000 well-preserved specimens dating from the Devonian Period (Age of the Fish). You can tour the inside of the museum, of course, but what is really exciting is to get out in the field and explore the Miguasha cliff, a treasure trove of fossils.

Located on a small peninsula with sweeping views of the Appalachians in the distance, the park is a picturesque spot to spend the night. There is also a good private campground right beside the park called **Camping l'érablière** (28

route Miguasha, 418/794-2913, May–early Oct., tent site $20).

FESTIVALS AND EVENTS

Not surprisingly, the Gaspé's main events revolve around its people's love for sweet nature and sweet music.

Outdoor Events

The **Raid Trans-Gaspésien Volkswagon** (www.raidtransgaspesien.com, mid-July) is a vigorous mountain bike race that runs between Carleton and Bonaventure. The race attracts more than 500 cyclists who come in from across the province. The **Fête du Vol Libre** (418/797-2222) is an international meet for hang-gliders and paragliders as well as other want-to-fly enthusiasts. It takes place annually in Mont-Saint-Pierre over 10 days at the end of July. And then, every winter the region's most challenging event takes place in mid-February. The award-winning **La Grande Traversée de la Gaspésie** (www.brisebise.ca/tdlg) is a six-day action-packed ski race that that covers more than 300 km on marked trails through the mountains, along the sea, and in open terrain.

Music Festivals

Throughout the summer months, there are plenty of music happenings in the Gaspé. Three of the best festivals are the **Festival en Chanson de Petite-Vallée** (www.festivalen-chanson.com) where traditional francophone singer-songwriters perform over 10 days at the end of June, the **Maximum Blues** (www.maximumblues.net) festival in Carleton in early August, which attracts good Québécois and Canadian blues acts, and the mid-August **Festival Musique du Bout du Monde** (www.musiqueduboutdumonde.com), which brings in music acts from all around the world that play everything from bluegrass to Brazilian.

INFORMATION AND SERVICES
Information

As you enter the Gaspé from the northern coast, the main **regional tourism office** (357 route de la Mer, 418/775-2223 or 800/463-0323, www.tourisme-gaspesie.com) will appear on your right directly on Route 132 in Ste-Flavie. The office is open year-round seven days a week, 8 A.M.–8 P.M. mid-June–mid-September, 8:30 A.M.–4:30 P.M. the rest of the year.

Emergency Services

You'll find hospital service in Sainte-Anne-des-Monts (418/763-2261), Gaspé (418/368-3301), and the closest one to Percé is in Chandler (418/689-2261). There is also a CLSC medical clinic in Percé. For pharmacies, there's Pharmacie Maryse Lepage (6 boul. Sainte-Anne Est, 418/763-7848) in Sainte-Anne-Des-Monts, Pharmacie Uniprix (167 rue de la Reine, 418/368-5595) in Gaspé, Pharmacie PJC Clinique (155 Place du Quai, 418/782-2550), and plenty of Pharmacie Jean Coutu all throughout the region.

Post Office

Canada Post has an office in most towns in the Gaspé, including Sainte-Anne-des-Monts (315 1ère avenue Ouest), Gaspé (98 rue de la Reine, 418/368-3666), Percé (147 rue Principale Ouest), and Carleton (716 boul Perron).

Banks and Money Exchange

For banking needs, head to Caisse Populaire Desjardins with ATMs in Haute-Gaspésie (10 1ère avenue Est, 418/763-2214), in downtown Gaspé (80 rue Jacques-Cartier, 418/368-5555), and Maria (554 boul. Perron Est, 418/759-3456), which serves the Baie-des-Chaleurs area. The only ATM available in Percé is located near the city hall.

GETTING THERE AND AROUND
By Air

You can book a flight from Montréal or Québec City on **Air Canada Jazz** (888/247-2262, www.aircanada.ca) to Mont-Joli Airport at the start of the peninsula or further east to the town of Gaspé. Québec's latest regional charter carrier, **Pascan Aviation** (888/313-8777, www.pascan.com), flies into airports in Mont-Joli or Bonaventure along the Baie-des-Chaleurs.

By Train

Probably the most spectacular way to travel to the region is to take one of the **VIA** (888/842-7245, www.viarail.ca) trains. The company offers an overnight service from Montréal to the Gaspé three times a week through the year on its *Le Chaleur* train. Following the north shore until Mont-Joli, the train then makes a dramatic turn south through the valley to the Baie-des-Chaleurs. It then passes through New Richmond, Chandler, and Percé before reaching its final destination in downtown Gaspé. Prices vary considerably between seats choices.

By Bus

The convenient **Orléans Express** (888/999-3977, www.orleansexpress.com) stops in almost every town along Route 132 with ticket offices and drop-off points at dépanneurs and gas stations. From Québec City to Percé, it's a grueling 12-hour trip and costs $89 one-way or $142 round-trip for adults. You can bring along a bike for a small fee.

Getting Around

Once you arrive in the Gaspé, the best way to get around is with a car. Car rentals are available in the main tourist towns including Percé (Thrifty 418/689-3739), Bonaventure (Thrifty 418/534-4848), Carleton (Armand Automobile 418/364-3384), and directly at the airport in Mont-Joli (National 418/775-3502 or 888/657-3032, Hertz 418/775-7077 or 800/263-0678) and in Gaspé (National 418/368-1541, Budget 418/368-1610 or 800/363-8111).

The more adventurous option is to bike—but make sure you are in good physical shape because there are lots of horrifying hills along both the north and east coasts.

Îles de la Madeleine

This archipelago located way out in the middle of the Gulf of Saint Lawrence (about 215 km from Gaspé), known as les Îles de la Madeleine (pop. 13,000) may just be Québec's best-kept secret. Green, grassy knolls and red cliffs create a dramatic landscape, especially when they are matched with the blue of the gulf waters and the vibrantly colored homes, which are scattered throughout the islands. The scene is completely unique and, arguably, consists of the most magical backdrop in the province. Composed of a dozen or so islands stretched out into a backwards "J," with two shallow lagoons etched into the line, les Îles extend about 100 km. Six main islands are connected to one another by long sand dunes and by a road, the spectacular Route 199, which runs 88 km.

Not surprisingly, fishing is the primary industry on the island and boats, nets, wharves, and traps often fill up the landscape. Up until a few years ago, sealing was also a major way of life for islanders, but ever since animal rights activists started flashing images of bloodied and battered baby seals, the industry has taken a major hit.

Although thankfully, winters can be milder here, summers can be cool and breezy. So if you've just left behind a Montréal heat wave, remember to bring along some light sweaters and wind breakers. The good news is that the

BEACHY KEEN

You don't typically think of Québec as being a sun worshipper's beach blanket hot spot, but with more than 300 kilometers of fine white sand, les Îles de la Madeleine possess some of North America's most pristine and scenic beaches. Granted, with the wind, it can get a little chilly out there, and you probably aren't likely to see a Baywatch parade of skimpy bathing suits of the bikini and thong variety, but there's much more to appreciate on these divine sandy spreads. Here's a rundown of the best.

Most Beautiful Beach: Largely considered to be the most spectacular beach on the islands, the Plage de la Grande Échouerie stretches about 10 kilometers and is the only one with a lifeguard on duty. It can get packed some days though.

Most Fun to Explore: The sensational Plage de la Dune-du-Sud offers impressive red cliffs, shelter from the winds, and a handful of caves to explore at low tide. Just watch out for the undertow!

Warmest Waters: It's not quite as balmy as its Caribbean name suggests, but Plage de la Martinique, located on Baie de Plaisance, has the islands' most temperate waters. It's also the favored beach for kite surfers.

Most Secluded: Located at the end of the Havre Aubert beach, Bout du Banc can only be reached after a long walk along Dune Sandy Hook. Once you get to the beach, you'll be rewarded with an incredible view of Île d'Entrée and, so long as not too many people have the same idea as you, all the privacy you could want.

Best Beach to Spot Wildlife: Located along Dune du Nord, Plage de l'Hôpital is famous for its seal sightings. It's also a favored spot for kite flyers – another wild species and much more colorful! But if it's bird-watching that you're after, the Zodiac trip out to the beaches of Bird Rock and Brion Islands are highly worthwhile.

Best Sand Castle Building: It's not that there's something magic in the sand, but Plage de Havre-Aubert plays host to the annual sand castle contest, which takes place every second weekend in August, so it must be doing something right.

Just remember before you head out: The dunes on les Îles are fragile creatures. Try not to trample through the beach grass, which actually plays the vital role of keeping the beach from further erosion. Stay on the marked paths as much as possible and keep cars far, far away.

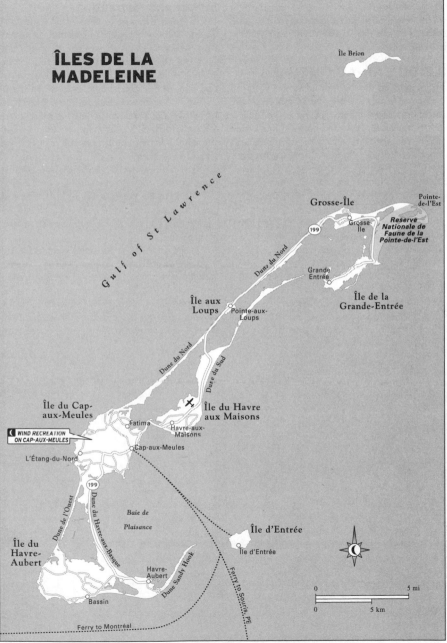

ÎLES DE LA MADELEINE

Île Brion

Gulf of St Lawrence

Grosse-Île

Pointe-de-l'Est

199

Grosse-Île

Reserve Nationale de Faune de la Pointe-de-l'Est

Dune du Nord

Grande Entrée

Île de la Grande-Entrée

Île aux Loups

Pointe-aux-Loups

Dune du Nord

Dune du Sud

Île du Cap-aux-Meules

Île du Havre aux Maisons

WIND RECREATION ON CAP-AUX-MEULES

Fatima

Havre-aux-Maisons

Cap-aux-Meules

L'Étang-du-Nord

199

Dune de l'Ouest

Dune du Havre-aux-Basque

Baie de Plaisance

Île d'Entrée

Île d'Entrée

Île du Havre-Aubert

Havre-Aubert

Dune Sandy Hook

Ferry to Souris, PE

Bassin

0   5 mi

0   5 km

Ferry to Montréal

GASPÉ AND LES ÎSLES

waters around the islands can be surprisingly warm, especially in the sheltered lagoons, so underneath that sweater, you can sport a bathing suit.

ÎLE DU CAP-AUX-MEULES

The main hub of activity and services, Île du Cap-aux-Meules is where the ferries from the mainland drop anchor, making it the busiest spot on the archipelago and home to more then half of the population of les Îles. The island consists of three villages: **Cap-aux-Meules** (pop. 1,659) where the ferry dock is located, **l'Étang-du-Nord** (pop. 2,944), known principally for its pretty port, its market, and its iconic memorial sculpture of seven fishermen called *Hommage aux pêcheurs,* and **Fatima** (pop. 2,686), a windswept town, established only in 1954.

Île du Cap-aux-Meules is where the main tourism information office is located and is the site of the only traffic light on les Îles. It's not the most attractive island of the archipelago, but it does have an impressive congregation of colorful homes and some worthwhile stops.

Sights and Recreation

Just beyond the port in Cap-aux-Meules, off Route 199, is the beautiful **chemin de Gros-Cap,** which runs parallel to the Baie de Plaisance. This is your first chance to see the islands' famous red cliffs. Situated between Cap-aux-Meules and l'Étang-du-Nord is the islands' oldest church, **Église Saint-Pierre de Lavernière** (1329 chemin de Lavernière, mass 4 P.M. Saturday). Made of shipwrecked wood, the white "little church that could" has been struck by lighting no less than four times.

Just a little bit north of the church, almost right in the center of the island, is the must-climb **Butte du Vent,** or Wind Hill. The hill provides a panoramic view of the area and on a good day, you can pretty much see the entire archipelago.

On the west side of the island is the beautiful 3.6-km **Belle-Anse** biking and hiking trail that runs along the coastside escarpment, showcasing grasses, red cliffs, crashing waves, and as nighttime approaches, some incredible sunsets. At the northern tip of the island, the **Barachois Trail** is a five-km interpretive hiking and cycling path

The archipelago is surrounded by the red cliffs of Gros-Cap.

© MICHEL BONATO

that cuts through wetlands and salt- and fresh-water marshes, a humid environment created because of the area's position between Fatima's lowlands and the sand dunes.

From the port in Cap-aux-Meules, you can catch the ferry, the *SP Bonaventure* (418/986-8452, adults $10, children 2–12 $7), which makes twice-daily trips to the treeless **Île d'Entrée** (pop. 130). The only inhabited is-land not connected to the rest of the chain, Île d'Entrée's population is almost entirely Eng-lish-speaking—the 50 or so families can trace their roots back to a small group of Irish and Scottish settlers who were shipwrecked here centuries ago.

You can easily explore the tiny, velvety green island on foot. The one must-do on the island is climbing the 170-meter **Big Hill,** the high-est point in les Îles. You'll get a great view of the surrounding hills with cows grazing, and you may see some wild horses. There's also a tiny local historical museum (Route Principale, 418/986-6622) that features objects donated by local families.

(Wind Recreation

With wind such a constant presence on the is-lands, it's no wonder that the locals have devel-oped numerous ways to channel it. **Aérosport** (1390 rue de La Vernière, 418/986-6677 or 866/986-6677, www.aerosport.ca, 8:30 A.M.–6 P.M. daily June–Sept., three-hour buggy in-troduction $50, three-hour kite surfing course $250) in l'Étang-du-Nord offers lessons and excursions in kite kayaking, buggy coasting, car sailing, and speed sailing (windsurfing on wheels). The owner, Eric Marchand, is a Ca-nadian snowboarding champion and a world snow sailing champion. If you love flying kites or have always wanted to try, check out **Au Gré du Vent** (Place du Marché, 418/986-5069, www.greduvent.com, 9 A.M.–9 P.M. June–Sept., 1 hour course $25), a little kite boutique also located in l'Étang-du-Nord. You can't rent kites and go out on your own here, but you can take an hour-long class or buy a kite outright (every kite purchase comes with a half-hour introductory lesson).

Accommodations and Food

In terms of camping accommodations on Île du Cap-aux-Meules, **(Parc de Gros-Cap** (74 chemin du Camping, 418/986-4505 or 800/986-4505, www.parcdegroscap.ca, tent sites $17–23, rooms $24–55 breakfast and linens included) is a great spot. Although you may feel a bit exposed here (there isn't much in the way of shade and shelter), the loca-tion on the peninsula is very impressive. The 100-site campground also holds a laid-back **International Youth Hostel** with three private rooms ($55 d) and six shared rooms ($28 per person). There are sea kayak rentals, courses, and organized tours available, too.

The island's legendary bistro/inn is **Les Pas Perdus** (169 chemin Principal, 418/986-5151, www.pasperdus.com, 8 A.M.–3 A.M. daily, rooms $40 for first person, $10 additional person, mains under $10). Located in a bright red building, the bohemian bistro has plenty of books, artwork from local artists, and a ca-sual menu with burgers and fajitas. Every Mon-day is jam night, and there are regular concerts happening at other times during the summer. The six rooms are basic, but clean and color-ful. Just up from here is **Café Wendell** (185 chemin Principal, 418/986-6002, www.chez-wendell.ca).

The island's finest dining is at **La Table des Roy** (1188 route 199, 418/986-3004, www .latabledesroy.com, 6–10 P.M., Mon.–Sat., June–Sept., table d'hôte $42), which serves up excellent seafood (fish, bouillabaisse, crab-cakes) and meat dishes (duck, grilled pork), with a solid wine list. The décor is elegant but cozy. The islands' brew pub, **À l'Abri de la Tempête** (286 chemin Coulombe, 418/986-5005) located in l'Étang du Nord serves up very tasty blond, red, and dark lagers made from Madelinot barley exposed to the island's salty air. There are no meals on hand, but they have a variety of light snacks.

ÎLE DU HAVRE-AUBERT

Moving south from Île du Cap-aux-Meules, onto the tip of the archipelago, is the beau-tiful and historic Île du Havre-Aubert, the largest but least populated of the six islands. Although joined to Île du Cap-aux-Meules by two long sand spits, it is only accessible via the eastern one: the 10-km Dune du Havre-aux-Basques. Île du Havre Aubert has two main communities: **Havre-Aubert,** the touristy but charming oldest village on the islands, and the wooded **Bassin.** You'll find most of les Îles' cultural attractions on this island. All around the island, notice the *baraques,* which are a unique and common feature of Havre-Aubert. These four-column sheds with slanted rooftops are used to shield haystacks from the effects of bad weather.

Sights and Recreation

As you come off the Dune du Havre-aux-Basques into Havre-Aubert, you'll spot the **Musée de la Mer** (1023 route 199, 418/937-5711, 9 A.M.–6 P.M. Mon.–Fri., 10 A.M.–6 P.M. Sat.–Sun. mid-June–mid-Sept., 9 A.M.–noon, 1–5 P.M. Mon.–Fri., 1–5 P.M. Sat.–Sun., adults $5, children 6–16 $3), which recounts the islands' maritime history with photos, miniature boats, and other relics. **Site Historique de La Grave** (990 route 199, 418/937-6625, 11:30 A.M.–5 P.M. daily in the summer, adults $1) is where, starting in 1762, Acadian families set up a post, drying and salting fish—a way of life that continued for close to 200 years. Unfortunately, only a small percentage of the original traditional fishing houses remain, but it's still pleasant to stroll the thin piece of land where they are located. You can do so on your own or by visiting the interpretation center to take a 45-minute walking tour. You'll find plenty of shops, cafés, and restaurants around the site.

One of the best places to go if you have kids traveling with you is the **Aquarium des Îles** (982 route 199, 418/937-2277, 10 A.M.–6 P.M. daily June–mid-Aug., 10 A.M.–5 P.M. daily mid-Aug.–mid-Oct.), which showcases different species of local fish, crustaceans, and mollusks. Some of the species are located in touch pools, which means that you can reach in and hold the critters. If you're lucky, you may even witness a crab race, which are held

sporadically throughout the summer. Another good stop is the **Économusée du Sable** (907 route 199, 418/937-2129, www.artisansdusable. com, 10 A.M.–9 P.M. daily in the summer), a shop and interpretation center run by a collective of artists called the Artisans du Sable. The artists transform sand into a solid matter, while creating objects such as clocks, bowls, small sandcastles, vases, and chess sets. The unique and tasteful items here are a good choice for a local souvenir.

Explore the rest of the island along the coastal **Chemin du Bassin,** which has stunning views off the southwestern coast and ends up at the beach. In Bassin, have a peek at l'Église Saint-François-Xavier (574 chemin du Bassin, mass Sunday 11:15 A.M.). The striking white-with-red-roof church and presbytery were originally built in 1875.

Accommodations and Food

Located in the old General Store, **(Restaurant Café de la Grave** (969 route 199, 418/937-5765, open 8:30 A.M. to close, mains $8–14) is a landmark on the islands. In addition to its warm ambience, friendly service, and crowd of as many locals as tourists, the restaurant also has to-die-for seafood pot pie and clam chowder in a bread bowl. There's homemade cake for desert.

Originally from Dijon, chef Patrcik Mahey fell in love with les Îles and decided to make it home. The inspired seafood cuisine served at his high-end restaurant and inn called **(La Marée Haute** (25 chemin des Fumoirs, 418/937-2492, www.ilesdelamadeleine.com/mareehaute, table d'hôte $25–50, rooms $75–125 d with breakfast) is a must-try. The dining room has a great view and is bright and airy. The inn's seven rooms are very cute and cozy with real wood paneled walls, colorful pillows and bedspreads, and private baths. Just a little ways away is **Auberge Chez Denis à François** (404 chemin d'En Haut, 418/937-2371, www.aubergechezdenis.ca, table d'hôte $29–33, rooms $115–125 d with breakfast). This beautiful yellow house has an interesting story: After a ship was washed ashore during a horrific storm in 1874, its lumber was pilfered and used to build the sizeable place, which today is an elegant restaurant and inn. You can sample seal, which you may see on the menu here and elsewhere on the islands as *loup marin,* literally "sea wolf." The rooms are simple and pleasant. You won't miss **Gîte le Marie Michel** (600 chemin du Bassin, 418/937-2621, www.lemariemichel.ca, $70 d with shared bath) in Bassin with its bright yellow exterior with red trim. Located right near the church and the beach, this B&B has four rooms that are small but quaint. The charming owner will pack you a picnic lunch upon request.

ÎLE DU HAVRE AUX MAISONS

Right in the middle of the archipelago is the magnificent Île du Havre-aux-Maisons (pop. 2,048). Although its landscape is shaved bare of trees due to excessive logging, many people consider this island the most picturesque of the archipelago. The island's most predominant feature is the expansive Lagune du Havre aux Maisons that separates the Dune du Sud from the isolated Dune du

Nord where the tiny community of **Île-aux-Loups** is located. The lagoon's warmer waters make it great for swimming.

To learn more about Île du Havre-aux-Maisons, there is a small interpretation center (69 route 199, 418/969-4849, 9 A.M.–4 P.M. daily June–Sept.), located just before the bridge leading to Île du Cap-aux-Meules. The center will give you an overview of island history.

Sights and Recreation

For a scenic hike, take Chemin de la Pointe-Basse and Chemin de Échoueries up to the lighthouse at Cap Alright and park there. Either take the rope path down to the beach to explore the island's famous **Buttes Pelées,** which are odd-looking rock formations, or hike up to the summit of **Butte Ronde.** Another places to visit is the impressive **La Meduse** (638 route 199, 418/969-4681, www.meduse.qc.ca, 9 A.M.–7 P.M. Mon.–Sat. mid-June–mid-Sept., guided tour $2), a glass studio and boutique housed in an old school house. Objects include plates, vases, and bowls along with the house specialty,

the red cliffs of the Île Boudreau in Grande-Entrée

jellyfish glass balls. You can get a tour of the place and witness glass blowing in action.

One of Québec's most famous raw-milk cheeses comes from the **Fromagerie du Pied-de-Vent** (149 chemin Pointe-Basse, 418/969-9292, 9 A.M.–5 P.M. daily). Stop by the cheese factory for a tasting and a tour and to pick up some of this delicious cheese made from milk of the Canadienne cow. Continuing on a bit of a savory tour, the grey-shingled **Fumoir d'Antan** (27 chemin du Quai, 418/969-4907, 8 A.M.–5 P.M. Mon.–Fri. Apr.–mid-June, Sept.–Oct., 8 A.M.–5 P.M. daily mid-June–Aug., $2) is a traditional herring smokehouse and economuseum dedicated to the islands' smoked herring industry, once a major way of life for many Madelinot families. There's a boutique on site where you can buy all kinds of herring products, including herring jerky. You can also sample the wares, see the photo exhibit, and get a tour. To explore the lagoon, try **Les Excursions de la Lagune** (418/969-4550, adults $27, children 12 and under $15, additional child $9), which offers an interpretive tour aboard the *Ponton II*, a glass-bottom boat. During the tour, you'll see grey seals and a lobster trap demonstration, and you'll also have the option of sampling some of the mussels, clams, and other creatures you'll be hearing about.

Accommodations and Food

Under the name **Le Grand Large** (326 and 341 chemin de la Pointe-Basse, 418/969-4940, www.grandlarge.ca, $84–98 d), the Arseneau family operates two inns: one is Maison Éva-Anne and the other is Auberge Grand Large. Between them are eight simply decorated rooms, some with private baths and others shared. Steve Arseneau also offers *cabarouette* (horse-drawn wagon) tours, which involve piling into a large boxlike wagon and being pulled by two horses to some of the island's prettiest sights. The beautiful stone building that houses the **Domaine du Vieux Couvent** (292 route 199, 418/969-2233, www.domaineduvieuxcouvent.com, 5–10 P.M. Thurs.–Mon. daily June–Sept., mains $12–16, rooms $175–225)

is a former convent that now functions as a restaurant and inn. The restaurant has tasty seafood fare including mussels, calamari, bouillabaisse, lobster bisque, and steak frites, while the inn has 10 renovated rooms and six apartments. You'll also find the rowdy bar **Chez Gaspard,** a great spot to hear live jazz, folk, and blues and to tie one on.

GROSSE-ÎLE AND ÎLE DE LA GRANDE-ENTRÉE

Accessed by a scenic drive along the upper part of the Dune du Nord, the islands of Grosse-Île (pop. 543) and Île de la Grande-Entrée (pop. 660) make up the east end of the archipelago. Grosse-Île, mostly anglophone, is characterized by softly rounded hills, marshes, ponds, beaches, and salt mines, while Île de la Grande-Entrée has a similar landscape, but is best known for its status as the lobster capital of Québec. Check out the interpretive center for the area, called **Le Centre d'Interprétation les Portes de l'Est** (56 chemin Principal, 418/985-2387, 9 A.M.–6 P.M. daily June–Sept.), situated right beside the salt mines. The center offers a natural interpretation of the area and tours on demand.

Sights and Recreation

The sandy 684-hectare **Réserve Nationale de Faune de la Pointe-de-l'Est** (377 route 199, 418/985-2833) straddles both islands and is the temporary home of many migrating birds including sandpipers, American black ducks, and mergansers, as well as the horned grebe and piping plover—both at-risk species. The fragile vegetation is composed mainly of beachgrass and low brush, which can be experienced from two short nature interpretation trails. The l'Échouerie Trail will lead you to the **Plage de la Grande Échouerie,** a gorgeous 10-km beach. Grosse-Île is proud of Old Harry, a tiny little community that for a long time held only one resident, Harry Clark. Now it also holds the **Council for Anglophone Magdalen Islanders** (787 route 199, 418/985-2116, 9 A.M.–4 P.M. Mon.–Fri.), located in a vibrant red schoolhouse. The council runs a museum, which outlines the history of the islanders' English-speaking population.

Route 199 ends at **Pointe de la Grande Entrée,** the islands' lucrative lobster port that at any one time can house over 100 colorful lobster boats. The busy port is a nice spot to browse the craft boutiques or grab a seafood snack. The well-run **Club Vacances de Îles** (377 route 199, 418/985-2833 or 888/537-4537, www.clubiles.qc.ca) offers all kinds of ecotours throughout the islands. Activities include nature walks, biking, clamming, and general tours of the islands. The Club also has its own inn and campground and provides shuttle service to and from the airport. This is the ideal way to go if you do not want to drive and want someone to show you around. Right on site is the **Centre d'Interprétation du Phoque** (377 Route 199, 418/985-2833, www.loup-marin. com, 10 A.M.–6 P.M. daily June–Sept.), dedicated to the four types of seals that frequent the area. Of course, the center is sympathetic to the local economic relationship to sealing and tells the stories of those involved in the industry. But it also takes great care to chronicle the lives of these impressive creatures through slide shows, exhibits, and artifacts.

EVENTS AND ENTERTAINMENT

One of the islands' best festivals is the **Châteaux du Monde...** (418/986-6863), which takes place every year over three days in mid-August. Teams of adults and families gather on the beach on Île du Havre-Aubert to create the most original and majestic sand castles they possibly can. Teams are allowed to prepare their mounds of sand on Friday night, while all of the action happens on Saturday. On Sunday the winners are announced.

Taking place over two weeks in the fall, the **Festival International Contes en Île** (330 chemin Principal, 418/986-5281, www.conteseniles.com) brings in French storytellers from all over the world. There are all kinds of events beyond the readings, including tall tale contests, conferences, workshops, and music. Throughout the summer, **Arrimage,** the islands' arts council publishes a calendar of all the cultural and musical events happening on the islands. Unfortunately, it's only available in French, but you should be able to make out a few titles and places.

INFORMATION AND SERVICES
Tourist Information

All of the islands' main services are located in Cap-aux-Meules. The islands' only tourism office (128 chemin Principal, 418/986-2245 or 877/624-4437, www.tourismeilesdelamadeleine.com, 7 A.M.–9 P.M. daily late June–Aug., 9 A.M.–8 P.M. daily Sept., 9 A.M.–5 P.M. Mon.–Fri. Oct.–June) is located here in a cute yellow beach pavilion within walking distance from the ferry terminal.

ISLAND MENUS

Madelinots have their own way of doing things and nowhere is that more apparent than their menu. Here's a primer on some of the islands' signature food and drink, so you can be prepared to make your order.

Okay, so "boiled dinner with salted meat" may not sound particularly appetizing, but *bouilli à la viande salée,* a stew made with succulent meat from locally raised livestock and fresh veggies, is divine on a cold, windy day. Putting an island spin on a classic French dish, *crêpes au homard* (lobster crepes) come with cheese, mushrooms, and plenty of butter.

Croquignoles, sweet little shell-shaped donuts, used to be fried in seal fat. Now, good ol' vegetable oil usually does the trick. With *ragoût de loup-marin,* you probably understand the *ragout* part, but the literal translation of *loup-marin* is "sea wolf" and actually refers to seal, which you will still see popping up in various incarnations on Madeleine menus. Probably the islands' most famous dish, *pot-en-pot* is a cross between pot pie and chowder and has seafood, potatoes, sauce, and a baked crust. It's delicious. For drinking, try *Bagosse,* a local brew.

Emergency Services

In case of emergency, the Centre Hospitalier de l'Archipel (420 chemin Principale, 418/986-2121) is up the road from the ferry dock. There's a pharmacy just across the street from the hospital called Pharmacie Aline Richard (445 chemin Prinicipal, 418/986-2700, 8:30 A.M.–10 P.M. Mon.–Fri., 9 A.M.–6 P.M. Sat.–Sun.).

Banks

For banking needs, international money exchange, and an ATM, go to the Banque Nationale (425 chemin Principal, 418/986-2335, Mon.–Fri.). Otherwise look for Caisse Populaire Desjardins ATMs in Havre-Aubert, Grande-Entrée, and Havre-aux-Maisons.

Laundromat

If you need to clean some clothes, there's Nettoyeur Arsenault (273 chemin Principal, 418/986-2516, 8 A.M.–5 P.M. Mon.–Fri., 7 A.M.–9 P.M. Thurs.–Fri., 9 A.M.–noon Sat.) in Cap-aux-Meules. Most of the campgrounds and the youth hostel also have laundry facilities.

Internet

You can get Internet access at Les Pas Perdus (169 chemin Principal, 418/986-5151, www.pasperdus.com, 8 A.M.–3 A.M. daily, $1 for 10 min.).

GETTING THERE AND AROUND

By Air

The fastest way to the islands is to fly by plane from Gaspé to the airport on Île du Havre aux Maisons (YGR). Air Canada Jazz (888/247-2262, www.aircanada.com) flights tend to vary in price but you should be able to get a round-trip flight for under $300 taxes included if you book far enough in advance. It's a pleasant one-hour flight with great views. Another option is on the local carrier, Pascan Aviation (418/877-8777 or 888/313-8777, www.pascan.

com), that leaves from either Montréal, Québec City, or right in the Gaspé at the airport in Bonaventure (flights from here cost about $400 round-trip).

By Boat

Groupe CTMA (888/986-3278, www.ctma.ca) offers trips to les Îles from Montréal, with a stop in Chandler in the Gaspé region just south of Percé, and from Souris, on the northeastern tip of Prince Edward Island. The Montréal ferry runs weekly late May–October, leaving on a Friday afternoons and arriving at les Îles on Sunday morning. The costs are $460–630 per person one-way from Montréal and $140 from Chandler to les Îles. Meals are included in the price, but cars aren't. They will cost you and extra $275 from Montréal and $150 from Chandler.

The Souris–les Îles run is a five-hour jaunt that runs daily July–August and every day except Monday April–July and September. There is limited service October–end of January. One-way rates are $40 for adults and $20 for children, plus $77 for a car.

By Car

You can rent a car to get around the island at Thrifty (188 chemin de l'Aéroport, 418/969-9006 or 800/367-2277) and National (205 chemin de l'Aéroport, 418/969-4209 or 800/227-7368, 9 A.M.–5:30 P.M. Mon.–Wed., 9 A.M.–9 P.M. Thurs.–Fri., 9 A.M.–5 P.M. Sat.), located right near the airport in Havre-aux-Maisons. Make sure that you book way in advance.

By Bike

Biking is a great way to make your way around the island. You can rent one from Le Pédalier (800 chemin Principal, 418/986-2965, www.lepedalier.com, one hour $6, four hours $18, 1–3 days $24 per day), just up the street from the tourism office next to the Place des Îles shopping mall. This place rents tandem and child carriers, too.

BACKGROUND

The Land

Everyone knows how enormous Canada is. Well, Québec, its largest province, is no exception. Covering a huge territory of 1,667,296 square kilometers (643,819 square miles), Québec is three times larger than France but has one-eighth of its population. It is seven times the size of the United Kingdom and twice the size of Texas. Close to 2,000 km separate the city of Montréal in the south of the province from its northernmost point, Ivujivik, which itself sits only 425 km from the Arctic Circle. Despite its immensity, the entire province has a population of only 7.5 million people (about 4.4 people per square km) with close to half of its citizens living within the Greater Montréal area.

Québec shares a border with the Canadian provinces of Newfoundland and Labrador to the east, New Brunswick to the southeast, and Ontario to the southwest. It is also the northern neighbor of the American states of Maine, New Hampshire, Vermont, and New York. There is a huge variety of landscapes in the province, but the land can be divided into three principal geological regions.

The **Laurentian Plateau** (also called the Canadian Shield) occupies more than 90 percent of the province from the Outaouais region in the west to the Saguenay in the east, where its mountains plunge dramatically into the St. Lawrence. One of the oldest mountain ranges in the world, the Laurentians are made up of Precambrian rock (more than 500 million years old) that forms the southern edge of the Canadian Shield. Through time, the range has been eroded by glaciers, which have replaced spiked peaks with rounded hills and mountains with summits mostly ranging from between 500 meters to just higher than 900 meter except for a few peaks, mostly in the Charlevoix region, that top 1,000 meters.

The mythic **Appalachians,** which actually run from Alabama straight through to Newfoundland, take up a strip of Québec land that runs diagonally between the St. Lawrence and the province's southern border, covering the entire Gaspé Peninsula. The Appalachians are more than 250 million years old with rocks dating to the Palezoic era. In the western part of the province the mountains are modest, while the Parc de la Gaspésie in the east contains the soaring Chic-Chocs (a Mic-mac word meaning "impenetrable") with its highest peak, Mont Jacques-Cartier, reaching 1,268 meters.

Lining the St. Lawrence, the fertile, mostly level, geological area known as the **St. Lawrence Lowlands** may be tiny in comparison to the two others, but it is significant in that it contains Québec's two major cities, Montréal and Québec City, and thus, most of the province's population. There are three sections of the Lowlands: the triangular St. Lawrence Plain, which stretches from Cornwall, just over the border in Ontario, to its apex in Québec City; the low-lying region around Lac Saint-Jean; and farther east, covering the southern section of the North Shore and île d'Anticosti.

Québec has no shortage of water resources. Groundwater covers 12 percent of the territory, including more than 130,000 rivers and one million lakes. Its coastline is extensive and stretches 9,000 km in length, taking in the Arctic Ocean, the Atlantic Ocean, the Gulf of St. Lawrence, the St. Lawrence River, James Bay, and Hudson Bay.

The province's most significant waterway is the **St. Lawrence River.** The third-longest river in Canada after the Mackenzie and the Yukon, it stretches roughly 1,200 km from Kingston on Lake Ontario straight through to the Atlantic. Considered North America's leading inland seaway, the St. Lawrence played a vital role in the development of Québec. The river also contains a 200-km border between Canada and the United States and at 65 km wide, the world's largest estuary.

CLIMATE

With such a huge land mass extending across five degrees of latitude, the province has three distinct climates: the humid continental climate, which is south of the 50th parallel (the area containing the overwhelming majority of the province's cities and towns), the subarctic climate between the 50th and 58th parallel, and the arctic climate north of the 58th.

The humid continental climate is characterized by extreme variations in temperature and four distinct seasons.

Spring (April and May) is an exhilarating time when the province comes to life again. Spring fever runs rampant, migratory birds make their return, fresh buds pop out on the trees, the snow starts melting, and of course, café and restaurant terraces all begin reopening. With rivers engorged from melting ice and snow, spring is also the best time for whitewater rafting. And of course, it marks the period when the sap starts running and people gather at the sugar shacks to gorge on meals of beans, ham, *tourtière* (meat pie), sugar pie, and *la tire* (hot maple taffy poured over snow and wound around a popsicle stick).

Summer (June, July and August) is lush, green, hot, and often very humid. July is the hottest month with the mercury regularly rising to 26°C (79°F), but feeling, with the humidity, more like 30°C (86°F). June and mid- to late August are probably the nicest times during the summer to visit, with the humidity far less of an issue and slightly cooler evenings. Summer means festival season in Québec. It is also, of course, its busiest tourist season and when most Quebecers take their vacations.

Autumn (September and October), with its orange, red, and yellow leaf colors, is a spectacular time of year in the province, especially in the Laurentians, Eastern Townships, Outaouais, and Charlevoix. With school back in after Labor Day, things get a little quieter and the days are often warm and sunny and the nights cool.

And then there's **winter** (November–March), ah... winter, the season that for better or worse gets the most attention. Although the mean temperature is -7 to -9°C, it can frequently get much colder than that. The good news is that when extremely cold weather arrives, it usually doesn't last very long. The season usually brings a healthy dose of snow (the average annual is three meters), which is always good news for the province's ski hills and snowmobile and cross-country trails.

Environment Canada has a website (www.weatheroffice.ec.gc.ca) where you can check on current conditions, seasonal forecasts, and marine and aviation weather.

Flora and Fauna

ECOZONES
Québec has five main ecozones (ecological areas that have their own climate, flora and fauna, and distinctive terrain). The **arctic** zone encompasses the northern reaches of the province. Despite the 10-month winters, extreme cold, and constant permafrost, perseverant plant species consisting mostly of mosses and lichens do survive here. Less barren than the tundra zone is the **taiga shield** zone, which is mostly made up of lichen and shrub, but which also includes some patches of stunted black spruce and jack pine. Next down is the **boreal forest,** the largest of Québec's forest zones, covering 27 percent of the province. Its largely softwood trees consist of pine, balsam fir, larch, and spruce. The fertile **mixed woods,** with its milder climate and growing season of close to 200 days, is the province's agricultural center. This zone consists of plains and rounded hills and tree species including the colorful maple, as well as birch, beech, oak, and ash. Finally, the **Atlantic maritime** zone, which encompasses the southeastern part of the province, is largely made up of the same trees as the mixed woods zone, but it has an abundance of spruce and balsam fir, along with many shrubs and wildflowers.

BIRDS
Québec is home to a diverse array of birds, including about 250 species of nesting ones. The province's emblematic bird is the beautiful and strong snowy owl. The largest owl in North America (its wingspan is between 4–5 feet), the snowy nests in the north of the province during the warmer months and makes its way south to the St. Lawrence valley for the winter. Males can be pure white while females typically have feathers marked with dark brown. Another owl making its home in Québec is the

Northern gannets congregate on the shores of Île Bonaventure.

more common and sedentary barred or "hoot" owl, known for its distinctive "Who cooks for you, who cooks for you all?" call. The barred owl has brown plumage with white streaks.

The province is also home to a wide variety of ducks, geese, and seabirds including the loon, king of the $1 coin, whose classic melancholic call is reminiscent of lakeside cottages, and the ever-honking, ever-pesky, and ever-growing in number Canada goose. The mallard, harlequin, and American black duck and the colorful wood duck also make their home in the province.

There are about 20 species of seabirds that breed along the shores of the St. Lawrence. They include black-legged kittiwakes, murres, razorbills, and even a small number of Atlantic puffins. The northern gannet makes up one of the largest seabird colonies in Québec. With its long neck, white plumage, jet-black wing-tips, and icy blue eyes, you'd think the gannet would be a graceful bird, but its stubby legs and webbed feet make it a bit of a clumsy waddler. Making their home on islands and cliff tops in the Gulf of St. Lawrence, and especially on Île Bonaventure off the coast of the Percé from late March until November, gannets are known for their cunning feeding techniques, which involve plunging at speeds of up to 100 km/hour.

LAND MAMMALS

Québec has a huge variety of land mammals, varying from the tiny (moles and shrews) to the massive (polar bear). Rodents include the chipmunk, squirrel (gray, red, and the bizarre-looking flying ones), muskrat, porcupine, and that ubiquitous symbol of Canada, the beaver. The industrious and hardworking beaver lives throughout Québec wherever deciduous trees are found. Using their sharp incisors, they gnaw away at trees until they fall, creating impressive dams that form shallow ponds so that the water won't completely freeze come winter. You'll often hear the *thwack* of a beaver's flat tail if you make yourself visible to one in the woods. This noise is to caution fellow beavers.

Carnivores include skunk and raccoon, both of which are present in the woods, as well as city backyards, much to urbanites' chagrin. There are also the mink, the red fox, which, despite the name also comes in black and brown, the gray wolf, the coyote, and the widespread and sometimes unpredictable black bear. Even the polar bear has been known to make an appearance around the James Bay and Hudson Bay areas. Three members of the cat family also share the Québec forests. They are the lynx, bobcat, and mountain lion (one of Canada's endangered species).

Québec's deer family is made up of three species. The white-tailed deer, the smallest species of deer in North America, is very common in the province and is also the most hunted of animals. Canada's other emblematic animal, the moose, is the largest member of the deer family and comparable in size to a horse. Distinguished by its size and the male's broad antlers, the moose also possesses a rounded schnoz and a furry wattle called the "bell." The moose population has experienced a growth spurt in recent years and now numbers approximately 100,000. They live in the Bas-Saint-Laurent, Gaspé, and the northern Abitibi region. Woodland caribou are unique among members of the deer family as all males and most females possess antlers. Found largely in the northern part of the province, every year hundreds of thousand caribou migrate across a range of more than one million square kilometers. There is also a tiny pocket of 200 caribou in the Parc National de la Gaspésie—the only remaining caribou south of the St. Lawrence River.

SEALIFE

Where the St. Lawrence River meets the Saguenay, along its northern shores and out into the Gulf of St. Lawrence, are some of the best places in the world to observe seals, porpoises, and whales.

Six types of seal can be spotted in the estuary and the gulf, including the harp seal, whose young are the well-known "whitecoats," the huge, black-headed gray seal, and the much smaller and lighter harbor seal, the only species

A seal rests on higher ground alongside Île Bonaventure.

© SUE MOORE

that lives in the St. Lawrence on a permanent basis—although its numbers are dwindling.

Despite major international flak from animal rights organizations, seal hunting is still practiced in Québec, especially in smaller northern villages and off the coast of les Îles de la Madeleine. Although sealing has occurred for centuries in Canada, and even longer amid First Nations groups, the practice came under severe scrutiny in the 1970s when graphic ads showing the killing of baby seals with blood splattered on white snow were shown on TV. The outcry forced the government to ban the hunting of whitecoat and blueback pups, impose quotas, and enforce the manner in which seals were killed. Recently, however, the government loosened the quota on harp seal, saying that their overpopulation is one of the reasons for the depletion of the cod stocks. The debate rages on.

With 13 species of cetaceans (whales, porpoises, and dolphins), Québec, and more specifically the waters around Tadoussac, is one of the few places in the world where such a wide variety lives. What attracts them here is the abundant food supply (plankton and krill) of the waters around the St. Lawrence Estuary. Whale species include the gigantic blue, which at 100 tons and 25 meters easily ranks as the largest mammal on the planet, the fin whale, which is second in size, the acrobatic humpback whale, the outgoing beluga, and the deep-diving sperm whale.

Four of the 13 cetaceans in the St. Lawrence have been deemed endangered or threatened. They include the beleaguered beluga, the right, the bottlenose, and the blue.

ENVIRONMENTAL ISSUES

With nearly half of Québec's territory covered in forests (750,300 square km to be exact), it's no surprise that forestry is a principal industry in the province. Close to 250 of Québec's municipalities are economically dependent on the harvest of forests (with pulp and paper being the main industry). Although clear-cutting has been curbed, the practice still exists. Québec's Forest Protection Strategy, introduced in 1994, is committed to protecting forest resources as well as encouraging their renewal. The strategy, which outlawed the use of chemical pesticides in forests in 2001, dictates that forest development must be sustainable and that conditions of the forest ecosystems must be maintained.

Although Canada is listed as a country that has some of the highest levels of greenhouse gas emissions (GHG) per capita, Québec is the province that produces the least amount of GHGs. This may be explained by the fact that the province's electricity is more than 95 percent hydraulic, and that it makes greater use of electricity as an energy source (second only to Norway). Nevertheless, emissions are expected to grow, largely because of energy consumption in the transportation industry, which accounts for 40 percent of emissions. The increase can already be felt in Montréal, where smog alerts are a regular occurrence and more and more people are suffering from allergies and asthma. The city, like many others in Canada, participates in a variety of initiatives aimed at promoting public transportation, such as World Car-Free day. Québec also played a key role in the 1997 Kyoto Accord, which involved the adoption of Canadian GHG reductive objectives.

Hydro-Québec is the only supplier of electricity in the province, with its most infamous project taking place in James Bay in northern Québec, on the southern end of Hudson Bay, home to several major hydroelectric projects. After a 25-year battle with the area's Cree residents regarding the environmental impact of the project, a deal was approved which saw the native people receiving cash payments from the provincial government. There remains an ongoing debate about the pros and cons of developing this area, which involved the devastation of millions of acres of forest. Further, the project caused ongoing flooding in northern Québec. Caribou migration routes were also affected, resulting in the deaths of more than 10,000 caribou in 1984. The positive side is the fact that the project has allowed for thousands of megawatts of electricity to be generated pollution-free to not only Québec, but to the rest of Canada and the United States as well.

History

EARLY INHABITANTS

Before England and France cast their imperial nets over the region, a diverse group of aboriginal peoples populated present-day Québec. Their ancestors were hunters who crossed the icy Bering Strait from Asia toward the end of the Ice Age. They slowly fanned out across the continent, especially after the glaciers retreated 10,000 years ago.

Québec's native peoples are descended from three linguistic factions: Algonquin, Iroquian, and Inuit. Most Algonquin and Inuit were seminomadic hunters, while the Iroquois were sedentary farmers. All three groups shared similarities: They all used the canoe to navigate the waterways, the family was the major social unit, although hunting societies centered on the father, agricultural societies centered on the mother, and political life was focused on the tribe, with chiefs governing through respect and by consensus.

When the Europeans dropped anchor and started settling along the shores of the St. Lawrence in the 16th and 17th centuries, they irrevocably changed not just the face of the province but the course of North American history.

EUROPEAN ARRIVAL

While the French were already exploiting the Newfoundland cod fishery, they dispatched explorers such as Jacques Cartier in 1534. Although Cartier's trips saw him chart new territory, make contact with the aboriginal peoples in the villages of Stadacona (Québec City) and Hochelaga (Montréal) and pepper the countryside with French names, they were deemed unsuccessful by the French king, who was disappointed that the explorer hadn't succeeded in his original mission to chart a route to Asia.

Exploration stagnated for many decades, until fur became the *de rigueur* fashion item of the French bourgeoisie toward the end of the 16th century. European merchants set sail up the St. Lawrence and stocked their ships with beaver pelts, attempting to also set up more permanent outposts. The first to succeed in establishing a trading post was Samuel de Champlain in 1608.

The arrival of the one-time laborer from the southwest of France, who from a young age was fascinated with the art of navigation, changed everything. Champlain chose to set up his trading post at a spot called "Kebec," an Algonquin word meaning "where the river narrows." Although Champlain, thanks to his successful alliances with the Huron, Algonquin, and Montagnais, was successful in establishing a little fur-trading empire, he soon set his sights further, to establishing a French colony.

STRUGGLE FOR CONTROL

In the mid-17th century, battles with the Iroquois, along with the expansion of England's own fur trade through the Hudson's Bay Company, threatened France's burgeoning venture. Until then, New France was being run and developed by the Compagnie des Cents Associés, a company set up by the King of France that brought together about 100 associates whose primary mission was to populate the colony. However, with trade threatened by the attacks of the Iroquois and the company's failure to populate the colony quickly enough, King Louis XIV assumed administration and beefed up defenses, most notably about 1,200 soldiers of the Carignan-Salières regiment.

The king's men in the New World were charged with keeping the peace and focusing on the future by populating the sparse territory. One of the king's most famous strategies included the envoy of almost 1,000 young women of childbearing age to the colony. They were called *les filles du roi* and had their passages and their dowries paid for by the French treasury.

With peace achieved with the Iroquois, it was the Brits who soon came calling, vying with the French for control of the colony. Intermittent battles dominated the 18th century, and vast expanses of French territory (including Newfoundland and parts of Québec and present-day New England, Nova Scotia, New Brunswick, and Prince Edward Island) were ceded to the English with the Peace of Utrecht in 1713. But it was Britain's triumph in the French and Indian War, sealed by the watershed battle on the Plains of Abraham in Québec City, that brought France's imperial dreams to an end. Out of that war came the 1763 Treaty of Paris, which secured British control of New France.

Although the British regime officially controlled New France, its campaign to make Québec a mini-England was a dismal failure. Britain knew that appeasing the largely Catholic French-speaking population would be necessary for political survival. To ensure French

© JENNIFER EDWARDS

The merchandise in Hodge's Store in the Eastern Townships dates back to World War II.

loyalty, the British Parliament passed the Québec Act of 1774, reestablishing the French civil code and granting free practice of Catholicism, enraging British settlers in the process. The move was none too soon: In the next year the American Revolution began, and American soldiers attempted to capture Montréal and Québec City. They were swiftly pushed back, receiving little local support.

CONFEDERATION

In the late 18th century, once the American colonies gained independence, a flood of 50,000 British loyalists emigrated to Québec. None too pleased with having to abide by the French civil code, these new citizens began to push for a repeal of the Québec Act. Instead, Britain passed the Constitutional Act in 1791, which divided its massive territory into Upper and Lower Canada, now respectively Ontario and Québec.

Although each province was given its own elected assembly, executive and legislative councils, and lieutenant governors, executive power was still the jurisdiction of the British governor-general. Discontent with their lack of political powers, Lower Canadians launched a series of rebellions. The French Patriots' insurgencies outside Montréal from 1837 to 1838, which led to the execution of 12 French Patriots in 1839, marked what has become a centuries-long power struggle between French and English Canada and is perhaps one of the earliest examples of Québec nationalism.

The revolts ultimately proved unsuccessful, but they did bring about the Act of Union, which brought Upper and Lower Canada back together under a joint legislature. Responsible government was established in the colony in 1848, giving the legislative assembly voting power and increasing the power of the Catholic Church in setting social and educational policies. It was followed in quick succession by Confederation in 1867, which unified New Brunswick, Nova Scotia, Ontario, and Québec under federal rule, while each maintained provincial power.

MODERN QUÉBEC

Although Québec had emerged as a largely rural, agrarian society—a process that began in the 18th century and grew through the next 200 years, near the end of the 19th century, the province emerged—despite a bumpy transition—as an industrial leader, and the transformation brought significant social, economic, religious, and political change. Factories, forests, and mines became the foundation of an emerging industrial capitalism. Cars, radios, and electricity sparked a surge of consumerism in the until-then largely conservative and devotedly religious society.

Montréal, Québec's most cosmopolitan city, grew rapidly in the early 20th century, though smaller communities such as Chicoutimi and Saint-Hyacinthe also prospered thanks to a boom in pulp and paper mills and leather and textile factories. In fact, before American investments in the Toronto Stock Exchange made that megalopolis the self-proclaimed center of Canada, Montréal was Canada's star city.

While things were looking up for the province, Québec women still had battles to fight. Although women in the rest of the country could vote in provincial elections by 1922, women in Québec had to wait until 1940. Talk about a glass ceiling: Women were recruited as cheap labor during the World War I but later in the decade they were ghettoized in traditional nursing, teaching, and clerical roles with little chance of promotion, earning only half of what men did. Of course, Québec's strong Catholic conservatism didn't help in the promotion of women's rights.

But slowly, the political and social landscape was changing. The Catholic Church's power started to wane after the Great Depression and a general discontent was starting to emerge. As early as the end of the 19th century, Quebecers were starting to think that Confederation was not the partnership it had hoped it would be, with the rest of Canada considering Québec just another link in the federal chain, that is, no more distinct than any other province. Fueling the resentment was the conscription of World War I. To many Quebecers, the idea of fighting in a war for the British Army, its for-

TOTAL REFUSAL

Penned by a group of artists and intellectuals who called themselves the Automatistes, the *Refus Global* (Total Refusal) manifesto was shocking, smart, and filled with bravado – all the ingredients required for an instant bestseller.

Launched on August 9, 1948 at a small bookstore on rue Sainte-Catherine in Montréal, the manifesto attacked the insularity, close mindedness, and conservatism of Québec society and called for an end to what they deemed the Catholic Church's stranglehold on the nation.

At the heart of the manifesto was a letter by a painter by named Paul-Émile Borduas. He had been practicing a style of painting called automatism, which relied on the subconscious to bring abstract images to the fore. Borduas had found a following amongst a group of young artists in Montréal and with it, the support he needed to go forth with his declaration.

When the manifesto hit the streets, it kick-started a huge debate that extended far beyond art circles. But its contentious statements ("We must refuse to serve, or to be used for such despicable ends. We must avoid deliberate design as the harmful weapon of reason. Down with them both! Back they go!") were almost too much for the Church-abiding populace. Borduas was immediately fired from his teaching position and could find no other job. His wife and kids moved out, and he was left alone, almost penniless.

Borduas moved to Paris in 1955, resumed painting, and soon became well known for his abstract style. It would only be a few years after Borduas died in 1960 that the ideas that he put forth would firmly take root in a little movement called the Quiet Revolution.

---

mer conqueror, was an abhorrent thought. Add to that stories of ill treatment among French soldiers who had already joined the mostly English Protestant battalions and the fact that Ontario had just banned French schools in the province, French Canadians seeking to serve instead chose to form French-speaking regiments, such as Les Fusiliers Mont-Royal. The first full-fledged French batallion created was the Royal 22nd Regiment, which still exists at the Citadelle in Québec City.

THE DUPLESSIS DARK AGES

Though he founded the Union Nationale, a provincial nationalist party, and balanced the provincial budget for almost two decades, the provincial rule of Maurice Duplessis, also known as *le chef*, was characterized by corruption, crippling favoritism, and, ultimately, a legacy as the province's most power-hungry and oppressive leaders. "The saying goes that after the death of every great man there's a long period of ingratitude. I find Maurice Duplessis' period is lasting pretty long," his niece told a newspaper reporter a few years ago.

In power almost successively from 1936 to 1959, the man who was chief literally sold out, allowing American corporations to snap up Québec resources. A big friend of big business, Duplessis employed violent methods to suppress strikes, while introducing the loosely defined Act Concerning Communist Propaganda in 1937, which was used to stifle unions and minority religious and political groups. (More than 20 years later, the Supreme Court of Canada declared the act unconstitutional.)

Duplessis was also very cozy with the Catholic Church, allowing it to assume great political, educational, and societal powers. His dictatorial reign cast a shadow over the province, which came to be known as La Grande Noirceur, or The Great Darkness.

THE QUIET REVOLUTION

After Duplessis died in 1959, the province reawakened, engaging in a defining movement that started in the early 1960s called the Quiet Revolution (la Révolution Tranquille). The term is said to have been coined by a Toronto journalist who, observing the widespread social, political, and economic changes that were taking place as a reaction against the religious and political oppression of the Duplessis regime, said that Québec society was going through a revolution, albeit a quiet one.

With the slogan, "It's time for a change," the Liberal Party under Jean Lesage returned to power, introducing large, centralized health, education, and social services and nationalizing private hydroelectric companies. The Liberals established provincial departments such as the Ministry of Culture and took a direct role in administering health and social services. But its single biggest move came when it demoted the Catholic Church from its seat at the head of the educational system. For the Catholic Church, it was the end of its long-held position of political and moral influence. The ties that once bound Québec society, ties to the land, to the church, and to tradition, were now becoming undone. That is all except for one: nationalism.

THE NEW NATIONALISM

During the 1960s and 1970s, Québec culture went through a full-blown renaissance. French artists, musicians, and writers were finally able to express themselves without the interference of the Catholic Church. The result inspired a new sense of pride in being Québécois.

Montréal received a major boost of confidence when it was chosen as the location of Expo '67. For a short while, the city became center stage of the world, a performance that would be repeated less than 10 years later when it won the bid over Moscow and Los Angeles to host the 1976 Olympic Games.

A robust civil service and valuable provincial assets such as Hydro-Québec saw growing numbers of French Canadians filling high-end jobs, positions they once claimed were unavailable to them.

Politically, Québec nurtured a friendship with France. On a visit to Montréal in the late 1960s, French President Charles de Gaulle sparked enduring controversy with his: "Vive le Québec! Vive le Québec libre!" cry, which he yelled from the balcony of the Hôtel-de-Ville. English Canadians were outraged that the French prime minister should stick his nose into Canada's affairs, while French Canadians took it as a major rallying cry, the almost-fatherly endorsement of their cause.

When the separatist Parti Québécois (PQ) under the leadership of René Lévesque was elected to office in 1976, French had already been declared the official language of Québec, but language legislation was extended further to include tough new restrictions on the use of French in business, schools, and in advertising. Politically and culturally, language became the hallmark of the separatist movement. Meanwhile, nationalist tensions grew as the federal government involved itself more in provincial affairs.

During this time, groups of radicals, such as the terrorist FLQ (Front de Libération du Québec) began making major noise. After a few bombing attempts, the FLQ kidnapped British diplomat James Richard Cross and Québec Minister of Labour Pierre Laporte. When government negotiations with the terrorists proved futile, Prime Minister Pierre Elliott Trudeau imposed the War Measures Act, sending the Canadian Armed Forces into several Québec cities. The FLQ assassinated Laporte the next day.

Although it was by far the most extreme demonstration of violence in the national unity debate, the event created a huge wedge between the two sides. That wedge was made even broader when the PQ announced plans for its 1980 referendum on secession. Leading up to the vote, the streets were flooded with rallying separatists and federalists, each wearing buttons, waving their respective flags and with their foreheads and cheeks painted with a *oui* or a *non*. Though ultimately the *non* side won out, acquiring 60 percent of the votes, the *oui* side garnered a majority of the francophone vote. During his emotional concession speech, René Lévesque addressed his supporters by saying: "If I understand you well, you're saying, 'Until next time.'"

POST-REFERENDUM

Québec was the only province to *not* sign a new constitution in 1982 that surrendered British title to Canada. Two high-profile attempts during the next decade to amend the constitution and include Québec ultimately failed. The results of a second referendum led by PQ leader Jacques Parizeau and the federal Bloc Québécois' Lucien Bouchard was held in 1995. Although early polls showed that a majority of Quebecers would vote "no," things began to shift leading up to the referendum. Watching the election coverage on the TV that night was a nail-biting affair. The end result? The "no" vote won... by one percentage point.

While the "nationalist question" has never really been answered, its prominence both provincially and nationally has been lessened. Fed up with the debate and the emotional toll it took, Quebecers have chosen to get on with their lives and focus on bettering the place in which they live instead of dreaming large. But separatism is never far away. For now, it's just riding along in the back seat.

GOVERNMENT

The National Assembly of Québec is the province's legislative body, which sits in residence at the Hôtel du Parlement in Québec City. The province is divided into 125 electoral ridings and during a general election, each riding votes in a candidate who becomes a member of the National Assembly. The party with the most elected officials forms the provincial government, led by a premier, the leader of the party.

The Executive Council (commonly referred to as the Cabinet) is selected by the premier and is responsible for all decision-making in the government. It is primarily composed of government ministers who hold portfolios such as finance, education, health and social services, transport, etc.). Along with the lieutenant governor, the Executive Council constitutes the government of Québec and is responsible for its direction, as well as overseeing and enforcing laws, regulations, and policies.

The province's major political parties consist of the Parti Libéral du Québec, the current party in power, led by Jean Charest, the Parti Québécois (PQ), whose members and supporters are frequently called *Péquistes,* and

the Action Démocratique du Québec. The Bloc Québécois is a federal party, meaning that it holds seats at the House of Commons in Ottawa.

The most invisible, yet profound, difference between Québec and the rest of Canada is that Québec functions under the Civil Code, derived from France's Code Napoléon, instead of the British system of Common Law. In Québec, interactions between neighbors or between a boss and employees or any other civil interaction such as buying goods in a store are governed under rules set out in a code, while Common Law is based on legal precedent.

The Civil Code has become an intrinsic part of a culture where the state has a say on how people interact—quite a departure from the Anglo Saxon approach of individual freedom without state interference. As a manifestation of that culture, the Québec government has created entities such as La Régie du Logement, a board that dictates the relationship between landlords and tenants, and La Société de l'Assurance Automobile du Québec, which runs a mandatory public insurance for all car accidents.

ECONOMY

Québec, along with Ontario, make up Canada's economic heart—although the province's economy has had a slower performance based, in part, on its slow demographic growth. Once largely dependent on its natural resources, Québec's economy has diversified and become highly industrialized through the past couple of decades. Today, the province's top industry is science and technology, with Montréal ranking fourth in North America in terms of the number of high-tech jobs. The province is a recognized world leader in the aerospace industry, with companies such as Bombardier and Pratt & Whitney headquartered in the province. Forestry is still a significant industry. The province ranks as the third-largest producer of newsprint in the world and softwood and wood pulp make up other major exports.

Although the massive ice storm of 1998,

shrinking water levels, and other environmental concerns have undermined public confidence in Hydro-Québec, a government-run corporation that administers 83 power-generating plants in the province, it is still a major performer in the province's economy and has allowed Quebecers to enjoy one of the lowest electricity rates on the continent.

The People

The second-most populous province in Canada, Québec has just over 7.5 million people, roughly 23 percent of Canada's total population. Just over 80 percent of Quebecers cite French as their mother tongue, making the province an island in a sea of English-dominated North America. Most of the six million French speakers descend from the original 10,000 settlers from France.

English-speakers make up 11 percent of the population. Most of them descend from British settlers but also from British Loyalists who fled the United States after the War of Independence. Allophones, those who count neither French nor English as their first language, make up 6 percent of the population and most of them live in Montréal. Some of the dominant groups include Greeks, Italians, Portuguese, German, Polish, Lebanese, Haitian, and Latin Americans.

The First Nations of Québec today account for roughly 1 percent of the population or just over 80,000 people. The population is divided between Amerindians (88 percent) and Inuit (12 percent). Most of the people who make up the 10 Amerindian nations live on reserves or land governed by a band council. The Inuit live in the northern reaches of the province in 14 villages with a political structure similar to the rest of the province's.

CULTURE

Although most Québécois descend from the original French colonists, they are true North Americans. Lise Bissonnette, one of the province's well-respected intellectuals, has a pointed way of describing Québec culture. She says that the reality of her people is undeniably North American, while its aspirations are more

European. In other words, the daily lives of Quebecers are just like those of other North Americans: They eat Kellogg's cereal bought at Costco, they drive to work, gobble down sandwiches or burgers for lunch, and wind down with *une bonne bière* (a tasty beer) at the end of the day.

But it's when Quebecers want to treat themselves that their French nature kicks in. Dining out means going to a fine, chef-owned restaurant and taking one's time. Driving a cool car means a European one (notice the preponderance of Volkswagen and Smart cars). And dreaming of a better society means look-

Antique shopping is a popular pastime in North Hatley.

© JENNIFER EDWARDS

DRINKING WITH THE DEVIL

Quebecers are legendary for loving a good drink. (And we're not talking milk.) So it's fitting that the stuff figures prominently in one of Québec's favorite legends: that of the Flying Canoe (*chasse-galerie* in French).

The story goes that one New Year's Eve, a lonely lumberjack named Baptiste Durand makes a deal with the devil so that he and his colleagues can make it back to their girlfriends in Montréal in time for the celebrations. The journey is more than 300 miles, but the devil ensures Baptiste that he can get them there by flying them through the skies in their canoe. The devil has certain conditions though: The crew must not mention the Lord's name nor touch the crosses on the tops of the steeples as they fly by.

To be sure that the others stay in line, Durand forbids the lumberjacks from touching another drop of alcohol and says that if they do, they will be forced into selling their souls to the devil. The flying canoe reaches Montréal without incidence, and the crew makes it to Batisette Auger's house where the party is in full swing. They all dance, drink, and become very, very merry.

As the very early morning sets in, the crew starts to panic, knowing that they have to make it back to camp in time for work. The only problem is that Baptiste, the canoe's navigator, is as drunk as a skunk. Things do not go well as they begin the return trip. Baptiste almost steers them into a steeple and soon, they end up crashing into a snow bank. Fearing that an expletive will soon escape from Baptiste's mouth, the lumberjacks gag him and get someone else to steer. As the canoe again takes flight, Baptiste shakes his gag loose and swears a blue streak. Terrified by the repercussions, the new navigator loses control and steers the canoe straight into a pine tree.

Found the next morning by other loggers who figure that they are simply sleeping off a drunken night at camp, the crew stays mum about the exploits and breathes a sigh of relief that the devil has seemingly not taken notice. The legend took such hold in Québec that Canada Post issued a 40-cent postage stamp with the image of the flying canoe and its crew in 1991. You can also catch a glimpse of the devilish depiction by seeking out a bottle of La Maudite (meaning damned one), a beer made by one of the province's mega-microbreweries, Unibroue.

ing to Europe for examples of good government programs.

Generally considered an open, vibrant, and creative population, Quebecers don't bother with Old World conventions and traditions; they are friendly. But like the French, they enjoy a good debate, good food, and a glass of good wine.

Religion

Although Roman Catholics account for 83 percent of the population, the dominance of the faith doesn't mean nearly the same thing as it would have before the Quiet Revolution. Before then Quebecers were devoted and obedient Roman Catholics, observing the church's role in all matters of public life, from local politics to health care to control over the province's school systems.

All that changed in the 1960s, however, when Quebecers started to question the role of the church and began to push for social change. As a result, the province became more secular, pushing the church out of administrative systems, and for a large part, out of daily life altogether. Today most Roman Catholic Quebecers consider themselves nonpracticing Catholics. The younger generations have deserted the churches. Québec's birth rate, which once was the highest in the country, is now the lowest, and more and more Quebecers don't even ponder marriage at all but prefer common-law relationships.

According to a Statistics Canada survey conducted in 2001, the number of Quebecers who declare that they are of no religion jumped almost two points to 5.6 percent between 1991 and 2001, making it the second denominational (or nondenominational) group in the province. Protestants are next with 4.7 percent, Muslims come in at 1.5, Christian Orthodox 1.4, and Jewish 1.3.

Language

Ahhh… the issue of language in Québec is a long, colorful, and, some would say, sordid one. Although the first laws governing language in the province date to 1910 with the Lavergne Law, which mandated that bus and train tickets be printed in both English and French, the real beginning of French-language protection made its debut in 1961 with the creation of the Office Québécois de la Langue Française, commonly referred to among Anglophones as the "Language Police."

Bill 22, passed by the Robert Bourassa–led Québec Liberals in 1974, was the first law to make French the official language of the province. Under the bill, businesses were required to have French incorporated names and prove that they could function in French, while school-age children had to prove that they had a basic understanding of English before being enrolled in the English school system. While Anglophones resented the law, Francophones thought that it didn't go far enough.

The Charter of the French language, usually referred to as Bill 101, came to pass under Parti Québécois (PQ) leader René Lévesque in 1977. The bill went much further than the previous one, stating that French was to be "the normal and everyday language of work, instruction, communication, commerce and business." The bill banned English from commercial signs, while education in English was granted to children who were already enrolled or those whose parents had received English-language instruction. The uproar from English-owned businesses was vocal and swift. It's still common today to see grafitti featuring anti- or pro-Bill 101 comments (and many far from polite) around the city.

Once Robert Bourassa was back as premier, the law was relaxed somewhat with Bill 178, which stated that only French could be used on exterior signs while interior signs could use both languages.

In 1993, however, the U.N. Human Rights Committee ruled that the province's sign laws broke international rules on civil and political rights and freedoms. Bourassa amended the law with Bill 86, which allowed for English on exterior signs as long as French was at least twice as big. The result of this legislation had representatives of the Office Québécois de la Langue Française running around with tape measures, ensuring that English lettering was no bigger than the law required while English shopkeepers tried to shoo them away.

Although Québec language laws have created bitter division through the years, many Quebecers (even English Quebecers) now see it as being a necessary step to protect what was becoming an increasingly threatened language in English-dominated North America, where English-language books, movies, TV shows, music, and American-based franchises were streaming into the province.

THE ARTS
Cinema

Many Canadians wonder why it is that English Canadian movies for the large part are so mediocre while Québec movies are so good. While movies from the rest of the country often flop at the box office, if they ever get released in theaters at all, Québec movies bring in huge numbers. Although some of this can certainly be explained by the fact that English cinema in Canada has to compete with the flood of blockbuster American movies, there is still an undeniable superiority in Québec moviemaking, which is at once funny, self-effacing, creative, and smart.

The Golden Age of Québec cinema occurred in the 1960s, born largely out of a dissatisfaction with the pro-Canada documentary films made by the National Film Board of Canada (NFB). Québec filmmakers employed by the NFB started making movies telling their own stories, influenced by the techniques of direct cinema. One of these films was *Le chat dans le sac,* a 1964 movie by Gilles Groulx, which chronicles the fading relationship between Claude, a sort of rebel without a cause in search of himself, and Barbara, his Jewish anglophone girlfriend who is in search of a career. The film is considered the beginning of modern fiction moviemaking in Québec.

Perhaps the province's most pivotal movie is *Mon Oncle Antoine* made by director Claude Jutra in 1971. The film is set in an asbestos mining town during the 1940s and tells the story of a 15-year-old boy coming of age. With its snowy scenes and dark, almost claustrophobic, interiors, close-knit family, and issues of repressed desires, the film expertly captures the feeling of Duplessis-era Québec.

More recently, Denys Arcand has made major strides toward a world-recognized Québec film industry. His acclaimed *Decline of the American Empire* was a sort of *Big Chill* of Québec. This 1987 film follows the conversations of a group of men gathered together to prepare dinner for that evening and women working out at the gym, cutting between the two as they discuss friendship, relationships, and mostly sex. Arcand's masterpiece however, was his followup to the film, the 2002 *Barbarian Invasions,* which won the Oscar for best foreign film. This time the group of friends have gathered around their friend who is dying of cancer, a man that many of them have to learn to forgive for his selfish, philandering ways. The film is poignant and powerful while never losing its robust sense of humor. You can catch some of these movies at the Cinérobothèque (1564 rue Saint-Denis, Montréal, 514/496-6887, www.nfb.ca, noon–9 P.M. Sat.–Sun., films $2 per hour, adults $3 for one hour or $5.50 for two hours, children and students $2 for one hour or $3.50 for two hours), the Cinémathèque québécoise (335 boulevard de Maisonneuve Est, Montréal, 514/842-9768, www.cinematheque.qc.ca, adults $6, students $5, children 6–15 $3), or by going to one of the Boite Noire (4450 rue Saint-Denis, Suite 20, Montréal, 514/287-1249, www.boite-noire.com, 10 A.M.–11 P.M. daily) movie rental outlets in Montréal.

Literature

Québec literature found its sure footing with the development of a slew of self-reflexive fiction that took place on the *terroir* (rural homestead) and the Québécois ties to the land, family, and community. One of these was the 1913 classic *Maria Chapdelaine* by Louis Hémon, which chronicles the life of a woman left to care for her family after her mother dies and the suitors who promise her very different lives. *Un homme et son péché* (1928) by Claude-Henri Grignon is another classic of Québec literature that looks at rural life, although this one is far less idealized. Taking place in Sainte-Adèle, the novel defines the hardships of small-town life more concretely with its portrayal of a young local woman who is forced to abandon her dreams of marrying the man that she loves in favor of the cruel and greedy mayor to save her father from bankruptcy.

The Québec novel turned to city life and the effects of industrialization and poverty with the internationally recognized *Bonheur d'occasion* (*The Tin Flute*) by Gabrielle Roy. Considered a classic of Canadian literature and a must-read on the list of many schoolkids, the book shows a young woman named Florentine, struggling to make it in the working-class Saint-Henri neighborhood of Montréal. Working-class life in Montréal also played an important role in the first novel published by Mordecai Richler, *The Apprenticeship of Duddy Kravitz* (1959), which follows a young opportunist striving to make a name for himself in the Jewish quarter of the Plateau, and the pivotal 1965 play by Michel Tremblay called *Les Belles-soeurs.* The play centers around the conversations of a group of woman who have assembled around the kitchen table of a woman who just won a million trading stamps and needs help pasting them into books. It was the first to incorporate *joual* (Québécois slang) into a major work. Although the play has become a classic both as a play and a piece of literature, the Québec government originally refused to sponsor the 1972 mounting of the play in Paris because of its use of base language.

In terms of poetry, the melancholic Émile

Nelligan, born in 1879, remains Québec's most well-known poet. Publishing his first lyrical and romantic poems at the age of 16, Nelligan had a psychotic breakdown after his only poetry reading at the age of 20. He never recovered, spending the rest of his years in and out of mental hospitals. Anne Hébert is known for her poems and her fiction, including her best-known work, the novel *Kamouraska*. Her poems were bleak, often depicting a stifling and oppressive Québec pre-Quiet Revolution. And, of course, there are the metaphoric poems of Leonard Cohen, poet, novelist, and singer-songwriter. Cohen's first collection of poems was *Let Us Compare Mythologies,* published in 1956.

Québec literature today is confident and individualistic. There's Nelly Arcan's somewhat shocking semiautographical book *Putain* (2001), a gritty tale of the life of a Montréal prostitute, Gil Courtemanche's *A Sunday at the Pool in Kigali,* about a romance set against the brutal backdrop of the Rwandan genocide, and Yann Martel's magical novel *The Life of Pi,* the tale of a 16-year-old who find himself adrift in the Pacific Ocean with a 450-pound Bengal tiger, which won major acclaim and the Booker Prize in 2002.

Music

Unfortunately, Québec music is recognized internationally as being the domain of the overwrought, overly emotional, chest-thumping Celine Dion. Quebecers have a funny relationship with the diva, recognizing that she is unbelievably *quétaine* (tacky), but they are in other ways quite proud of the local girl done good.

Two legendary Québec musicians of the folk realm who made their mark in the 1950s and 1960s were Félix Leclerc, the king of the Québécois *chanson,* credited with reviving the province's folk genre, and Gilles Vigneault, who achieved major acclaim with his anthemic song *Mon pays,* a rallying cry for Québec nationalism. The late '60s and '70s also brought forth a mother lode of musicians, including the folk sisters Kate and Anna McGarrigle, rockers Michel Pagliaro and Robert Charlebois, with his legendary album *Québec Love,* the liter-

ate musings of Leonard Cohen, the harmony-driven Beau Dommage, the progressive rock of Harmonium, and who can forget Gino Vanelli with his 1978 *I Just Wanna Stop,* a guilty pleasure song for Montrealers.

In the 1980s, everyone was fawning over the pouty Corey Hart, Men Without Hats, who had their one-hit wonder with "Safety Dance," Luba, Mitsou, Villain Pingouin, The Box, and the late '80s and '90s ushered in the fresh rocking sounds of Jean Leloup, Les Colocs, Bran Van 3000, and Daniel Bélanger.

Recent releases have included a wealth of francophone artists, including Steffie Shock, Les Trois Accords, Les Cowboys Fringants, and Ariane Moffat, while anglophone music has been drawing particular attention. Sam Roberts, Stars, Simple Plan, the Dears, and particularly the critical darlings, the Arcade Fire, have been leading charges of Montréal's designation as the next big music scene.

Jazz performers have also had a strong influence in Montréal, including the city's most famous jazz musician, Oscar Peterson, the legendary pianist. Peterson grew up in the poor,

ECONOMUSEUMS

During your travels throughout the province you'll probably notice signs stating that the paper-making locale, cheese factory, or doll maker's shop that you're visiting is an economuseum. Created in 1992, the economuseum network consists of food and craft artisans who demonstrate a unique or traditional technique in creating their wares and combine their businesses with interpretation offerings like guided tours and explanatory panels.

There are 34 economuseums in Québec, from the Vignoble de L'Orpailleur winery in the Eastern Townships and the Papeterie Saint-Gilles in Charlevoix to the Artisans du Sable in les Îles de la Madeleine. You can get a complete list of all the places included in the network, along with descriptions of the goods and activities, by visiting the Economuseum Network at www.economusees.com.

working-class neighborhood of Saint-Henri and made his mark on the local jazz scene as a young teenager. One of Peterson's pupils was Oliver Jones, who used to hang out as a kid on Peterson's porch to listen to him play. Jones made a name for himself as well, recording many albums and regularly performing at the Festival International de Jazz de Montréal.

Visual Art

It would seem somewhat obvious that a population so dependent on the land and affected by the change of the seasons would produce some of the country's best landscape artists. Among them are Clarence Gagnon (1881–1942), known for his colorful, bright paintings of rural Charlevoix and Île d'Orléans and his illustrations of the novel *Maria Chapdeleine,* and the luminous landscapes of René Richard (1895–1982) and Marc-Aurèle Fortin (1888–1970). All three of these artists were drawn to the Charlevoix region to paint, making it one of the richest landscape representations in Québécois art.

Although Jean-Paul Lemieux (1905–1990) started his career as a landscape painter, his pieces became more abstract later on, typically showing well-dressed individuals or families set against expansive, minimalist backgrounds. One of Lemieux's closest friends was the abstract painter and sculptor Paul-Émile Borduas (1905–1960), one of the authors of the *Refus global* manifesto. Borduas also became leader of the *automatistes,* who believed that art should not be thought out but automatic and a liberation of the subconscious. One of the artists who signed Borduas's *Refus global* and who was a member of the *automatistes* was Jean-Paul Riopelle (1923–2002), commonly regarded as the father of Canadian contemporary art. Riopelle was most famous for his series of mosaics, which involved squeezing tubes of color onto huge canvases and shaping it with a palette knife.

ESSENTIALS
Getting There

BY AIR
Airports

Most travelers arriving by air will fly into **Montréal-Trudeau International Airport (YUL)** (514/394-7377 or 800/465-1213, www.admtl.com) in the western suburb of Dorval, about 20 km from downtown Montréal. Formerly known as Montréal-Dorval Airport, the airport was renamed for former Prime Minister Pierre Elliott Trudeau on January 1, 2004, a few years after he died.

Montréal-Trudeau is the province's biggest airport with more than 50 carriers, but it is in the process of expanding. To offset the cost of major renovations the terminal will under-take during the next few years, the airport has implemented a departure tax of $15, which is included in the price of your ticket.

Those wanting to fly directly to Québec City will arrive at the **Jean Lesage International Airport (YQB)** (418/640-2700, www.aeroportdeQuébec.com). This airport handles a substantially smaller number of domestic and international carriers and flights than Montréal. Air Canada and other Canadian charter companies do fly into smaller cities in Québec but most are handled by flights via Montréal.

Air Canada

Canada's national carrier, Air Canada (888/

247-2262, www.aircanada.ca) is one of the world's largest airlines with service to more than 150 destinations throughout the world. Air Canada has five new fare options that increase in price according to service and flexibility. For the lowest available fare, ask about Tango or Tango Plus. These tickets will have limited allowable changes, but they are the best value. Air Canada Jazz, Air Canada's regional airline, offers daily direct flights to Montréal and Québec City from cities across North America. Direct flights to Montréal are available from all major cities in Canada and from the following U.S. destinations: Boston, New York, Philadelphia, Washington, various Florida cities, Detroit, Las Vegas, San Francisco, and Los Angeles.

Travelers coming from Europe can fly directly to Montréal from London, Paris, and Frankfurt with other city connections throughout Europe. Air Canada also partners with other airlines throughout the world through Star Alliance.

From the South Pacific, Air Canada operates flights from Sydney and Auckland to Toronto via Los Angeles through its Star Alliance partnership with New Zealand Air. Asian travelers can fly Air Canada directly from Hong Kong, Tokyo, and Delhi to Toronto before continuing to Montréal. Other Asian cities such as Beijing, Shanghai, and Taipei have service to Montréal via Vancouver.

Air Canada continues to expand its service into Latin America. It offers flights routed through Toronto from more than 31 destinations in Latin America, including Brazil, Chile, Argentina, and now Venezuela, Columbia, and Peru. There are flights from Mexico City directly to Montréal.

Other Canadian Airlines

In the last couple of years a number of discount airlines have emerged, offering competitive fares. **CanJet** (800/809-7777, www.canjet.com), based in Halifax, services central and eastern Canadian cities and has expanded to the United States with flights from New York La Guardia and several Florida loca-

tions to Montréal. **WestJet** (888/937-8538, www.westjet.com), originally established as a low-cost airline serving western Canada, has expanded its operations to serve the rest of Canada, including Montréal. It also offers flights from certain U.S. cities including Los Angeles, Los Vegas, Phoenix, Fort Lauderdale, Orlando, and Tampa.

Air Transat (877/872-6728 from North America, 870/556-1522 in the United Kingdom, www.airtransat.com) is a Montréal-based, charter airline that offers a wide variety of seasonal flights to Montréal from Europe. With direct flights from cities in France, England, Belgium, Italy, and Greece and reasonably priced fares, Air Transat is worth looking into. The airline also offers twice-weekly flights to Québec City from Paris. Its website has last-minute deals.

U.S. Airlines

Montréal is served by the following U.S. airlines or their subsidiaries: **American Airlines** (800/433-7300, www.aa.com) has flights from Chicago, New York, and Miami, **Continental** (800/231-0856, www.continental.com) from New Jersey and Cleveland, **Delta Airlines** (800/361-1970, www.delta.com) from New York, Atlanta, and Cincinnati, **Northwest** (800/225-2525, www.nwa.com) from Detroit and Minneapolis, and **US Airways** (800/428-4322, www.usairways.com) from Philadelphia, Pittsburgh, and Charlotte.

Northwest and Continental are the only U.S. carriers that fly directly into Québec City. Both offer daily flights from Newark, New Jersey.

International Airlines

Montréal-Trudeau is well serviced by the major European airlines including: **Air France** (800/667-2747, www.airfrance.ca), **British Airways** (800/247-9297, www.britishairways.ca), **KLM** (800/225-2525, www.klm.com), **Lufthansa** (800/563-5954, www.lufthansa-ca.com), and **Swiss** (877/359-7947, www.swiss.com). These international airlines all offer a wide variety of direct flight options to Montréal from cities within the United Kingdom and continental Europe.

For those traveling from the South Pacific and Asian locations, Air Canada is typically the best bet. However, some international carriers that fly into the United States and other parts of Canada have established partnership alliances to offer connecting flights to such cities as Montréal. International carriers that provide this service are: **Japan Airlines** (888/525-3663, www.japanair.com), **New Zealand Air** (800/663-5494, www.airnz.com), and **Qantas** (800/227-4500, www.qantas.com).

From the Airports

Montréal-Trudeau Airport (YUL) (514/394-7337 or 800/465-1213, www.admtl.com) is 22 km west of downtown. Depending on the time of day, it will take you approximately 30 minutes to travel this distance (longer during rush hour). A taxi ride will cost about $31 and a limousine will be about $50.

If you prefer a more economical option, a shuttle service is offered by **L'Aerobus** (514/842-2281) to six downtown locations, including the Terminus Autobus, the bus station, and various hotels, including the Fairmont Queen Elizabeth, which is attached to the Gare Centrale, the train station. It leaves from Arrivals level every 20 minutes daily. The one-way cost is $13 for adults and $9.25 for children aged 5–12 years. You can buy tickets at the dispatch counter or from the bus driver directly.

Jean Lesage Airport (YQB) (418/640-2700, www.aeroportdeQuébec.com) is 19 km northwest of downtown Québec City. The only way to get there is by taxi, which will cost between $24 and $28.

If you're looking to rent a car, the following companies are at both airports: Alamo (800/327-9633, www.goalamo.com), Avis (800/321-3652, www.avis.com), Budget (800/268-8900, www.budgetmtl.com), Hertz (800/263-0678, www.hertz.com), National (800/387-4747, www.nationalcar.com), and Thrifty (800/367-2277, www.thrifty.com).

BY RAIL

If you have the time to spare, the train is an excellent alternative to flying. **VIA** (888/842-7245, www.viarail.ca), Canada's passenger-train service, links the country from coast to coast and has undergone major changes in recent years. Trains and schedules have been improved and more competitive pricing put into place. Montréal and Québec City as well as stops in between are accessible along the Windsor/Québec Corridor. This is VIA's most traveled line with many daily trains, including an overnight train between Toronto and Montréal.

Although it's long, nothing will give you a better sense of the country's landscape than the **Canadian,** a three-day journey that leaves three times a week from Vancouver, hitting Jasper, Edmonton, Saskatoon, Winnipeg, and Sudbury before finally pulling into Toronto. You can then hop another train for Montréal.

For those starting from points east, the **Ocean** links Halifax to Montréal. Visit the VIA website for the most up-to-date information on schedules and fares.

Special rates are available to all passengers if tickets are booked at least five business days in advance. However, these lower rates are limited to a number of seats per train. The earlier you book, the better chance you have of securing one. VIA also offers special student and senior rates on all seats as well as a number of promotional offers.

An excellent alternative if you are traveling a great distance and planning to make many stops is the **CanRail Pass.** This pass provides unlimited travel on the VIA Rail system for a period of 12 days within a 30-day period. The price of this pass depends on the season: for off-peak travel (mid-Oct.–June) an adult pass is $460 and student/child pass is $415. For high-season (June–mid-Oct.), it's $741 and $667.

Amtrak (800/872-7245, www.amtrak.com) offers a daily service to Montréal on the Adirondack line with service from New York City's Penn. It's a bit of a milk-run trip, taking about 10 hours, but it is a scenic one. Amtrak offers some discounts to students and seniors as well as special promotional offers that include a discount if the ticket is booked online.

Amtrak and VIA have joined to offer the **North American Pass,** which offers 30 consecutive travel days with unlimited stopovers. For off-peak travel (mid-Oct.–June.) an adult pass is $667 and student/child pass is $600. For high season (June–mid-Oct.), it's $941 and $846.

BY BUS

Greyhound (Canada 800/661-8747 or U.S. 800/231-2222, www.greyhound.ca) has more than 2,500 stops in North America and with partnering bus companies provides an extensive network from which to reach Québec. Arrive in Montréal from western Canada via Toronto or from the United States via Burlington, Vermont, which connects directly with New York and Boston. Discount fares are offered on a regular basis with special rates for children, students, and seniors. The bus ride from Toronto to Montréal takes about eight hours, as does Boston to Montréal, and from Washington 13 hours. Reservations are not required but it is recommended that travelers be at the bus station at least 45 minutes before departure.

Like the train, Greyhound and other participating bus companies offer a hop-on, hop-off tour option called the **Discovery Pass.** There are many variations of this pass and the cost is dependent on the number of days you choose to buy (anywhere from four to 60).

Another option is **Adirondack Trailways** (800/858-8555, www.trailwaysny.com), which has about seven daily departures from New York City to Montréal, and then there's **Rout-Pass** (514/842-2281, www.routpass.com), a bus company that runs from May to October only. This pass offers holders unlimited bus travel for seven, 14, or 18 consecutive days within Québec and Ontario. The 18-day pass is also good for travel to/from New York City.

BY BOAT

Québec can be reached by boat from within Canada via the Great Lakes, the Ottawa River, or the St. Lawrence River. Arriving from the United States, boaters can travel up the Hudson River through Lake Champlain, joining the St. Lawrence at Sorel, 80 km northeast of Montréal. Boaters requiring more information can buy navigational charts from Canada's Federal Publications. Visit www.fedpub.com, where you will find a link for Nautical Charts under Maps and Charts. Information on area marinas is best found at www.marinamap.com.

BY CAR

Many roads lead to Montréal. If you are coming from Toronto, there's the trusty 401, the 504-km highway that runs between the two cities, hitting Belleville, Kingston, Brockville, and Cornwall in between. The city is only 47 km away from the New York border, which is accessible from New York City via I-87. At the border the expressway links with Route 15, which will take you right into the city. The trip is 644 kilometers. The 500-km trip from Boston runs along I-91 to the border. It then picks up on Route 55, which in turn links into Route 10 though the Eastern Townships before heading into Montréal.

To get to Québec City, you can either get to Montréal and then take the fast, but bland, Route 20 or the slower but nicer Route 40. If you are coming from the east via New Brunswick, you can get to Québec City via Route 2 in the south or Route 11 in the north, which both join to Route 20. I-91 and 93 from Hartford and Boston also link up to Route 20 at Drummondville, about halfway between Montréal and Québec City. Route 201 from Portland, Maine, represents part of the Kennebec-Chaudière International Corridor, linking it directly with Canadian highways that head directly to Québec City. If you are traveling in the winter, check the road conditions by calling 418/648-7766.

You can also check on the wait times at several highway border crossings by visiting the **Canadian Border Services Agency** (877/226-7277, www.cbsa-asfc.gc.ca) website or the Québec government's **Inforoutière** (888/355-0511, www.inforoutiere.qc.ca).

Getting Around

Trains, planes, and automobiles are the options for exploring Québec, while the more adventurous may opt to cycle through some of Québec's most scenic rural landscapes along **La Route Verte.**

BY AIR

Air Canada's regional carrier is **Air Canada Jazz** (888/247-2262, www.aircanada.ca), which has service throughout the entire province, including numerous direct flights to and from Montréal and Québec City daily, including places such as Gaspé and les Îles de la Madeliene. These flights are booked through Air Canada's website. If there is a Jazz option available, you'll see it in the flight results. The earlier you book the more likely you'll be able to secure a Tango fare, which are the cheapest seats on any Air Canada flight. **Pascan Aviation** (450/443-0500 or 888/313-8777, www.pascan.com) offers charter service Monday to Friday from both Montréal and Québec City to airports in Bonaventure and les Îles de la Madeleine. Tickets don't come cheap, though. Expect to pay more than $900 for a return flight to les Îles from Montréal.

BY TRAIN

VIA (888/842-7245, www.viarail.ca) is a great way to make your way through much of the province. It travels regularly between Montréal and Québec City and the fares are reasonable, especially if you book five days in advance (about $90). You can also head farther east aboard VIA's **Chaleur** train, which runs between Montréal all the way to Gaspé three times a week, passing through the villages of Charny just outside Québec City, Rivière-de-Loup, and Percé. Leaving Montréal in the evening, the train travels along the south shore of the St. Lawrence, arriving in Gaspé the next morning. It's about 18 hours and costs about $102 one-way.

BY CAR

Québec has a major network of roads crisscrossing the entire province. Despite what people from neighboring Ontario will tell you, Québec drivers really aren't that bad. Watch out for the occasional speed demon, however.

Québec's Official Road Map provides a compete overview of the highway and road system. You can order a free copy by calling the tourism department at 877-BONJOUR (877/266-5687) or by downloading the map online at www.bonjourquebec.com under the Road Map section. Look for the blue tourist signs on all major roads and highways, as they indicate the name of the region that you're in and provide directions to attractions and services. Distances and speeds are posted in kilometers. The maximum speed limit on major highways is 100 kph (60 mph) and remember, once you cross any bridge onto the island of Montréal, there will be no turning right on a red light for you!

© JENNIFER EDWARDS

When the stairs just won't do, hitch a ride on the Funicular.

DISTANCE IN QUÉBEC

Chart in kilometers (to convert to miles multiply by 0.6)

	H	MT	M	S	Q	T	R	G	I*
Hull	-	149	207	347	451	670	633	1124	1345
Mont Tremblant	149	-	131	276	369	584	556	1045	1268
Montréal	207	131	-	147	253	468	432	930	1144
Sherbrooke	347	276	147	-	240	428	392	915	1104
Québec City	451	369	253	240	-	220	205	700	917
Tadoussac	670	584	468	428	220	-	115	515	772
Rivière-du-Loup	633	556	432	392	205	115	-	491	727
Gaspé	1124	1045	930	915	700	515	491	-	827
Iles de la Madeleine*	1345	1268	1144	1104	917	772	727	827	-

* This takes into consideration the distance on the road network only. Add 147 km for the distance traveled by ferry.

If you want to calculate a distance to or from another destination within Québec, visit the Inforoutière website at www.inforoutiere.qc.ca, and click on Road Information. Once there, you'll see a link entitled Distance Between Cities.

BY BUS

A few bus companies travel throughout the province. The granddaddy, **Greyhound** (Canada 800/661-8747 or U.S. 800/231-2222, www.greyhound.ca) provides service between Ottawa and Montréal and throughout the region. Smaller bus companies include **Orléans Express** (888/999-3977, www.orleansexpress.com), which provides service between Montréal and Québec City as well as to the Bas-Saint-Laurent and the Gaspé Peninsula. To reach the Charlevoix region and the Saguenay, try **Intercar** (418/627-9108 or 888/861-4592, www.intercar.qc.ca). **Limocar** (514/842-2281, www.limocar.ca) will take you from Montréal to the Eastern Townships with stops in Granby, Magog, and Sherbrooke. And **Autobus Galland** (514/842-2281, www.galland-bus.com) runs from Montréal to Saint-Sauveur, Sainte-Adèle, Sainte-Agathe, Saint-Jovite, and Mont-Tremblant.

The Moose Travel Network (888/816-6673, www.moosenetwork.com) bills itself as the bus for backpackers. Offering a jump-on, jump-off service, the bus company offers a number of tours within Québec from May to October. The *Loonie Pass,* from $239 per person, provides travelers with a four- to five-day trip from Montréal to Québec City, continuing to Tadoussac. Its *Big East Pass* is a nine-day tour starting from Toronto and heading to Québec City and then returning via more northern spots such as Mont-Tremblant, Ottawa, Fort Coulonge, and Madawaska in Algonquin Park before returning to Toronto. Prices start at $479.

BY BOAT

Most of the ferry crossings in the province are operated by the Québec government under a department called **Société des Traversiers du Québec** (877/787-7483, www.traversiers .gouv.qc.ca), including the little Lévis to Québec

City ferry, Saint-Joseph-de-la-Rive to Isle-aux-Coudres, the Rivière-du-Loup to Saint-Siméon ferry, Baie-Sainte-Catherine to Tadoussac, and the pip-squeak ferry between Île d'Entrée and Cap-aux-Meules in les Îles de la Madeleine.

Private ferries and boat tours also chug through the province. Two of the biggest operators are **Les Croisières AML** (800/563-4643, www.croisie-resaml.com) and **Croisières Famille Dufour** (800/463-5250, www.groupedufour.com). AML offers sightseeing tours around Montréal and Québec City and whale-watching and Saguenay Fjord tours near Tadoussac. Dufour offers similar tours around Québec City, whale-watching tours, and tours to historic Grosse-Île, near Île d'Orléans, and a Montréal to Québec City tour that you either can take one-way or return the next day. The trip starts in Montréal at 7:30 A.M. and arrives in Québec City 6.5 hours later at 2 P.M.

The small cruise ship **CTMA Vacancier's** (888/986-3278, www.ctma.ca) has seven-day cruises running from May to October from Montréal all the way up the St. Lawrence to les Îles de la Madeleine. Passengers have close to three full days to visit the islands before the ship returns to Montréal. The cost varies depending on the type of cabin and meal plan selected.

BY BICYCLE

La Route Verte (800/567-8356, www.route-verte.com) is Québec's great cycling network of roads. It is already extensive, but once it's completed, it will stretch across 4,279 kilometers and will rival the great cycling routes from around the world. Run by the cycling association Vélo Québec, La Route Verte consists of more than 3,000 kilometers. The routes use a variety of courses, including paved highway shoulders, designated roadways, and actual bike paths.

La Route Verte is well marked with signs that are often accompanied by route information and tourist signs highlighting nearby services or attractions. Québec has many services available specifically to accommodate cyclists. You can get a Carte Vélo (cycling map) at most tourist offices or by visiting the Route Verte website.

Vélo Québec (800/567-8356, www.velo.qc.ca) itself offers an extensive variety of bike tours for all fitness levels throughout the province. Its jaunts through the province include the Eastern Townships, Charlevoix, and longer trips to the Bas-Saint-Laurent and along the Gaspé Peninsula.

Visas and Officialdom

ENTRY FOR U.S. CITIZENS

Citizens and most permanent residents of the United States may enter Canada with a birth, baptismal, or voter-registration certificate. Naturalized citizens should carry a naturalization certificate, U.S. passport, or other citizenship evidence. Proof of residence may also be required; check with the nearest Canadian Consulate General office. A passport is the easiest such proof and will speed re-entry into the United States. As of January 1, 2007, a passport will be required by U.S. citizens re-entering the United States via land borders. At press time, the U.S. government was developing alternatives to the traditional passport. For further information, see the website http://travel.state.gov/travel. For current entry requirements to Canada, check the Citizenship and Immigration Canada website (www.cic.gc.ca).

OTHER VISITORS

All other foreign visitors must have at least a valid passport. Some countries require a Temporary Resident Visa. Citizens of the United States, British Commonwealth, or Western Europe are exempt. To determine if you require a visa to enter Canada, visit the Citizenship and Immigration website at www.cic.gc.ca or contact the local Canadian embassy in your home country directly. To apply for a Temporary Resident Visa fill out the application online. It is very important to note that this visa must be obtained before your arrival in Canada.

EMPLOYMENT AND STUDY

In most cases you will need a valid work permit to earn money in Canada. You can obtain one only after you have a job offer from an employer, Human Resources and Skills Development Canada approves the position, and you fill out an Application for Work permit, available on the Citizenship and Immigration website (www.cic.gc.ca). This permit must be obtained before entering the country.

If you are coming to Canada for study and plan on doing so for longer than six months, you may also require a permit. Contact a Canadian embassy or consulate in your home country and ask for the pamphlet called Entering Canada to Study or to Work (RC4220) or visit the Citizenship and Immigration website for the online application.

CUSTOMS

Canada's customs are handled through the **Canadian Border Services Agency** (877/226-7277, www.cbsa-asfc.gc.ca), a newly established branch of the Canadian government since 9/11. Visitors can bring certain goods into Canada for their personal use during their stay. If these goods are declared upon arrival and taken back, no duties or taxes will need to be paid.

In terms of **alcohol and tobacco,** travelers arriving in Québec who are older than 18, the age of majority in the province, are allowed to bring in the following items without having to pay duty and taxes into Canada: 1.5 liters of wine or 1.14 liters of liquor or 8.5 liters of cans or bottles of beer or ale; in terms of tobacco, up to 200 cigarettes, 50 cigars, 200 grams of tobacco, and 200 tobacco sticks.

Dogs and cats from the United States are welcome as long as they are accompanied by a veterinary certificate stating that they have received a rabies vaccination within the last three years. Contact the Canadian Food Inspection Agency if you plan to bring other kinds of pets

from the United States, or if you are bringing any type of animal from another country, contact the **Canadian Border Services Agency** (877/226-7277, www.cbsa-asfc.gc.ca).

If you are bringing any food or plants into the country, your best bet is to declare it at customs to make sure that what you have with you is allowed. The regulations are somewhat confusing: Fresh veggies are generally allowed, while root crops are regulated. Coffee, teas, herbs, and spices are fine and so are all fish and seafood, except puffer fish and any from China. Any wood products and carvings must be stripped of bark and free of insects. Have a look at the Canadian Food Inspection Agency website (www.inspection.gc.ca) or call the Automated Customs Information Services at 800/461-9999 for further information before you travel.

CONDUCT AND CUSTOMS

Etiquette in Québec closely follows that of the rest of Canada and resembles the same general conduct principles as in the United States. People are generally a little bit more left-leaning here and have a live-and-let-live attitude.

Terms of Address

Although you will probably find that most Quebecers will respond to you in English even if you attempt to speak to them in French, making the effort will be much appreciated. Quebecers, on the whole, are a welcoming people who like to see foreigners appreciating their province... and especially their language.

When addressing someone you do not know, except for a child, always use the *vous* pronoun, which is a sign of respect. You can switch to using *tu* when you get to know them better or by asking them if you can address them that way. Chances are they won't have a problem with it and will be happy that you want to have less formal dealings.

All men can be addressed as Monsieur. It gets a bit trickier when addressing women. In theory, a woman who is married is Madame and one who isn't is Mademoiselle, although this of course gets blurred when you do not know the marital status of the person. So, the rule generally is to use Madame for someone who appears older than 25 years old. Unfortunately, there is no common form of address such as Ms. Another thing to note is that women in Québec do not change their surname when they get married. The law actually states that women keep their names.

Tips for Travelers

GAY AND LESBIAN TRAVELERS

Québec, especially its cities, is a gay-friendly place. Montréal's "The Village" is a vibrant tourist destination for gays and lesbians worldwide. The area covers a distance of two km, focused around Beaudry metro stop. Boundaries extend from rue Saint-Denis in the west to avenue Papineau in the east and rue Sherbrooke in the north to boulevard René-Lévesque in the south.

In existence for more than 30 years now, Montréal's gay village is home to more than 100 gay establishments, including trendy clothing stores, upscale restaurants, B&Bs, bars, nightclubs, and even saunas. Many gay and lesbian visitors descend upon the city during the renowned seven-day Divers/Cité festival every summer. The event kicks off with the Pride Parade, which runs along boulevard René-Lévesque, and continues with a multitude of shows and dance parties.

Québec City has a much smaller gay community, which tends to focus on the Quartier Saint-Jean-Baptiste, just outside the walls. The annual Gay Pride festival, called La Fête Arc-en-Ciel, happens there on a weekend in early September.

SENIOR TRAVELERS

Seniors will be well accommodated in Québec even though it is not a destination that specifically caters to them. Most museums and other attractions do have special rates for seniors; expect to prove that you're of age (55 years and older) in order to qualify for the price break.

TRAVELERS WITH DISABILITIES

On average, you'll find that Québec has the same mobility access as the rest of North America, with sloping sidewalks, wheelchair ramps, and special-access elevators. **Kéroul** (514/252-3104, www.keroul.qc.ca) is an organization that works with the Québec government to make tourist attractions more accessible to people with limited mobility. It keeps an online database of accessible facilities across the province for travelers with disabilities and publishes the data in a guidebook that it sells for $15.

Health and Safety

Canada, including Québec, is a safe place to live and visit. Crime is relatively low, it's generally safe to walk the streets at night, and you shouldn't get any major illnesses from eating what's on your plate. Although once in a blue moon people can get a bout of food poisoning, this is very rare.

BEFORE YOU GO
Insurance

Before leaving home, ensure that your current health-insurance plan covers both medical and hospital costs for incidents that may occur during your visit to Québec. If it doesn't, it is recommended that you seek medical coverage from a private company that provides overseas medical coverage to travelers before arriving in the province. Find a travel medical insurance company that provides Canadian coverage online or by calling a local travel agent. The insurance will provide you 24-hour telephone assistance. In either case, it is important to verify whether you will be expected to pay the bill up front or whether the insurance company will look after payment immediately.

Prescription Drugs

Be sure to bring enough prescription drugs with you. It has become very common in the last few years for Americans to buy less-expensive prescription drugs when visiting Canada; however, new rules now require a Québec doctor's prescription before purchase. Make sure all the prescription drugs that you carry with you are clearly labeled and in their original containers.

WHILE THERE

Should you need to visit a doctor while you are in Québec, a local phone book or the front desk at your hotel will be able to direct you to the nearest health clinic, called a **CLSC**, or doctor's office. Larger cities are equipped with CLSCs that welcome walk-in patients and provide reliable medical attention. Hospital emergency rooms should be avoided if possible because of long lines. However, if you have an emergency, dial "911" anywhere in Québec.

Mosquitoes

Those planning to camp while in Québec should be aware of the newest virus to hit North America, the West Nile virus. This virus is transmitted through mosquitoes who catch it from infected birds and transmit it to humans through bites. Although the risk of contracting the illness is extremely low, it is important to protect yourself during mosquito season (May–October). Use insect repellent and avoid dense mosquito areas from dusk till dawn, when they are most active. If you know you will be traveling through heavily wooded areas, wear mosquito netting, long sleeves, and long pants.

Wild Animals

If you are driving anywhere outside the city, especially in or near wooded areas, you should beware of deer and moose crossings, especially at dusk or dawn when visibility is low. Watch for warning signs that will indicate a known crossing and if you should spot an animal at the side of the road, make sure you slow down until you pass it as animals will sometimes bolt suddenly.

Crime

Canada is a safe place to visit. In fact, the province of Québec has one of the lowest crime rates in North America. However, as in most tourist destinations, large cities and main attractions can attract pickpockets and petty thieves. Be conscious of your wallet and purse and refrain from carrying large amounts of cash. Plane tickets and passports can be placed in hotel security boxes for extra peace of mind. Remember to lock your car doors and conceal any purchases in the trunk of the car.

WINTER TRAVEL CONSIDERATIONS

Yes, winters in Québec are cold... some would even say freezing. If you are dressed properly and take precautions, though, you shouldn't have any problems, except for the odd red nose.

Winter Driving

Sleet, ice, freezing rain, and heavy snow—oh, the joys of winter driving in Québec. Although some days can be smooth and worry-free, there are plenty of times when the roads can get treacherous. The first thing to do before heading out is to call **Inforoutière** at 888/355-0511 or visit www.inforoutiere.qc.ca to get the day's road conditions. Make sure that your car has snow tires, extra windshield washer fluid, a snowbrush, and scraper. If the weather is bad, sit out the storm.

Hypothermia

Hypothermia sets in when the body loses heat faster then it generates it. If you notice someone start to shiver, bring him or her inside to warm up. When the body's core temperature to drop, it provokes a series of symptoms including shivering, blue lips, mumbling, lethargy, and if untreated, slowed respiration and heartbeat and, ultimately, death.

Remember that 30 percent of heat loss occurs through the head and neck, so wear a hat and scarf if you are outside for long periods. Avoid contact with cold surfaces (e.g., sitting on the ground) and remember that the key to keeping warm is keeping dry. Wool is a good choice of clothing as it will insulate even if wet. Synthetic fibers such as microfleece will help to wick away moisture and when coupled with a GoreTex shell, provide one of the best protections. Dress in layers so that items can be removed during periods of physical activity.

Frostbite

It begins as a numbness, tingling, or pain experienced somewhere on your body that has not been properly protected from the cold. Extremities such as hands, feet, nose, and ears are particularly vulnerable and when exposed to severe cold will turn from red to white. Immediately get out of the cold and cover the affected area. Never rub the skin because this will further aggravate it.

Information and Services

MONEY
Currency

Canadian currency comes in dollars and cents, with 100 cents equal to one dollar. Dollar bills come in denominations of five, 10, 20, 50, and 100 notes. It is best to carry smaller notes as $50 and $100 bills are not always accepted, especially at local stores or cafés. Coins come in denominations of one, five, 10, and 25 cents, and $1 and $2. The $1 gold-colored coin is known as the loonie because of the picture of the Canadian loon on one side. The $2 coin, which was released a few years later, immediately became known as the toonie. It is silver with a gold-colored center.

Credit Cards and ATMs

Major credit cards such as Visa, MasterCard, American Express, and Diners Club are accepted in most places, while travelers checks can be cashed at foreign-exchange offices or banks and in some hotels, stores, and restaurants in major cities. Banks generally offer the best exchange rate. American dollars can be used in major tourist areas throughout Québec, but this does not guarantee a favorable rate.

Once you arrive in Québec, the most convenient way to obtain Canadian dollars is by using your ATM bank card. A network of automatic banking machines is available throughout the province, with most linked to Interac, Cirrus, or Plus System banking systems.

Taxes

You can't escape taxes when traveling in Canada, and Québec is no exception. Expect to pay tax—7 percent federal tax known as the Goods and Services Tax (GST, TPS in French) and 7.5 percent Québec Sales Tax (QST, TVQ in French)—on most goods and services. These taxes will appear on your receipt after you make a purchase and not on the original price tag. They are cumulative so it is important to remember that they will be added to most purchases, including meals and accommodation. In addition, most regions in Québec (except the Laurentians) charge a Québec lodging tax of $2 per night on all accommodations, with the exception of stays longer than 31 days and campsite rentals.

Those traveling to Québec from outside Canada may be entitled to a GST rebate on goods you are taking home with you and on the price of accommodation. To qualify for a refund, each receipt must amount to at least CAN$50 before taxes, with a total purchase amount with all receipts added of at least CAN$200. If you are leaving Canada via one of the Canada-U.S. borders, you can claim your GST cash rebate at the duty-free shop; otherwise your rebate will be sent to you in the form of a check. Those leaving from any international airport in Canada will need to have their receipts stamped and verified by the customs clerks on hand. Attach these receipts to your completed *Tax Refund for Visitors* booklet, available at most hotels, large retail stores, tourist information centers, and airports, or by contacting **Revenue Canada** directly at 800/959-2221 from within Canada and the United States or www.ccra.gc.ca/visitors.

Be sure to ask for the official Tax Refund booklet published by the Government of Canada and not one produced by a private company. This will ensure that no mysterious "processing fee" gets deducted from your claim.

Costs

The cost of living in Québec is generally higher than in the United States. The cost per day of your stay will, of course, depend on how well you like to treat yourself when you travel. If you plan to camp or stay at hostels and to prepare most of your own food, you should be able to get by on less than $50 per day. Québec is graced with many affordable inns *(auberges)* and B&B's *(gîtes),* similar to what you would find in Europe but without the exorbitant costs. Meals at smaller family-run restaurants are reasonably priced and it is not uncommon to enjoy a good table d'hôte (three-course meal) for $15–25 per person. Gasoline prices in Québec are much higher than what you would pay in the United States but are cheaper than in European countries. In Québec, gas is sold in liters (3.79 liters equals one U.S. gallon) and the cost has jumped in recent years, fluctuating between $0.90 cents to $1 a liter for regular unleaded. This amount climbs the farther you travel away from the major cities.

Tipping

Tipping charges are not usually added to your bill, unless you are dining in a large group. For meals, a haircut, or a taxi ride, 15 percent of the bill (before taxes) is a normal gratuity. If you want help figuring out the 15 percent, simply add the two taxes (GST and QST). In a bar, a $0.50 tip per drink is standard and bellhops and porters generally receive $1 per item.

MAPS AND TOURIST INFORMATION
Maps

MapArt (www.mapart.com) and **Cartotek Géo** (www.cartotekgeo.com) are the most detailed maps available for the entire province, the regions, or for the province's major cities. You can buy them for for a reasonable price at most grocery stores, pharmacies, or gas stations throughout Québec. To receive a free copy of *Québec's Official Road Map,* call Québec's tourism board at 877/BONJOUR (877/266-5687).

Tourism Information

You can reach the provincial tourism office by calling 877/BONJOUR (877/266-5687) or by visiting its website at www.bonjourquebec.com. For more specific trip planning, contact or visit the regional tourism offices: Montréal (www.tourism-montreal.org), Outaouais (www.tourisme-outaouais.ca), Laurentians (www.laurentides.com), Eastern Townships (www.tourismecantons.qc.ca), Québec City (www.quebecregion.com), Charlevoix (www.tourisme-charlevoix.com), Gaspé (www.tourisme-gaspesie.com), Îles de la Madeleine (www.tourismeilesdelamadeleine.com).

COMMUNICATIONS
Postal Services

Canada Post (www.canadapost.ca) is the government agency that presides over the Canadian postal service. The only way to mail anything from Québec or Canada is to buy Canadian stamps. Despite popular belief, U.S. stamps won't work here. Postcards and letters mailed within Canada cost $0.52. They cost $0.90 to the United States and $1.50 to any other international destination accessible by plane. Prices increase if the envelope is heavier than 30 grams. You can buy stamps at post offices, most front desks at hotels, some grocery stores, pharmacies, airports, and train stations. You'll spot the red mailboxes on many street corners in cities and in the downtown core of smaller towns.

Telephones

The area code for the island of Montréal is 514, although starting in June 2006, that area code was to be supplemented with a 438 area code, requiring that all 10 digits be dialed whenever making a local call. The areas surrounding Montréal have their own 450 code. Outside this main urban area, the rest of the western part of the province uses 819. Québec City and the regions to the east all share the 418 area code. These prefixes must be used when dialing long-distance calls, including those made within the province, and must begin with 1, the country code for Canada. For an overseas call, dial 011 plus country code plus area code plus local number. Phone numbers with 800, 866, 877, and 888 codes are toll-free within Canada and often the United States.

Public phones cost $0.25 for an unlimited length (or until someone waiting kicks you off). They all take small change and $1 coins. They do not, however, return change. Long-distance calls start at an outrageous $2.50 per minute. Your best bet is to buy an international prepaid phone card such as Gold from a convenience store; it will allow you to call home anywhere in the world for substantially less money. Do a little research when selecting a phone card, as some apply an extra fee every time you make a call.

Internet

In Québec, Internet access is commonly available at most hotels and hostels, although the more rural the location the more likely you'll be able to find it only at the larger hotels… if at all. Both Montréal and Québec City have a number of Internet cafés.

Newspapers and Magazines

For the most part, local newspapers in Québec are in French. The exception is Montréal, which has an English-language newspaper covering local, national, and international news called *The Gazette*. It also has two English entertainment weeklies, *The Mirror* and *Hour,* which can be found on street corners and various establishments as of Thursday of every week. Both papers offer information on movies, music, dance, and art happenings throughout the city. All of these, along with Canada's two national dailies, *The Globe and Mail* and the *National Post,* should be available at newsstands in the city and bookshops in larger centers across the province.

Smaller English-language papers include Sherbrooke's *The Record,* Stanstead's *Stanstead Journal,* and Québec City's *Québec Chronicle-Telegraph.* If you can read French, have a look though *La Presse,* the province's biggest French-language paper, *Le Devoir,* the more intellectual daily, or *Le Journal de Montréal* or *Le Journal de Québec,* the sensationalist ones. *Voir* (available in both Montréal and Québec City) and *Ici* (Montréal) are the French entertainment weeklies.

Two good English-language magazines are *Maisonneuve,* a cultural/literary magazine written and produced in Montréal, and *Québec: Lifestyle and Travel Magazine,* a translation of the original French version, which includes compelling travel, historical, and cultural information about various locations throughout the province.

Radio and TV

There are a number of English-language radio stations in Montréal, including CHOM 97.7 for classic rock, MIX 96 for pop tunes, CKUT 90.3, the eclectic McGill University radio station, and Q92 for everything that's light and breezy. On the AM band are CJAD 800, the talk-radio station, and The Team 990, the sports channel.

You can listen to or watch the CBC (www.cbc.ca) and the French-language Radio-Canada (www.radio-canada.ca) throughout the province. All the big American stations will be picked up at most hotels in Montréal and Québec City, but for English-language local (Montréal) news, turn to CTV, CBC, or Global. All three have nightly newscasts.

WEIGHTS AND MEASURES
The Metric System
Although Canada converted to the metric system 20 years ago, it is still not uncommon to hear mention of pounds, ounces, acres, and miles. Road signs are all in kilometers, though (multiply by 0.6 to get the equivalent in miles), and gas is sold by the liter (one American gallon equals 3.8 liters, and one Canadian gallon equals 4.5 liters).

Time and Time Zones
Time in Québec is told on the 24-hour system, so that 7 A.M. reads 7 h (*sept heures*) and 7 P.M. reads 19 h (*dix-neuf heures*). The rule is that after noon, you simply add 12, so that 1 P.M. becomes 13 h, 6 P.M. becomes 18 h, and so on. When speaking casually, however, and there is no mistaking the time of day you are referring to, you are welcome to use the 12-hour system.

All of Québec lies within the Eastern time zone, save for les Îles de la Madeleine, which fall within the Atlantic time zone, one hour ahead of the rest of the province.

Electricity
Voltage (110 volts) is consistent throughout Canada and is the same as in the United States. The frequency of electrical current is 60 Hz. People visiting from other countries can buy adapters in travel stores and department stores.

RESOURCES

Glossary

amuse-gueules appetizers
auberges inns
autoroute expressway
banh mi sandwich pork or chicken topped with veggies on a baguette
bière beer
boîte à chansons sing-along bars
branché in the know
BYOW bring your own wine
cabane-à-sucre sugar shack
cabourettes horse-drawn wagons
caisse populaires credit unions
carte map or menu when in a restaurant
calèches horse-drawn carriages
canard duck
carré public square
chemin road
5 à 7 happy hour
cipaille de grand-mère meat pie with pheasant, rabbit, caribou, veal, and pork
croque-canard toasted baguette with duck and melted cheese.
croque-monsieur toasted baguette with ham and melted cheese.
dépanneur corner store
duc duke
est east
été summer
FLQ Front de Libération du Québec
fougasse flat bread topped with herbs
fresque fresco
friperies second-hand stores
frites fries
fromage cheese
gîtes B&Bs

joual Québécois slang
la tire hot maple taffy poured over snow and wound around a popsicle stick
loups marin seals
marché market
metro subway
morceau piece
moules mussels
mow the part of a barn where hay or straw is stored
nautique nautical, relating to water
n'est-ce pas? don't you think?
nord north
ouest west
pétanque French version of the game bocce
pain bread
pavillon pavilion
place public square
pont bridge
potage soup
poutine fries topped with gravy and cheese curds
quétaine tacky
quai quay, wharf
rue street
séjour vacation, a stay
sûreté police
saison estival summer season
seigneuries long parcels of land distributed to colonists by the intendant of the King of France
seigneurs land owners
steamie a steamed hot dog
sud south
table d'hôte fixed-price meal with a set number of courses

tam-tams Sunday congregation of bongo players and dancers at Parc Mont-Royal
tonkinoises Tonkinese
tour tower

tourtière meat pie
viande meat
vieux old
voie route or lane

Phrasebook

Québec's French grew apart from the French from France in a way that is similar to American English's diversion from British English. Québec's written French is essentially the same as the French from France, but spoken French in Québec is where things get a bit more complex and colorful.

Although Quebecers are now increasingly mindful of their *anglicismes,* the influence of English in definitely present. For instance, you'll hear Quebecers present themselves by saying *"Mon nom est... ,"* which is a direct translation of "My name is... " while the French would say *"Je m'appelle... "* (which is like "I am called... ").

PRONUNCIATION GUIDE

French isn't the easiest language to pronounce, but it certainly isn't the toughest. The trickiest part about pronouncing French words is learning which letters are silent and which ones to utter with gusto. Accented letters are easy once you get the hang of them. But then there's also that pesky rolling "r" to contend with.

Consonants

c as in **car** before a, o, or u *(café);* like **s** before e, i, or y *(cinema)*
ç the little squiggly line at the bottom (called the cedilla) always denotes an **s** sound *(garçon)*
ch always like **sh** *(chemin)*
g as in **garden** before a, o, or u *(garde robe);* like the **s** in **decision** before e, I, or y *(gentile)*
h always silent *(hotel)*
j like the **s** in **decision** *(jus)*
qu always like **k** *(quatre)*
r strong and rolled *(rouler)*

s like a **z** between vowels *(chemise;)* silent at the end of words *(à propos)*
th always like a simple **t** *(theater)*
x silent at the end of words *(voix)*
y on its own like **ee** *(on y va);* in the word **yeux** like **z;** then a regular **y**

Vowels

a usually as in **that** *(bateau)*
â as in **car** *(pâté)*
ai like **e** in **red** when at the beginning or within words *(aider);* like **a** in **make** when on its own or at the end of words *(quai)*
au/eau like **o** *(gateau)*
e as in **bet** before two or more consonants *(miette);* like the long **a** in **able** when before an **r** at the end of a word *(marcher);* silent at the end of words *(pomme)*
é like the **a** in **take** *(rosé)*
è like the first **e** in **element** *(près)*
ei as in **bet** *(reine)*
eil like the **a** in **rate** *(orteil)*
eu like the **e** in **perky** *(heur)*
euil, ueil same as above, but followed by a **y** as in **yellow** *(écureuil)*
i sometimes like **ee** in **meet** *(vitrine);* sometimes like **i** in **interest** *(ouvrir)*
o sometimes like **o** in **glove** *(comme);* sometimes like **o** in **home** *(numéro)*
ô like **o** in **home** *(hotel)*
oi like **w** in **water** *(oiseau)*
ou like **ew** in **dew** *(genou)*
u like **uh,** but with pursed lips *(mur)*
ui like **we** *(nuit)*

BASIC AND COURTEOUS EXPRESSIONS

Generally Quebecers are very courteous in their business and everyday speech, opting for a more formal tone. After a basic transaction in a store, most people will wish each other a good day *(Bonne journée).*

Hello. *Bonjour.*
Hi. *Salut.*
Good morning. *Bonne journée. (all day)*
Good evening. *Bonsoir. (after 6pm)*
Good night. *Bonne nuit.*
How are you? *Comment ça va? (familiar)/ Comment allez-vous? (formal)*
I'm fine./Fine. *Je vais bien./Ça va.*
I'm doing well, thank you. *Ça va bien, merci.*
Not well. *Ça ne va pas bien.*
Not bad. *Pas mal.*
So-so. *Comme ci, comme ça.*
please *s'il vous plaît*
Thank you. *Merci.*
Thank you very much. *Merci beaucoup.*
You're welcome. *De rien.*
yes *oui*
no *non*
OK *d'accord*
and/or *et/ou*
Excuse me. *Excusez-moi.*
Pardon me. *Pardon.*
I'm sorry. *Je suis désolé(e).*
Goodbye. *Au revoir.*
See you tomorrow. *À demain.*
See you later. *À tout à l'heure.*
I speak a little bit of French. *Je parle un peu de français.*
Do you speak English? *Parlez-vous anglais?*
What does... mean? *Que veut-dire... ?*
How do you say... in French? *Comment dit-on... en français?*
Repeat, please. *Répétez, s'il vous plaît.*
I don't understand. *Je ne comprends pas.*
I don't know. *Je ne sais pas.*
Where is the bathroom? *Où sont les toilettes?*

TERMS OF ADDRESS

Always start with the more formal "vous" when addressing someone in the third person except when it's a child.

I *je*
you *tu (familiar)/vous (formal and plural)*
he/him *il*
she/her *elle*
we/us *nous*
they/them *ils (masculine)/elles (feminine)*
Sir, Mr. *Monsieur (M)*
Madam, Mrs. *Madame (Mme)*
Miss *Mademoiselle (Mlle)*
friend *ami(e)*

TRANSPORTATION

Where is... ? *Où se trouve... ?/Où est... ?*
How far is it to... ? *À quelle distance se trouve... ?*
From... to... *De... à/au...*
I would like to buy a ticket to... *Je voudrais acheter un billet pour...*
I want to get off at... *Je veux descendre à...*
Here, please. *Ici, merci.*
Where is this bus going? *Cet autobus va où?*
information *les renseignements*
subway *le métro*
subway stop *station de métro*
bus stop *arrêt d'autobus*
airport *l'aéroport*
train station *la gare*
ferry terminal *gare du traversier*
prix/prices *le prix/les tarifs*
ticket *le billet*
round-trip ticket *un billet aller-retour*
one-way ticket *un billet simple*
map *une carte*
downtown *centre-ville*
highway *l'autoroute*
road/street *la rue*
kilometer/mile *kilomètre/mille*
straight ahead *tout droit*
to the right *à droite*
to the left *à gauche*
beside *à côté*
right here *juste ici*
address *l'adresse*
luggage *valises*
north *nord*
south *sud*
east *est*
west *ouest*

ACCOMMODATIONS

hotel *hôtel*
inn *auberge*

B&B *gîte*
I would like a room... *Je voudrais une chambre...*
for one night/two nights *pour une nuit/ deux nuits*
for one person *pour une personne*
for two people *pour deux personnes*
What is the rate? *Quel est le prix de la chamber?*
1st floor *le rez-de-chausée*
2nd floor *le premier étage (known as the 1st floor in Québec)*
key *la clef*
bathroom *la toilette*
shower *la douche*
bath *le bain*
manager *gérant(e)*
bath *le bain*
towel *la serviette*
soap *le savon*
toilet paper *le papier de toilette*
blanket *une couverture*
air-conditioning *air climalisé*
no vacancy *complet*

FOOD

I'm hungy. *J'ai faim.*
I'm thirsty. *J'ai soif.*
I would like... *Je voudrais...*
breakfast *petit déjeuner*
lunch *dîner*
dinner *souper*
menu *la carte*
fixed-price meal *le menu*
happy hour *5 à 7*
glass *un verre*
fork *une fourchette*
spoon *une cuillère*
knife *un couteau*
napkin *une serviette*
drinks *les breuvages*
water *l'eau*
bottled water *eau embouteillée*
soft drink *liqueur douce*
juice *le jus*
beer *la bière*
wine *le vin*
coffee *le café*

tea *le thé*
mlik *le lait*
cream *la crême*
sugar *le sucre*
eggs *les œufs*
bread *le pain*
butter *le beurre*
jam *la confiture*
pancakes *les crêpes*
steak *le bifteck*
chicken *le poulet*
snails *les escargots*
fish *le poisson*
fries *les frites*
fries, gravy, and cheese *la poutine*
pasta *les pâtes*
salt *le sel*
pepper *le poivre*
the bill *l'addition*
tip *le pourboire*
tip (not) included *service (non) compris*
patio *terrasse*
Enjoy your meal! *Bon appétit!*

SHOPPING

I need... *J'ai besoin du/de/de la...*
I want... *Je veux un/une...*
I would like *J'aimerais avoir...*
How much does... cost? *Combien coûte... ?*
What is the exchange rate? *Quel est le taux de change?*
Can I see... ? *Est-ce que je peux voir... ?*
This one *celui-là/celle-là*
currency exchange *un bureau de change*
convenience store *dépanneur*
money *de l'argent*
traveller's cheque *un chèque de voyage*
credit card *une carte de crédit*
ATM card *une carte bancaire (carte de guichet is more familiar)*
out of service *hors service/en panne*
store *magasin*
open/closed *ouvert/fermé*

HEALTH

Help me please. *Aidez-moi s'il vous plaît.*
I am ill. *Je me sens malade.*

I need to see a doctor. *J'ai besoin de voir un médecin.*
fever *la fièvre*
stomach ache *mal à l'estomac*
vomiting *vomir*
diarrhea *diarrhée*
medicine *médicament*
pill, tablet *une pilule*
birth control pills *pillule anticonceptionnelle*
condom *un condom*

NUMBERS

0 *zéro*
1 *un (masculine), une (feminine)*
2 *deux*
3 *trois*
4 *quatre*
5 *cinq*
6 *six*
7 *sept*
8 *huit*
9 *neuf*
10 *dix*
11 *onze*
12 *douze*
13 *treize*
14 *quatorze*
15 *quinze*
16 *seize*
17 *dix-sept*
18 *dix-huit*
19 *dix-neuf*
20 *vingt*
21 *vingt-et-un*
22 *vingt-deux*
30 *trente*
40 *quarante*
50 *cinquante*
60 *soixante*
70 *soixante-dix*
71 *soixante-et-onze*
72 *soixante-douze*
80 *quatre-vingts*
81 *quatre-vingt-un*
82 *quatre-vingt-deux*
90 *quatre-vingt-dix*
91 *quatre-vingt-onze*
100 *cent*

200 *deux cents*
201 *deux cent un*
1,000 *mille*
10,000 *dix mille*
1,000,000 *un million*
a billion *un milliard*

TIME AND DAYS

Quebecers officially use a 24-hour time clock and do not use A.M. or P.M., which means that as soon as one o'clock in the afternoon hits, you should add 12 hours, i.e. 13h00. In conversation, people will more casually do away with the 24-hour time clock and just say use the words *matin, après-midi,* or *soir* after the hour. And sometimes, when there is no question as to what times of day you're referring to, you can just say, *"Il est trois heures,"* without further clarification.

What time is it? *Quelle heure est-il?*
It's one o'clock. *Il est une heure.*
It's 1:10. *Il est une heure dix.*
It's 3:30. *Il est trois heures et demie./Il est trois heures trente.*
It's 4:15. *Il est quatre heures et quart./Il est quatre heures quinze.*
It's 4:45 A.M. *Il est cinq heures moins quart/4h45/Il est quatre heures quarante-cinq.*
It's 7 A.M. *Il est sept heures du matin/7h00*
It's 3 P.M. *Il est trois heures de l'après-midi/15h00/Il est quinze heures*
It's 6 P.M. *Il est six heures du soir/18h00/Il est dix-huit heures*
It's noon. *Il est midi/12h00*
It's midnight. *Il est minuit/0h00*
today *aujourd'hui*
tomorrow *demain*
yesterday *hier*
last night *hier soir*
next day *le prochain jour*
Monday *lundi*
Tuesday *mardi*
Wednesday *mercredi*
Thursday *jeudi*
Friday *vendredi*
Saturday *samedi*
Sunday *dimanche*

Suggested Reading

Most of these books are widely available at English bookstores throughout the province and country. You can order many of them online as well though Chapters (www.chapters.ca), Indigo (www.indigo.ca), or Amazon (www.amazon.ca). Many should also be available at Barnes and Noble (www.barnesandnoble.com) and the U.S. Amazon (www.amazon.com).

HISTORY AND POLITICS

Bothwell, Robert. *Canada and Quebec: One Country, Two Histories.* Vancouver: The University of British Columbia, 1999. This book by historian Bothwell chronicles Canadian and Québécois history. It includes interviews with prominent politicians and scholars.

Cooke, Ramsay. *Watching Quebec: Selected Essays.* Montréal and Kingston: McGill-Queen's University Press, 2005. A solid attempt to explain the complex relationship between Québec and Canada through essays that examine both historical and contemporary events.

Dickinson, John and Brian Young. *A Short History of Quebec.* Montréal and Kingston: McGill-Queen's University Press, 2003. A weighty, yet completely readable, overview of the province's history written by two history professors, who teach in Québec.

Fraser, Graham. *René Lévesque and the Parti Québécois in Power.* Montréal and Kingston: McGill-Queen's University Press, 2001. This book captures one of Québec's most exciting and dramatic periods and one of its most charismatic leaders.

Parkman, Francis. *Montcalm and Wolfe, The French and Indian War.* New York: Da Capo Press, Revised Edition 2001. A chronicle of the French and Indian War and a look at the two opposing generals of Québec's most famous battle.

Stacey, C. P. and Donald E. Graves. *Quebec, 1759: The Siege and the Battle.* Toronto: Robin Brass Studio, Revised Edition, 2002. The entire run-down of the events leading up to and during the Battle on the Plains of Abraham.

CULTURE

Carrier, Roch, Sheldon Cohen and Sheila Fischman. *The Hockey Sweater.* Montréal: Tundra Books, 1985. It's fiction, but it's a Canadian classic that beautifully and simply illustrates (in the literal and figurative senses of the word), the differences between English and French Canadians.

Grescoe Taras. *Sacré Blues: An Unsentimental Journey Through Quebec.* Toronto: MacFarlane Walter & Ross, 2001. A humorous but honest look at Québec culture with treatises on why Quebecers love ketchup-flavored chips and small cars and what the deal is with yellow margarine.

MacLennan, Hugh. *Two Solitudes.* Mass Market Paperback, 2003. This Canadian classic novel delves into the troubled relationship between the country's "two solitudes" by focusing on the lives of one family.

LANGUAGE

Canadian French for Better Travel. Montréal: Ulysses Travel Publications, 2004. This Québec-based publisher has produced a nifty little book that includes slang, regional varieties, and pronunciation explanations.

Timmins, Steve. *French Fun: The Real Spoken Language of Quebec.* Montréal: John Wiley & Sons Canada Ltd., 1995. An insider's look at Québec French with all its color, expressiveness, and sometimes even naughtiness.

OUTDOOR RECREATION

Callan, Kevin. *A Paddler's Guide to the Rivers of Ontario and Quebec.* Erin, Ontario: Boston Mills Press, Updated Edition 2003. For the canoeing or kayaking type of paddler, this well-written and well-researched book has detailed information on some of the best river trips throughout Ontario and Québec.

Hiking in Quebec. Montréal: Ulysses Travel Publications, 2003. The only English guide that devotes itself to hiking in the province explores more than 100 trails in all the regions of the province.

Take a Ride on the Green Side: Official Guide to Bicycling on Quebec's Route Verte. Québec: Les Éditions Tricycle, 2003. This book is a great resource for anyone looking to explore a few or many of the trails that make up Québec's biking network.

OTHER GUIDEBOOKS AND MAPS

Armstrong, Julian. *A Taste of Quebec.* Montréal: John Wiley & Sons Canada Ltd., 2001. Written by the *Montréal Gazette*'s food editor, this book includes travel information on where to sample the province's prized delicacies, some history, and recipes, including a number of takes on *tourtière.*

Chesterman, Lesley. *Flavourville: Lesley Chesterman's Guide to Dining Out in Montreal.* Toronto: ECW Press, 2003. Written by another *Gazette* foodie—this time the food critic—this guide to Montréal's restaurants provides in-depth critiques of food, décor, and service written in colorful, opinionated language.

Montreal Art Maps. Société Carte Option Art. These free maps available at tourist centers and libraries include everything an art lover could desire including listings of art galleries, museums, design shops, and craft centers for the greater Montréal area and Old Montréal.

Symon, John. *The Lobster Kid's Guide to Exploring Montreal.* Montréal: Lobster Press Ltd., 2000. This helpful guide for parents includes many family-fun activities and itineraries. It also tells you where to take your kids for dinner and what the best family attractions are.

Internet Resources

TRAVEL

Bonjour Quebec
www.bonjourquebec.com

On the Québec government's official tourism site you can explore the province by region or do an overall search for accommodations and restaurants. The site has some good sample itineraries, panoramas of popular attractions (like the interior of the Basilique Notre-Dame), and answers to FAQ.

Made in MTL
www.madeinmtl.com

This beautiful, engaging website explores Montréal and its neighborhoods, restaurants, bars, and cultural and heritage attractions with compelling editorial written by locals, photos, and video so you can get a real look and listen of the place.

Tourisme Montréal
www.tourisme-montreal.org

The City of Montréal's official tourism site has all the local information on accommodations and food. It also has a complete events calendar and many last-minute deals on hotels. This is also the best place to get online maps of the city.

Tourisme Charlevoix
www.tourisme-charlevoix.com

This official Charlevoix tourism site does a

good job of showcasing the region, especially with its "trails" section, which explores the area according to scenic views, food, painters, maritime heritage, religious heritage, etc.

Québec City and Area
www.quebecregion.com
The Québec City region's main site has good panoramas of the city's must-sees, shopping suggestions organized by category, and the regular hotel and restaurant lists. It has a good selection of walking tours.

St. Laurence Touring
www.circuitsaint-laurent.com
This new site outlines four sections of the St. Lawrence River: in and around Québec City, Charlevoix, Bas-Saint-Laurent, and Chaudière-Appalaches. Ferry listings, events, and places to stay along the river are also listed.

Old Montréal
www.vieux.montreal.qc.ca
The graphics aren't great, but Old Montréal's tourism site has practical information on how best to explore the district and good write-ups and photos on each of its main attractions.

Société des Musées Québécois
www.smq.qc.ca
The Société des Musées Québécois' website provides a complete overview of the province's museum offerings with thematic routes organized by religious heritage, science and technology, and architecture and design.

HISTORY

Quebec Heritage
www.quebecheritage.com
This excellent site chronicles all of Québec City's architectural jewels, including religious, military, and archaeological sites.

Canadian Museum of Civilization
www.civilization.ca
The Canadian Museum of Civilization's website has in-depth features on Canadian

moments in history and a virtual museum exploring the developments of New France.

McCord Museum
www.mccord-museum.qc.ca
Montréal's McCord Museum has a virtual exhibitions section, including the compelling *Urban Life Through Two Lenses,* which looks at Montréal locations taken by two photographers, a century apart.

CULTURE

Virtual Museum of Canada
www.virtualmuseum.ca
The Virtual Museum of Canada is a complete online museum with plenty of exhibits, including one on the French explorers, another that compares Christmas traditions between France and Canada, and an excellent one showcasing francophone artists in Canada called *Gestures and Words.*

Musée de la Civilization
www.mcq.org
Québec City's Musée de la Civilization has plenty of online exhibits from the first encounter between French explorers and the first nations peoples to the province's fascination with hockey.

National Film Board of Canada
www.nfb.ca
The National Film Board of Canada specializes in documentaries and animation. You can watch some animation shorts on the website and order videos. The works of some of Québec's first filmmakers are available here.

NEWS SITES

The Gazette
www.montrealgazette.com
The website of Montréal's main English-language daily, *The Gazette,* has the news, entertainment, and classifieds, but it also has

some good special features like the Food & Wine guide and a collection of web cams situated in different parts of the city.

The Montreal Mirror
www.montrealmirror.com

One of the city's two English-language alternative weekly papers, *The Montreal Mirror* has a good site with entertainment listings, local news, and restaurant reviews.

Hour
www.hour.ca

The other English weekly belongs to *Hour*. It too has entertainment listings, news, and food reviews, along with features on topics like where to shop for appliances.

Canadian Broadcasting Corporation
www.cbc.ca/montreal

The Canadian Broadcasting Corporation has a Montréal-focused satellite site that covers the major events affecting the city and the province.

INFORMATION

Government of Québec
www.gouv.qc.ca

The Québec government offers a portrait of Québec with facts and figures on the population, geography, economy, and its place in the world.

Le Grand Dictionnaire Termonologique
www.granddictionnaire.com

Run by the Québec government, Le Grand Dictionnaire Termonologique is an online dictionary that translates words from English to French and vice versa. It's the last word on Québec French.

Environment Canada
www.weatheroffice.ec.gc.ca

Environment Canada has the latest weather updates for the entire country, including Québec. Forecasts are for five days.

Inforoutière
www.inforoutiere.qc.ca

Inforoutière, run by Transports Québec, offers road maps, information on road conditions, road distances, and the locations and services offered by all the provincially run wayside parks.

Index

HIKING

MUSEUMS

PARKS

WINTER SPORTS

Bromont: 146, 151
Eastern Townships: 15
Gaspé: 260
La Malbaie: 235
Laurentians: 15, 120-122, 125-127, 129, 134-135
Le Massif: 226
Mont-Sainte-Anne: 215-216
Mont-Tremblant: 137

North Hatley: 173
Outaouais: 14
Owl's Head: 166
Parc de la Gatineau: 110
Parc Mont-Royal: 53
Parc National du Mont-Orford: 162
Parc National du Mont-Tremblant: 144
Sutton: 159
La Traversée de Charlevoix: 226-227

149; Sainte-Adèle 127; Saint-Sauveur-des-Monts 117, 122
water resources: 272
water sports: 109-110
weather: 18-19, 272-273
websites: 308-310
weights and measures: 300-301
Westmount: 56, 91
Westmount Library: 56
Westmount Square: 56
West Nile virus: 297
wetlands: 215
whales/whale-watching: general discussion 239, 275, 294; Parc Marin du Saguenay-Saint-Laurent 16, 221, 240-241; Tadoussac 238-239

white-water rafting:see river rafting
wildlife: 273-275, 297
wind recreation: 245, 265
Windsor Station: 50
wind turbines: 249
wine/wineries: drinking regulations 88; Dunham 155; Eastern Townships 15, 153-156; Île d'Orleans 217
winter travel: 297-298
Wolfe House and Redoubt: 214
woodland caribou: 251
work permits: 295
yoga camps: 128-129
zoos: 149

Acknowledgments

This book came together through the help of many people. Whether they researched, wrote, passed along newspaper clippings, or simply kept me sane, they all provided valuable insight and shared their love of Québec. Thank you to Marie-France Chassé, Anne-Marie Curatolo, Craille Maguire Gillies, Julie Roy, and Chantal Tranchemontagne for your inspired contributions. And a very special thank you to Sue Moore for her hard work on the Gaspé, Québec City, and Outaouais chapters.

Thank you to Roland-Yves Carignan for answering my barrage of questions, for the historical input, and for the late-night counsel. Thanks to dad, Joy, Dan, and Dick for helping me keep up the momentum, and a big, big, heartfelt thank you to mum for keeping the rest of my life together so that I could sit down and write.

Finally, thanks to Grace Fujimoto for her skilled and sensitive edit.

www.moon.com

For helpful advice on planning a trip, visit www.moon.com for the **TRAVEL PLANNER** and get access to useful travel strategies and valuable information about great places to visit. When you travel with Moon, expect an experience that is uncommon and truly unique.

MAP SYMBOLS

Expressway		Highlight		Airfield		Golf Course
Primary Road	○	City/Town		Airport		Parking Area
Secondary Road	◉	State Capital	▲	Mountain		Archaeological Site
Unpaved Road	⊛	National Capital	✛	Unique Natural Feature		Church
Trail	★	Point of Interest				Gas Station
Ferry	•	Accommodation		Waterfall		Glacier
Railroad	▼	Restaurant/Bar	▲	Park		Mangrove
Pedestrian Walkway	■	Other Location		Trailhead		Reef

CONVERSION TABLES

$$°C = (°F - 32) / 1.8$$
$$°F = (°C \times 1.8) + 32$$

1 inch = 2.54 centimeters (cm)
1 foot = 0.304 meters (m)
1 yard – 0.914 meters
1 mile = 1.6093 kilometers (km)
1 km = 0.6214 miles
1 fathom = 1.8288 m
1 chain = 20.1168 m
1 furlong = 201.168 m
1 acre = 0.4047 hectares
1 sq km = 100 hectares
1 sq mile = 2.59 square km
1 ounce = 28.35 grams
1 pound = 0.4536 kilograms
1 short ton = 0.90718 metric ton
1 short ton = 2,000 pounds
1 long ton = 1.016 metric tons
1 long ton = 2,240 pounds
1 metric ton = 1,000 kilograms
1 quart = 0.94635 liters
1 US gallon = 3.7854 liters
1 Imperial gallon = 4.5459 liters
1 nautical mile = 1.852 km

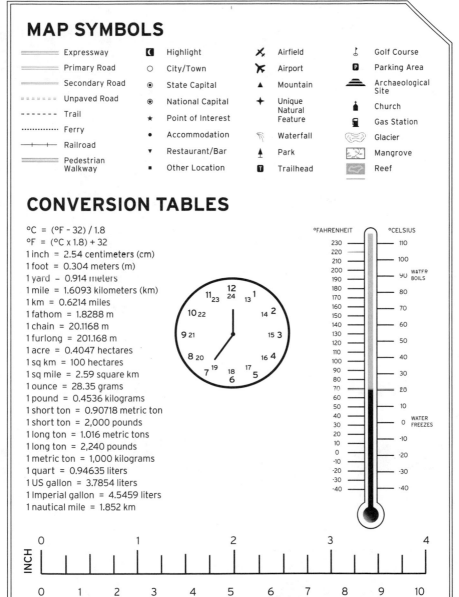

MOON MONTRÉAL & QUÉBEC CITY

Avalon Travel Publishing
An Imprint of
Avalon Publishing Group, Inc.

AVALON
publishing group incorporated

1400 65th Street, Suite 250
Emeryville, CA 94608, USA
www.moon.com

Editors: Grace Fujimoto, Cinnamon Hearst
Series Manager: Kathryn Ettinger
Acquisitions Manager: Rebecca K. Browning
Copy Editor: Karen Gaynor Bleske
Graphics Coordinator: Stefano Boni
Production Coordinator: Domini Dragoone
Cover & Interior Designer: Gerilyn Attebery
Map Editor: Kat Smith
Cartographers: Suzanne Service, Kat Bennett,
   Christine Markiewicz
Cartography Manager: Mike Morgenfeld
Indexer: Judy Hunt

ISBN-10: 1-56691-779-4
ISBN-13: 978-1-56691-779-7
ISSN: 1559-3479

Printing History
1st Edition—May 2006
5 4 3 2 1

KEEPING CURRENT

If you have a favorite gem you'd like to see included in the next edition, or see anything that needs updating, clarification, or correction, please drop us a line. Send your comments via email to feedback@moon.com, or use the address above.